ELIOT'S DARK ANGEL

Eliot's Dark Angel

INTERSECTIONS OF LIFE AND ART

RONALD SCHUCHARD

New York   Oxford

OXFORD UNIVERSITY PRESS

1999

Oxford University Press

Oxford   New York

Athens   Auckland   Bangkok   Bogotá   Buenos Aires   Calcutta
Cape Town   Chennai   Dar es Salaam   Delhi   Florence   Hong Kong   Istanbul
Karachi   Kuala Lumpur   Madrid   Melbourne   Mexico City   Mumbai
Nairobi   Paris   São Paulo   Singapore   Taipei   Tokyo   Toronto   Warsaw

and associated companies in
Berlin   Ibadan

Published by Oxford University Press, Inc.
198 Madison Avenue, New York, New York 10016

Oxford is a registered trademark of Oxford University Press

Library of Congress Cataloging-in-Publication Data
Schuchard, Ronald.
Eliot's dark angel : intersections of life and art
/ Ronald Schuchard.
p.   cm.
Includes bibliographical references and index.
ISBN 0-19-510417-X
1. Eliot, T. S. (Thomas Stearns). 1888–1965—Psychology.
2. Eliot, T. S. (Thomas Stearns). 1888–1965—Knowledge—Popular
culture.   3. Poetry—Authorship—Psychological aspects.   4. Poets,
American—20th century—Psychology.   5. Popular culture in
literature.   I. Title.
PS3509.L43Z86352   1999
821'.912—dc21   98-54730

Frontispiece: Saint Sebastian and the Angel,
Fogg Art Museum, Harvard University

1 3 5 7 9 8 6 4 2

Printed in the United States of America
on acid-free paper

FOR A. WALTON LITZ

ACKNOWLEDGMENTS

I wish to express my deepest thanks to Mrs. Valerie Eliot for her interest and assistance during the preparation of this book, for her permission to examine restricted materials, and for allowing me to quote from unpublished writings by T. S. Eliot in the Yale Collection of American Literature, Beinecke Rare Book and Manuscript Library, Yale University; the Berg Collection of English and American Literature, the New York Public Library, Astor, Lenox and Tilden Foundations; the Brotherton Collection, Leeds University Library; the Modern Archive Centre, King's College Library, Cambridge; the Harry Ransom Humanities Research Center, University of Texas at Austin; the Houghton Library, Harvard University; the Manuscripts Division, Department of Rare Books and Special Collections, Princeton University Library, and the Herbert Read Archives, McPherson Library, University of Victoria, British Columbia. All such quotations are reprinted by permission of Mrs. Valerie Eliot and Faber and Faber Ltd., © Mrs. Valerie Eliot, 1999, and the respective libraries. I am further grateful to Mrs. Eliot and to Faber and Faber for permission to quote generously from numerous uncollected literary writings by T. S. Eliot, and for permission to quote from *The Waste Land: A Facsimile and Transcript by T. S. Eliot*, edited by Valerie Eliot. Material is reprinted by permission of Faber and Faber, Ltd. from the following books by T. S. Eliot: *After Strange Gods; The Complete Poems and Plays of T. S. Eliot; For Lancelot Andrewes; Inventions of the March Hare: Poems 1900–1917; Knowledge and Experience in the Philosphy of F. H. Bradley; The Letters of T. S. Eliot*, vol. I; *On Poetry and Poets; The Sacred Wood*, second edition; *Selected Essays; To Criticize the Critic; The Use of Poetry and the Use of*

Criticism, second edition; *The Varieties of Metaphysical Poetry*. Versions of some sections of this book first appeared in *ELH*, the *Modern Schoolman, Orbis Litterarum, PMLA*, the *Review of English Studies*, and the *Southern Review*. Versions of some paragraphs in the prelude first appeared in *Yeats: An Annual of Textual and Critical Studies*, the *Recorder*, and *Princeton University Library Chronicle*. I am grateful to the respective editors for permission to reprint the material. Versions of other sections first appeared in *T. S. Eliot: Essays from the* Southern Review, ed. James Olney (Oxford: Clarendon Press 1988); *The Southern Review and Modern Literature, 1935–1985*, ed. Louis P. Simpson, James Olney, and Jo Gulledge (Baton Rouge: Louisiana State University Press 1988); *The Placing of T. S. Eliot*, ed. Jewel Spears Brooker (Columbia and London: University of Missouri Press 1991); *Words in Time: New Essays on Eliot's* Four Quartets, ed. Edward Lobb (London: Athlone Press 1993); *Modernist Writers and the Marketplace*, ed. Ian Willison, Warwick Gould, and Warren Chernaik (London: Macmillan; New York: St. Martin's Press 1996). I am grateful to the respective editors and publishers for permission to reprint this material.

For assistance in locating Eliot's syllabuses and records relating to his Extension lecturing, I am grateful to the late F. W. Jessup and A. E. W. Ingram of the Department of External Studies, Oxford University; T. F. Evans and J. M. Pavey of the Department of Extra-Mural Studies, University of London, and A.R. Neate of the Greater London Record Office. I am also grateful to Sharon Adamczak Schmidt, archivist for the Harcourt Brace and Company archives in Orlando, Florida, for providing me with copies of correspondence related to the publication of *Selected Essays* and for permission to quote from archival material. I should like to thank librarians Cathy Henderson, Harry Ransom Humanities Research Center, University of Texas, and Eric R. Nitschke, Woodruff Library, Emory University, for valuable research assistance. I am indebted to Richard Mangan, administrator of the Raymond Mander and Joe Mitchenson Theatre Collection, and to Max Tyler, historian of the British Music Hall Society, for providing me with photographic illustrations of music-hall performers.

For assistance and advice of various kinds I am indebted to the late William Arrowsmith; John Bodley, Faber and Faber; Jewel Spears Brooker, Eckerd College; Miriam Chirico, Emory University; T. Susan Chang, Oxford University Press; the late Alan Cohn; Ann Margaret Daniel, University of Richmond; Stephen Enniss, Emory University; Edward Lobb, Queen's University, Kingston, Ontario; Thomas Pinney, Pomona College; Christopher Ricks, Boston University, and Chris Buttram Trombold, Sam Houston State University. Warwick Gould, Programme Director of the Institute of English Studies, and Terence Daintith, Dean of the School of Advanced Study, University of London, provided me with a visiting research fellowship and facilities that enabled me to bring this study to completion. The Emory University Research Committee and Graduate School of Arts and Sciences further supported the preparation of this volume. I owe thanks to A. Walton Litz of Princeton University for persuading me to pause and put together in book form my ongoing study of Eliot's life work. My intellectual and scholarly debt to Professor Litz over twenty-five years of discussing modern literature together is only faintly marked in the dedication. Each chapter of this book bears the impress of my most discerning reader and critic, Keith Schuchard.

CONTENTS

Illustrations appear after page 108

ABBREVIATIONS

Principal editions cited or quoted

PUBLISHED

By T. S. Eliot

ASG	*After Strange Gods.* London: Faber and Faber, 1934.
CPP	*The Complete Poems and Plays of T. S. Eliot.* London: Faber and Faber, 1969.
FLA	*For Lancelot Andrewes.* London: Faber and Gwyer, 1928.
IMH	*Inventions of the March Hare: Poems 1909–1917*, ed. Christopher Ricks. London: Faber and Faber, 1996.
KEPB	*Knowledge and Experience in the Philosophy of F. H. Bradley.* London: Faber and Faber, 1964; New York: Farrar, Straus, 1964.
L1	*The Letters of T. S. Eliot*, vol. 1, ed. Valerie Eliot. London: Faber and Faber, 1988. New York: Harcourt Brace Jovanovich, 1988.
OPP	*On Poetry and Poets.* London: Faber and Faber, 1957; New York: Farrar, Straus and Cudahy, 1957.
SE	*Selected Essays,* 3rd enl. ed. London and Boston: Faber and Faber, 1986.

SW	*The Sacred Wood*, 2nd ed. London: Faber and Faber, 1997.
TCC	*To Criticize the Critic.* London: Faber and Faber, 1965. New York: Farrar Straus Giroux, 1965.
UPUC	*The Use of Poetry and the Use of Criticism,* 2nd edition. London: Faber and Faber, 1964.
VMP	*The Varieties of Metaphysical Poetry*, ed. Ronald Schuchard. London: Faber and Faber, 1993. New York: Harcourt Brace, 1994.
WLF	*The Waste Land: A Facsimile and Transcript of the Original Drafts,* ed. Valerie Eliot. London: Faber and Faber, 1971. New York: Harcourt Brace Jovanovich, 1971.

Other Works

CFQ	Helen Gardner, *The Composition of Four Quartets.* London: Faber and Faber, 1978.
CWTEH	*The Collected Writings of T. E. Hulme,* ed. Karen Csengeri. Oxford: Clarendon Press, 1994.
Gallup	Donald Gallup, *T. S. Eliot: A Bibliography*, rev. and extended ed. New York: Harcourt, Brace and World, 1969.
Harries	B. A. Harries, "The Rare Contact: A Correspondence between T. S. Eliot and P. E. More," *Theology* 75 (March 1972), 136–44.
TLS	*Times Literary Supplement*
TSE	Lyndall Gordon, *T. S. Eliot: An Imperfect Life,* rev. ed. London: Vintage, 1998.

PUBLISHED

Bodleian	The Bodleian Library, Oxford University
Berg	The Berg Collection of English and American Literature, the New York Public Library, Astor, Lenox and Tilden Foundation
Brotherton	The Brotherton Collection, Leeds University Library
Chapel Hill	The Wilson Library, University of North Carolina, Chapel Hill
Emory	The Robert W. Woodruff Library, Emory University
Houghton	The Houghton Library, Harvard University
King's	Modern Archive Centre, King's College Library, Cambridge University
MS VE	Private collection, Mrs. Valerie Eliot, London

Princeton	Paul Elmer More Papers, Manuscripts Division, Princeton University Library
Texas	Harry Ransom Humanities Research Center, University of Texas at Austin
Victoria	The McPherson Library, University of Victoria, British Columbia
Yale	The Beinecke Rare Book and Manuscript Library, Yale University
HBA	Harcourt Brace and Company Archives, Orlando, Florida

Our age was forced, by his inimical genius, to become aware of inner tensions which it would have preferred to ignore, to sharpen the terms of its most troubling dialectic. That genius forced us, with particular severity, and regardless of our personal opinions and dogmas, to look at the ambiguities of our age and to struggle to make sense of them, or pass beyond them. Consider the *Four Quartets*. Who else, in that noisy and angry time, tried to define the anguish of the need for stillness? . . .

His power lay in the capacity to see the world as a personal drama of ultimate meanings. The shadow of our unspecified human story—the need to move to meaning and toward peace through the ruck of the world—was at the center of his work, and even for those who doctrinally or temperamentally had little sympathy for him the dramatic force of the implied story was nigh overwhelming. He had the charisma of any man who is struggling for reality.

—Robert Penn Warren,
1965 television obituary
for T. S. Eliot (Emory)

ELIOT'S DARK ANGEL

PRELUDE

The Dark Angel

Dark Angel, with thine aching lust
To rid the world of penitence:
Malicious Angel, who still dost
My soul such subtile violence!

—Lionel Johnson,
"The Dark Angel"

T S. Eliot inherited the dark angel that tormented Lionel Johnson's spiritual
life. Its visitations began early in Eliot's manhood, and it stayed long to ter-
rorize a creative sensibility rich in sensual and spiritual antinomies. The outwardly happy Harvard undergraduate, who loved philosophy and art, poetry and
drama, minstrel shows and melodramas, college songs and bawdy ballads, gradually gained a malicious companion. Hovering and whispering, Eliot's dark angel
descended as an agent of temptation and messenger of damnation. Under the
shadow of its wings, the poet's spiritual impulses were desecrated by sexual fantasies, while his sexual desires were short-circuited by the chatter of madness or
chuckle of death. Turning desire itself into a psychological mechanism of spiritual terror and bodily disgust, the dark angel dislocated the poet's consciousness
from ordinary reality, took him to the edge of the abyss, and led him to phantasmal planes. Under its louring presence, the suffering poet conceived of himself
as Arnaut, his lustful soul wrapped in purgatorial flames; as Sebastian, his spiritual
love wracked by bodily arrows; as Hamlet, his rational will locked in spiritual
paralysis; as Faust, his self-inverted mind on the brink of dissolution. The dark
angel would appear again in the consciousness of the London bridegroom and
banker who loved teaching and reviewing, music halls and the Russian ballet,
ragtime and jazz, the Chicken Strut and the Grizzly Bear. Eliot's dark angel was
at once his fury and his muse, causing and conducting the internal drama of
shadows and voices that inhabit his acutely personal poems and plays.

3

When Eliot discovered that other poets had suffered from this dark angel, he went searching for its manifestations in Dante, Marlowe, Shakespeare, George Chapman, John Webster, Donne, Baudelaire, and Ernest Dowson. He found traces of its presence in the "deeper psychology" and "merciless clairvoyance" of Hawthorne, James, Flaubert, Stendhal, Dostoyevsky, and Turgenev. Eliot searched everywhere in western literature for signs of visitations and possessions; he gathered the afflicted into his company and wrote out of the reality of the violence described by Johnson and felt by all of them. No one, however, had sensed that angel's increasing presence in the post-romantic world more than Matthew Arnold, and no one studied his destructive effects with greater disinterest than William Butler Yeats.

Arnold was the first English poet to describe a disturbing new phenomenon in modern letters, a "mysterious malady" that had affected him in the composition of "Empedocles on Etna" (1852), in which his persona struggles with "some root of suffering in himself, / Some secret and unfollowed vein of woe."[1] Arnold's Empedocles, his spirit exhausted and senses benumbed, becomes "dead to life and joy." The victim of a "devouring flame of thought" and an "eternally restless mind" (*PMA* 200), he succumbs to despair and throws himself into the fiery volcano. When Arnold explained his decision to exclude the poem from the first edition of his *Poems* (1853), he pointed to the presence of a destructive subjectivity that had infected modern writers: "the calm, the cheerfulness, the disinterested objectivity have disappeared: the dialogue of the mind with itself has commenced; modern problems have presented themselves; we hear already the doubts, we witness the discouragement, of Hamlet and of Faust."[2] Reminding the reader of Schiller's assertion that "all art is dedicated to Joy," Arnold explained that Empedocles, who serves as an ancient mask for the modern lyric poet, belongs to a joyless class of situations from which no enjoyment can be derived:

> They are those in which the suffering finds no vent in action; in which a continuous state of mental distress is prolonged, unrelieved by incident, hope, or resistance; in which there is everything to be endured, nothing to be done. In such situations there is inevitably something morbid, in the description of them something monotonous. When they occur in actual life, they are painful, not tragic; the representation of them in poetry is painful also. (*CPW1* 2–3)

Four years before the appearance of Baudelaire's *Les Fleurs du Mal* (1857), Arnold had found depression and ennui stamped on the literary minds of his time; looking back to Goethe's Faust and Byron's Manfred, he had taken the pulse of febrile writers whose descents into the self led only to paralysis and despair. Like Empedocles, he wondered whether modern poets

> will once more fall away
> Into some bondage of the flesh or mind,
> Some slough of sense, or some fantastic maze
> Forged by the imperious lonely thinking-power.
> And each succeeding age in which we are born

Will have more peril for us than the last;
Will goad our senses with a sharper spur,
Will fret our minds to an intenser play,
Will make ourselves harder to be discerned.

. . .

And we shall feel our powers of effort flag,
And rally them for one last fight—and fail;
And we shall sink in the impossible strife,
And be astray for ever. (*PMA* 202–3)

In identifying Hamlet and Faust as the literary prototypes of this morbid poetic temperament, Arnold foretold the appearance a half century later of the personae in "The Love Song of J. Alfred Prufrock," "Gerontion," and *The Waste Land,* whose minds are sunk in insidious dialogue with the self, their spirits exhausted. More immediately, Arnold betokened the sensual-spiritual malaise visited upon members of Yeats's generation; Dowson, Johnson, Beardsley, and Wilde all knew the dark angel.

Yeats was the sole inheritor of Arnold's dialectic of morbidity and joy, and he was an even closer observer of the spiritual ills of his literary friends. In *The Trembling of the Veil* (1922), he looked back painfully on his association with what he calls the "the tragic generation," that accursed group of 1890s poets and artists whose lives were consumed by spiritual despair and whose careers were wrecked early by melancholia, dissipation, madness, and suicide. For more than thirty years he had puzzled, like Arnold before him, over the "morbid effort" of their religious pursuits. Disturbed by the terrible waste of genius, he asks, "Had not Matthew Arnold his faith in what he described as the best thought of his generation?" Drawing a line from Coleridge to Rossetti through Count Stenbock and Beardsley to Dowson and Johnson, he laments that their Christianity "but deepened despair and multiplied temptation."[3] Mulling the dark psychology of his defeated friends, he quotes the opening stanzas of Johnson's "The Dark Angel," as though Johnson had fingered the common cause of suffering:

Dark Angel, with thine aching lust,
To rid the world of penitence:
Malicious angel, who still dost
My soul such subtil violence!

When music sounds, then changest thou
A silvery to a sultry fire:
Nor will thine envious heart allow
Delight untortured by desire.

Through thee, the gracious Muses turn
To Furies, O mine Enemy!
And all the things of beauty burn
With flames of evil ecstasy.

Because of thee, the land of dreams
Becomes a gathering-place of fears:
Until tormented slumber seems
One vehemence of useless tears.[4]

Yeats then asks of the present time, "Why are these strange souls born every-where to-day, with hearts that Christianity, as shaped by history, cannot satisfy?" (*Aut* 315). In his dismay at the continued morbidity of modern poetry, he wist-fully recalls his almost apocalyptic belief during the 1890s that Cabalistic magic would soon displace the strange Catholic mysticism that had enveloped his friends in gloom. It was Yeats's father who gave his son's friends "their right name," echoing Arnold in telling him that "they are the Hamlets of our age."[5]

In his youth Yeats had begun the "strange pursuits" that led him into the vi-sionary company of the Order of the Golden Dawn, who, he says, "taught me methods of meditation that had greatly affected my thought" (*Aut* 411). At the same time, several of his literary friends were caught up in the Catholic revival that had made its way through France into England, and these two rival visionary traditions found coexistence among the intimate members of the Rhymers' Club. His Catholic friends were men of genius whose strong spiritual drives were accompanied by equally strong passions, but their inability to annihilate or sublimate passion in the mystical process made them subject to destructive lives and an overwhelming sense of guilt and remorse. Through the Cabala, however, which integrates passion and ecstasy, sexuality and visionary experience, Yeats found the disciplined techniques that enabled him to ward off the dark angel, whose "envious heart," as Johnson described it, will not "allow / Delight untor-tured by desire." In "The Two Trees" (1892), Yeats had symbolically distinguished the two concepts of self and their separate pathways to sanctity: the poet-mage who ascends the holy branches of the sephirotic Tree of Life toward a visionary joy is not subject to the "subtile guile" of the mirror-wielding demons that await the poet-mystic, who may find in the treacherous branches of the Tree of Knowledge of Good and Evil a "fatal image" of the self, a self that is violently consumed by "The ravens of unresting thought."[6]

Yeats continued to bear witness to the devastating toll of the decade, observ-ing firsthand his friends' descents into the abyss of the self. Aubrey Beardsley, who said to Yeats, "I have always been haunted by the spiritual life," was dead in 1898, a victim of consumption and subverted sexual and spiritual passion. "His disease," Yeats observed, "presented continuously before his mind . . . lascivi-ous images, and he drew them in their horror, their fascination, and became the first satirist of the soul English art has produced."[7] Yeats was also aware of the ef-fects of a morbid spiritual emotion that wreaked its "subtile violence" on Wilde's life, which Yeats believed was "an attempt to escape from an emotion by its exag-geration" (*Aut* 287). Dowson and Wilde were both dead in 1900, the year, said Yeats from a long perspective but with no loss of exasperation, in which "every-one got down off his stilts; henceforth . . . nobody went mad; nobody com-mitted suicide; nobody joined the Catholic church; or if they did I have forgot-ten" (*OBMV* xi).

Yeats would brood upon and write about the morbid condition of modern writers for the rest of his life. In October 1909, after attending Martin Harvey's production of *Hamlet* in Dublin, he wrote to Harvey that "the play should seem to one, not so much deep as full of lyric loftiness & I feel this all the more because I am getting tired of our modern delight in the Abyss."[8] The following year he delivered lectures on the "melancholy mysticism" of what he now called "the doomed generation," observing that in making entry into the abyss of the self they did not realize, as the Cabala taught, that such a descent requires a change from contemplative to active thought. Yeats had become fond of quoting Goethe's admonition that "a man only learns to know himself by action, by contemplation never,"[9] a maxim reaffirmed by Arnold, the champion of Goethe. In his preface to *Poems* (1853), Arnold implies that "Empedocles on Etna" is analogous to *Faust,* a "defective" piece of work that, he says, Goethe himself describes as "something incommensurable" with the rest of his work (*CWP1* 8). Yeats explains the Rhymers' morbid effort toward vision and sanctity through the analogy of Christian mystics, particularly St. John of the Cross, in the wilderness. Finding that wilderness, Yeats declares, is the beginning of sanctity, but the saint, in encountering the dark night of the soul, can more readily pass safely through the despair and gloom than the poet, for the saint has only to renounce and annihilate his passions. In the wilderness of the mystical process, Yeats explains,

> the passions become infinite and powerful energy because they are no longer controlled and limited by circumstance and habit but must be faced in the depth of the mind. To enter into the mind, to renounce all but the mind or what excites it to its highest intensity, that is the toil of the saint and the lyric poet. But all those passions which the saint may at last tame the poets need in their wildness. I can understand that generation, for I was of it. I almost shared its curse without any excess to help the strain of the emotion which was the foundation of our work. (*YT* 69)

Yeats avoided their destructive excess through his Cabalistic meditation techniques. He had learned to harness the energy of passion to the chariot of vision and to seek not the self but the anti-self, which discloses to the poet, as he affirms in "Ego Dominus Tuus," "All that I seek" (*VP* 371). Yeats came to believe that the mystical process becomes destructive when the poet encounters his personal passions in the depths of the mind and surrenders to the temptation to sing them. "He separates himself from all else, for like the Saint he has his wilderness, he knows that there is nothing that sings but passion and that the greatest passions are one's own" (*YT* 80). When these intense moments subside, however, the poet may become enveloped by a horrifying darkness: "Melancholy desire, strange hatreds, these will father about him always and he will often hear about him before the darkness has fallen terrifying voices." Yeats thus attributed the spiritual suffering of his Catholic friends to "that hidden meditation wherein they lost or saved their souls and certainly lost the world" (*YT* 81), and he would soon place Eliot among their company.

In compiling *The Oxford Book of Modern Verse* (1936), Yeats summoned

Arnold once again to help him characterize the extension of the morbid tradition from the Rhymers to the present day. In excluding the work of some wartime poets who made the suffering of their comrades their own suffering, he declared: "I have rejected these poems for the same reason that made Arnold withdraw his *Empedocles on Etna* from circulation; passive suffering is not a theme for poetry" (*OBMV* xxxiv). Through Arnold, and through his understanding of the Rhymers, Yeats had also come to comprehend the postwar poets, particularly Eliot. "If I understand aright this difficult art," he wrote, "the contemplation of suffering has compelled them to seek beyond the flux something unchanging, inviolate, that country where no ghost haunts, no beloved lures because it has neither past nor future" (*OBMV* xxxviii).

It was Eliot's absorption in passive, purgatorial suffering that stood behind much of Yeats's criticism of Eliot's poetry. When he read *The Waste Land* in 1924 he noticed immediately, as he wrote to Lady Gregory, that Eliot "writes but of his own mind. That is the kind of insoluble problem that makes the best conversation, and if you will come and visit me, I will call the Dublin poets together, and we will discuss it until midnight" (*VP* 854). Yeats, like others, saw the change signaled by *Ash-Wednesday* (1930) as coming from an emotional enrichment from religion, and it led him to again associate Eliot with his Catholic friends, though not without asserting that Eliot's religious suffering, compared to that expressed in Johnson's "The Dark Angel," "lacks all strong emotion; a New England Protestant by descent, there is little self-surrender in his personal relation to God and the soul" (*OBMV* xxii). Whatever one's response to his estimation of Eliot's religious emotion and spiritual surrender, Yeats had identified him as a modern member of the fatal mystical tradition that moved from France into England late in the nineteenth century. It is perhaps one of the great ironies of modern criticism that Yeats saw Eliot as a morbid romantic poet lost in the wilderness of the self. What truth is in it?

I

At the age of sixteen Eliot discovered James Thomson's "The City of Dreadful Night" and Ernest Dowson's "Impenitentia Ultima," poems that provided him, he later affirmed, with "a new and vivid experience" of a London phantasmagoria and an intense admixture of religious and sexual emotion.[10] He was soon captivated by John Davidson's "Thirty Bob a Week," and he began reading the poems of Lionel Johnson, Arthur Symons, Francis Thompson, and other English poets of the 1890s. "I cannot help wondering," Eliot later reflected,

> how my own verse would have developed, or whether it would have been written at all, supposing that the poets of the 'nineties had survived to my own time and had gone on developing and increasing in power. . . . I certainly had much more in common with them than with the English poets who survived to my own day—there were no American poets at all. Had they survived they might have spoken in an idiom sufficiently like my own to have made anything

I had to say superfluous. They were in contact with those of France, and they might have exhausted the possibilities of cross-fertilisation from Symbolist Poetry (as they called it) before I had a chance.[11]

Eliot read the English poets of the 1890s before he read Dante or Baudelaire, and he later credited them with preparing him for "initiation into the work of some of the French symbolists, such as La Forgue [Laforgue], whom I came across shortly after."[12] Though Eliot pointed only to their technical innovations and their attempts to bring a more modern idiom and rhythm to Victorian verse, their collective impact on Eliot's mind was more substantive than aesthetic. In the early poems now published in *Inventions of the March Hare,* the cross-fertilization between the English and French poets is already evident in Eliot's morbid fascination with the conflicts of desire and beatitude, body and soul, flesh and Absolute. His deepest emotional affinity was with the English poets: he had already begun to feel the stirrings of Johnson's dark angel.

In his "First Debate between the Body and Soul" (January 1910), Eliot's youthful persona is "devoted to the pure idea," but he is thwarted in his search for the Absolute by the debilitating persistence of "Imaginations / Masturbations / The withered leaves / Of our sensations" (*IMH* 64). His "sluggish brain" is dulled not only with remembered sensations but with sexual temptations from "twenty leering houses that exude / The odour of their turpitude." Unable to extricate himself from the "emphatic mud" of his senses, and disturbed by the "cosmic smudge" imprinted on his soul by the thumb of God, he appeals in his lassitude to a shabby old blind man, "a supersubtle peasant," to help him apprehend the Absolute and teach him to regard his own nature "without love or fear / For a little while." As the poet's lascivious imagination is the source of his spiritual frustration, he finally aborts the poem itself as a further profanation of the soul, as yet another of his "Imagination's / Defecations."

The several poems that chronicle the torture of the soul by the body eventuate in a poem that traces the violent metamorphosis of the poet as Saint Narcissus into the poet as Saint Sebastian, as though only a metaphor of martyrdom could convey the extremity of emotion, only the semblance of sainthood could bring relief. In "The Death of Saint Narcissus" an ominous narrative voice summons the persona's attention to the strange shadow of a desert rock that is "something different" from any familiar bodily or temporal shadow. Under the shadow of the gray rock the phantom narrator reveals not only the bloody cloth and limbs of Narcissus, who becomes Sebastian when the burning arrows pierce his smooth white body, but the "gray shadow" of a kind of death that now suffuses Sebastian's lips.

In recounting the stages of the saint's metamorphosis, his death and rebirth, the narrator records the moment at which Narcissus was first "struck down" by self-conscious knowledge of his own sensual beauty, causing him to abandon "men's ways" and become "a dancer before God." In the streets of the city, however, God's dancer suffers horrific sensations of treading on an orgiastic humanity, of walking on a virtual sea of "faces, convulsive thighs and knees." He thus flees the teeming city for the barren sands of the desert and the shadow of the gray rock. Once in the shadow he has hallucinative visions of what he believes to be the succession of his previous Ovidian metamorphoses: first as a tree, "tangling its roots among each other"; then as a fish, "With slippery white belly held tight in his own fingers"; and finally as a young girl sexually violated by a drunken old man, a vision in which Narcissus suddenly comes to know "the taste of his own whiteness / The horror of his own smoothness." Under the shadow, Narcissus has an overwhelming sense of the vanity of lust and the reality of damnation. The spiritual terror turns him into a dancer to God once again, waiting to embrace the arrows that will transform him into Sebastian:

> Because his flesh was in love with the burning arrows
> He danced on the hot sand
> Until the arrows came.
> As he embraced them his white skin surrendered itself to the redness of
>   blood, and satisfied him. (*CPP* 606)

The welcome arrows drain the body of the blood's desires and release the soul from fear of spiritual death. Though Narcissus is dead, the poet, like Saul becoming Paul, is alive, ritually reborn as Sebastian, "green, dry and stained" but with a heavy birthright. He now lives permanently "With the shadow in his mouth," the shadow of a destructive power so palpably tasted that it will suddenly activate a sense of horror when certain desires and temptations rise to frighten the soul.

The violent conflict of body and soul had become not only a malady but a madness for Eliot's personae, as evident in the early drafts of "Prufrock," where in the original epigraph Arnaut Daniel speaks for the first time from his purifying flame in the purgatorial circle of lust: "'Sovegna vos al temps de mon dolor'— / Poi s'ascose nel foco che gli affina" (*IMH* 39).[13] Prufrock, rigidly pacing the streets like a Roman sentinel on his nightwatch, his "Pervigilium," passes by women "spilling out of corsets," prostitutes whose "evil houses" point "a ribald finger" at him and "chuckle" at him in the darkness. At midnight he awakens in a fever-dream to see a figure darker than the night moving before him in the form of an octopus, or devilfish. In terror he describes

>   the darkness
> Crawling among the papers on the table
> It leapt to the floor and made a sudden hiss
> And darted stealthily across the wall
> Flattened itself upon the ceiling overhead
> Stretched out its tentacles, prepared to leap

When dawn finally breaks, Prufrock fumbles to the window "to experience the world / And to hear my Madness singing." His Madness is personified in the form of "A blind old drunken man" (now a recurring figure of degradation in the mind) sitting on the curbstone before him. When his Madness begins to sing, Prufrock's world "began to fall apart," dissolving before his eyes. His devastating encounter with the tentacled darkness in the aftermath of sexual temptation (not

unlike Wilde's encounter with the phantom of desire in "The Sphinx"), leads to
a declaration of his elect experience, as though none other was worse:

> —I have seen the darkness creep along the wall
> I have heard my Madness chatter before day
> I have seen the world roll up into a ball
> Then suddenly dissolve and fall away. (*IMH* 44)

Eliot subsequently canceled this attempt to portray an extreme emotional
experience, as though the explicit madness was unworthy of such models as
Dostoyevsky's Raskolnikov, Shakespeare's Hamlet, and even the poems of Gérard
de Nerval, discovered through Symons's *Symbolist Movement in Literature* (1908).[14]
As an observant student, Eliot subtly brought Nerval's mastery of phantasmal visions and narratives of madness to bear upon and modulate Prufrock's horrific
visions—of his head upon a platter (at some Salome's behest) and of the snicker-
ing figure of death attending him during his forays among the many lovely arms,
"braceleted, white and bare." Eliot's identification with the melancholy persona
of Nerval's "El Desdichado"—"Le prince d'Aquitaine à la tour abolie"—led him
to use the disconsolate prince's descent into the Siren's dreamcave ("J'ai rêvé dans
la grotte où nage la sirène") to describe the alluring "chambers of the sea" from
which the ageing Prufrock knows that he, too, must inevitably awaken, or in the
dream of whose fatal songs he must inevitably drown. Preoccupied with both
Arnaut's canceled sigh and the prince's lament, Eliot would temporarily turn
them under, eventually to retrieve them both for the maddened concluding lines
of *The Waste Land*. Meanwhile, they were superseded in Eliot's mind by the
painters of a secret Christian, Saint Sebastian.[15]

Eliot began searching for paintings that reflected the relation of the physical
body to spiritual turmoil on his Italian tour in July–August 1911, just after completing the final version of "Prufrock," and by 1914 he could identify the Sebastians of Andrea Mantegna, Antonello of Messina, and Hans Memling as
his favorites, particularly Mantegna's lissom saint, whose physical and spiritual
agony are lit by a burning candle tagged with a motto indelibly imprinted on
Eliot's mind: "nil nisi divinum stabile est; caetera fumus."[16] "I have studied
S. Sebastians—" he wrote to Conrad Aiken, "why should anyone paint a beautiful
youth and stick him full of pins (or arrows) unless he felt a little as the hero of
my verse?" (*L1* 44). By the summer of 1914 he had begun another ironic love
song, "The Love Song of Saint Sebastian," in which Eliot's delirious martyr fan-
tasizes the death of his white-gowned beloved, an embodiment of the desire he
must extinguish. Eliot was uneasy about the poem, asking Aiken if he thought it
"morbid, or forced?" (*L1* 44). In a monologue reminiscent of the deranged lovers
in Browning's "Porphyria's Lover" and "My Last Duchess," Sebastian envisions
coming before her in a hair shirt, in a self-flagellating state of madness brought
on "after hour on hour of prayer /And torture and delight." He would follow
her white feet to her bed, where in white gown and braided hair she would let
him die with his head between her breasts. But this fantasy dissolves in another,
of Sebastian strangling his beloved while perversely observing the unique curl
and curve of her ears:

I think that at last you would understand.
There would be nothing more to say.
You would love me because I should have strangled you
And because of my infamy;
And I should love you the more because I had mangled you
And because you were no longer beautiful
To anyone but me. (*IMH* 78–9)

Eliot carries the imagery and conflicts of the Sebastian poems into "The Burnt Dancer" (June 1914), a poem deeply informed by the context of the epigraph ("sotta la pioggia dell' aspro martiro"), taken from the description of the crimson river of flame that rains upon tormented souls damned for ungoverned desire in the seventh circle of hell (*IMH* 62). There Dante speaks with the burnt forms of three Florentine shades who break off from a troop that passes "beneath the rain of the sharp torment" (*Inferno* 26, line 6).[17] When the shades, their bodies twisted together into a wheel for awkward propulsion, ask Dante if the virtues of courtesy and valor have been lost in the "perverse country" of Florence, he affirms that they have indeed succumbed to materialism, pride, and excess. After asking Dante to remember them to friends above, they break from their wheel, "and, as they fled, their nimble legs seemed wings."

Eliot's winged creature, his "papillon noir," is similarly "caught in the circle of desire" as its beating wings dramatize in a "twisted dance" the flight of the poet's own wayward soul. The "black moth," strayed from the whiter, benign flames and "vital values" of an ideal star, has been drawn into the orbit of a lesser, earthly star and become distracted by the merely "golden values" in a dangerous "yellow ring of flame." As the poet observes his dark dancer, he insistently urges it to intensify the dance. Bewildered in a world become "too strange" for virtues defined by the reality of good and evil, pride and shame, he would have the strayed visitant reveal in the dance what virtue he uses in the circle of desire, what secret he brings to the whimpering children of this world, what warning of disaster he signals from his distant star. As the dance proceeds in "the circle of my brain," the poet describes the dancer with the metaphors of a divided self: he is, on the one hand, like Sebastian, "The patient acolyte of pain," who "expiates" his heedless flight through tireless beating of wings; and on the other he is "The singèd reveller of the fire," flying in abandon to the burning flame. Caught on and tossed between the horns of spiritual and sensual desire, the poet's black moth, losing sight of the end of desire, desires the loss of desire itelf. Once burnt, however, he becomes a "broken guest who may not return," forever separated from his hidden star. Recognizing his own soul fallen on the "ragged teeth" of the yellow ring, the poet desperately redoubles his hopeless cry to dance an exit from the burning flame: "O danse danse mon papillon noir!" As Johnson's dark angel tortured delight with desire, and as Sebastian's prayers were wrought with "torture and delight," so Eliot's papillon noir brings "Agony nearest to delight." In a world of desire, the dancer before God is a burnt dancer, like Dante's shades ever under the rain of the sharp torment, denied the unadulterated delight of divine vision.

More than any biography could, these and other early poems show the young poet and student of philosophy trying to represent and control in his art the intensity of his internal conflicts, able to create poems but unable to subli-mate passions, and they place him in the company of that morbid brotherhood that Arnold and Yeats had observed so intently in France and England. Emily Hale, whom Eliot met in Boston in 1912, and with whom he played in amateur theatricals in 1913, would not have been privy to his internal sexual drama. Be-fore leaving for Germany and England in the summer of 1914, he professed his love to her. But after a year of philosophical studies at Oxford, he confessed to Aiken the dramatic effect of having arrived in London alone: "How much more self-conscious one is in a big city! Have you noticed it? Just at present this is an inconvenience, for I have been going through one of those nervous sexual at-tacks which I suffer from when alone in a city. Why I had almost none last fall I don't know—this is the worst since Paris. I never have them in the country" (*L1* 75). The poems themselves illuminate the spiritual terror triggered by those attacks over the previous three years and arrest any easy speculation about Eliot's sexual life that his letter may invite. Those "nervous" attacks, with their repellent visions of carnal coupling in the city streets, were not unknown to Prufrock and Narcissus. And from the beginning, it was in the city, not in the country, that Eliot would stage the drama of a spiritual consciousness under sensual assault. As he subsequently explained, in yet another Dantean vision of a squalid humanity covered in glutinous secretions, "Some poets, such as Baudelaire, similarly pos-sessed by the town, turn directly to the littered streets, the squinting slums, the grime and smoke and the viscid human life within the streets, and find there the centre of intensity."[18]

The dark angel had descended on Eliot in the streets of Boston, Paris, and London; after his sudden marriage to Vivienne (soon abbreviated to Vivien) Haigh-Wood and removal to London in the summer of 1915, the city would gradually become for him as "Unreal" as Baudelaire's Paris. Under the surface of his daily life, Eliot the teacher, banker, and critic was living in a phantasmagoria of shadows and specters. When he returned to Baudelaire in 1919, he was struck by a line in "Les Sept Vieillards"—"Où le spectre, en plein jour, raccroche le pas-sant!" "I knew what *that* meant," Eliot wrote, "because I had lived it before I knew that I wanted to turn it into verse on my own account" (*TCC* 127).[19] The gradually disclosed reality of sexual betrayal in his marriage had magnified his sense of spiritual dispossession, and when he began to transform the voices of his spectral dreamscapes into *The Waste Land,* the most imperious voice heard by his persona among the broken images and allusions of sexual betrayal was again the desert voice that summoned Narcissus to the shadow:

> (Come in under the shadow of this red rock),
> And I will show you something different from either
> Your shadow at morning striding beside you
> Or your shadow at evening rising to meet you;
> I will show you fear in a handful of dust. (*CPP* 61)

In this poem of memories mixed with desires, the fragments of sexual memory overwhelm the fragmented spiritual memory, but the fearsome biblical voice in the shadow resounds through *The Waste Land* into *Ash-Wednesday* and *Four Quartets,* reminding all that "desire shall fail" and admonishing all to "Fear God" (Ecclesiastes 7:5).

Eliot was moved to personify the reality of the shadow that terrifies his personae in "The Hollow Men," where those who reside in "death's dream kingdom" live with the knowledge that across their actions of desire "Falls the Shadow."[20] And the paralyzing mental states wrought in art by those living under the Shadow are not to be slighted or misrepresented by the psychological descriptions of unperceiving critics and translators, as Eliot makes clear when he comes to Baudelaire's defense in his review of Arthur Symons's translation of *Baudelaire: Poetry and Prose* (1926), where Symons says that Baudelaire's poetry issues from "nerves" and "hysteria." "And hysteria!" Eliot impatiently exclaims in violent protest against Symons's psychological portrait, "was any one ever less hysterical, more lucid than Baudelaire? There is a difference between hysteria and looking into the Shadow."[21] Appalled by Symons's textbook analysis, Eliot quotes for the reader Symons's assertion that Baudelaire's poetry was driven by "a deliberate science of sensual and sexual perversity, which has something curious in its accentuation of vice with horror, in its passionate devotion to passions." To Eliot, Symons fails to perceive the spiritual mechanism at work in Baudelaire's "accentuation of vice with horror," fails to comprehend that Baudelaire's sense of the Shadow was so strong and terrifying in the presence of persistent passions that his poetry was driven not by nerves and hysteria but by his failure to master passion in a desperate search for the divine.

Eliot's Shadow had now become a constant player in his poems and plays. In "Animula" the "misshapen" soul becomes in its deformity the "Shadow of its own shadows," a "spectre in its own gloom." In working on the drafts of *Sweeney Agonistes,* he came across a passage in the letters of Junius that he temporarily added as an epigraph, as if to suggest that the characters in the play he could not finish issued from a drama of personal shadows: "These are the gloomy companions of a disturbed imagination; the melancholy madness of poetry, without the inspiration."[22] As the Chorus in *Murder in the Cathedral* affirm in their portentous statement, "We have all had our private terrors, / Our particular shadows, our secret fears," and they sense that the "great fear" that may come upon them is "A fear like birth and death, when we see birth and death alone / In a void apart" (*CPP* 244). Thomas Becket, too, knows that in the face of threatening events "the substance of our first act / Will be shadows, and the strife with shadows. / Heavier the interval than the consummation" (*CPP* 246). In *The Family Reunion,* Harry describes his sudden awareness of the imminent onset of the Eumenides as

> That apprehension deeper than all sense,
> Deeper than the sense of smell,
> . . . a vapour dissolving
> All other worlds, and me into it. (*CPP* 311)

In Harry's description of his phantasmal world, Eliot gives full voice to the violent drama he has lived for thirty years:

> Now I see
> I have been wounded in a war of phantoms,
> Not by human beings—they have no more power than I.
> The things I thought were real are shadows, and the real
> Are what I thought were private shadows. O that awful privacy
> Of the insane mind! (*CPP* 334)

In *The Cocktail Party* Edward externalizes his private shadows when he says to Lavinia,

> And then you came back, you
> The angel of destruction—just as I felt sure.
> In a moment, at your touch, there is nothing but ruin.
> O God, what have I done? The python. The octopus. (*CPP* 398)[23]

Nowhere, however, does Eliot describe more vividly the shadow of the dark angel coming upon him than in *East Coker*, but there he waits, at last, not in fear but in stillness, faithfully waiting for the darkness to become the light:

> I said to my soul, be still, and let the dark come upon you
> Which shall be the darkness of God. As, in a theatre,
> The lights are extinguished, for the scene to be changed
> With a hollow rumble of wings, with a movement of darkness on darkness
> And we know that the hills and the trees, the distant panorama
> And the bold imposing façade are being rolled away—(*CPP* 180)

Here again is the sense of "darkness on darkness" that Prufrock had tried to describe in madness after his pervigilium thirty years earlier, and the "hollow rumble of wings" is meant to suggest the arrival of the angel of darkness in the mind as much as the rumbling away of side-scenes in the drama.

When Eliot began to reflect anew on the creative process after his conversion, he came to feel in himself, and to find confirmed in others, a strange relation between certain kinds of morbid illness and creativity, as if a certain dependency existed between analogous states of body and imagination.[24] A. E. Housman had made such an observation about his own writing in *The Name and Nature of Poetry* (1933), where he admits that much of his poetry was written in ill health and that the process had been "agitating and exhausting." Declaring that the production of poetry "is less an active than a passive and involuntary process," Housman defines poetry itself as "a secretion," his own and much other poetry as "a morbid secretion, like the pearl in the oyster." Eliot reviewed Housman's printed lecture in the *Criterion,* stating there that

> Observation leads me to believe that different poets compose in very different
> ways: my experience (for what it is worth) leads me to believe that Mr. Hous-

man is recounting the authentic processes of a real poet. "I have seldom," he says, "written poetry unless I was rather out of health." I believe I understand that sentence. If I do, it is a guarantee—if any guarantee of that nature is wanted—of the quality of Mr. Housman's poetry. (*Cr* 12: 154)

Eliot found confirmation in Housman of what he had written in his Norton Lectures, *The Use of Poetry and the Use of Criticism,* several months earlier—that "there is an analogy between mystical experience and some of the ways in which poetry is written." It is clear that for Eliot some morbid blockage in the mystical process precedes and is completed by the creative process, which closely parallels or reenacts the mystical struggle. He had attempted to characterize the process in "Dante" (1920), his first essay on that author: "The contemplation of the horrid or sordid or disgusting, by an artist, is the necessary and negative aspect of the impulse toward the pursuit of beauty" (*SW* 143). Now he went further:

> To me it seems at these moments, which are characterised by the sudden lifting of the burden of anxiety and fear which presses upon our daily life so steadily that we are unaware of it, what happens is something *negative:* that is to say, not "inspiration" as we commonly think of it, but the breaking down of strong habitual barriers—which tend to reform very quickly. Some obstruction is momentarily whisked away. The accompanying feeling is less like what we know as positive pleasure, than a sudden relief from an intolerable burden. (*UPUC* 144–5)

As Eliot explains, a poem that quickens when the poet is in ill health has usually undergone a long period of incubation, and thus, he says, it "cannot be suspected of being a present from a friendly or impertinent demon." The poem itself may not be a present from a demon, but a demon is certainly present for the inception of the poem. It is in the mystical process that the poet's demon implants the dark seed of the poem; it is in the creative process that the poet, according to Eliot's shifting metaphors, exorcises or gives birth to the consequent "burden" within. Eliot would continue to alternate and combine these metaphors in his discussions of the creative process, for they were indicative of the inextricably close relation of the mystical-creative struggle.

Early in 1933, in the midst of delivering his Norton Lectures, he paused to write a critical preface for the collected poems of Harold Monro. Moving beyond his previous knowledge of individual poems by Monro, Eliot was struck by how his patient immersion in the whole work made him aware of a "personal vision" that distinguished Monro from his Georgian contemporaries. Eliot identified Monro as being among those poets whose originality is dictated "not by the idea—for there is no idea—but by the nature of that dark embryo within him which gradually takes on the form and speech of a poem."[25] Eliot suddenly recognized in Monro a rare contemporary in his own tradition; he saw in Monro's poetry, as in Housman's, the authentic process that led to "the real right thing," describing it as though it were his own:

I feel always that the centre of his interest is never in the visible world at all, but in the spectres and the "bad dreams" which live inside the skull, in the ceaseless question and answer of the tortured mind, or the unspoken question and answer between two human beings. . . . The external world, as it appears in his poetry, is manifestly but the mirror of a darker world within. . . . Under the influence of this sincere and tormented introspection, the warm reality dissolves: both that for which we hold out our arms, and that at which we strike vain blows.[26]

When Eliot revisited the creative process twenty years later in "The Three Voices of Poetry" (1953), he continued to describe the poet's struggle with the "dark embryo," which represents, he says, some "unknown, dark *psychic material—* we might say, the octopus or angel with which the poet struggles" (*OPP* 100).[27] It was a startling analogy, as if from a distance he could finally identify Prufrock's octopus and the poet's dark angel as both the agon and the muse of his morbid art. Under the pressure of this "rude" negative mass, the creative process begins; the poet finds himself

oppressed by a burden which he must bring to birth in order to obtain relief. Or, to change the figure of speech, he is haunted by a demon, a demon against which he feels powerless, because in its first manifestation it has no face, no name, nothing; and the words, the poem he makes, are a kind of form of exorcism of this demon. In other words again, he is going to all that trouble, not in order to communicate with anyone, but to gain relief from acute discomfort; and when the words are finally arranged in the right way . . . he may experience a moment of exhaustion, of appeasement, of absolution, and of something very near annihilation, which is in itself indescribable. (*OPP* 98)

Here is the mystic-poet drawn into that demonic wilderness of the self that Yeats had described. Over and over again Eliot wrestled with embryo and demon in a continuous spiritual-poetic process. Even in the midst of writing the *Four Quartets* he did not feel that the creative process was "authentic" unless the one preceded the other, writing to Bonamy Dobrée on 6 August 1941 that "as my natural way of writing verse seems to require a long period of germination for each poem, before I address myself to the machine, I have been afraid that I have been overproducing, and at last trying to make poetry out of unseasoned material" (Brotherton). Only in the completion of *Four Quartets* did Eliot finally exorcise his personal demon—his octopus, his python, his moth, his angel—bringing the long struggle of the flesh and the dark angel in his poetry to an exhausting dénouement. No verse defines more sharply the heart of Eliot's personal struggle than the canceled invocatory stanza of Lionel Johnson's poem:

Dear and dread God, Thou sendest me
This Angel of the dark, that I
From out the dark may cry to Thee,
Fear, and adore, and love, and cry.[28]

II

In centennial retrospect, we can see how close Eliot was to the 1890s poets in temperament, how singularly he took up their spiritual burden, how immersed he was in their work before and after he discovered the French symbolists. As I will show, when he left America in 1914 he carried them with him to Georgian London, followed them into the music halls, and mulled their blasphemous cries. Moreover, he soon began lecturing—not only on Arnold (including "Empedocles on Etna"), Thomson, "The Nineties," the *Yellow Book*, aestheticism, and "art for art's sake," but on John Davidson, Dowson, Johnson, Symons, Thompson, and Wilde as poets of doubt and belief. Their spiritual sensibilities remained crucial to him before Baudelaire came back into his life, especially when he found himself, as on a darkling plain, surrounded by Georgian poets who were writing, as he said, a poetry that "belongs to the sensibility of the ordinary sensitive person" and static poems that "failed to show any very interesting development in the mind and experience of the author."[29] By the mid-1920s, however, Eliot began to distance himself from the English "decadents," not only because their personal lives had become prominently portrayed on the garish fin de siècle canvas (even Yeats had been painted with the decadent brush),[30] but because the nature of their spiritual lives had begun to pale before his intensive study of Baudelaire.[31] As Dowson and Johnson receded, Baudelaire became his sole contemporary. Thus, when Eliot reviewed Symons's translation and criticism of Baudelaire in 1927, he declared that it revealed little about Baudelaire and much about the religious "childishness" of the 1890s—and of the 1900s as well:

> What is right in Mr. Symons's account is the impression it gives that Baudelaire was primarily occupied with religious values. What is wrong is the childish attitude of the 'nineties toward religion, the belief—which is no more than the game of children dressing up and playing at being grown-ups—that there is a religion of Evil, or Vice, or Sin. Swinburne knew nothing about Evil, or Vice, or Sin—if he had known anything he would not have had so much fun out of it. For Swinburne's disciples, the men of the 'nineties, Evil was very good fun. Experience, as a sequence of outward events, is nothing in itself; it is possible to pass through the most terrible experiences protected by histrionic vanity; Wilde, through the whole of the experiences of his life, remained a little Eyas, a child-actor. On the other hand, even to act an important thing is to acknowledge it; and the childishness of the 'nineties is nearer to reality than the childishness of the nineteen-hundreds. But to Baudelaire, alone, these things were real. (*FLA* 91–2)

The Eliot who made these harsh comparisons had just come through his own Baudelairean night with the reality of evil, vice, and sin. His opportunistic review of Symons's book in the *Dial* was meant to inform his American readers that English critics from Swinburne to Symons had misrepresented Baudelaire to English readers. To Eliot, Swinburne's review of *Les Fleurs du Mal* in 1862, in which he portrayed Baudelaire as an exemplar of art for art's sake and the beauty of evil, had largely determined the misperception of Baudelaire in the 1890s. And now Symons, a survivor of that decade, the critic who had omitted Baudelaire from his *Symbolist Movement in Literature* until the third edition appeared in 1919, had come forth to perpetuate the crime, enshrouding Baudelaire "in the Swinburnian violet-coloured London fog of the 'nineties" (*FLA* 94). In effect, Eliot had declared himself the new interpreter of Baudelaire "in our time"; he had drawn a direct line of descent from Baudelaire to himself, bypassing all the Victorians.[32] And yet, whatever "infection of decadence" he had come to see in the religious poets of the 1890s, he could not deny the importance of their own connection to Baudelaire. These poets, he wrote, "are nearer to us than the intervening generation—I date in *literary* generations; and the fact that they were interested in Baudelaire indicates some community of spirit" (*FLA* 86–7). However blasphemous their ways and destructive their lives, Eliot knew that they, too, had suffered under the shadow of the dark angel, who had driven them all toward Catholicism through the *via negativa* of despair and degradation. "How else but through a broken heart," asked Wilde in "The Ballad of Reading Gaol," "My Lord Christ enter in?" Even as Eliot broke through the darkness himself, he invoked prayer in *Ash-Wednesday* for those who, walking and waiting in darkness, "are terrified and cannot surrender" (*CPP* 97). He had already begun to affirm in his criticism the continuing importance of their spiritually ill lives in a spiritually vacuous world. As critical as he could be of Wilde, for example, he was not deceived by Wilde's Satanic poses and blasphemous postures, affirming in his Clark Lectures (1926) that the currents of religious feeling that flow from Baudelaire in France and Cardinal Newman in England proceed "even in a degraded and popularised form to Oscar Wilde" (*VMP* 162). The existence of a pose, Eliot declares, "implies the possibility of a reality to which the pose pretends. One of the constant by-products of this revival of morality is Satanism; but even Satanism—the cultivation of Evil—in any of its curious forms, in part of Baudelaire, in Barbey d'Aurevilly, in Huysmans, in Wilde's *Pen, Pencil and Poison*—is a derivative or an imitation of spiritual life" (*VMP* 209).

As this and other passages confirm, Eliot's frame of reference in his writing is not only to the French symbolists discovered in Symons's book but to the whole complex of French and English decadents, to all the men of Baudelaire. And yet, though Eliot drew on technical innovations from each side of the channel, he was more ambivalent toward the French poets than toward the English poets of the 1890s. He had already begun to challenge the philosophical romanticism of Jules Laforgue and his contemporaries. In his poetic dialogue with them, he probed the foundation of their spiritual hunger, the operation of their sense of good and evil, their awareness of the Shadow. If he found his early aesthetic inheritance primarily on the French side of Baudelaire, in Laforgue, Tristan Corbière, Théophile Gautier, and Stéphane Mallarmé, he found his spiritual inheritance primarily on the English side, in Johnson, Dowson, Thompson, Wilde. He too knew and recognized the states of mind engendered by subverted passion and unresting thought, by demonic possession and spiritual dispossession; he too made them the source and substance of his art. Quite apart from his association with all the young modernists in London and Paris after 1914—Pound,

Wyndham Lewis, Joyce—Eliot was the last of the poets of the 1890s, like them a Hamlet of his age, strangely a romantic poet with a classical sensibility, caught up in that deeply introspective tradition that Arnold and Yeats eschewed. Eliot's poetry, we come to see, is not only richer for being immersed in that tradition but greater for having transcended it. Yeats, who did not live to read *Four Quartets,* had underestimated the intensity of Eliot's struggle with Johnson's dark angel, for Eliot broke through the mystical obstructions and barriers that defeated his predecessors; he claimed in spiritual and creative exhaustion a victory of the soul; he embodied in contemplative poetry the liberating joy and vision that Arnold and Yeats had not thought possible through passive suffering.

The dark angel governs but one plane of Eliot's complex spiritual, intellectual, and creative life, but the succeeding chapters of this book assume the reality and operation of that plane at all times. Eliot was himself drawn to authors whose characters lived in a "double world," authors who could intimate the existence of several planes of reality and who possessed the skill to keep them intersecting. He knew too that it was the most difficult art for both the poet and the audience. Most people, he has Harry say to Amy, "don't understand what it is to be awake, / To be living on several planes at once / Though one cannot speak with several voices at once" (*CPP* 324). When we first read Eliot as students, when we first hear "Prufrock" or *The Waste Land* or *Little Gidding,* we may not know what the poems mean, but we may sense that they mean something terribly important, that they speak to us on a personal level and touch a substratum of our selves that we may not have visited before. "It is a test," Eliot affirms, "that genuine poetry can communicate before it is understood" (*SE* 238). But when that initial excitement leads us to the critics in an attempt to better understand the compelling poetic voice, we may be dismayed to read that it is not personal at all, that it is deliberately impersonal, employs objective correlatives, relies on the mythical method, mines the most obscure recesses of the classical-Christian tradition, and expresses primarily the dissociation of sensibility in the modern world. If we read further, we are told that his voice is in reality misogynistic, homoerotic, elitist, racist, fascist, absolutist, orthodox and, in the view of one recent critic, "terribly malignant," until we are intimidated into believing that the voice we must have misheard was not a voice we want to hear at all.[33] In view of the swelling barrier reef of reductive and formulaic criticism, we may never hear the low and high registers of despair and love, horror and vision; we may never awaken to the intersecting planes and voices of a life lived intensely in art.

It is often remarked that if only we had an authorized biography of Eliot we would see him steadily and see him whole. Eliot did not want a biography written about himself because he did not believe that a poet's life is as important as his poetry, and he did not want readers to be distracted from the life of the poetry. Even if we had a greatly detailed biography of Eliot, much of the imaginative and intellectual life would be lost to the the demands of chronology and narrative; the biographer could hardly hope to portray the several planes lived simultaneously and keep them communicating. When a group of distinguished literary biographers recently met to respond to Helen Vendler's provocative statement that "The biography of an author ought to take as its centre the imaginative dynamic by which one can make sense of the oeuvre," they were uniform in declaring the difficulties of doing so.[34] "The real problem," writes John Haffenden, "may be that the art of narrative—the heart of biography—is fundamentally embarrassed by literary criticism. Too many biographers evidently fear that narrative momentum will be interrupted or skewed by what (they have little doubt) will turn out to be essayistic excursions." Lawrence Lipking, concerned with how the life and the art can be held in balance, asserts that "In practice they seldom are. Notoriously, the quality of the author's best work tends to bleach out in literary biographies," and consequently most biographers "usually deepen the mystery they set out to solve: how did that singular person create this body of work that seems to belong to us all?" Isobel Grundy concurs that in the necessity of constructing narratives the biographer is inevitably impelled to "flatten and simplify" the multiple selves of the artist: "None can escape the constant friction between the narrative drive to coherence and the moments-of-being drift to fragmentation." And Max Saunders voices the general conclusion that "literary biography is a hybrid form that has two objects of knowledge: facts about the life, and criticism of the works; and the two stories it tells can't be persuasively integrated."[35] Summaries and sacrifices effecting the shaping of the life and the art are made at every turn, as R. F. Foster reveals in his authorized biography of Yeats: "Most biographical studies of WBY are principally about what he wrote; this one is principally about what he did."[36] There are times in the study of an author when a detailed biography is crucial to certain kinds of critical, historical, and cultural interest, and this is certainly such a time for Eliot. But if we cannot look to the biographer to explore and map the planes and intersections where life and art meet, then the the job of constructing the imaginative dynamic falls to the biographical critic.

There is no doubt that the theorists of the New Criticism greatly stymied the development of biographical criticism in the last half-century. In their *Theory of Literature* (1948), René Wellek and Austin Warren, attempting to make such criticism totally extrinsic to and disreputable in the interpretation of the artistic object, declared dogmatically that "it seems dangerous to ascribe to [biography] any specifically *critical* importance. No biographical evidence can change or influence critical evaluation."[37] If that was not a sufficient deterrent, the postmodern proclamation of the Death of the Author all but emptied the literary archives. Most critics lost all confidence in exploring the difficult and delicate relation of art and life, leading more than one generation to shirk, in Yeats's words, "The spiritual intellect's great work," in Eliot's, "the progress of the intellectual soul." Dissuaded from tainting the pure literary object with the stains of sensibility, consciousness, intellect, and spirit, we have since found ways to make it the legitimate wellspring of political concerns and cultural bias. Certainly, some bold attempts to discover patterns of behavior or disposition in Eliot's poems fail as the result of an ulterior critical motive or a tenuous manipulation of word and image without factual support. Still, for all the caveats and known excesses, the reluctance to trace the transfiguration of life into art makes criticism of Eliot less humanistic and arresting than it might be, for our strongest intimation from the first reading is that all the work is intensely personal. That was Eliot's own intimation in reading any great author; much of his criticism derives from his steady pursuit of the personal voice.

Moreover, the charge of the biographical critic is larger than earlier academic concerns with authorial intention and textual indeterminancy would indicate; the charge is to explore the ways in which art and personality, art and consciousness, are indissolubly linked, the ways in which the reconstruction of biographical and intellectual contexts may indeed change or influence critical evaluation. The critic probes those aspects of the life that have exerted tremendous pressure on the art, the intersections or nodes where life events have become the material of art (and criticism) under intensive creative pressure and transformation. Unconstrained by the chronological and narrative necessities of the biographer, the biographical critic is free to return again and again to the same period, to plumb and connect the several planes of consciousness that operate there and that may converge in a creative point, in what Eliot calls the point of escape from the "acute discomfort" of personality into the impersonality of art. As he says, "only those who have personality and emotions know what it means to want to escape from these things" (SE 10–11). The critic aims not only to record the unique complex of personal and artistic voices but to uncover the obscure figures and chart the forgotten events that once operated with significant effect on the artist's work. In effect, the critic becomes a kind of cartographer, constructing not a single map but a layered atlas of artistic and intellectual life, gradually erasing from terra incognita the grotesque emblems of reductive criticism. In the process, the chronology is often reordered, the contours of intellectual and artistic life reshaped. Ultimately, however, the biographical critic aims to complement the biographer, gradually defining the imaginative dynamic to which the biographer can but partly attend, for their common aim is to place a representation of the art and life of the artist not only in academia but in the larger world of serious readers.

The chapters in this book were written as interconnected layers in an ongoing atlas of Eliot's life, poetry, and criticism. Though the study encompasses the origins and endings of Eliot's creative and critical career, the separate chapters are ordered not by linear progression but by events of significance and intensity in Eliot's life and work. They defer to "the moments-of-being drift to fragmentation" rather than to "the narrative drive to coherence," to "essayistic excursions" in literary criticism rather than to narrative momentum. They attempt to fill glaring gaps on an intellectual grid, beginning with a full account of Eliot's immeasurably important experience of teaching Extension classes to working students. Even as he prepared his first lectures, however, he discovered the poetry and criticism of T. E. Hulme, who must now be dramatically relocated on the grid as one of the most important and influential figures in Eliot's intellectual life. As we see the remarkable consolidation in 1916 of Eliot's broad classical point of view in the concept of Original Sin, we discover that his twenty-five-year debate with romanticism had begun eight years earlier in his intensive philosophical engagement with Jules Laforgue, a figure previously seen only on an aesthetic plane of Eliot's early poetic life.

As Eliot lectured on French and English literature and on Hulme's poetry and criticism, his marriage to Vivien and his friendship with Bertrand Russell got under way. Russell, his former teacher and permanent intellectual antagonist, was to become one of the darkest angels in Eliot's life when a shock of marital betrayal in a shared cottage in Marlow triggered a sequence of horrific moments that were to influence his poetry and criticism for the next thirty years. And yet, at this same devastating time Eliot was deeply immersed in his favorite pastimes, the music halls and the ballet, two of the most important components of his developing theory of poetic drama, both largely neglected in the biographical and intellectual records. When this plane comes into play, when we see Eliot's love of the performers, their songs and dances and methods of acting, indeed, when we see his immersion in popular culture and its lifelong effect on his art and life, some of the calcified attitudes toward his work may begin to dissolve.

Eliot's rediscovery of Baudelaire in 1919 coincided with a walking tour of southern France, an event that was to bear heavily on the composition of *The Waste Land*. On that tour with Ezra Pound he experienced another of the horrific moments that fueled the composition of this poem, where the voices on every plane of consciousness vie to be heard, but he had so learned from Webster, Baudelaire, and others how to use and control personal horror in his poetry that evidence of controlled horror became a primary interest and criterion of his criticism. As his estrangement from Vivien deepened in the 1920s, he renewed his contact with Emily Hale; as he wrote *Sweeney Agonistes,* he became an ascetic follower of St. John of the Cross. The invitation to give the Clark Lectures on metaphysical poetry was, he revealed, "a ray of hope just at the *blackest moment of my life*" (*VMP* 6). When these planes of life converge in *Ash-Wednesday,* we see that it is less a poem of conversion and more the beginning of a deeply regretful love poem, a *Vita Nuova* eventually completed in *Four Quartets.*

Through his awe of Baudelaire's profound sense of good and evil, Eliot began to formulate his moral criticism in the 1920s, gradually lifting the conflict of classicism and romanticism begun with Laforgue to a higher plane of absolute values and adopting orthodoxy and heresy as critical terms. In his simultaneous personal struggle with doubt and the problems of belief, however, he became intrigued by the symbolic importance of what he calls Baudelaire's blasphemy, a submerged but crucial concept that significantly alters our perception of Eliot's unique attempt to provide for the moral valuation of literature. Concurrently, even deeper in the substrata of his intellectual life, he had entered into a difficult and uncertain evaluation of the *Spiritual Exercises* of St. Ignatius, through whom he completed his long engagement with the classic-romantic theme. Just as that conclusive moment came, he rediscovered George Herbert, whose poetry was to dramatically reshape the direction of Eliot's creative and critical life. At that point he dropped the hand of Baudelaire, who could take him no further, and made Herbert his closest poet-companion. In Herbert's *The Temple* Eliot found a structure of human love and hard-won faith that he carried into *Four Quartets,* where visionary gain is set against the hardly bearable pain of personal denial.

Most of the chapters in this book have had earlier lives as lectures and as independent essays, though chapters 5 and 8 have not been published previously in any form. All have been continuously expanded and renewed as archival and other research materials have become available, piece by piece, year by year. The appendix is a related part of this critical atlas, for the plot of a poet-critic's relation to his publishers and the editions of his work represents the most continuous and often the most culturally revealing plane of a great literary life.

IN THE LECTURE HALLS

When sunlight glows upon the flowers,
Or ripples down the dancing sea:
Thou, with thy troop of passionate powers,
Beleaguerest, bewilderest, me.

Who ever thinks about T. S. Eliot as a classroom teacher, preparing lectures late at night and marking the papers of working-class adults who came exhausted from their jobs to attend his classes? Who ever considers how crucial was his teaching experience to the development of his poetry and criticism? Most of Eliot's readers are quite familiar with the succession of his wartime activities after he arrived in England in September 1914—postgraduate student, new husband, dissertation writer, assistant editor, poet, reviewer, and banker. Biographical accounts of this period usually make passing mention of his brief tenure as a schoolmaster, begun out of financial necessity when he made the decision to marry and remain in England, but there is seldom the slightest notice of his Extension lectures for workers. He took his first position at the High Wycombe Grammar School in September 1915, earning £140 per annum, with dinner, until he found a slightly more remunerative position at the Highgate Junior School, which brought him £160, with dinner and tea. "I stayed at that for four terms," he reported to his Harvard classmates, "then chucked it because I did not like teaching."[1] Even so, before he fled from the middle-class adolescents he had already applied for lecture and tutorial classes for adults with the Oxford University Extension Delegacy, and with the University of London Joint Committee for the Promotion of the Higher Education of Working People; his financial difficulties required him to continue teaching on a part-time basis. What has been missing from the record of Eliot's intellectual life is the fact that for the next three years he was steadily employed and deeply engaged as an Extension lecturer and tutor for five Workers Educational Courses on Elizabethan, Victorian, and modern French literature. The recovered syllabuses for those courses provide an astonishingly rich map of Eliot's reading life: they show how thorough was his grounding in French and English literature, literary criticism, social and intellectual currents, moral and philosophical attitudes, political and economic theories, as he began to formulate his own critical positions. Eliot's Extension courses were the source of the great watershed of readings that he would draw on continuously for his highly allusive poetry and criticism. The letters and records related to those courses show not only what "immense pleasure" his teaching brought to him in a difficult personal life but how deeply affected the twenty-eight-year-old American was by the war-torn lives of his working-class students.

I

Eliot evidently applied to the Oxford University Extension Delegacy in the autumn of 1915, for he appears in the Delegacy's list of lecturers published in February 1916. He is shown as offering six separate courses on modern French literature, only one of which was requested for the following autumn.[2] In April, Eliot completed his dissertation on F. H. Bradley, and in August, having decided to forego an awaiting assistant professorship in philosophy at Harvard, he wrote to Conrad Aiken: "This autumn will find me busier than ever, as I am preparing a set of six lectures on contemporary intellectual movements in France to deliver under the auspices of Oxford to the general public—mostly, I believe, ladies. If they come off, I ought to be able to secure plenty of lecturing, at least enough to keep us" (*L1* 144). In the summer of 1916, as Ezra Pound led him to anticipate the publication of *Prufrock and Other Observations,* Eliot hoped to find sufficient lecturing and reviewing to become fully self-supporting while pursuing his literary career. Only then could he plan to abandon full-time teaching at Highgate and free up more time for his own work.

Eliot's lectures and classes on modern French literature were held in the afternoons from 3 October to 12 December 1916 at Ilkley, in Yorkshire, an experience that would soon be recorded in his poem "Mélange Adultère de Tout" (1917), in which he catalogues his recent vocational roles: "En Yorkshire, conférencier." His journeys to Ilkley to teach Extension students also afforded him his first introduction to Yorkshire's wealthy manufacturing class, many members of which were known to Vivien as old family friends. On 11 October 1916 she described them to Eliot's brother Henry as "most dreadful people really—very *very* rich manufacturing people—so *provincial* that my American friends tell me they are very much like Americans!! Tom has just met a few at Ilkley (in Yorkshire) when he went for his first lecture—and *he* says the same—he was struck with how much more like Americans they are than the South of England people" (*L1* 154). This encounter in Ilkley, near the manufacturing town of Bradford, was to be translated into Eliot's description of "the young man carbuncular" in "The Fire Sermon": "One of the low on whom assurance sits / As a silk hat on a Bradford millionaire."

Eliot's course was arranged by the Local Committee for the Extension of

University Teaching in connection with the "Literary and Scientific Society." As was customary, the Delegacy provided for free distribution the *Syllabus of a Course of Six Lectures on Modern French Literature* (Oxford, 1916), "by T. Stearns Eliot, M.A. (Harvard)." In a letter to his former Harvard professor, J. H. Woods, Eliot explained that the lectures were "on Social, Philosophical and Religious Problems in Contemporary France (the syllabus is given as 'Literature' and the course is advertised as 'Contemporary France,' but that is what it really is" (*L1* 152). His syllabus and reading list follow.[3]

LECTURE I

The Origins: What Is Romanticism?

Contemporary intellectual movements in France must be understood as in large measure a reaction against the "romanticist" attitude of the nineteenth century. During the nineteenth century several conflicting tendencies were manifested, but they may all be traced to a common source. The germs of all these tendencies are found in Rousseau.

Short sketch of Rousseau's life.
His public career consisted in a struggle against
    (1) *Authority* in matters of religion.
    (2) *Aristocracy* and *privilege* in government.

His main tendencies were
    (1) Exaltation of the *personal* and *individual* above the *typical*.
    (2) Emphasis *upon feeling* rather than *thought*.
    (3) Humanitarianism: belief in the fundamental goodness of human nature.
    (4) Depreciation of *form* in art, and glorification of *spontaneity*.

His great faults were
    (1) Intense egotism.
    (2) Insincerity.

Romanticism stands for *excess* in any direction. It splits up into two directions: escape from the world of fact, and devotion to brute fact. The two great currents of the nineteenth century—vague emotionality and the apotheosis of science (realism) alike spring from Rousseau.

LECTURE II

The Reaction against Romanticism

The beginning of the twentieth century has witnessed a return to the ideals of classicism. These may roughly be characterized as *form* and *restraint* in art, *discipline* and *authority* in religion, *centralization* in government (either as socialism or monarchy). The classicist point of view has been defined as essentially a belief in Original Sin—the necessity for austere discipline.

It must be remembered that the French mind is highly theoretic—directed by theories—and that no theory ever remains merely a theory of art, or a theory of religion, or a theory of politics. Any theory which commences in one of these spheres inevitably extends to the others. It is therefore difficult to separate these various threads for purposes of exposition.

The present-day movement is partly a return to the ideals of the seventeenth century. A classicist in art and literature will therefore be likely to adhere to a monarchical form of government, and to the Catholic Church. But there are many cross-currents. Our best procedure is to sketch briefly the relation of politics, literature, and religion, and then consider the work of a few representatives of these three interests.

A. Politics: General feeling of dissatisfaction with the Third Republic, crystallizing since the Dreyfus trial. Hence two currents: one toward syndicalism, more radical than nineteenth-century socialism, the other toward monarchy. Both currents express revolt against the same state of affairs, and consequently tend to meet.

Nationalism is an independent movement, but tends to associate itself with monarchism.

B. Religion: Neo-Catholicism is partly a political movement, associated with monarchism, and partly a reaction against the sceptical scientific view of the nineteenth century. It is very strongly marked in socialistic writers as well. It must not be confused with modernism, which is a purely intellectual movement.

C. Literature: Movement away from both realism and purely personal expression of emotion. Growing devotion to form, finding expression in new forms. Disapproval of dilettantism and aestheticism. Expression of the new political and religious attitudes in literature.

We shall consider men of letters only as they represent political, religious, or philosophical tendencies.

LECTURE III

Maurice Barrès and the Romance of Nationalism

Barrès illustrates the transition between the nineteenth and twentieth centuries. His two phases:

    (1) Begins as an exponent of egotistic aestheticism in the "nineties," comparable to J. K. Huysmans and Oscar Wilde. His early novels. Novels of Italy. *Bérénice.*

    (2) His entrance into politics as a deputy. In his later novels he returns to the scenes of his childhood—Lorraine. Becomes the champion of the irreconcilables of Alsace-Lorraine.

Barrès' later novels: *Les Bastions de l'Est: Colette Baudoche.*

These novels illustrate two features of nationalism: growing spirit of revenge against Germany, and the cult of the soil—the local, as contrasted with the Parisian spirit—which has been taken up by many modern writers.

While the gulf that separated France from Germany always widened, French writers turned more and more to England. Evidences of the Anglophile sentiment in French letters.

Besides the loyal band of traditional royalists there are several intellectuals who have been led to the royalist position largely as a protest against all the conditions in art and society which seemed to be due to the Revolution.

The two most noteworthy of these men are Pierre Lasserre and Charles Maurras.
    Characteristics of their work:
        Their reaction fundamentally sound, but marked by extreme violence and intolerance.

Contemporary socialism has much in common with royalism. Growth of proletariat, as contrasted with bourgeois socialism. Causes of this: conservative and compromise character of official socialism.

A peasant journalist: Charles Péguy.
        Sketch of his life. Celebrity due to his death on the battlefield.
        His relations with Jaurès. Foundation of the *Cahiers de la quinzaine.*
        His writings and literary style.

Péguy illustrates nationalism and neo-Catholicism as well as socialism; and the fusion of nationalism and Catholicism in his *Jeanne d'Arc.*[4]

A more violent reaction against bourgeois socialism is found in Georges Sorel, the initiator of syndicalism.
        His philosophic creed.
        His theory of the general strike.
        His development toward royalism.

Both of these men—Péguy and Sorel—were strongly influenced by Bergson.

Reaction against the positivism of Taine and the scepticism of Renan, the two chief intellectual leaders of the nineteenth century. Tendency of the French intellectual to return to orthodox Christianity.
    Modernism is merely a compromise between the point of view of historical criticism—inherited from Renan—and orthodoxy.

This return to the Church is illustrated in authors of all types.

Among poets by—

Francis Jammes. Sentimental Christianity, really romanticist.

And especially by—

Paul Claudel. Claudel is also nationalist. His Christianity is that of medieval philosophy. The national and the Christian sentiments are the mainspring of his poems and his poetical dramas. Claudel a writer of great force and great influence, but often falls into rhetoric and verbiage.[5]

Contrast between the Catholicism of twentieth-century men of letters and that of the nineteenth century. It is more social and political, less individualistic and ascetic.

LECTURE VI

Before and After the War: Questions for the Future

The philosophy of 1910.[6]

Henri Bergson was then the most noticed figure in Paris. The leading idea of his philosophy. Comparison with Maeterlinck: the two men have in common

(1) The use of science against science.

(2) Mysticism.

(3) Optimism.

Influence of Bergson upon some of the men already mentioned. Is this influence good or bad? Whether it is likely to persist.

Summary of contemporary tendencies. Influence of the war.

Forecast of French thought after the war.

BOOKS

ROUSSEAU: *The Social Contract* (Everyman's Library, 1s.3d. net); *Confessions* (3s.net, in French 2s.10d. net); *De l'origine de l'inégalité* (in French, 2s.net).[7]

LEMAÎTRE: *Jean-Jacques Rousseau* (Heinemann, 10s. net).

BARRÈS: Novels: For the first period, *Le Jardin de Bérénice* (3s.3d. net). For the later period, *Colette Baudoche; La Colline inspirée* (each 3s.3d. net). Political writings: *Scènes et doctrines du nationalisme* (3s.3d. net); *La Patrie française* (6d. net); *Pages choisies* (2s.).

MAURRAS: *L'Avenir de l'intelligence; La Politique religieuse.*

LASSERRE: *Le Romantisme français* (3s.3d. net).

PÉGUY: *Œuvres choisies, 1900–10* (3s.3d. net); *Le Mystère de la charité de Jeanne d'Arc* (3s.3d. net); *Notre Patrie* (3s. net).

SOREL: *Reflections on Violence* (Allen & Unwin, 7s.6d. net); French text, 4s.6d. net).

CLAUDEL: *Art poétique* (3s.3d. net); *The Tidings Brought to Mary* (Chatto & Windus, 6s. net; French text, 3s.3d. net); *The East I Know* (H. Milford,

5s.6d. net; French text, 3s.3d. net).
BERGSON: *Introduction to Metaphysics* (2s. net).
MAETERLINCK: *Wisdom and Destiny, The Life of the Bee* (Allen & Unwin, 2s.6d. net each).
SABATIER, PAUL: *Modernism* (5s. net); *Disestablishment in France* (3s.6d. net); *France To-Day: Its Religious Orientation* (6s. net).
LOISY: *The Gospel and the Church* (1s.6d. net); *War and Religion* (1s.6d. net).

Recommended for special subjects:

> For Rousseau: Lord [John] Morley, *Rousseau,* 2 vols.; Frederika Mac-
> donald, *Rousseau.* For the influence of Rousseau and the ideas of the
> Revolution outside of France, such books as [H. N.] Brailsford's *Shel-
> ley, Godwin and their Circle* (Home University Library, 1s.3d. net), or
> [Sydney] Waterlow's *Shelley* (People's Books, 6d. net).
> For the leading ideas of the nineteenth century: Renan, *Souvenirs d'en-
> fance et de jeunesse* (Nelson, 1s.3d. net); Taine, *Introduction à l'histoire de la
> littérature anglaise* (D. C. Heath & Co.); Babbitt, *Masters of Modern French
> Criticism* (Constable); Bourget, *Essais de psychologie contemporaine* (2 vols.,
> 3s.3d. net each).
> For exposition and criticism of contemporary ideas (neo-classicism,
> neo-Catholicism, &c.): various works of Ferdinand Brunetière, Émile
> Faguet, and Jules Lemaître will be referred to in the course of the lec-
> tures, and especially Anatole France, *La Vie littéraire* (4 vols., 3s.3d. net).
> For contemporary literature: Amy Lowell, *Six French Poets;* Jacques
> Rivière, *Études* (3s.3d. net); Henri Ghéon, *Nos Directions* (3s.3d. net);
> Ezra Pound, *The Approach to Paris.*[8]
> For Bergson: H. Wildon Carr, *Bergson* (People's Books, 6d. net).
> For recent publications of French men of letters in connexion with
> the war: Loisy's *War and Religion* and Barrès' *Pages choisies,* mentioned
> above, and Romain Rolland, *Above the Battle* (2s.6d. net); André Suarès,
> *Péguy, Nous et eux* (3s. each); Lasserre, *Le Germanisme et l'esprit humain*
> (1s.3d.).
> The best short history of French literature is G. L. Strachey's *Landmarks
> in French Literature* (Home University Library, 1s.3d.net).

The average attendance at each of the lectures was fifty-eight, with an average of fifteen attending the discussion classes that followed. In his formal report
on the lectures Eliot noted two main difficulties in measuring the reaction of his
audience: the absence of student papers and the novelty of the material, which
was "difficult and involved." The students' general lack of familiarity with the authors and material discussed "precluded any discussion of an argumentative nature," though Eliot modestly felt that his audience "showed a highly intelligent
interest in the material, was keen and critical, and followed the lectures with
closer attention than they merited." In a separate general critique of the class,
Eliot reveals the frustrations of a first-year lecturer: "The audience seemed ex-

tremely intelligent, but somewhat passive; it seemed to consider the subject rather as interesting information than as matter to provoke original thought. It did not wish mere entertainment, but was not prepared for study." Eliot concluded his report by regretting the diminutive "male element" at the lectures. The scarcity of men was of course due to the war, and its effect on the performance of the class is reflected in the Local Secretary's report, which tempers Eliot's criticism of the students' lack of energy and initiative:

> The hour of the lectures was unpopular—It also made it impossible for most teachers to attend the course—The subject was difficult, and it was all new ground—Lectures much appreciated by the better educated members of the audience, who used the Library hard—The war has affected the centre adversely—Many of our members are away nursing and so on—others are too busy or tired to attend regularly or to read—.

The war continued to have adverse effects on Eliot's courses for the next three years.

II

While Eliot was preparing his Ilkley lectures he was making application to the University of London Extension Board, listing among his qualifications his Harvard M.A. in English, his study at the Sorbonne, his position as assistant to the department of philosophy at the Harvard Graduate School, his Sheldon Traveling Fellowship at Merton College, Oxford, and his position as Oxford Extension lecturer. On 19 October 1916 the university's Joint Committee for the Promotion of Higher Education for Working People approved his application for tutorial work, added his name to its list of lecturers, and resolved "that Mr. Eliot be the tutor for the Southall I class provided that there is satisfactory evidence that he will be remaining in England for a reasonable period." After the printing of his *Syllabus for a Tutorial Class in Modern English Literature* (London, 1916), he began, concurrently with his Yorkshire lectures and his final term at Highgate, the first year of a three-year Tutorial Class at Southall, Middlesex.[9] His classes were held on Monday evenings for twenty-four weeks during the autumn and winter of each year. Each class met for two hours, with the first hour devoted to lecture and the second to questions and discussion. The sixteen-part syllabus is "divided by subject and not by lecture."

MODERN ENGLISH LITERATURE

I. Tennyson

Survey of the Romantic Period. Influences upon Tennyson. Temper of his time. His personality. Early verse (1830–42). Technique. Read: *Lady of Shallott, Lotos-*

Eaters, Mariana, Morte d'Arthur, Ulysses, Locksley Hall, The Two Voices, The Palace of Art.

Tennyson's longer poems. Tennyson's scientific interests. Politics. Moral teaching. Religious views. Relations with his contemporaries. Read: *Maud, In Memoriam, Idylls of the King.*

II. Browning

Contrast with Tennyson. His personality. Influences upon him. Early verse. Read: *Pauline.*

Dramatic qualities of Browning. Characterisation. Range of emotion. His mature technique. Read: *Dramatic Lyrics, Dramatic Romances, Dramatis Personae, Men and Women.*

Browning's residence and study in Italy. His thought. Moral ideas. Examination of *Sordello* and *The Ring and the Book.* Read: *The Ring and the Book* (especially I, V, VI, VII, X).

The dramas. Survey of Browning's later work. Read: *Pippa Passes, A Blot on the 'Scutcheon.*[10]

III. Elizabeth Barrett Browning

Quality of her genius. Marriage and correspondence. Social interests. Read: *Rime of the Duchess May, Lady Geraldine's Courtship, The Lost Bower, The Cry of the Children, The Dead Pan, A Musical Instrument, Sonnets from the Portuguese.*

IV. Carlyle

Life and personality. Carlyle and Jane Welsh. Carlyle and Froude. Early influences. Study in Germany. Style. Read: *Sartor Resartus, John Sterling.*

Carlyle as moralist and social reformer. Relation to Chartism. His political views. Read: *Chartism, Past and Present, Heroes and Hero Worship.*

Carlyle as historian and critic. Historical methods. Comparison with Macaulay. Read: *French Revolution.*

V. John Henry Newman

His temperament, with regard to his change in religious attachment. Relation to the Oxford Movement. Reasons for joining the Church of Rome. His thought. Style. Read: *Apologia, Idea of a University.*

VI. Dickens

Reasons for his greatness. Comparison with earlier novelists and humorists. Development of his work. Plot and situation. Examination of some of his characters. Influence, especially in Russia. Read: *Pickwick Papers, David Copperfield, Bleak House.*

VII. Thackeray

Contrast with Dickens. Education. Influences upon his style. Satire and senti-ment. Characterisation. The historical novel. The novel of society. Comparison with other novelists' handling of similar material. Read: *Esmond, Vanity Fair, Pendennis.*

Thackeray as critic and essayist. Read: *English Humourists, The Four Georges, Roundabout Papers, Poems.*

VIII. George Eliot

Life and personality. Her philosophy of life: moral views. The tragic spirit. Ex-amination of a few of her characters. Eliot, Thackeray, and Dickens as representa-tive of their age. Read: *Scenes of Clerical Life, Romola, Mill on the Floss.*

IX. Matthew Arnold

Prose:

Survey of literary criticism in England. French influence upon Arnold. Arnold as a guide to taste. Importance of the *Essays in Criticism.*

Arnold as a moralist. His view of society. Comparison with Carlyle and Emerson. Attitude toward Christianity. Read: *Essays in Criticism, Culture and Anarchy.*

Poetry:

The elegiac spirit. Technique. Quality of emotion. Classical tastes. Restraint. Read: *Scholar Gipsy, Rugby Chapel, Dover Beach, Sonnets, Stanzas from the Grande Chartreuse, Heine's Grave, Tristram and Iseult, Empedocles on Etna.*

X. Minor Novelists

DISRAELI: Relation of his novels to his political life. Read: *Coningsby.*
PEACOCK: Satire and wit. Peacock as a precursor of Meredith. Read: *Nightmare Abbey, Headlong Hall.*
CHARLES READE: The historical novel. The novel of social reform. Read: *Peg Woffington, or The Cloister and the Hearth, It is Never Too Late to Mend.*
TROLLOPE: The novel of country society. Compared with Jane Austen. Read: *Barchester Towers.*

XI. The Brontës

Work of the three sisters compared. Comparison with Jane Austen and George Eliot. Read: *Jane Eyre, Wuthering Heights, Shirley.*[11]

XII. George Borrow

Unique position of Borrow in literature. His eccentric personality. The novel of gipsy life. His relation to the "picaresque" novel. Unevenness of composition. Read: *Lavengro, The Romany Rye, The Bible in Spain.*

XIII. Ruskin

Life and personality. Ruskin's work as an art critic. His emphasis upon moral values in art. Survey of art criticism in England. Ruskin's greatness and limitations as a critic. Admiration for the painting of Turner. Read: *Stones of Venice, Modern Painters* (selections), *Lectures on Art* (selections).

Ruskin as a stylist. Unevenness and extraordinary brilliance of his writing. W. C. Brownell on Ruskin's style.

Ruskin as a moralist and social reformer. Compared to Carlyle. Read: *Unto This Last, Crown of Wild Olive, Munera Pulveris.*[12]

XIV. Edward Fitzgerald

Isolation. Scholarship. Merit as a translator. Comparison of the two versions of *Omar Khayyám.* His prose works. Letters. Read: *The Rubaiyat of Omar Khayyám, Euphranor.*[13]

XV. George Meredith

Influences. Originality and difficulty of his style. Meredith as a critic and essayist. Read: *Essay on Comedy.*

Meredith as a poet. Verse technique. His sonnet sequence compared with Mrs. Browning's and others. Read: *Modern Love, Love in the Valley.*

Meredith as a novelist. Wit and epigram. Brilliance of dialogue. Irony. Portraits of women. Read: *Richard Feverel, Beauchamp's Career, The Amazing Marriage.*[14]

XVI. Retrospect

View of earlier and later Victorian literature.

SUPPLEMENTARY READING

G. K. Chesterton, *The Victorian Age in Literature* (Home University Library);[15] W. C. Brownell, *Victorian Prose Masters;* A. C. Bradley, *A Commentary on Tennyson's "In Memoriam";* Hallam, Lord Tennyson, *The Life and Works of Alfred, Lord Tennyson; Tennyson and His Friends;* David Duff, *An Exposition of Browning's "Sordello";* Edmund Gosse, *Robert Browning, Personalia;* Sir Henry Jones, *Browning as a Philosophical and Religious Teacher;* Alexandra L. Orr, *A Handbook to the Works of Robert Browning;* Arthur Symons, *An Introduction to the Study of Browning;*

J. A. Froude, *Thomas Carlyle; My Relations with Carlyle;* Wilfrid Meynell, *Cardinal Newman;* S. P. Cadman, *The Three Religious Leaders of Oxford and Their Movements;* W. P. Ward, *The Life of John Henry Cardinal Newman;* G. K. Chesterton, *Charles Dickens;* John Forster, *The Life of Charles Dickens;* Anthony Trollope, *Thackeray;* C. K. Shorter, *The Brontës;* Robert A. J. Walling, *George Borrow: The Man and His Work;* A. C. Benson, *Ruskin: A Study in Personality;* J. A. Hobson, *John Ruskin, Social Reformer;* Thomas Wright, *The Life of Edward Fitzgerald;* Richard Le Gallienne, *George Meredith: Some Characteristics;* G. M. Trevelyan, *The Poetry and Philosophy of George Meredith;* Stopford A. Brooke, *Four Poets: Clough, Arnold, Rossetti, Morris;* J. M. Robertson, *Modern Humanists: Sociological Studies of Carlyle, Mill, Emerson, Arnold, Ruskin and Spencer;* R. W. B. Browning, ed., *The Letters of Robert Browning and Elizabeth Barrett Barrett, 1845–46;* S. R. T. Mayer, ed., *Letters of Elizabeth Barrett Browning to R. H. Horne;* Charles E. Norton, ed., *Letters of Carlyle; The Correspondence of Thomas Carlyle and Ralph Waldo Emerson, 1834–72;* Alexander Carlyle, ed., *New Letters and Memorials of Jane Welsh Carlyle;* G. Hogarth and M. Dickens, eds., *The Letters of Charles Dickens;* Mary Dickens, *Charles Dickens: By His Eldest Daughter; A Collection of Letters of William Makepeace Thackeray, 1847–55;* W. A. Wright, ed., *Letters of Edward Fitzgerald;* W. M. Meredith, ed., *Letters of George Meredith.* The *English Men of Letters* is the best series of biography.

Eliot wrote to members of his family with great enthusiasm about his lectures and students. "One of the class told me that I was the best literature tutor they had ever had in that class," he told his father. "I enjoy it immensely, and the Monday evening is one of the moments of the week that I look forward to. The class is very keen and very appreciative, and very anxious to learn and to think. These people are the most hopeful sign in England, to me" (*L1* 161). Later in the month he wrote to tell his cousin Eleanor about his new position and duties at Lloyds Bank:

> My greatest pleasure however is my workingmen's class in English Literature on Monday evenings. I have steered them through Browning (who arouses great enthusiasm), Carlyle, Meredith, Arnold, and am now conducting them through Ruskin. There are not many working *men* at present, except one very intelligent grocer who reads Ruskin behind his counter; most of them are (female) elementary schoolteachers, who work very hard with large classes of refractory children all day but come with unabated eagerness to get culture in the evening (stimulated, I hope, by my personal magnetism). (*L1* 168)

He delighted in describing the characters in his classes, especially two women who may have been the real prototypes of Madame Sosostris:

> I sit at the head of a table flanked by Mrs. Howells and Mrs. Sloggett. Both are mad. Mrs. Howells is a spiritualist, and wanted to give me mental treatment for a cold in the head. She writes articles on the New Mysticism etc., for a paper called the *Superman,* and presents them to me. Mrs. Sloggett writes me letters beginning Dear Teacher, Philosopher and Friend, and her special interests are astrology and politics. She has written a character study of me (very flattering)

which I should like to send you; and spends some of her time writing letters to cabinet ministers. Still, at the present time she does not seem to me much madder than most people. The rest of the class are quite sane, and some of them are remarkably clever, and I have to do my best to keep up with them in discussion. (*L1* 168)

Eliot's weekly journeys to Ilkley and Southall were his first ventures into working-class England, and he was quick to champion his students' attitudes toward learning as he began to make national comparisons. "In America," he wrote to his sister,

there would, I think, be less chance for this sort of class. Education is so diffused, and it is so easy for almost anyone to get a so-called "college education," that education is less prized. A young man who will work himself to death to "go through college" usually works himself to death making money afterwards. The idea of people studying all their lives is unknown, as also among the more prosperous classes in England. But my class is entirely *disinterested* in its devotion to study and thought. (*L1* 166)

His growing admiration of and affection for his students led him to make English class comparisons as well. "This class of person," he wrote to his cousin, "is really the most attractive in England, in many ways; it is not so petrified in snobbism and prejudice as the middle classes, and yet is very humble. To an American, the English working classes are impressive because of their fundamental conservatism; they are not, as a whole, aggressive and insolent like the same people in America" (*L1* 168-9). When he wrote to Professor Woods about his lectures, stating that he found the working class "the most agreeable in England to me," he was much less restrained about the English middle class: "The middle class—including most of the people one knows, or at least their families, is hopelessly stupid. Its family life is hideous. When of sufficient means, the middle classes want their sons to go to public schools; but the only motive is snobism, [*sic*] and the lack of respect for education is amazing" (*L1* 171).

In his formal half-session report to the Joint Committee, Eliot stated that he was "very well pleased with the work of the majority of the class." Many of his students, however, had been unable to keep up with their reading for the lectures, and Eliot found it necessary to depart somewhat from his syllabus:

I ask the students *all* to read some particular work on the current author, in order that there may always be a common basis for discussion; but when (as is usually the case), a student has very little time, I recommend further reading of one author in whom the student is interested, rather than a smattering of all. Because of the students' lack of time . . . it seems to me on the whole desirable to devote more time to fewer authors, even if it is necessary to sacrifice altogether some of those named in the syllabus.

Fortnightly essays were standard requirements in Extension courses, and though it was a written condition of attendance that all essays be completed, tutors generally had considerable difficulty extracting student papers. Of his twenty-four students Eliot reported: "The most conscientious members of the class number about twelve or fourteen. There are others who need constant stimulation, and about half a dozen who have so far written no essays. I am writing personal letters to each of these, as well as making appeals in the meetings." Eliot was particularly conscientious in marking and assessing his students' papers, and in reporting their progress in written reports to the Joint Committee. By the end of the year only three students had satisfied the writing requirements,[16] and one of his best students had been summoned to the war. "Of the three writers who fulfilled the requirements," Eliot reported,

> I think that on the whole Miss Gardner deserves the most praise. Her work showed a careful and intelligent grasp of the subject, and her eager interest was an unfailing support. Miss Hastie's work was less even. Miss Hastie already had a far wider store of reading than any other member of the classs—is in fact remarkably well read—and this was a distinct advantage to her especially in more purely literary criticism, where she did her best and most original work. Mrs Howells is far below these two, but showed some improvement in composition, and read faithfully. Of the others Miss Bickle's work is distinctly good; it is crude and miniature, but often thoughtful and original. She entered late, and was overworked, or she might have done still better. Miss Allder was interested but commonplace. Mr Coltman's work was first-rate, refreshingly vigorous and independent, and his summons to the Army deprived the discussion of a good deal of its liveliness. Miss Radcliffe wrote two papers one extremely good, but was ill or in poor health a large part of the winter. I regret not having had more papers from the others who wrote, as several were quite promising.

Quite apart from the writing requirements, and the weekly reading assignments, the lectures themselves were demanding of student attention after a long working day. In his final assessment of the year's work Eliot indicated that he had interwoven several thematic subjects into the discussion of various authors:

> We devoted at the end four evenings to Ruskin and one to George Borrow. In retrospect, I believe that I might have co-ordinated the work better; so far as I was concerned, the work was largely experimental and tentative. It was possible, however, to call attention to the background of Victorian literature; the importance of such phenomena as the Oxford Movement, Utilitarianism, the Manchester School, Darwinism and Renanism, especially in dealing with Arnold, Carlyle, and Ruskin. It would be an advantage I believe if the Library might include such books as Mill's *Utilitarianism,* or Renan's *Life of Jesus,* besides those of the men actually dealt with, and also a few historical works covering the period. . . . In proceeding, I think there is ample material for a year on the rest of the nineteenth century, without dealing with living authors, which I do not favour. I do not wish to slight the personal element, but if the course can be arranged on the basis of subjects—instead of passing from one man to another, I think more papers would be written; as the members are deterred by thinking that

before they can read a book and write about it, the author will have been dropped.

III

On 19 March 1917, near the end of his first-year tutorial, Eliot had gone to work for Lloyds Bank, "as a stop-gap" he told Professor Woods. "Literature and journalistic work is not in great demand, nor is lecturing or teaching, except school teaching, which I refuse to return to—it is altogether too exhausting" (*L1* 171). In May he became assistant editor of the *Egoist,* and in June *Prufrock and Other Observations* was published by the Egoist Press. Eliot planned to continue his tutorial class at Southall in the autumn, and to further supplement his income he arranged to give a course on Victorian literature under the auspices of the London County Council.[17] On 12 September, after the completion of *Ezra Pound: His Metric and Poetry,* Eliot described the preparation of his lectures to his mother:

> I have begun to be very busy the last few days preparing my lectures. One set covers very much the same ground as my lectures at Southall last year, but more broadly, beginning with "The Makers of Nineteenth-Century Ideas," lectures on Carlyle, Mill, Arnold, Huxley, Spencer, Ruskin, Morris—then the poets, and then the novelists. I have never read much of George Eliot, the Brontes, Charles Reade, or the Kingsleys. (*L1* 194)

This course of twenty-five lectures was given on Friday evenings at the County Secondary School, High Street, Sydenham, beginning 28 September. Eliot received a flat fee of a pound a lecture, with no expense allowance. His syllabus for *A Course of Twenty-Five Lectures on Victorian Literature* (London, September 1917), which misprints the lecturer as "T. G. Eliot," lists only the titles of the lectures.[18]

COURSE OF LECTURES
ON
VICTORIAN LITERATURE

1. Introductory—The Social Framework.

The Makers of Nineteenth-Century Ideas

2. History and Criticism—Thomas Carlyle.
3. A Contrast in Ideas: John Stuart Mill and Matthew Arnold.
4. The Influence of Science—Darwinism in T. H. Huxley and Herbert Spencer.
5. Art and Economics—John Ruskin and William Morris.

The Development of English Poetry

6. Characteristics of Victorian Verse—Some Comparisons.
7. Tennyson as a Representative of his Age.
8. Robert and Elizabeth Browning—Poets of Love and Life.
9. Browning and his Men and Women.
10. Three Poets of Doubt—Matthew Arnold, Edward Fitzgerald, James Thomson.
11. Philosophy in Poetry—George Meredith.[19]
12. The Pre-Raphaelite Movement—D. G. Rossetti and William Morris.
13. A Poet of Liberty—A. C. Swinburne.
14. Poets of Religious Faith—Christina Rossetti, Francis Thompson, Lionel Johnson.

The Development of English Fiction

15. General Survey.
16. The Brontës and their Special Significance in the History of the Novel.
17. Charles Dickens and his Social Types.
18. Thackeray and Social Satire.
19. Kingsley, Reade, and the Novel of Social Reform.
20. George Eliot.[20]
21. George Meredith—A Critic as Novelist.
22. Thomas Hardy and Realism.

Byways of Victorian Literature

23. The Gipsy Pateran—George Borrow, Richard Jefferies and others.
24. Aestheticism—Walter Pater and Oscar Wilde.
25. The Laureates of Nonsense—Edward Lear, Lewis Carroll, and the Makers of Light Verse.

IV

"The other course," Eliot wrote of his Southall tutorial, "is a continuation of last year's; they want me to start with Emerson, go on to Samuel Butler and William Morris, then the Pre-Raphaelites, and so on. Both of these courses depend for their continuance upon the enrolment at the first few lectures, so I am waiting anxiously" (L1 194). On 14 October Eliot wrote to say that "enough members have enrolled for each; whereat I am much rejoiced, as it is rather a compliment to a class to exist at all at the present time, and also, we shall need the money very much this winter" (L1 199). Though he was conducting two separate courses, Eliot entered his second year of lecturing as a more efficient teacher and effective speaker. "I am very busy with my lectures," he wrote to his father, as I give one on Fridays and one on Mondays, I have hardly finshed one before I begin to think of the next. But they cost me far less in effort and time than they used to; I only make a couple of pages of notes now, and I can talk away for an hour or more. When I began, I used to try to get too much into the time, which I believe made the lectures difficult to follow. . . . The feeling of power which you get by speaking from very brief notes is pleasant. I remember that the first lecture I gave, in Yorkshire, I had written all out and tried to memorise, and when I came to deliver it I found that I had quite enough for two hours talk! (*L1* 204)

When the second-year tutorial began, the war, illness, and other misfortunes had reduced the number of students to fifteen; only twelve remained at the beginning of the second term. Eliot's *Syllabus for a Tutorial Class in Modern English Literature, Second Year's Work* (London, 1917) is again "divided by subjects and not by lectures."

MODERN ENGLISH LITERATURE

I. Emerson

Characteristics of New England literature of the time. Emerson's relation to English men of letters. The society in which he lived. Religious and philosophical environment: Unitarianism and Transcendentalism.

Emerson's style as an essayist. His aloofness; contrast with Carlyle, Arnold, and Ruskin. Quality of his thought. Read: *Essays, Nature,* and *The Conduct of Life.*[21]

Emerson as a poet. Read: *Selected Poems.* Suggested Reading: Thoreau, *Walden;* Hawthorne, *The Scarlet Letter;* chapter in *Great Writers of America,* in the "Home University Library."

II. William Morris

Original impulse and meaning of "Pre-Raphaelitism." Its relation to Ruskin. Morris's life and personality. His place as a poet; obligations to Tennyson. His mediævalism. Morris as a ballad writer and as a writer of narrative verse. Read: Selections from the *Defence of Guenevere* and from the *Earthly Paradise.*

Morris's attitude towards art. His experiments; beginnings of the arts and crafts movement. Read: *Hopes and Fears for Art; Architecture, Industry, and Wealth; Signs of Change.*

Morris as a prose writer. His prose romances. Read: *The Roots of the Mountains, The Glittering Plain.*

Morris's social philosophy. Communism. Comparison with Ruskin. His original contribution towards social progress. Read: *News from Nowhere, A Dream of John Ball.*[22]

III. Dante Gabriel Rossetti

Transition of the mediæval movement in literature from Ruskin to Rossetti. Rossetti the individualist, and detached artist. Temperament. His use of ballad form. Read: *The Blessed Damozel, The White Ship.*

Rossetti as poet and painter. His aesthetic creed. Read: *The House of Life.*

IV. Swinburne

The pure romantic. Relation to Pre-Raphaelitism. "Paganism." His early attitude. His championship of liberty. Merits and faults of his poetry. Read: Selections from *Poems and Ballads; Atalanta in Calydon,* selections from *Songs Before Sunrise.*

Swinburne as prose writer. Comparison with Shelley, as a poet.

V. Walter Pater

The pure aesthete: "art for art's sake." Qualities of his style; its elaborateness. His works of imagination, his criticism, and his gospel of life. His influence. His enthusiasm for art at the opposite pole from Ruskin's, though both react against industrialism. Read: *Studies in the Renaissance* (especially the Conclusion), *Imaginary Portraits.*

VI. Samuel Butler

A solitary figure, neglected until he received the enthusiastic praise of Shaw. His eccentric career. Versatility: Butler is important for his theories of Evolution, his social satires, his novels, and for his ideas on all subjects as found in his "Note-Books." Complete independence of mind. No political, social, or literary movement to forward. Short sketch of his theory of Evolution, opposed to Darwinism. Read: *Life and Habit.*

Butler's social satires. His influence upon Shaw. His wit. His philosophy of life. Read: *Erewhon.*

Butler as a novelist. Read: *The Way of All Flesh.*

Butler's criticisms of art, science, literature, life. His greatness as a satirist. Read: Selections from the *Note-Books.* Also suggested: Bernard Shaw's *Cashel Byron's Profession, An Unsocial Socialist;* Gilbert Cannan's *Satire.*[23]

VII. Robert Louis Stevenson

A dilletante of letters. His reputation as a prose writer. Influence of Meredith. Characteristics of his generation: Stevenson and Henley. His style, and rank as a novelist. The novel of adventure: a predecessor of the sevenpenny, but better written; comparison with the popular novels of a previous generation. Stevenson and the short story. Read: *Treasure Island; Kidnapped; Markheim.*

Stevenson as an essayist and letter writer. His philosophy of life. Read: *Vailima Letters, Travels with a Donkey, Virginibus Puerisque.*

Stevenson as a poet. Read: *A Child's Garden, Collected Poems.*

VIII. The "Nineties"

Characteristics of the group of the "Yellow Book." Influence of Walter Pater. Their attitude toward life. Some personalities: Wilde, Ernest Dowson, Lionel Johnson, Aubrey Beardsley, Francis Thompson, W. B. Yeats, and Bernard Shaw (in his earlier phase). The "Celtic Movement": Yeats, Synge, A. E., Fiona Macleod. Read: Oscar Wilde: *Intentions; The Importance of Being Earnest; The Ballad of Reading Gaol;* Selected poems of Dowson, Johnson, Thompson, Symons, Yeats, Davidson; Synge: *The Playboy of the Western World.*

IX. Thomas Hardy

Hardy's conception of tragedy: comparison with Greek tragedy. Importance of the local background of his novels: studies of the effect of circumstance and environment upon character. Relation of man to the world; necessity and chance. The naturalistic attitude in modern fiction and verse. Hardy's philosophy as seen in his poems. Read: *Poems* (Selections).

Hardy as a prose master. Irony, and absence of humour. His style. Relation of plot to character. Analysis of some leading characters. Read: *Jude the Obscure, The Return of the Native, The Mayor of Casterbridge.*

X. Conclusion

Comparison of the later part of the nineteenth century with the earlier. Growth of the naturalistic attitude: influence of science. Development of Socialism and Aestheticism. Changes in religious outlook. Different ideals in prose fiction: continental influence. Different ideals in poetry.

SUPPLEMENTARY READING

On Emerson: Oliver Wendell Holmes, *Ralph Waldo Emerson;* Charles E. Norton ed., *The Correspondence of Thomas Carlyle and Ralph Waldo Emerson, 1834–72;* Emerson's *Journal* (10 vols.) is well worth reading parts of, to obtain a more intimate knowledge of the man.[24]

William Morris: J. W. Mackail, *The Life of William Morris; William Morris and His Circle;* Holbrook Jackson, *William Morris: Craftsman, Socialist.* The best short and comprehensive account of Morris and his work, by a sympathetic critic and disciple, is A. Clutton Brock's *William Morris,* in the "Home University Library."

Rossetti: William Sharp, *Dante Gabriel Rossetti: A Record and a Study;* A. C. Benson, *Rossetti;* W. M. Rossetti, *Dante Gabriel Rossetti: His Family Letters.*

Swinburne: Edward Thomas, *Algernon Charles Swinburne: A Critical Study.*

Walter Pater: Ferris Greenslet, *Walter Pater;* A. C. Benson, *Walter Pater;* Thomas Wright, *The Life of Walter Pater.*

Samuel Butler: Gilbert Cannan, *Samuel Butler: A Critical Study.*

Stevenson: Walter Raleigh, *Robert Louis Stevenson.*

Oscar Wilde: A. Ransome, *Oscar Wilde: A Critical Study.*

The Celtic Movement: Yeats's *Synge and the Ireland of his Time* and *Poetry and Ireland;* F. L. Bickley, *J. M. Synge and the Irish Dramatic Movement;* Lady Gregory, *Our Irish Theatre.*

Thomas Hardy: H. C. Duffin, *Thomas Hardy: A Study of the Wessex Novels.*[25]

SUGGESTIONS FOR PAPERS

Subjects will be proposed in connection with each lecture, but it is also suggested that those who are specially interested in any particular aspect or phase of later Victorian literature should plan three or more papers on related subjects. In this way writers could be studied who are not directly dealt with in lectures, and reading could be concentrated. Such work might result in papers which could profitably be read before the class. The following are suggested:

> Emerson and his Circle (the point of view of Emerson, Thoreau, Hawthorne, etc.).
>
> Socialism in Literature (the various forms of socialism expressed by Ruskin Morris, Shaw, and others).
>
> "Art for art's sake" (a valuation of this attitude, as shown by Pater, Wilde, Whistler, Arthur Symons).
>
> Mediæval influence in poetry and prose (either the mediæval ideal as expressed by Carlyle, Ruskin, Morris, or mediæval themes and manners in the verse of Morris, Rossetti, and the Irish poets).
>
> Naturalism (the materialistic view of John Davidson, the fatalism of Hardy).
>
> The Celtic Revival (Yeats, Synge, A. E., and others: nationalism and literature: definition of the Celtic spirit).
>
> The Drama (Shaw, Wilde, Synge, and the Abbey Theatre in Dublin, the influence of Ibsen).

Despite dwindling numbers and "a larger proportion of ill health," Eliot felt that his class had "maintained a very satisfactory activity" during the second year. "Miss Gardner deserves high commendation for her written work," Eliot reported to the Joint Committee, "and so also, considering her illness, does Miss Hastie. Mrs Howells and Mrs Sloggett have both shown considerable improvement, and the other papers have been of at least as good quality as last year." Though there had been less writing, more books had become accessible, and the students had done more reading. "The subjects covered," he wrote, "have proved more interesting to the Class than last year's, and especially Samuel Butler. Considering the difficulties with which we have had to contend, including a number of evenings when there were raids, and evenings suitable for raids, the attendance has been very faithful."

V

The Tutorial Class completed its second year at Easter, 1918, and on 10 May, Eliot wrote to his mother: "My Southall people want to do Elizabethan Literature next year which would interest me more than what we have done before, and would be of more use to me too, as I want to write some essays on the dramatists, who have never been properly criticised" (*L1* 231). Eliot approached the substance of these new lectures, which involved "considerable preparation," with renewed enthusiasm, for his preparations began to refuel and sustain his long preoccupation with and movement toward a career in poetic drama. The projected essays on Elizabethan dramatists would soon form a substantial part of his first volume of prose, *The Sacred Wood* (1920). But when the class reorganized in the autumn the small enrolment placed the continuance of the course in jeopardy. In December the Joint Committee reported that of the seven tutorial classes in their third year all were "proceeding satisfactorily" except for Eliot's Southall class, which had fewer original students than required by the Board of Education. Eliot, who had a strong sense of responsibility to his students, had also become so absorbed in the material that he wrote to the Joint Committee requesting permission to continue the course for a reduced fee if the Board of Education refused to pay grant on it. As the Southall center was one the Committee wanted to encourage, special approval for continuance was finally granted.[26] Though the lectures were on Elizabethan literature, the cover of the syllabus retained the general title of the Tutorial Class: *Syllabus for a Tutorial Class in Modern English Literature* (London, 1918).[27]

ELIZABETHAN LITERATURE

I. *The Earliest Forms of Drama.* (1)

Popular festival and religious rite. The "liturgical" drama. The Guild plays. Difference between "miracle" plays, "moralities," and "interludes." Examination of several examples. Their peculiar charm and their essential dramatic qualities. Read: *Everyman, Abraham and Isaac,* and the *Second Shepherds' Play.*

II. *The Revival of Learning.* (2)

The Renaissance in England, and its effect upon the Drama. John Bale and Heywood. Influence of humanism not always beneficial. Study of Latin literature: Seneca and Plautus. Beginnings of blank verse. Development of set tragedy and comedy. Italian influence. Read: *Gorboduc* or *Ralph Roister Doister.*

III. *The Elizabethan Stage.* (3)

Popularity of the Theatre. The theatres of Shakespeare's time: their construction, the audience, its character and its demands, the players and their life. The playwright: his task and his life. The continuous adaptation of old plays to current needs. Why Elizabethan life and thought found its most adequate expression in the theatre. Read: The first chapters of G. P. Baker: *Development of Shakespeare as a Dramatist*.[28]

IV. Kyd: The First Important Dramatist. (4)

His *Spanish Tragedy* analysed. Its great popularity. The "tragedy of blood." Comparison with *Titus Andronicus* and *Hamlet*. First appearance of stock situations. Kyd the probable author of *Arden of Feversham*, a unique attempt at tragedy based on contemporary events. Why was this kind of realism not more popular? Read: *The Spanish Tragedy* or *Arden of Feversham*.

V. Christopher Marlowe. (5-6)

The greatest poet since Chaucer and the greatest dramatist before Shakespeare. What is known of his life. His originality. His verse in *Tamburlaine*. His intellect in *Faustus:* comparison with Goethe's handling of the same legend.

Importance of the "chronicle play." Marlowe's *Edward II* compared with Shakespeare's *Richard II*.

Marlowe's *Jew of Malta* compared with the *Merchant of Venice*. Characterisation in the work of the two dramatists. Monotony of Marlowe's dramatic verse compared with Shakespeare's at his best. Read: *Dr. Faustus,* and either *Edward II* with *Richard II,* or the *Jew of Malta* with the *Merchant of Venice*.

Marlowe's minor plays: *Dido Queen of Carthage*. Two men influenced by Marlowe: Peele and Greene, and their relation to him. Read: *James IV* (Greene) or the *Old Wives' Tale* (Peele).

VI. The Chronicle Play. (7)

Examination of the *True Tragedy of Richard Duke of York* with *Richard III* and *Henry VI* for traces of Marlowe, Peele, Greene, and Shakespeare. *Henry IV* as a play by Shakespeare.

VII. Euphuism. (8)

The work of John Lyly. The style of *Euphues* and of Lyly's plays. Its Spanish sources; its popularity. Influence upon Shakespeare. Read: Lyly's *Endymion* and Shakespeare's *Love's Labour's Lost*.

VIII. Shakespeare. (9–10)

The early Shakespeare and his relation to the foregoing summed up. His work as an adapter; its value for his progress. In what ways are his early plays inferior and superior to Marlowe's work? His early use of sources. Read: *Two Gentlemen of Verona* or *Comedy of Errors*. Criticism of these two plays.

The mature Shakespeare. Study of a mature play: *Measure for Measure;* the thought and the versification. His early faults and their disappearance. *King Lear:* comparison with the original play of that name. Read: *Measure for Measure.*

The later Shakespeare. Do the great tragedies exceed the possibilities of the stage? Lamb's views on this subject. Characteristics of Shakespeare's old age. Read: *Coriolanus,* or the *Winter's Tale,* or *Antony and Cleopatra.*

Shakespeare's relation to his time.

IX. Non-Dramatic Poetry. (11)

English poetry after Chaucer. Tudor verse, and verse translation: Gawain Douglas, Golding, the poets of "Tottel's Miscellany." Surrey and Wyatt. Blank verse. Marlowe as poet: his *Hero and Leander* compared with Shakespeare's *Venus and Adonis.* Read: Marlowe's *Hero and Leander,* Canto I. Poems of lesser men in various anthologies, especially Arber's *Surrey and Wyatt Anthology* and *Spenser Anthology.*

X. Spenser. (12)

French and Italian influence. His earlier poems. The *Epithalamion.* The *Faery Queene;* type to which it belongs. Limitations and unique merits of Spenser's verse. His place with Milton and Tennyson.

XI. The Lyric and the Sonnet. (13–14)

The song and music in Tudor times. Shakespeare's and Campion's lyrics. Read Selections from Arber's *Shakespeare Anthology.*

The sonnet; its Italian origin. Popularity of Petrarch. Usual artificiality of the sonnet. Differences between the Italian and the English. Comparison of Shakespeare's with Spenser's, Sidney's and others. Read: A few translations of Italian sonnets in *Golden Treasury* or in the *Oxford Book of English Verse.*

Lyrics of Ben Jonson. Transition to the Jacobean poetry of Marvell, Donne, and others.[29]

XII. The Beginnings of Prose

Tudor Prose. The place of Malory. Work of Elyot and other Humanists. How English prose grew up: effect of theological writing, books of travels, history. The Prayer Books of Edward VI. Fox.

XIII. Sidney and Raleigh

Lives of these two courtiers. Fulke Greville's Life of Sidney. Importance of the *Apology for Poetry* and Raleigh's *Fight of the "Revenge."* A new kind of prose. Read: The two essays mentioned above.

XIV The Elizabethan Romance

The beginnings of the novel. Why less important than the drama, and less mature. Lyly, Lodge, Sidney, Nash, Greene, and their work.

XV Montaigne

Life of Montaigne: his importance in French literature and his importance in English literature. His influence on Elizabethan England. On Shakespeare. The translation of John Florio. The first essayist. Other important translations: Holland's *Plutarch*. Read: Several of Montaigne's essays in Florio's translation.

XVI. Bacon

His life. Importance as a philosopher. His English prose, the *Advancement of Learning*. The *Essays,* compared with Montaigne's. Development of philosophic prose after Bacon. The work of Hooker. Survey of prose from Bacon to Hobbes. Sir Thomas Browne. Read: Select essays of Bacon, Browne's *Religio Medici*.

XVII. Ben Jonson

Difference from all other dramatists. His vast importance in English letters. His erudition, theories about drama. The interest of *Every Man in his Humour*. His satiric ability. Comparison with Molière. Quarrels of the time.

Jonson's view of historical tragedy. *Sejanus* and *Catiline*. Their inferiority to his comedies: *Volpone, The Alchemist, Epicœne*. His non-dramatic work.

Construction of Jonson's plays. Read: *Volpone,* or the *Alchemist,* or *Bartholomew Fair*.[30]

XVIII. The Later Drama

Influence of Shakespeare. The various merits of Chapman, Dekker, Heywood, and Middleton. Development and decline of the drama after Shakespeare. The gifts of Beaumont and Fletcher on the whole better exhibited in the scene than in the complete play. The greatest of Shakespeare's followers is undoubtedly John Webster. His skill in dealing with horror; the beauty of his verse. Each of these men could deal marvellously with certain types of situation. The work of Ford. Each of the later dramatists has some unique quality, and in them English blank verse reaches its highest point. Read: Webster, the *Duchess of Malfi*. Ford, the *Broken Heart*. Beaumont and Fletcher, the *Maid's Tragedy* and the *Knight of the Burning Pestle*.

READING

Drama

The "Everyman" edition of *Everyman* contains the early plays mentioned, and others. Also in J. M. Manly: *Specimens of Pre-Shakespearian Drama*. E. K. Chambers:

The Mediæval Stage gives a very scholarly and complete account of the conditions; and J. J. Jusserand: *English Wayfaring Life in the Middle Ages* is useful and very interesting. For the early plays the work of Manly, mentioned above. Particular use will be made of the "Everyman" *Minor Elizabethan Drama,* Vol. I., Tragedy; Vol. II., Comedy, which contains all the Pre-Shakespearian plays to be discussed, with the exception of those of Marlowe, which are found in a separate volume of the "Everyman" edition. There is very little good criticism of Elizabethan and Jacobean drama, but J. A. Symonds: *Predecessors of Shakespeare* is useful, and Swinburne: *Age of Shakespeare* and *Study of Ben Jonson,* as well as Rupert Brooke: *John Webster,* are interesting, though misleading. The "Mermaid" edition of most of the dramatists is good. Ben Jonson and Beaumont and Fletcher are to be had in the "Everyman" edition. For Shakespeare, Sir Sidney Lee's *Life* is the standard biography, and Professor G. P. Baker's *Development of Shakespeare as a Dramatist* is very useful. The best Shakespeare criticism is Coleridge: *Lectures on Shakespeare,* which also contains notes on Jonson and Beaumont and Fletcher. A. C. Bradley: *Four Tragedies of Shakespeare* is an excellent study. Thomas Seccombe and J. W. Allen: *Age of Shakespeare.* F. E. Schelling: *Elizabethan Drama* is thorough. The *Shakespeare Apocrypha,* plays attributed to Shakespeare, is edited by C. F. T. Brooke. Many of the Elizabethan plays are well edited separately in the "Temple Classics." The "Temple" and the "Arden" editions of separate plays of Shakespeare, and the "Globe" edition in one volume, are good; the finest critical edition of Shakespeare is Furness's "Variorum" edition.

Poetry

Marlowe's *Hero and Leander* is in the "Everyman" edition of his works. His admirable translations are difficult to obtain. Edward Arber's edition of "Tottel's Miscellany," and the Arber *Surrey and Wyatt, Spenser, Shakespeare,* and *Jonson Anthologies* contain many fine poems unobtainable elsewhere. Bullen: "England's Helicon," the "Golden Treasury," and the "Oxford Book" contain many lyrics and sonnets. Campion's poems are in the "Muses' Library." For Spenser the Oxford edition. There are cheap editions of Chapman's translation of Homer.

Prose

Sir Thomas Elyot's *Gouvernour,* Edward VI.'s Prayer Books, are in the "Everyman" edition. Select writings of Raleigh recently published by the Clarendon Press, Oxford. Sidney's *Apologie* is easily obtainable. So are Florio's *Montaigne,* Holland's *Plutarch,* Bacon's *Essays,* Hooker's *Ecclesiastical Polity.* Hobbes: *Leviathan,* and Sir Thomas Browne: *Religio Medici* are not exactly in the period, but may well be read in connection with it.

Note: For the general history of the Tudor reigns, including that of Elizabeth, the various volumes of Froude are of permanent value, and are many of them obtainable in the "Everyman" edition.

V

Eliot's syllabuses suggest that he approached his Extension lectures as seriously as he would have a course of lectures at Harvard, and though in his reports he consistently balanced his remarks on adverse class conditions by commenting on the high intelligence and receptiveness of his students, in other places, when he was writing for a sophisticated literary audience, he became rather condescending toward his Extension audience. In April 1918, he referred disparagingly to a passage on Tennyson in Alice Meynell's *Hearts of Controversy* as "what a University Extension audience would like; but it is not criticism."[31] On 28 October 1919, in a lecture entitled "Modern Tendencies in Poetry," Eliot's opening remark was no less derogatory of his fellow lecturers: "A popular theme of Extension lectures and the like is the Relation of Poetry to Life. Poetry has been interrogated a good many times by these conscientious educators, who have exerted considerable ventriloqual ingenuity in the replies that they have pretended to extract from it."[32] Later, in "The Function of Criticism" (1923), Eliot revealed the impatience that apparently drove him out of the classroom: "I have had some experience of Extension lecturing, and I have found only two ways of leading any pupils to like anything with the right liking: to present them with a selection of the simpler kind of facts about a work—its conditions, its setting, its genesis—or else to spring the work on them in such a way that they were not prepared to be prejudiced against it." (*SE* 32).

In the disparity between his public comments and his private letters and reports, it is probable that Eliot's sense of his students' general lack of commitment to literature clouded his remembrance of the immense pleasure his lectures once gave him. At any rate, whatever may have been his later attitude toward Extension courses, his own courses were vital to his development as a poet-critic, even though he wrote to his mother that the "only permanent good" that would come from his lectures was "a vast amount of miscellaneous reading and a certain practice in public speaking" (*L1* 200). The necessities that forced him to lecture from 1916 to 1919 also forced him into a three-year period of intensive reading and selective organizing. His courses required him to articulate his developing critical concepts, to exercise his taste, and to reorder the poets of the English tradition into his own aesthetic and moral hierarchy when he would not otherwise have done so. Though his classes were time consuming and doubtless kept him from original work, Eliot's lecturing helped spur him out of creative dryness into new poetic and critical activity. His preparations expanded the obvious erudition that he brought to his first critical efforts, and they provided a tremendous personal storehouse of allusions for his poetry.

In May 1919, as the Tutorial Class came to an end, the Hogarth Press published *Poems* (1919), and at the end of the year *Ara Vos Prec* (1920)—published in America as *Poems*—was in press. The new poems in these volumes, written between 1917 and 1919, are filled with allusions to authors and works listed in the syllabuses: Chapman, Shakespeare, Sidney, Webster, Donne, Browning, Emerson, Ruskin, to name only the obvious. Several of the works provide the epigraphs with which Eliot set the mood and moment of such poems as "Gerontion"

(*Measure for Measure*), "Sweeney Erect" (*The Maid's Tragedy*), "Mr. Eliot's Sunday Morning Service" (*The Jew of Malta*), and "Burbank with a Baedeker" (fragments from *Othello* and Browning's "*Toccata of Galuppi's*"). Numerous allusions in *The Waste Land* and in Eliot's notes to the poem were to come directly from the syllabuses. Collectively, they reveal a striking relation between his personal intellectual experience and his creative imagination.

In the aftermath of his lectures, Eliot wrote, among other important essays and reviews, "Tradition and the Individual Talent," " 'Rhetoric' and Poetic Drama," "Some Notes on the Blank Verse of Christopher Marlowe," "Swinburne and the Elizabethans," "Hamlet and His Problems," "Ben Jonson," "Swinburne as Poet," "Philip Massinger," "The Perfect Critic" (in part a review of Arthur Symons's *Studies in Elizabethan Drama*), and "The Possibility of a Poetic Drama," all of which were related extensions of his lectures. After 1920, Eliot continued to draw upon the subjects of his lectures, many of which provided a partial basis for later essays.[33] The course on Elizabethan literature became vital to Eliot's critical imagination from 1919 through the *Elizabethan Essays* of 1934, and the germs for many of his interim formulations on Elizabethan poets, dramatists, and poetic drama may be found in his topic and reading outlines. The courses on modern literature point to an unbroken continuity between Eliot and the Victorians, a continuity that many scholars have long suspected but insufficiently confirmed, and to the cross-currents of nineteenth-century French and English intellectual traditions, of which he was deeply conscious and which partially directed his subsequent critical interests.

After his final tutorial lecture, Eliot's faithful students presented him with several books to mark the completion of their three-year course, including a copy of the *Oxford Book of English Verse,* inscribed "with the gratitude and appreciation of the students of the Southall Tutorial Literature Class May 1919" (MS VE). "Eliot informed his mother that, "to my great relief," his lectures had ended. "I don't know whether it will be desirable for me to continue them from any point of view, as perhaps I can make more money as well as more reputation from the *Athenaeum*" (*L1* 295). He also wrote to his brother that he hoped to be able to give up his lecturing next year: "I feel very played out at present," he confessed (*L1* 273).

As important as they were, Eliot's Extension lectures constitute only one of several missing layers in a complex emotional and intellectual life that had left him "played out" at the end of the war. As I will show, his life also had been rapidly enriched by the discovery of T. E. Hulme, and gradually darkened by the friendship of Bertrand Russell.

2

HULME OF ORIGINAL SIN

Within the breath of autumn woods,
Within the winter silences:
Thy venemous spirit stirs and broods,
O Master of impieties!

Some of us who include Eliot in our own syllabuses have to contend with a number of entrenched attitudes toward his life and work, especially the alleged discontinuity of the poetry and criticism written before his religious conversion with that written after. Since the 1920s the cumulative criticism of Eliot's development as a poet, critic, and Anglo-Catholic has persuaded most classroom teachers to accept the following assumptions and chronology: that the poems written from "Prufrock" to "The Hollow Men" are those of a despairing, sceptical poet probing spiritual bankruptcy in the modern world; that from "Tradition and the Individual Talent" (1919) to his formal conversion in 1927 Eliot's theory of tradition and criticism spring from literary rather than moral concerns; that in 1928, when in the preface to *For Lancelot Andrewes* Eliot announces that his attitude is "classicist in literature, royalist in politics, and anglo-catholic in religion," there is a rather sudden turn from an aesthetic and literary theory of tradition to a moral and religious doctrine of orthodoxy; that in *After Strange Gods* (1934) and later Eliot not only sins against literature by employing his dogmatic religious beliefs as the narrow touchstone of his criticism but yearns nostalgically for the unified sensibility and moral security of a lost medieval world. Few would accept the assertion that by 1916 Eliot's classical, royalist, and religious point of view was already formulated. A first step toward establishing this assertion is to examine evidence of Eliot's critical and religious position in 1915–16, and especially the role of T. E. Hulme in defining that position.

That Eliot's critical attitudes were considerably influenced by Hulme has long been a well-exercised fact, and there was no surprise when in "To Criticize the Critic" (1961) Eliot stated: "The influence of Babbitt (with an infusion later of T. E. Hulme and of the more literary essays of Charles Maurras) is apparent in my recurrent theme of Classicism versus Romanticism"(*TCC* 17). Since J. R. Daniell in 1933 examined Eliot's relation to Hulme in general,[1] almost every modern literary history and individual study of Eliot's critical theory has outlined the similarities of their positions. Nonetheless, the crucial question of when Eliot came under Hulme's so-called later influence has never been resolved; consequently, the full chronology and depth of Eliot's debt to Hulme have remained uncharted. With the help of the Extension syllabuses, however, it can now be shown that Hulme had a significant impact on Eliot's critical and spiritual development at a much earlier date than previously supposed.

Critics of Eliot's early development and later theory have not successfully established any clear connections in the cloudy relationship between Eliot and Hulme before the publication of Hulme's *Speculations* in 1924. Since 1932 the numerous opinions concerning their association in wartime London and the possibility of Eliot's familiarity with Hulme's ideas on romanticism, democracy, progress, modernism, and Original Sin have been largely speculative and contradictory. In the earliest comprehensive study of Eliot's critical theory (1932), Ants Oras examines the likelihood of an early Eliot-Hulme relationship and states inconclusively that "the belated publication of his [Hulme's] posthumous papers makes it questionable how far Eliot knew his ideas before bringing out his [Eliot's] first collection of essays."[2] But in 1935 F. O. Matthiessen excludes the possibility of any early or important formative influence and says that "Eliot had not known Hulme personally, though he had heard much about him from Pound; and he had not read any of Hulme's essays before they were published, by which time Eliot's own theory of poetry had already matured."[3] He attributes the acknowledged similarities of their ideas to "an emerging general state of mind." Succeeding critics have taken Matthiessen's statement of Eliot's ignorance of Hulme's ideas as fact, understandably so, for he was presumably informed by Eliot himself. Most of these critics, however, glimpsing affinities between Hulme and Eliot before the publication of *Speculations,* cautiously suggest or assert the probability of their association in spite of Matthiessen's authoritative disclaimer.[4]

Others have been less cautious. Victor Brombert, in outlining several antiromantic influences on Eliot, says that Hulme, "whom he [Eliot] was to meet in London," strongly impressed Eliot with his pronouncements, but Brombert cites no evidence for the meeting nor any reference to Hulme by Eliot before 1929.[5] It is well known that after spending an academic year in Paris in 1910–11 Eliot returned to study philosophy at Harvard, where he remained until June 1914, but Enid Starkie erroneously states: "After Paris Eliot went to Oxford for a year, and then arrived in London in 1912, just as the Imagist Movement was getting into its stride" and then associates Eliot and Hulme in the "first real grouping of the Imagists" in 1913.[6] In the wake of this misinformed account have followed numerous claims to the effect that "Eliot had been associated with Hulme in the Imagist movement and . . . must have been familiar with his ideas."[7] Rising out of these conflicting accounts is the prevalent feeling that though it "seems" that some sort of familiarity with the "spirit" of Hulme's ideas is possible, whether or not Eliot directly knew Hulme or his ideas before 1924 is, in the words of David Daiches, "a question not very easy to determine and not of any great importance."[8] And further, that it was not until the late 1920s and after, when Eliot openly avowed the principles of Hulme's "religious attitude" in several essays, that his critical theory owes any of its essential features to Hulme. This biographical uncertainty, not to say confusion, has thus tended to make critics dismiss what they cannot ascertain, so much so that one influential study—Herbert Howarth's *Notes on Some Figures behind T. S. Eliot* (1964)—does not even mention Hulme.

It is thus time, in the light of new archival material, to revisit the biographical and bibliographical basis in fact for the suspicions of an early Eliot-Hulme relationship. Could it be that Eliot actually knew Hulme and talked with him about poetic and philosophical principles? The mounting circumstantial evidence points very strongly to this possibility. Moreover, careful reconstruction of Eliot's and Hulme's activities in London from 1914 to 1916 shows (1) that Eliot had not only read but was in fact teaching Hulme's poetry and philosophy in 1916; (2) that he had in fact so assimilated Hulme's ideas to those of Irving Babbitt and Charles Maurras that his broad classical point of view was already clearly focused; and (3) that his classicism even in 1916 was as much moral and "religious" in its formulation and attitude as it was aesthetic and literary.

In the years immediately preceding Eliot's arrival in London in 1914, the two philosopher-poets were moving independently along remarkably parallel lines. In 1909, while Hulme was giving theoretical impetus to the imagist movement and directing his friends toward radical experiments in verse, Eliot was studying nineteenth- and early-twentieth-century French literary criticism under Irving Babbitt, reading Symons's *The Symbolist Movement in Literature* and writing poems after Jules Laforgue. Hulme had become a student and follower of Henri Bergson, whose metaphysics he temporarily used to circumvent the dogmas of scientific determinism while he constructed his anti-romantic, anti-humanist, anti-democratic philosophy on the dogma of Original Sin. In 1911, while studying philosophy at St. John's College, Cambridge, he began defending Bergson's ideas in lectures and translating his *Introduction to Metaphysics*. In the same year, Eliot was at the Sorbonne and visited the Collège de France to hear Bergson's lectures, which were similar to those Hulme heard Bergson deliver at the Bologna Congress in April 1911, and, like Hulme, Eliot underwent "a temporary conversion to Bergsonism,"[9] though by 1916 Eliot, like Hulme, viewed Bergson's metaphysics as a romantic "infection" incompatible with his classical position.[10] Eliot, who had heard of Charles Maurras in Babbitt's classes, read Maurras's *L'Avenir de l'intelligence* in Paris in 1911. After his return he subscribed to the *Nouvelle Revue Française* and closely followed literary and intellectual developments in France for the next several years. Hulme was also avidly preoccupied during this period with the critical ideals of the French reactionaries, especially Georges Sorel, Maurras, Pierre Lasserre, and others connected with *L'Action Française,* many of whom provided a common reading ground for Eliot and Hulme. In 1913

A. R. Orage, Hulme's close friend and editor of the *New Age,* which had been publishing most of Hulme's essays since 1909, asserted that Babbitt's *Masters of Modern French Criticism,* which comprised the lectures given in the Harvard criticism course that Eliot attended, expressed a view of literature substantially the same as that of the *New Age.*[11] Both Hulme and Eliot attended lectures on philosophy at Marburg during their respective visits to Germany in 1912 and 1914, and both were indebted to Pound for getting their first poems into print. The affinities between these two lines of development, both of which were following the major movements and directions of the international reaction against romanticism—the reaction that Matthiessen called "an emerging general state of mind"—made their eventual confluence highly probable.

By 1912 Hulme had assimilated the rapid influx of reactionary ideas into a declaration that Eliot would soon reiterate. In the opening sentence of "A Tory Philosophy" (1912), Hulme states that it is his intention to explain "why I believe in original sin, why I can't stand romanticism, and why I am a certain kind of Tory"(*CWTEH* 232). Armed with his modified Pascalian theory of discontinuity and the concept of Original Sin, which he linked to the classical spirit, and believing like Babbitt and Maurras that all romanticism springs from Rousseau, Hulme was the first twentieth-century Englishman to take an important critical stance against the ubiquitous forms of romanticism and liberalism. The cornerstone of his position was Original Sin: as Wyndham Lewis describes Hulme in literary London, "If men of letters had *sobriquets* or nicknames . . . then Hulme would probably be called 'Hulme of Original Sin.'"[12] Ezra Pound has warned, however, that "The critical LIGHT during the years immediately prewar in London shone not from Hulme but from Ford (Madox etc.) in so far as it fell on writing at all," though he allows that "Hulme's critical broadside may have come later as a godsend when published."[13] Since Pound was close to Hulme and Eliot in London during the war, this passage has often been cited as a further indication that Hulme's philosophical influence on Eliot and others came after the publication of *Speculations* in 1924, but Hulme's "broadside" was actually first published in the *New Age* in 1915–16. Soon after Eliot's arrival in London, then, there was still enough of Hulme's light to show Eliot that Original Sin was the basic element in the classical compound.

In the spring of 1914 Eliot received a Sheldon Traveling Fellowship from Harvard and went to study philosophy at Marburg, but in August the outbreak of war forced him to leave for London and Merton College, Oxford. When Eliot arrived in London, Hulme had already joined the Honourable Artillery Company, but there were to be many opportunities for them to cross paths in 1915–16. Eliot, meanwhile, began to encounter the literary figures who would later ensure his knowledge of Hulme. By 22 September 1914 Eliot knew Pound, and in October he ran into Bertrand Russell, whose course in symbolic logic he had taken at Harvard the previous spring. Russell had been impressed by Eliot in the seminar, and during the next five years he was to figure dramatically in Eliot's personal and literary life. In December, during the Christmas holidays, Pound introduced Eliot to another close friend of Hulme, Wyndham Lewis, and on the 30th Hulme's infantry unit departed Southampton for the trenches in France.

After the holidays Eliot returned to his study of Aristotle, Bradley, Meinong, and Husserl. On 2 February 1915 Eliot wrote Pound to thank him for his continual efforts to publish his poems and for introducing him to the Arnold Dolmetsch family (*L1* 86).[14] Eliot disclosed that he had recently been reading some of Pound's work, referring specifically to his article on the Vortex, which, following "Arnold Dolmetsch," was the second of Pound's several "Affirmations" articles published in the *New Age* during January. In the article Pound refers to Kandinsky, about whom Eliot inquires in the letter, and in the third article in the series, "Jacob Epstein," which Eliot undoubtedly read, Pound refers to Hulme. Through a combination of meetings, essays, and letters, Eliot was being rapidly exposed to Pound's literary world. In closing, Eliot said he was not likely to be in London again until March, at which time he hoped to meet Yeats, with whom Pound and his wife were spending the winter of 1914–15. As spring approached, Lewis accepted two of Eliot's poems for the second number of *Blast* (July 1915).

Hulme, meanwhile, was writing the letters that comprise his "Diary from the Trenches." Shortly after the final entry on 19 April 1915 he was wounded in the arm and sent home for a brief recovery period in St. Mark's College Hospital, Chelsea, where he was visited by Pound, who recorded Hulme's escapades there in Canto 16.[15] Aside from the authority of Matthiessen's statement, the assumption that Eliot did not know Hulme is based in part on Herbert Read's erroneous statement in his introduction to *Speculations* that upon recovery from his wound Hulme was immediately "gazetted to the Royal Marine Artillery" and "returned to the front late in 1915." But after his dismissal Hulme was in fact "lost" by the War Office and, telling his friends that he saw no reason for returning until he was located, lived in London "trying to pick up his old life again."[16] Hulme moved back into his renowned 67 Frith Street salon, the Tuesday evening center of London literary activity from 1912 till the outbreak of war, and lived there until late March 1916. In the company of John Middleton Murry, C. R. W. Nevinson, and others, as Hulme's friend and suite-mate Ashley Dukes recounts, the conversation ranged from Ezra Pound's verse to Wyndham Lewis's *Blast:* "We knew of the work of T. S. Eliot, though he never came himself to these gatherings."[17] Though Eliot may not have ventured into Frith Street, it is certain that he knew a great deal about the work of Hulme, to the point that he wrote about him with the familiarity of friendship. On 4 April 1915 he wrote to the Boston hostess Isabella Stewart Gardner about his London friends: "there are at least a dozen people whom I like in London, and that is a great deal. I have been seeing a good deal of some of the modern artists whom the war has so far spared. One of the most interesting of the radicals—Gaudier-Brzeska—do you know him?— is in the trenches (as is the interesting T. E. Hulme)" (*L1* 94). Hulme, soon back at Frith Street with his friends, would have eagerly awaited and discussed the second number of Wyndham Lewis's *Blast,* which included Eliot's "Preludes" and "Rhapsody on a Windy Night," his first poems published in England. Dukes, who said he never lost touch with Hulme during his "forgotten" period, asserted forty years later, in a self-contradictory account: "Only at this time could he have gained any knowledge of Joyce; but certainly none of Eliot." To further prevent Hulme from being enveloped in an "aura of romance" about his alleged friendships, Dukes declared dogmatically that "it was only much later that he [Eliot] knew what this philosophic forerunner and interpreter had aimed to accomplish. All of this deserves to be accurately set forth."[18] The accumulated evidence, however, prevents an over-confident friend from enforcing the belief that Hulme knew nothing of Eliot in his lifetime and that Eliot knew nothing of Hulme's work until the publication of *Speculations*.

During the autumn of 1915 Eliot's contacts with Hulme begin, most conspicuously in *Catholic Anthology 1914–15*, edited by Pound and published in November. Pound included five poems by Eliot and one by Hulme.[19] It is difficult to believe that Pound had not brought them together by this time, especially since Pound's principal purpose in making the collection was "to get 16 pages of Eliot printed" in London.[20] On 14 October Hulme had published in the *New Age* his translator's preface to Sorel's *Reflections on Violence*, which expressed the essential ideas of his philosophy in condensed form. Then, from 2 December 1915 to 10 February 1916, while still in London, Hulme elaborated these ideas in a series of essays published under the general title "A Notebook." These are the influential essays that were later collected in *Speculations* as "Humanism and the Religious Attitude." It is doubtful that Eliot overlooked them, for in 1915 Orage's *New Age* was the weekly review that all serious writers read to keep abreast of current developments in literature, art, and politics. Orage often met with Hulme, Pound, and other contributors and writers at the Café Royal in Piccadilly to discuss their work. Moreover, Orage had published Pound's essays regularly since 1912 and, as previously noted, Eliot was reading some of Pound's *New Age* essays in 1915.[21] Finally, writing in 1934 on the death of Orage, Eliot revealed that he had known him and read the *New Age* diligently during that period. Eliot's meetings with Orage, "over a period of some eighteen years, had been infrequent and in public places," but Eliot remembered him as "the best literary critic of that time in London" and "the benevolent editor who encouraged merit and (what is still rarer) tolerated genius."[22] If Eliot was not introduced to Hulme by Pound in Frith Street, he may have met him at the Café Royal with Orage. In any event, Bertrand Russell would also have directed Eliot's attention to Hulme and his essays.

In the months following their meeting in October 1914, Russell and Eliot became reacquainted. Eliot wrote to Isabella Stewart Gardner in his letter of 4 April 1915: "I see the charming Bertie Russell from time to time; having in fact been to Cambridge recently" (*L1* 94–5). That spring, after completing the academic year at Oxford, Eliot made the decision to remain in England. On 26 June he married Vivien Haigh-Wood, and early in July they went to dinner at Russell's London flat. "As they were desperately poor," says Russell, "I lent them one of the two bedrooms in my flat, with the result that I saw a great deal of them."[23] He saw much more of Vivien, for later that month Eliot sailed alone for America and the Eliot summer home, where the family was obviously anxious about his recent decision not to return to an assistant professorship in philosophy at Harvard. During his six-week absence, Vivien took dictation for Russell, and as they formed a close relationship they decided to inform Eliot upon his return that the newlyweds would take a spare room in Russell's flat after a delayed honeymoon to Eastbourne. After the couple arrived in Eastbourne, Vivien sent Russell what he described to his lover, Lady Ottoline Morrell, as "a desperate letter":

> It seems their sort of pseudo-honeymoon at Eastbourne is being a ghastly failure. She is quite tired of him, & when I got here I found a desperate letter from her, in the lowest depths of despair & not far removed from suicide. I have written her various letters full of good advice, & she seems to have come to rely on me more or less. I have so much taken them both in hand that I dare not let them be. I think she will fall more or less in love with me, but that can't be helped. I am interested by the attempt to pull her straight.[24]

Ottoline warned him immediately of the risk to the Eliots and himself of becoming overly involved, but he assured her that he was acting out of the "purest philanthropy" for the couple, would not have any scandal, and regretted giving her the wrong impression of his motives.

After they moved into Russell's flat on 15 September, Eliot accepted a teaching position at the High Wycombe Grammar School for the autumn term, a position that required him to stay overnight during the week. On 10 November Russell gave Ottoline an update of his intermediary role in the new marriage:

> Eliot had a half holiday yesterday and got home at 3.30. It is quite funny how I have come to love him, as if he were my son. He is becoming much more of a man. He has a profound and quite unselfish devotion to his wife, and she is really very fond of him, but has impulses of cruelty to him from time to time. It is a Dostojevsky type of cruelty, not a straight-forward every-day kind. I am every day getting things more right between them, but I can't let them alone at present, and of course I myself get very much interested. She is a person who lives on a knife-edge, and will end as a criminal or a saint—I don't know which yet.[25]

Russell's interest in Vivien increased over the autumn, and for the next year he spent considerable time helping Eliot with what Russell called Vivien's "readjustment," bestowing lavish gifts on her and providing money for her dancing lessons. He also introduced Eliot to his side of the London literary world and got him a job reviewing for the *Monist* through his influence with the editor, Philip E. B. Jourdain.

Russell had known of Hulme's activities since 1911 when Hulme "let it be known in Cambridge that he was translating Bergson and this news aroused considerable feeling in Cambridge where the philosophy school was dominated by G. E. Moore and Bertrand Russell."[26] Russell knew of Hulme's translation and of his 1911–12 *New Age* articles on Bergson, in the last of which Hulme had expressed contempt for Russell's "A Free Man's Worship." Hulme's persistent advocacy of Bergson probably contributed to the antagonism that led to Russell's famous paper attacking Bergson's philosophy before the Heretics' Club at Cambridge in March 1913. From 11 November 1915 to 2 March 1916, while Russell was writing pacifist pamphlets and lectures, Hulme was publishing in the *New Age* his anti-pacifist "War Notes" along with his essays on humanism and the religious attitude. It was in one of the latter essays that Hulme began to set up Russell's philosophy as a target for his own writings. What Russell has to say on the subject of a *Weltanschauung* in "A Free Man's Worship," says Hulme on 23 December, "is so extremely commonplace, and is expressed in such a painful piece of false and sickly rhetoric, that I have not patience to deal with it here" (*CWTEH* 436). Two weeks later Hulme continued to probe the philosophical assumptions of Russell and G. E. Moore (*CWTEH* 440–3). In mid-January 1916 Russell began giving a series of lectures in Caxton Hall, Westminster, on "The Principles of Social Reconstruction," and Hulme attended some of these lectures. So did Eliot, who had written to Russell from a hotel in Torquay, where Russell was providing the Eliots with a holiday (having spent five days there with Vivien before Eliot replaced him), that he was "anxious to hear all the lectures" (*L1* 128). Due to Vivien's unexpected illness, however, Eliot was forced to miss the first lecture. Then, on 27 January, in an article entitled "The Kind of Rubbish We Oppose," Hulme began to criticize the premises of Russell's lectures in his "War Notes" series, and for two months thereafter, as they engaged in a weekly exchange of attacks and heated rejoinders, Hulme censured Russell's pacifism and progressivist views as a form of "faded Rousseauism . . . based on an entirely false conception of the nature of man, and of the true hierarchy of values; the hierarchy is not objective, but is merely the result of an uncritical acceptance of the romantic tradition" (*CWTEH* 395).[27] Eliot, who certainly followed this public controversy, would have privately relished Hulme's renewed attack on "A Free Man's Worship" and his portrayal of the romantic premises of Russell's values.[28]

On 16 March 1916 Hulme's translation of Georges Sorel's *Reflections on Violence* was reviewed in the *Times Literary Supplement* (*TLS*); four days later Hulme finally received a commission in the Royal Marines Artillery through the aid of Sir Edward Marsh. For the next six months Hulme was stationed at Eastney barracks in Portsmouth, but during this period he frequented London to see his friends and to sit for Jacob Epstein, who was sculpting a head of him. Eliot, meanwhile, was teaching, reviewing books, and writing his dissertation on Bradley, which he completed and mailed to Harvard in April. In May, Eliot's mother wrote to Russell, urging him to use his influence to persuade Eliot to pursue a career in philosophy rather than in "the vers libre" (*L1* 139). Pound, however, had already called him in to plan what soon became *Prufrock and Other Observations*. Eliot, committed to a literary life in London, nonetheless complained to Conrad Aiken on 21 August 1916 of the effects of war on his literary friendships: "Nearly everyone has faded away from London, or is there very rarely. . . . T. E. Hulme has been in France for ages" (*L1* 144–5).

Eliot had meanwhile committed himself to the course of Extension lectures on modern French literature for the autumn. Though Hulme was away, Eliot was preparing his lectures, it turns out, with Hulme's translations and ideas close at hand.

I

Eliot's *Syllabus of a Course of Six Lectures on Modern French Literature* shows his first course to be partly a synthesis of the dominant ideas embodied in the neoclassicism of Babbitt, the royalist-Catholic authoritarianism of Maurras, and the "religious attitude" of Hulme. The unifying theme of the lectures is the general twentieth-century reaction against romanticism and the specific directions this reaction was taking in French literature, politics, and religion at the time. "It must be remembered," says Eliot in an early lecture, "that the French mind is highly theoretic—directed by theories—and that no theory ever remains merely a theory of art, or a theory of religion, or a theory of politics. Any theory which commences in one of these spheres inevitably extends to the others. . . . Our best procedure is to sketch briefly the relation of politics, literature, and religion, and then consider the work of a few representatives of these three interests." The first lecture is entitled "The Origins: What Is Romanticism?" in which Eliot, following Babbitt, Maurras, and Hulme, locates the germs of nineteenth-century romanticist tendencies in Rousseau. Eliot describes Rousseau's public life as a struggle against *"Authority* in matters of religion" and *"Aristocracy* and *privilege* in government," and he lists Rousseau's main tendencies as: "(1) Exaltation of the *personal* and *individual* above the *typical.* (2) Emphasis upon *feeling* rather than *thought.* (3) Humanitarianism: belief in the fundamental goodness of human nature." This last tendency, rooted in the Renaissance, is at the core of Hulme's anti-Rousseauism. In one of his essays on humanism in the *New Age* for 27 January 1916, Hulme, while distinguishing the two conflicting conceptions of the nature of man, writes that the humanitarian or "humanist" attitude underlying romanticism is best described as "a heresy, a mistaken adoption of false conceptions" (*CWTEH* 450). When the romantic becomes blind to the fact of his limited and imperfect nature, he turns inward to establish and glorify a hierarchy of values originating within himself and based on the fact of his own "unlimited" existence. This error falsifies the true nature of both the human and the divine; consequently, it "creates the bastard conception of *Personality"* and "distorts the real nature of ethical values by deriving them out of essentially subjective things, like human desires and feelings." From Hulme's opposed "religious attitude," Eliot in this lecture derives his first Hulmean definition of romanticism as *"excess* in any direction. It splits up into two directions: escape from the world of fact, and devotion to brute fact." It is against the directions and assumptions of Rousseau and romanticism that Eliot constructs the succeeding lectures on the French and international reactions.

In the second lecture, "The Reaction against Romanticism," Eliot examines the tendencies in and the relation of politics, religion, and literature. He describes neo-Catholicism as "partly a political movement, associated with monarchism, and partly a reaction against the sceptical scientific view of the nineteenth century," and he sees a corresponding "Expression of the new political and religious attitudes in literature." Throughout the lectures Eliot considers men of letters "only as they represent political, religious, or philosophical tendencies." In the fourth, "Royalism and Socialism," he examines the specific nature of the royalist position of Maurras and Pierre Lasserre, the fusion of nationalism and Catholicism in the work of Péguy, and the syndicalist position of Sorel. In the fifth, "The Return to the Catholic Church," he examines the causes behind the tendency of the French intellectuals to return to orthodox Christianity, contrasts the "really romanticist," sentimental Christianity of Francis Jammes with the "medieval philosophy" of Paul Claudel's Christianity, and distinguishes the neo-Catholicism of many twentieth-century men of letters as being "more social and political, less individualistic and ascetic" than that of the nineteenth century. In the final lecture, "Before and after the War: Questions for the Future," he discusses the philosophy and influence of Bergson, questions its value and the likelihood of its enduring, and ends with an assessment of the influence of the war and a forecast of French thought after the war. Interestingly enough, for his text of Bergson's *Introduction to Metaphysics* Eliot uses Hulme's translation. Moreover, for part of his discussion of "The Philosophy of 1910" and the fundamental philosophical tenets of Bergson, who "was then the most noticed figure in Paris," Eliot probably went to Hulme's "Notes on Bergson" series, which had appeared in the *New Age* in 1911–12, just as the reading list shows he recommended Ezra Pound's "Approach to Paris" series, which had appeared there in September–October 1913.

"The Reaction against Romanticism" is the pivotal lecture in the series in that it delineates the anti-Rousseauistic tendencies that are explored and illustrated in the succeeding lectures, but for the aims of this inquiry it is more immediately important in that Eliot refers to Hulme's particular definition of classicism and indicates that the central strands of his own classicism were already woven together long before the classicist-royalist-Catholic declaration in 1928. Eliot begins his 1916 lecture in startlingly similar terms:

> The beginning of the twentieth century has witnessed a return to the ideals of classicism. These may roughly be characterized *as form* and *restraint* in art, *discipline* and *authority* in religion, *centralization* in government (either as socialism or monarchy). . . . The present-day movement is partly a return to the ideals of the seventeenth century. A classicist in art and literature will be likely to adhere to a monarchical form of government, and to the Catholic Church.

And while discussing the ideals of classicism he reduces the classicist attitude to its basic assumption in this unmasking statement: "The classicist point of view has been defined as essentially a belief in Original Sin—the necessity for austere discipline." Here is the first mention of the religious dogma that had already begun to inform the sensibility underlying Eliot's attitudes toward literature, politics, religion, and humanism, and it is Hulme's definition to which Eliot refers. One of the primary books for the course is Sorel's *Reflections on Violence* (London: Allen and Unwin, 1916), published in March. The translator of this edition is T. E. Hulme, and, conclusively, it contains Hulme's translator's preface, which had been published in the *New Age* the previous fall.[29]

Eliot had received a review copy of Hulme's translation from Bertrand Russell's friend and former student Philip Jourdain, English editor of the *Monist*.

Jourdain had become, for Eliot, "the most satisfactory employer I could wish. I have only to suggest an article and he clamours for it, and any book I see advertised and want to review he will send for, for me" (*L1* 149). Eliot dated his review copy of *Reflections on Violence* "May 1916" and later inscribed it: "This was my first introduction to Hulme and Sorel" (MS VE). The review had been completed and submitted by mid-July, for Jourdain wrote to the American editor on 25 July to say that three days earlier he had sent Eliot's two essays on Leibniz and other items for later issues, including "Reviews by Eliot (η) of books by Merz and Sorel."[30] Eliot described the book as one that "expresses that violent and bitter reaction against romanticism which is one of the most interesting phenomena of our time," Sorel himself as "representative of the present generation, sick with its own knowledge of history, with the dissolving outlines of liberal thought, with humanitarianism. . . . He longs for the pessimistic, classical view. And this longing is healthy. . . . It is not surprising that Sorel has become a Royalist." Equally striking is Eliot's concluding remark on Sorel's anti-romantic editor: "Mr. Hulme is also a contemporary. The footnotes to his introduction should be read."[31]

Even if the chances of circumstance were such that Eliot read no other essay by Hulme before 1916, Hulme's preface and footnotes to *Reflections on Violence* were sufficient to provide him with the basic tenets of Hulme's classical philosophy. Hulme finds in the political thinking of Sorel another application of the idea of Original Sin, and, as in his 1915–16 essays on war, he uses the essay as a vehicle to reiterate in political terms what he says elsewhere about philosophy, art, and poetry. In introducing Sorel's book, noting that in previous examinations of the work critics have shown "a complete inability to understand its motives," Hulme examines as an essential element in the romantic movement the two-centuries-old "democratic ideology" with which he associates the "doctrine of inevitable *Progress"* and the conception of man as being fundamentally good and of unlimited powers. Sorel's anti-democratic ideology he associates with classicism and the writers connected with *L'Action Française,* and with the idea that man is by nature bad or limited and requires the discipline of authoritarian institutions:

> What is at the root of the contrasted system of ideas you find in Sorel, the classical, pessimistic, or, as its opponents would have it, the reactionary ideology? This system springs from the exactly contrary conception of man; the conviction that man is by nature bad or limited, and can consequently only accomplish anything of value by disciplines, ethical, heroic, or political. In other words, it believes in Original Sin. We may define Romantics, then, as all who do not believe in the Fall of Man. It is this opposition which in reality lies at the root of most of the other divisions in social and political thought. (*CWTEH* 249–50)

Hulme separates Original Sin from its formal theological moorings in Christian dogma and faith and uses it as his primary assumption for discussion and revaluation of literature, metaphysics, politics, and aesthetics. The intellectual "sense of the dogma" to which he adheres is a firm belief in the futility and the tragic significance of life. The "religious attitude" toward man, toward ultimate values, and toward religious discipline is not only necessary for uprooting the presuppositions underlying romanticism, a way of feeling that "confuses both human and divine things by not clearly separating them," it is the necessary attitude for the whole transformation of society, which Hulme and his French forerunners believe is possible only by adhering to the objective and absolute ethic concomitant with this conception of man. In his preface to Sorel he states: "From the pessimistic conception of man comes naturally the view that the transformation of society is an heroic task requiring heroic qualities . . . virtues which are not likely to flourish on the soil of a rational and sceptical ethic. This regeneration can, on the contrary, only be brought about and only be maintained by actions springing from an ethic which from the narrow rationalist standpoint is irrational, being not *relative,* but absolute" (Hulme's ellipsis, *CWTEH* 250). In concluding the essay Hulme moves from his pessimistic conception of man to his recurring optimistic belief that a new "religious" humanism is emerging, basing his belief on various indications that "the *absolute* view of ethics . . . is gradually being re-established" *(CWTEH* 252). Once convinced that the assumptions of the dogma were fact, Hulme called for a full neoclassical revival, for a reactionary and revolutionary transformation of the deluded romantic assumptions that had been in accretion in Western culture since the Renaissance.

We need not surmise how carefully and thoroughly Eliot read these and other passages of analysis, assertion, and prophecy or how immediate and complementary was their impact in combination with the classical principles of Babbitt and Maurras. In his formula for the renewal of a misdirected civilization, Hulme isolated a working first principle for the new classicism. In so doing he became in effect for Eliot the magnetic antipode to Rousseau and romanticism. And as Eliot's broad classical and moral point of view began to cohere around the concept of Original Sin, his aesthetic interest was also strongly attracted by Hulme's poetic field.

If critics have been somewhat uncertain about Eliot's debt to Hulme as thinker, they have almost totally neglected his debt to Hulme as poet: Eliot was teaching Hulme's poetry as well as his philosophy in the Extension lectures. In a curiously neglected statement in "The Function of Criticism" (1923), Eliot looks back to his "experience of Extension lecturing" and remembers that "the poems of T. E. Hulme only needed to be read aloud to have immediate effect" (*SE* 32). The effect that Hulme's poetry continued to have on Eliot becomes apparent in Eliot's first essay on aesthetic problems, "Reflections on *vers libre,*" published in the *New Statesman* on 3 March 1917, six months before Hulme's death. In this well-known essay Eliot is primarily "concerned with the theory of the verse-form in which imagism is cast" (*TCC* 184). Without giving the names of the authors or the poems, Eliot quotes, "because of their beauty" and because of the mastery of their "constant evasion and recognition of regularity," two passages exemplary of *vers libre.* The first unidentified passage, which Eliot describes as "a complete poem," is Hulme's "The Embankment." And I. A. Richards recalled that

Eliot told him he taught Hulme's "The Embankment" in his 1916 Extension lectures, describing it to Richards as a "most successful poem to give an audience."[32]

Eliot had clearly studied Hulme's poems and verse experiments closely, having discovered the five poems that comprise "The Complete Poetical Works of T. E. Hulme" in an addendum to Ezra Pound's *Ripostes* (1912), a copy of which Eliot had in his library.[33] It would seem that Eliot's unqualified praise of Hulme as a poet was based on more than the five published poems. In his uncollected review of E. B. Osborn's *New Elizabethans* (1919), subtitled "a first selection of the lives of young men who have fallen in the great war," Eliot regrets that "Mr. Osborn has omitted one soldier who was a real poet—T. E. Hulme."[34] And on 9 July 1919 he wrote to his friend Mary Hutchinson: "I am not sure whether you thought that Hulme is a really great poet, as I do, or not. I can't think of anything as good as two of his poems since Blake" (*L1* 311). The following year Eliot was sufficiently dismayed with the state of contemporary verse to write, "Let the public . . . ask itself why it has never heard of the poems of T. E. Hulme."[35] From 1916 to 1920 Hulme stands just as close to the surface of Eliot's critical thoughts as he does from 1929 to 1934, and during the earlier period Hulme the poet rises as a conspicuous model in the aesthetic criticism just as Hulme the philosopher stands quietly behind the developing moral criticism.

II

Late in 1916 Hulme left for France, to return to England only once again, on a brief leave in August–September 1917, before he was killed at Nieuport, near Flanders, on 28 September. Perhaps Eliot and Hulme never met, though the opportunities during the eighteen months they were both in London, together with Eliot's use of Hulme's translations and poems during the latter part of this period, make that possibility seem unlikely. However, in a letter (Texas) of 23 March 1954 to Samuel Hynes, editor of Hulme's *Further Speculations,* Eliot wrote in response to a series of questions that he never met or corresponded with Hulme and that Bertrand Russell's recollection that Vivien had introduced her husband to Hulme must be in error. Eliot was confident that Vivien did not know Hulme; he surmised that she may have introduced Russell to the poems, which she admired, but not to the man. Further, Eliot replied that he did not remember reading any of Hulme's essays in the *New Age,* and that the first work he read of Hulme's, excepting the poetry, was *Speculations.* In an afterthought, without regard to date, he recalled reading the introduction to *Reflections on Violence.* Three years later he wrote decisively to the editor of *TLS,* "I never met Hulme, and in 1914 had not met Pound or Lewis."[36] But if Eliot told Matthiessen at Harvard in 1933 that he did not know Hulme *or* Hulme's work before 1924, then his memory failed him, as it did on other occasions.[37] Pound would have known of their relationship, but he did not reply to requests for information about it. Ultimately, we must accept Eliot's word, forty years on, that he never met Hulme during their very close encounters; however, the crucial facts remain: Eliot assiduously sought Hulme out and eagerly awaited his return from the trenches in

1915–16; he requested a copy of *Reflections on Violence* in May 1916, reviewed it enthusiastically for the *Monist,* and placed it on his syllabus that autumn; he studied, taught, and wrote about Hulme's poems, all with sufficient knowledge and admiration to describe Hulme as "a contemporary." In 1916, even if the two contemporaries had not become physical acquaintances, Hulme had become Eliot's close intellectual companion. Eliot knew Hulme's ideas well, and in them he found the keystone for his classicism, Original Sin. Later, when Eliot noticed the appearance of *Speculations* in his "Commentary" for the April 1924 *Criterion,* he did not review the book but discussed its import as an observer who has long since absorbed its premises. Appropriately, Eliot's discussion of the book, "which appears to have fallen like a stone to the bottom of the sea of print," is much like Hulme's introduction to Sorel, for he notes with characteristic scorn the deluded public's inability to comprehend the classical, reactionary, and revolutionary attitude that informs it:

> With its peculiar merits, this book is most unlikely to meet with the slightest comprehension from the usual reviewer: With all its defects—it is an outline of work to be done, and not an accomplished philosophy—it is a work of very great significance. . . . In this volume he appears as the forerunner of a new attitude of mind, which should be the twentieth-century mind, if the twentieth century is to have a mind of its own. (*Cr* 2: 231)

Here Eliot is not discovering Hulme. He is beginning to acknowledge the influence that he had felt for the previous eight years.

Eliot had received an advance copy of *Speculations* from the editor, his friend Herbert Read, who had withheld from the published volume a folder of manuscript notes that he had offered unsuccessfully to Wyndham Lewis for *Tyro.* When Eliot learned about the notes, he asked Read to edit them for a proposed Hulme issue of the *Criterion,* which he hoped would contain essays on the poetry by Richard Aldington and on the prose by Ramon Fernandez. Though the issue did not materialize, Read complied: his edited version of Hulme's "Notes on Language and Style" appeared in the *Criterion* for July 1925. As Eliot wrote to Read on 7 July, looking back to 1917 and succeeding years at Lloyds bank, "Hulme's book awakened in me certain desires of exploration which had slumbered during many years of Lombard Street" (Victoria).[38]

Eliot now began to reawaken his enthusiasm for Hulme's classicism. In his attempt to define the modern tendency toward classicism in "The Idea of a Literary Review," written to inaugurate the *New Criterion* (January 1926), Eliot listed Sorel's *Reflections on Violence* and Hulme's *Speculations* among the books "which to my mind exemplify this tendency." He also listed Bertrand Russell's *What I Believe* among those books "which represent to my mind that part of the present which is already dead," adding parenthetically, "I am sorry to have to include the name of Mr. Russell, whose intellect would have reached the first rank even in the thirteenth century, but when he trespasses outside of mathematical philosophy his excursions are often descents" (*Cr* 4: 5–6). In the second of his Clark Lectures, delivered at Cambridge University in February 1926, Eliot described Hulme as "the most *fertile* mind of my generation and one of the glories of this University" (*VMP* 82). There Eliot pointed out the importance of Hulme's distinctions between the philosophical "categories" of the thirteenth and nineteenth centuries; later, in "Second Thoughts about Humanism" (1929), he would quote Hulme in expressing agreement with his distinctions:

> "I hold the religious conception of ultimate values to be right, the humanist wrong. From the nature of things, these categories are not inevitable, like the categories of time and space, but are *equally objective*. . . . What is important, is what nobody seems to realize—the dogmas like that of Original Sin, which are the closest expression of the categories of the religious attitude. That man is in no sense perfect, but a wretched creature, who can yet apprehend perfection. It is not, then, that I put up with the dogma for the sake of the sentiment, but that I may possibly swallow the sentiment for the sake of the dogma." (*SE* 490–1; *CWTEH* 455)

In his review of *The Future of Futurism* (1926), written by his friend John Rodker, who had published Eliot's *Ara Vos Prec* at his Ovid Press, Eliot declared that he was "glad to find" Hulme's influence on Rodker's thought.[39] In "Mr. P. E. More's Essays" (1929), Eliot found More's dualism "remarkably similar to the theory of discontinuity put foward by the late T. E. Hulme," and he quoted extensively from "Humanism and the Religious Attitude" to illustrate the importance of what Eliot called Hulme's "theory of gaps." It is clear here that Eliot strongly believed that, quoting Hulme, "Our principal concern, then, at the present moment, should be the re-establishment of the temper or disposition of mind which can look at a gap or chasm without shuddering."[40]

Thus, in "The *Pensées* of Pascal" (1931), Eliot took pains to inform his readers: "An important modern theory of discontinuity, suggested partly by Pascal, is sketched in the collected fragments of *Speculations* by T. E. Hulme" (*SE* 416). For Hulme, who declared indifferently "that he was a member of the Church of England and left it at that,"[41] the dogmas and theories were more important than personal belief or association with any ecclesiastical system of belief. For Eliot, Hulme had become his model for thinking about the future direction of religious poetry: "The tendency is toward something more impersonal than that of 'the last romantics,'" he wrote in an unpublished lecture, "and I think away from decorative or sensuous aestheticism. It will be much more interested in the dogma and the doctrine; in religious thought, rather than purely personal religious feeling. The precursor of this attitude was T. E. Hulme, killed in 1917; he was not a religious poet but his critical ideas took this direction" (King's).[42] What had become important to Eliot was not Hulme's belief but his "religious attitude," his "orthodoxy of sensibility."

Hulme's *Speculations* had clearly become a desk-top handbook for Eliot, who had himself become the standard-bearer for Hulme's religious attitude. As the champion of the new classicism, he did not hesitate to carry the standard into his literary criticism, taking the opportunity to conclude his essay "Baudelaire" (1930) with a passage from Hulme to which Baudelaire, too, Eliot believed, would have subscribed: "In the light of these absolute values, man himself is

judged to be essentially limited and imperfect. He is endowed with Original Sin"
(*SE* 430). Nor did Eliot hesitate to defend Hulme against his critics, as evident in
his letter of 6 November 1931 to John Middleton Murry: "I am a little puzzled
because I believe that you are rather severe on Hulme's notion of discontinuity"
(Berg). So important to Eliot were Hulme's religious attitude and theory of gaps
that he described Hulme as "the most remarkable theologian of my generation"
(*L1* 94n).

Eliot's high valuation of Hulme's poetry did not decrease after his Extension
lectures. Indeed, Eliot considered Hulme of such importance to modern poetry
that he included a lecture on Hulme in his course on "Contemporary English
Literature (1890 to the Present Time)," taught in the spring of 1933 at Harvard
University, where he spent the academic year as Norton lecturer. In his surviving
outline and notes for the lectures, Eliot introduced Hulme as "the founder of
Imagism," provided the students with "His history," read Hulme's poems to them,
and then discussed "Hulme on the Fancy" (Houghton).[43] Eliot derived the last
part of the lecture from Hulme's "Romanticism and Classicism," in which
Hulme sets out to prove "two things, first that a classical revival is coming, and,
secondly, for its particular purposes, fancy will be superior to imagination"
(*CWTEH* 59). Hulme concludes his provocative lecture, delivered in 1912 and
printed in *Speculations,* with the emphasis on poetic precision that had attracted
Eliot to his poetic theory: "Fancy is not mere decoration added on to plain
speech. Plain speech is essentially inaccurate. It is only by new metaphors, that is,
by fancy, that it can be made precise" (*CWTEH* 71).

On 31 March 1933, while his course was still in progress, Eliot delivered the
conclusion to his Norton Lectures, published later in the year as *The Use of Poetry
and the Use of Criticism.* In examining the "kinds of defect and excess" in various
theories of poetry, such as that of Abbé Brémond, which is preoccupied with
mysticism, and that of I. A. Richards, which reveals a lack of interest in theology,
Eliot turns to a theory that expresses his own bias: "One voice was raised, in our
time, to express a view of a different kind; that of a man who wrote several remarkable poems himself, and who also had an aptitude for theology. It is that of
T. E. Hulme" (*UPUC* 149). To illustrate "the claims of a particular kind of poetry
for the writer's own time," Eliot again draws upon "Romanticism and Classicism," where Hulme defines the aims of the "dry classical spirit" in modern poetry. "The great aim is accurate, precise and definite description," Eliot quotes
Hulme. "The first thing is to realise how extraordinarily difficult this is. . . .
Language has its own special nature, its own conventions and communal ideas. It
is only by a concentrated effort of the mind that you can hold it fixed to your
own purpose" (Eliot's ellipsis). Thus, Eliot not only carried his admiration for
Hulme's poems into his Extension lectures and essays; he made Hulme's theory
of poetic language essential to the "dry classical spirit" of his own poetry.[44]

III

Eliot's exposure to Hulme in 1915–16 was decisive in the formulation of his literary theory and religious attitude. Eliot's first critical writings in 1916—reviews of

books treating philosophical, religious, and social problems—directly reflect specific Hulmean critical principles and echo ideas in nearly all of Hulme's work published before his death. The evidence strongly suggests that, in addition to Hulme's poetry and his translator's preface to Sorel, Eliot sought out and became closely familiar with his "Notes on Bergson" series, his essays on humanism, his "War Notes," and his controversy with Russell. It also suggests that these essays, and perhaps Hulme himself, collectively precipitated, in Eliot's mind, the classical, authoritarian, and reactionary ideas absorbed from Babbitt, Maurras, and "an emerging general state of mind" into what Eliot called a "coherent" view of life. Even more specifically, Hulme's Pascalian theory of discontinuity and his Catholic conception of the human soul had a signficant effect on the direction of Eliot's spiritual development. It appears that by 1916, following a three-year philosophical-spiritual journey that carried him through the metaphysics of Babbitt, Bergson, Patanjali, Bradley, and Russell in a rigorous inquiry into the nature of the Absolute, Eliot had already abandoned even Bradley's vision for a Christian humanism.[45] Once Bradley's theory of judgment is accepted, Eliot wrote in 1923, "you are led . . . to something which, according to your temperament, will be resignation or despair—the bewildered despair of wondering why you ever wanted anything, and what it was that you wanted, since this philosophy seems to give you everything that you ask and yet to render it not worth wanting."[46] Russell, who had himself been a disciple of Bradley from 1893 to 1899, chose to remain resigned to the intellectual limits of knowledge, while Eliot despaired of apprehending the Absolute in his company. Russell offered "A Free Man's Worship," but Eliot took Original Sin. Bradley had shown Eliot the way out of despair—submission of the human to the divine will—but for Eliot the corrosive forces of scientific rationalism made crossing the threshold of faith intellectually unjustifiable until he encountered Hulme, who was undergoing his own "nightmare" of mechanism (*CWTEH* 142).[47] Hulme's theory of discontinuity, Eliot later said, asserts "in effect that there is a gap between psychology and ethics; and that any so-called reconciliation between religion and science is nugatory, because there are no common differences to be reconciled."[48] In Hulme, who "found out for himself that there is an *absolute* to which Man can *never* attain," Eliot found—as he himself describes the process—rational assent, intellectual conviction, and a way toward orthodoxy and "complete spiritual freedom" (*SE* 490-1).

Though Eliot's formal conversion to Anglo-Catholicism was eleven years away, his *sensibility* was religious and Catholic, and his primary critical concerns were moral in 1916, as his reviews for that year show.[49] And the paralysis of will resulting from the tension between scepticism and the religious impulse was a motivating factor in his early poetry, as Eliot's poetic notebook, *Inventions of the March Hare,* and the poems from "Prufrock" to "The Hollow Men" show. After 1916 Eliot appears to turn more toward aesthetic problems, or at least that emphasis is predominant in the essays collected in *The Sacred Wood* (1920), but the moral current continues to run throughout the lesser known writings of this period. As Eliot was not ready to disclose his position, he continued to conceal his hand, trying to work out the paradoxical nature of modern belief and writing poetry that records the struggle with mechanism of a man in search of God. When in the 1920s numerous forces led him to return more openly and explicitly to spiritual problems, both personal and social, he naturally returned to Hulme to work out in his criticism what he had already worked out in his mind. Discussing his attitude toward the new humanism with Allen Tate, Eliot acknowledged in a letter of 22 February 1929: "Hulme has influenced me enormously" (Princeton). Eliot was deeply indebted to Hulme in and after 1916, to the extent that Hulme finally begins to emerge as the chief figure among those who stand behind the formulation of Eliot's moral and aesthetic canon. With these new pieces of the Eliot–Hulme puzzle in place, we can now step back and see how early the pattern of his critical and spiritual development reveals itself, and by pushing back the pivotal year from 1928 to 1916 we can continue to remove some of the critical distortions through which we have seen Eliot, darkly.

3

"OUR MAD POETICS TO CONFUTE"

Laforgue and the Personal Voice

The ardour of red flame is thine,
And thine the steely soul of ice:
Thou poisonest the fair design
Of nature, with unfair device.

Eight years before he encountered Hulme in London, Eliot discovered the young French poet who was the first to draw his developing sensibility into play—Jules Laforgue. In December 1908, during his junior year at Harvard, Eliot became intrigued by Arthur Symons's quotations from Laforgue in *The Symbolist Movement in Literature;* he went directly to Schoenhof's and ordered the two-volume *Oeuvres Complète de Jules Laforgue* (4th ed., Paris: Mercure de France, 1909). When his copies arrived, he signed them "Thomas Eliot 1909." A year earlier he had picked up the poems of Baudelaire, and though Baudelaire's images of the city had a "great impact" on him, he found Baudelaire too overwhelming at the time and put him down.[1] In Laforgue, however, Eliot experienced a shock of recognition: here was a poet with a seemingly similar temperament, a poet experiencing similar difficulties and desires, a poet whose voice was more intimate and less intimidating than Baudelaire's. Laforgue showed him how poetry could make much more use "of contemporary ideas and feelings, of the emotional quality of contemporary ideas, than one had supposed."[2] Eliot immersed himself in the study of Laforgue and later declared that he was "the first to teach me how to speak, to teach me the poetic possibilities of my own idiom of speech" (*TCC* 126). For the next two years Eliot filled his notebook with poems written mostly in the manner of Laforgue. At some point he tipped in an undated leaf, evidently intended as an epigraph page, on which he had inscribed a four-line invocation:

O lord, have patience
Pardon these derelictions—
I shall convince these romantic irritations
By my classical convictions. (*IMH* 83) 3

The young poet who wrote this quatrain had just emerged with a more confident, maturing voice from a long internal conflict; he was a masked rebel who had worked his way through the cloying romanticism of his Emersonian, Unitarian world, subtly exercising his classical convictions against romantic irritations, his own included. In his Laforguean poems he had discovered and activated his personal voice for the first time. And yet when Eliot's critics pore over these poems they note only the formal resemblances—his borrowing and adaptation of Laforguean irony, imagery, rhythmic patterns, dramatic situations—and then move on, satisfied that the poetic relation is technical and mimetic, adolescent and obscure, "too much Laforgue's to be quite Eliot's."4 Though one senses that a personal chord has been struck in the poems, that Eliot's relation to Laforgue is more complex than technical innovation, the notion of any personal emotion has been excluded from the criticism of a poet who declared early in his career that poetry is an escape from emotion. Before we attempt to hear the personal voice in these and later poems, we must rattle the cage of "impersonality" that imprisons it and free Eliot's falsely indicted theory of interpretation.

I

At the time of Eliot's death in 1965 the criticism of his work had been policed and contained for three decades by fallacy-minding New Critics whose textual tenets were the guardians of the poet's private life. Students were uniformly catechized in the institutional view of his depersonalized career: that of a deeply sceptical poet whose early poetry expresses the spiritual aridity of the modern sensibility and whose post-conversion poetry records with philosophical detachment and abstraction the Christian spiritual quest of a man who became the pope of modern letters. Eliot scholarship, in the absence of challenging biographical matter, at least enjoyed interpretive consistency within this dogmatic schema, but critical readings of his work eventually became exhausted at the hands of impersonality. The first crack in the veneer occurred just before the fiftieth anniversary of *The Waste Land,* when Eliot was quoted in the facsimile edition (1971) as saying that his celebrated poem "was only the relief of a personal and wholly insignificant grouse against life" (*WLF* [1]), a clear signal to critics that it was time to pry into origins. During the festivities T. S. Matthews's incendiary biography *Great Tom* (1974) finally blew the seal off Eliot's privacy. The sudden appearance of psychobiographical and psychopathological essays, subjecting to analysis Eliot's "fear and hatred" of women and sex, opened the door for looking at his poetry and criticism as the exorcism of neurosis.

The heretical interest in Freudian analyses of Eliot's allegedly neurotic voices gradually gave way to the determined deconstruction of his social and political voices. Psychologies were displaced by ideologies; the attempts to show that homosexuality, misogyny, or a divided psyche were the governing forces of the poetry got pushed aside to show that a complex of race, class, gender, and religious bias—made particularly unsavory by fascist sympathies and an aesthetic anti-Semitism—makes up the true voice encoded in the work. Now that the appalling poetic voice has been exposed for what it is, one zealous poet-critic recently proclaimed, we can see that we are at "the beginning of a long process of revisionist criticism which should diminish the overwhelming, the stifling cultural authority which Eliot's oeuvre has acquired."[5]

Eliot was himself aware of the plurality of analytical languages that constantly vie for critical audience and of the loss of focus that often leads literary critics into reductive criticism. "The ideal literary critic," Eliot wrote of the critic seeking the personal voice in the work before him, "should have both an intense concentration and an indefinite awareness":

> He should not be primarily concerned with sociology, or with psychology, or with politics, or with theology, or with any other ology; he should be primarily concerned with the word and the incantation. . . . He should differ from the practitioners of other sciences, not so much by what he needs to know and what he does not need to know—for indeed he needs to know everything—as by his centre of values: in the beginning was the word. (*VMP* 287–8)

Though he saw no reason why sociologists should not scrutinize poetry or why psychologists should not analyze it, he had no hesitation in saying, "but this is not literary criticism" (*VMP* 289). There is, of course, no richer grid than Eliot's oeuvre for working out the relation of impersonal form and personal voice, for Eliot, himself a master of the mask in his poems, was in his criticism a masterful pursuer of the personal voice through "intense concentration" and "indefinite awareness." Though Eliot greatly envied Shakespeare the enduring privacy of his life, ever elusive of intense biographical curiosity and psychological probing, he still brooded upon Shakespeare's secret mind during the whole of his career, longed to perceive and even empathize with the intense personal moments that haunt the surface of Shakespeare's work. It is thus rather astonishing that after seventy-five years of criticism, between the uses and abuses of "impersonality" on the one hand, and of "personality" on the other, the personal voice of T. S. Eliot, too, waits to be heard.

There are several explanations for such an unlikely assertion. In impersonal theories of art, according to which the poet projects his personal emotional experience into the collective human experience of his audience, the criticism proceeds in a linear direction away from the poet: the poetry tends to be interpreted in terms of its reflection of the values and sensibility of that audience, and the poet eventually becomes known as a "spokesman for his age" or as having expressed "the voice of a generation." Thus, following the publication of *The Waste Land,* we begin to hear Eliot described as a poet who voices "the disillusionment of a generation," and over forty years later critics were still saying that "in Eliot's poetry we find the intimate voice of the modern sensibility."[6] The intimidating voice of the New Criticism, which was largely a critical extension of Eliot's impersonal theory, so successfully separated the poet from the poem that for fifty years we almost forgot he was there. In isolating the poem from the poet (and this was one of the dangers of the New Criticism all along) we reduced Eliot's unique poetic voice to a modern mode. "Our practice," wrote Hugh Kenner, "when we are thinking about Eliot's poetry rather than his critical theory, is to attach Eliot's poems to Eliot, and then invent ourselves an Eliot to go with them."[7] Postmodern criticism of Eliot's poetry has since served to intensify the perceived fragmentation of Eliot's dislocated voices. What we have overlooked ever since we established "Tradition and the Individual Talent" as the gospel of Eliot's critical theory is that while we were separating the poetry from the poet and describing objective correlatives, Eliot, in his own criticism, was working back down the line from the poetry to the poet. Ironically, at the same time that he was developing a theory of depersonalization in the creative process, he was defining a method of repersonalization for the critical process.

Eliot began developing his theory of interpretation in a review–essay entitled "Ben Jonson," published in November 1919 just as the second part of "Tradition and the Individual Talent" was published in the *Egoist*. In the former essay Eliot directed critical attention away from biographical and historical concerns by delimiting them as precritical activities that must not disrupt critical engagement with the center of the work itself. However, Eliot's opposition to biographical and historical criticism did not imply a separation of poet from poem. To Eliot, the center of the work contains the essence of the poetic temperament that struggles with emotional experience to express a vision of life, and his primary interest as a critic was in unearthing the personal emotional tone beneath the objective surface of the work. In defending Jonson against the charge that his poetry springs solely from the intellect, Eliot declares that "The creation of a work of art . . . consists in the process of transfusion of the personality, or, in a deeper sense, the life, of the author into the [work]," and the "ways in which the passions and desires of the creator may be satisfied in the work of art are complex and devious" (*SE* 157–8). The emotional tone of Jonson's highly impersonal poetry is revealed not in the single poem but in the design of the poetry as a whole. Getting to Jonson's temperament requires what Eliot calls "intelligent saturation" in the whole, moving beyond the surface forms into an apprehension of the subjective preoccupations that unify and sustain the whole body of work. Once we dig beneath the theory, the surface observations, the deliberate inventions and elaborations of Jonson's poetry and drama, we find, says Eliot, "a kind of power . . . which comes from below the intellect" *(SE* 156), an organizing power that arranges objects in a way that reflects the unique emotional world of the poet. Until the pattern that this power makes is perceived by the critic, the full aesthetic value of the work cannot be realized. Knowledge of Jonson's poetry, says Eliot, requires knowledge of Jonson's temperament, and that knowledge is to be found not in his biography but in his poetry, which reveals the depth and dimension of the biography. Within the poetry itself, as Eliot says later, the poet will "give the pattern, or we may say the undertone, of the personal emotion, the personal drama and struggle, which no biography, however full and intimate, could give us" *(SE* 203).

In 1919, and for the next eleven years, Eliot devoted much of his critical energy to defining the nature and importance of the personal voice in "impersonal" works of art. Most of Eliot's readers are familiar with his chemical analogy for the creative process in "Tradition and the Individual Talent," where he portrays the poet's mind as a transforming catalyst that separates "the man who suffers and the mind which creates" *(SE* 18), but few have seen his important expansion of the analogy in "Modern Tendencies in Poetry" (1920). "The great scientist submerges himself in what he has to do," says Eliot, "forgets himself":

> But if he is a great scientist there will be . . . a cachet of the man all over it. No one else could have drawn those inferences, constructed those demonstrations, seen those relations. His personality has not been lost, but has gone, all the important part of it, into the work. Yet the inferences seem to have drawn themselves, the demonstrations constructed themselves, the relations flown into each other's arms; but without him it would not have happened. There is this same inevitability and impersonality about the work of a great poet . . . the greater the poet, the more evident his hand in every line, and the more elusive his personality. . . . What consitutes the terrible authenticity of Villon's testaments is that he *saw* his feelings, watched them, as coldly as an astronomer watches a comet; and without this cold and scientific observation he could never have given his feelings their permanent intensity.[8]

Eliot's intent was not only to clarify the relationship between the personal and the impersonal but, in defining the levels of value in the creative process, to define the essential levels of critical engagement. As Eliot explained in his introduction to Paul Valéry's *Le Serpent* (1924), "not our feelings, but the pattern which we may make of our feelings, is the center of value." Poetry, he affirms, "is impersonal in the sense that personal emotion, personal experience, is extended and completed in something impersonal—not in the sense of something divorced from personal experience and passion. No good poetry is the latter."[9] In the creative process what is essential to the poem, the personal pattern, is organically united with the superficies of the poem—a conventional form, a philosophical system, and so on—to create in the objective structure what Eliot calls a distinctive emotional undertone or pattern, and a major responsibility of the critic is to detect and define the presence or absence of that pattern as it pervades and enhances the aesthetic value of the work. Accordingly, during that same period Eliot criticized Philip Massinger and Thomas Heywood for a "defect of personality" while saying that in the work of most of their Jacobean contemporaries "there is at least some inchoate pattern; there is, as it would often be called, personality" *(SE* 175). Such statements are often seized by those who insist that Eliot contradicts his impersonal theory throughout his critical prose, but the creative and critical theories are distinct, complementary, and unopposed.

Throughout the 1920s Eliot discussed only briefly the critical principles that he was fully exercising in his own criticism. But in 1930 G. Wilson Knight's *Wheel of Fire,* comprised of essays on the interpretation of Shakespeare's tragedies, afforded Eliot an opportunity to further delineate his concept of the double pattern of art and to indicate ways in which the critic can approach the consciousness of the poet. In his introduction to that volume, Eliot insists that "the greatest poetry, like the greatest prose, has a doubleness; the poet is talking to you on two planes at once." The essay describes the difficulty of tracing the personal pattern in Shakespeare's work, but it also explores the ways in which the critic perceives the individual pattern of a poet working within the confines of an overt philosophical system. The poet, says Eliot, "has something to say which is not even necessarily implicit in the system, something which is also over and above the verbal beauty." In the poetry of Dante, whom Eliot uses to exemplify his method, "the pattern is interwoven chiefly with the systematic pattern which he set himself, and the mystery and excitement lies in trying to trace its relations and differences—the relation, and the personal variations in another mode, between for example the Thomist doctrine of Love, the poetic provençal tradition, and the direct experience of Dante with its modifications under philosophical and literary influences." The systematic pattern is a priori a guide to the personal, for it serves the critic initially as a "criterion of *consciousness,*" defining the emotional and spiritual range the poet is exploring.

After grasping the aesthetic design, the duty of the critic, says Eliot, is to read *below* the level of objective forms, below the level of philosophical system, conventional structure, dramatic situation, and personae in the understanding of what he calls "subterrene or submarine music."[10] In moving from the objective reality of the poem to the subjective reality of the poet within the poem, the critic observes the ways in which the poet's imagination plays upon and takes liberties with the given philosophical ideas, the proportion of invention, borrowing, and adaptation, the ways in which he manipulates the ideas for his own purposes and synthesizes from the emotional-ethical order those emotions and values that are most central to his own experience. Contemplating the manner in which the poet's selected equivalents are arranged and given a special coloring, language, and order, the critic seeks to experience the poet's creation of a wholly individual aesthetic and moral world within a wholly impersonal system. Further, he attempts to relive the recurring emotional preoccupations of the personae who inhabit this world, for if the pattern is there, says Eliot, the personae will be "dramatizing, but in no obvious form, an action or struggle for harmony in the soul of the poet" *(SE* 196). Ultimately, the critic strives to transcend the objective reality, to comprehend, as far as it is ever possible, the inner experience, the personal and private agonies, that the poet, in the process of creation, transmutes "into something rich and strange, something universal and impersonal" *(SE* 137). All this leads toward what Eliot calls "the real pattern," but how the link between the two worlds is made, beyond the fact that it involves "instinct" and is characterized by "mystery and excitement," he does not say, though much of what is perceived is obviously lost through the medium of critical language, so that we are always at some remove from the actuality of personal experience. Nonetheless, "intelligent saturation" in the work requires an engagement of the critical

with the creative imagination. It demands more than an analytical power of tracing the organic interdependence of objects in the objective surfaces of a poet's
works; it demands an additional power of concentration, absorption, and synthesis that enables the critic to penetrate the deepest layers of the work, to know
when the voice of the poem and the voice of the poet are in harmonious or
ironic equilibrium. It requires sustained critical intensity, but as he says in "Ben
Jonson," "not many people are capable of discovering for themselves the beauty
which is only found after labour" (SE 148).[11]

In effect, Eliot was defining an objective critical method for expressionist
criticism, which he regarded an essential part of aesthetic evaluation. He directs
the critic to the interior world of the poet because an insignificant poet can be
"too objective, without having that large and intricate pattern which objectivity
requires," thereby presenting "a world with no particular interesting man inside
it."[12] Criticism of Eliot's poetry was for years too objective as well, a consequence of misapplying his theory of impersonality to the critical act, and in reaction the criticism has for years been too psychological, too ideological, too
much in the service of individual and cultural agendas. Eliot was foremost a
critic of the personal voice—of Dante, Shakespeare, Donne, Jonson, Herbert,
Baudelaire, Laforgue, Yeats; he was continuously in pursuit of the personal pattern of the artist within the objective structures of his art. At the same time that
he was describing the "process of depersonalization" in the creative act, he was
lamenting as a critic that in reading most contemporary poetry "one never has
the tremendous satisfaction of meeting a writer who is more original, more independent, than he himself knows. No dead voices speak through the living
voice; no reincarnation, no re-creation."[13] In his memorial address for Yeats, Eliot
regrets that the early poems reveal "only in a line here or there, that sense of a
unique personality which makes one sit up in excitement and eagerness to learn
more about the author's mind and feelings" (OPP 255).[14] As the long misguided
arc of impersonality finally comes full circle, it is time to seek, in his formal,
instinctive way, the particularly interesting man inside Eliot's own poetry and
criticism.

II

To approach the personal voice in Eliot's own "impersonal" poetry, we must heed
his often-repeated corollary to the necessity of apprehending the design of the
whole work: that in searching for the personal pattern the critic must not focus
solely on the major works and neglect those works of apprenticeship or decline
that initiate and complete the pattern. Accordingly, we must begin with the
poems of his first productive period, the poems written "under the sign of
Laforgue" between 1909 and 1911. Several of these poems, "Nocturne," "Humouresque," "Spleen," and "Suite Clownesque," were omitted from Prufrock and
Other Observations when Eliot and Pound began to plan the makeup of the volume in April 1916, and most have been summarily dismissed as slight, derivative
detritus of Eliot's attempts to master Laforgue's symbolist techniques.[15] But for

the entirety of his career Eliot never ceased to reiterate and rethink the importance of Laforgue to him in his periodic discussions of influences. "I do feel
more grateful to him than to anyone else," he wrote to a correspondent who
praised the publication of *Prufrock and Other Observations,* "and I do not think
that I have come across any other writer since who has meant so much to me as
he did at that particular moment, or that particular year" (*L1* 191). Two years later,
discussing the nature of early poetic influence, implicitly in context of his relation to Laforgue, he insisted that "we do not imitate; we are changed; and our
work is the work of the changed man; we have not borrowed, we have quickened, and we become bearers of a tradition."[16] His sense of the importance of a
writer's "first passion" for another poet is measured not in terms of technique
but in terms of the transformative, maturative effect on the poetic voice. "When
a young writer is seized with his first passion of this sort," says Eliot, "he may
be changed, metamorphosed almost, within a few weeks even, from a bundle of
second-hand sentiments into a person. The imperative intimacy arouses for the
first time a real, an unshakeable confidence." Eliot did not slight the technical importance of Laforgue "as a laboratory study for the young poet,"[17] and though
he describes the early relation between Laforgue and himself as " a sort of possession by a stronger personality,"[18] the primary importance of Laforgue to Eliot
was the sudden discovery of his own poetic voice. In 1909, after having discovered Laforgue, and after having become an apostle of Irving Babbitt, who was at
the forefront of the neoclassical reaction against romanticism and Rousseauistic
sentimentalism in all its forms, Eliot became, as he says, "engrossed in working
out the implications of Laforgue."[19] As it turns out, Eliot was as engrossed with
the philosophical implications of Laforgue as with the artistic. He *was* intrigued
by the Laforguean method of subtly mocking or ironically undercutting the explicit, implicit, or expected sentimentalism of a dramatic situation, but he turned
the ironic technique of deflating the emotional sentimentalism in the poem
against Laforgue by further mocking the philosophical sentimentalism underlying Laforgue's lunar symbolism. All the poems are too much Eliot's to be quite
Laforgue's.

When the melancholic sensibilities of Laforgue's truth-seeking lunar dandies
confront the sordid realities and illusory, maddened surfaces of the solar, daylight
world, they turn away from and scorn the sun, which is symbolic of a rational, empirically defined absolute. They then take flight to the nocturnal realm of Our
Lady the Moon, who in Laforgue's poetry is symbolic of a higher inner reality, of
what Laforgue calls, after Eduard von Hartmann, the Unconscious, which harbors
within the individual psyche a divine, metaphysical Absolute.[20] In Laforgue's third
volume of poetry, *L'Imitation de Notre-Dame le Lune* (1886), which constitutes what
Laforgue called "a contribution to the cult of the moon,"[21] the moon is explicitly
addressed as the soul, the Unconscious, and is celebrated by a masquerade of
clowns who serve as priests of the Unconscious. In their *dandysme lunaire,*
Laforgue's clownish retinue has faith that a fulfilling Absolute exists *within* the romantic self rather than in a supernatural reality external to the fallen self. In the
adopted lunar symbolism of Eliot's poems, however, the Laforguean lunar lady is
consistently mocked and debased, and the priests of the Unconscious have be-

come her betrayed victims. She is symbolic not of the enlightening Unconscious but of the deluding Inner Light, of the romantic, sentimental attitude toward the nature of man and the Absolute.[22] To Eliot, whose classical premises are defined in the Laforguean poems, the world is moonstruck with sentimentalism. The Laforguean personae that inhabit his early poems are seen, from an aesthetic distance, as anxious creatures of feeling. In their inner moonlit journeys into the Unconscious, their empty souls are filled not with perceptions of the Absolute but with deluding emotional sentiments and distorted visions that the abhorrent sunlight inevitably turns into disillusionment and despair.

Eliot's first Laforguean poem, "Nocturne," appeared in the *Harvard Advocate* on 12 November 1909 (*CPP* 601). In the poem the poet describes his own modern recreation of the prototypal Romeo-Juliet romance, which he not only strips of the sentimental conclusion expected by his "female readers" but also turns into a parody of *dandysme lunaire* in particular and of *poésie des départs* in general. Eliot's effete counterparts are pictured "in the usual debate / Of love, beneath a bored but courteous moon." Their flagging conversation and Romeo's banal nocturne are woefully inadequate to the demands of the traditional romantic scene. In sympathy for their ordinary, unromantic "fate," the poet contrives dramatic action by having a hidden servant stab Juliet, whose blood "looks effective on the moonlit ground." But the "hero," rather than plunging into despair, surprisingly "smiles" in apparent relief. Suddenly released from temporary and unfulfilling earthly sentiments that are insufficent to his ideal needs and that bore the onlooking moon, he takes excited flight to the sublime lunar lady, who has patiently awaited his departure. The poet, in his "best mode oblique," an ironic mode designed to mask his underlying attitude toward the actions of his romantic personae, lets his mocking attitude emerge in the parodic description of his moonstruck hero, who, in the manner of Laforgue's Pierrot, "Rolls toward the moon a frenzied eye profound." With the depiction of that lunar impulse the nocturnal scene is closed; it is not necessary to provide the stock sentiments and "perfect climax" for which the tearful ladies cry, for though he is derisive of their emotional expectations, his focus remains on Romeo's ludicrous philosophical sentimentalism, of which his feminine readers are unaware.

In "Conversation Galante," originally entitled "Short Romance" and dated November 1909, Eliot places his own contemptuous persona among the followers of the moon. The poem is modeled roughly on the dramatic dialogue in Laforgue's "Autre Complainte de Lord Pierrot," where the meditative male, who keeps "One eye intent upon the Unconscious," talks to a threatening representative of all womankind. In Eliot's poem the male lover digresses from his amorous pursuits to point out derisively "Our sentimental friend the moon," which he debunks as an "old battered lantern" whose purpose is "To light poor travellers to their distress" (*CPP* 33). The lady, annoyed and bored by his metaphysical drift, further suffers his scorn against the sentiments of moon-inspired music, against "'That exquisite nocturne, with which we explain / The night and moonshine; music which we seize / To body forth our own vacuity.'" The lady asks if this acidulous portrayal of the sentimental mind refers to her, but his oblique reply elevates her to a symbolic position alongside their sentimental friend the moon:

"Oh no, it is I who am inane."

"You, madam, are the eternal humorist,
The eternal enemy of the absolute,
Giving our vagrant moods the slightest twist!
With your air indifferent and imperious
At a stroke our mad poetics to confute—"

The lady is Eliot's counterpart of Laforgue's portrayal of the Eternal Feminine, whose enigmatic, worldly intricacies and powers of enchantment wreck the antennae of the poet's truth-seeking soul. Eliot's persona sees not only the earthly lady but the moon who rules her as the "eternal enemy of the absolute," for together these embodiments of sentimentalism hold seductive power over mind and reason, engulf the soul and heart with delusive sentiments and feelings, and "light poor travellers to their distress." The fervid mood of Eliot's asentimental pilgrim of the Absolute, whose lunar-feminine invectives in a sentimental world make him appear "inane" and his poetics "mad," is then slightly twisted by the indifferent sublunary lady: "Are we then so serious?" In the Laforguean spirit of self-deprecation, Eliot mocks the heavy-handed manner of his impassioned persona, but the classical premises of his mad, anti-romantic poetics are sharply revealed.

In "Humouresque," parenthetically subtitled "(After J. Laforgue)" and published in the *Harvard Advocate* in January 1910, a similar contemptuous persona appears as the puppeteer-poet's favorite marionette. The germ of the poem is in a single stanza of Laforgue's "Locutions de Pierrot, xii," where one of the poet's clowns, described as having a lunar dandy's heart in a ludicrous little body, dies of chronic orphanhood. However, Eliot's marionette, a metaphor for one of his artistically manipulated voices, is a philosophical orphan of a different cast. He has a grimacing face, a "Half bullying, half imploring air," and his "who-the-devil-are-you stare" is inevitably "Translated, maybe, to the moon" (*CPP* 602). At the beginning of the poem the poet laments the puppet's death, but he is dead only in the sense that his supposedly weak-headed logic and his imploring voice are thought to be useless and dead on earth. He is therefore placed in Limbo, but his insistent, jack-in-the-box voice continues to rail against the earth's latest philosophical fashion: "'Your damned thin moonlight, worse than gas—'". To which the poet ironically remarks: "Logic a marionette's, all wrong / Of premises; yet in some star / A hero!" In this romantic world, however, Eliot's heroic marionette-persona is a mad, intellectual outcast, and the poet knows that his classical voice and vision, if they are to survive, must be masked in irony.

Eliot takes his Laforguean masquerade to its most oblique theatrical heights in "Suite Clownesque," dated October 1910. The setting is a Victorian-Edwardian version of a Greco-Roman amphitheatre, a modern coliseum complete with painted colonnades, orchestra pit, and manicured lawns studded with terra cotta fawns and potted palms, all lit up by cigarettes, stars, and a ring of lights. On this mock-classical stage appear the debased counterparts of *commedia dell'arte*, the popular Italian comedy of masked characters featuring Harlequin and his beloved mistress Columbine. In Eliot's outlandish harlequinade, the characters enact a four-scene play of "philosophy and art," a comic melodrama in which the comedian, in various guises, diabolically embodies and caricatures the nature of romantic sentimentalism (*IMH* 32). It is indeed a burlesque of the suite, an instrumental musical form derived from dance and consisting of a series of movements in contrasting rhythm and mood. In the hands of Eliot's orchestra, the musical compositions of the suite have degenerated into the nightmusic of romantic serenades; in the sequence of scenes we hear evoked the popular incidental music of vaudeville sketches, minstrel shows, and Gilbert and Sullivan operettas. The audience, full of suspense about the hero's quest for his Columbine and implicated in the pervasive sentimentalism by the characters, is finally too impatient to stay for the classic saraband that incongruously concludes this dubious suite. At the close of the play the comedian returns yet "again"—not before a final curtain, but under a threatening shadow that suddenly falls upon the romantic stage.

In the opening scene, Eliot's ubiquitous comedian bounds onto the stage "again," now as a corpulent caricature of Laforgue's moonlit Pierrot (a descendant of Harlequin). He struts the stage, donned in a "dogmatic vest" that envelops his immense and sparkling "belly," a vest that proclaims him the embodiment of the self and its absolute truths—a priest of the Unconscious in a ringmaster's vestments. Sceptical of truth in the external world, he points his scarlet nose in contemptuous interrogation of the stars in constellations above, no less than of the human "entities" in the "ring of lights" below. The poet's comic narrator sardonically informs us that somewhere in the vortex of that dogmatic vest and scarlet nose resides his "soul," one that self-assuredly has the world "at rights." He "gets away with it," his haughty solipsism, by exhibiting his animal antics, the clown's simple art of spreading the toes, a comic gesture of self-deprecation. But the narrator sees through the comedian's "self-embodied rôle" and sets about the comic deflation of his pretentious pose as "The most expressive, real of men." Below the cocksure egotism, our portly hero is made out to be a restless and anxious poltroon, all self and no will, a spineless "jellyfish" lacking self-control.

In the second scene the comedian is succeeded on stage by seven singleminded school girls in the midst of a truant adventure. Evidently surprised by the onlooking audience as they mount stools, they greet the people and shake their fingers in reverse reprimand of their presence, revealing in unison that they are on "a peek about the town." Ready to go, they jump in a street car, opportunistically descending when they see soldiers on whom they use their wiles to fund their romantic spree. The seven soubrettes may be tired of their school texts, but they peevishly tell the audience that they are "perplexed" and "vexed" by the poetic text in which they find themselves. "Where shall we go to next?" one asks, and we soon discover that they have followed the comedian to the streets of New York, where they have taken roles as members of his romantic retinue, playing young Pierrettes to his Pierrot in the third scene.

Eliot's comedian undergoes a striking transformation in New York, casting off his sparkling dogmatic vest for the "quintessential flannel suit." In impeccable sartorial conformity, he leads a double solar/lunar life. If we meet him walking down "the avenue" (Fifth Avenue) in the afternoon, he will "very likely" give a cordial greeting and a gentlemanly nod of recognition, but should we later meet him walking up Broadway "Under the light of the silvery moon" (sounding the lyrics of the popular vaudeville song in the suite),[23] we find him in true demeanor, gleefully parading his young cult of the moon:

> You may find me
> All the girls behind me,
> Euphorion of the modern time
> Improved and up to date—sublime

Euphorion, the Arcadia-born son of Goethe's Faust and the classical Helen, is aptly portrayed for Eliot as being "a young genius, classical in aspect, but wildly romantic and ungovernable in temper."[24] Under the silvery moon, Eliot's "Improved and up to date" Euphorion is "Quite at home in the universe," scornful of death, a carpe diem romantic "Shaking cocktails on a hearse." Now in his moonlit element, exclaiming in liberation from his solar mask that "It's Broadway after dark!" he gives a stage direction to the orchestra, calling for a minstrel melody to accompany the lunar revelry: "Here let a clownesque be sounded / on the sandboard and bones."

With the return of daylight we find him on the beach, immaculately attired in his flannel suit, compelling the attention of his audience, which exclaims in unison, "Look at him!" He returns the stare to his onlookers as his nymphs prepare for a swim, now making the ultimate romantic assumption—that he is the "First born child of the absolute." Euphorion in pure flannel has now altered his parentage: he is divinely sent, an earthly manifestation of the Absolute in his own right. Under his searching gaze a member of his audience protests, "I guess there's nothing the matter with us!" In Laforguean fashion, however, a wave of self-doubt sweeps over the protester, leading him to close the scene in search of self-assurance: "But say, just be serious, / Do you think that I'm all right?"

In the final scene the stately steps of the minuet have been displaced by the "last contortions" of a modern operetta, in which the frivolous truants play pastoral milkmaids and village girls who "Withdraw, advance" on city boys with rattan canes. The climax of the piecemeal play comes when the Harlequin-hero finally "captures the Columbine." This is what the sentimental audience wanted, and it wants no more. Its members rise "hat in hand" to depart, satisfied, disdaining to stay for the anticlimatic sarabande, the unmasking of the masquerade, the lighting up of cigarettes and the exchange of compliments. As the stage and lawns empty, however, a massive shadow darkens the coliseum: "But through the painted colonnades / There falls a shadow, dense, immense." It is yet another early instance of the many ominous shadows that eclipse the mindscapes of Eliot's poetry and plays. Out of this mysterious shadow, as dark and dense as the fearsome hovering of a wing, the comedian springs forward again in vest and nose for his finale, exploding in demonic laughter, spreading his toes. The masked poet has played the clown, directed the play, and conducted the suite with his mad poetics and mock-heroics: his is the last laugh of irony, the last hint (locked in parentheses) of illusion ("The most expressive, real of men"), the last animal gesture (anticipating Sweeney's spreading of the knees) in mockery of the romantic illusion of self-divinity.

When a more familiar poem of the same period, "Rhapsody on a Windy Night" (dated March 1911), is placed in its proper position with the other Laforguean poems, the developing pattern of Eliot's voice, previously inaccessible through the lunar symbolism of the one poem in isolation, becomes quite clear. In this poem Eliot is detached from the persona, who is, in effect, a Laforguean lunar traveler unmasked. His world and mind are "Held in a lunar synthesis," and as he struggles to resuscitate his paralyzed memory, all the clear relations and distinctions of the mind are dissolved by the seductive charms and delusions of "lunar incantations" (*CPP* 24). As he continues his sublunary journey toward a lost image of truth, the memory throws up only images of broken, twisted, artificial things, and toward the end of the hallucinatory night a sputtering streetlamp directs the persona's attention to the moon, uttering in French a slightly revised and ironically used line from Laforgue's "Complainte de cette bonne lune":

> Regard the moon,
> La lune ne garde aucune rancune,
> She winks a feeble eye,
> She smiles into corners.
> She smooths the hair of the grass.
> The moon has lost her memory.
> A washed-out smallpox cracks her face,
> Her hand twists a paper rose,
> That smells of dust and eau de Cologne,
> She is alone
> With all the old nocturnal smells
> That cross and cross across her brain.

Here the anxious image of Our Lady, symbol of the Unconscious, or Inner Light, is poxed and deflated; the moon, who has also lost her memory, has led her man into a rhapsody of spiritual despair.

Interwoven with these mock-serious lunar diatribes are what might be called the solar poems, in which Eliot confronts those daylight actualities of existence that Laforgue's dandies eschew, and he begins to explore the relation of the tormented individual soul to an external, redemptive Absolute. In "Preludes," in which the four sections alternate between night and day, the "grimy" approach of evening and the ritual lighting of the lamps signals not a rhapsodic escape into the Unconscious but a painful reminiscence of "The burnt-out ends of smoky days" (*CPP* 22). At sunrise, "The morning comes to consciousness / Of faint stale smells of beer," and the despondent persona imagines a masquerade of other isolated, rootless souls pouring out of "a thousand furnished rooms" onto the street. As night returns, the mind is again filled with "The thousand sordid images / Of which [the] soul was constituted," images that become even more nightmarish at dawn:

> And when all the world came back
> And the light crept up between the shutters
> And you heard the sparrows in the gutters,
> You had such a vision of the street
> As the street hardly understands.

As reminiscence gives rise to sordid images of the soul and to a Dantean vision of "a blackened street" of lost souls, the despairing persona entertains and clings to the idea and possibility of an external, redeeming savior:

> I am moved by fancies that are curled
> Around these images, and cling:
> The notion of some infinitely gentle
> Infinitely suffering thing.

But this vague, momentary hope in the midst of torment is regarded as "sentiment" by the policing rational mind, which immediately undercuts it by affirming the aimless, Godless nature of existence:

> Wipe your hand across your mouth, and laugh;
> The worlds revolve like ancient women
> Gathering fuel in vacant lots.

Yet the notion of redemption and the Absolute persists. In "Spleen," published in the *Harvard Advocate* in January 1910, a masquerade of pious churchgoers consciously going through their ritual social graces plunges the "mental self-possession" of the poet into splenetic dejection (*CPP* 603). Collectively they conjure the image of a personified abstraction named Life, who, "Languid, fastidious, and bland" and anticipating Prufrock, waits anxiously "On the doorstep of the Absolute." The spleen results not from the Sunday guises and pretensions but from an acute awareness of spiritual torpor and inaction. It arises from the utter inability of the intellect to find a way out of the self to the Absolute. In these early poems, only Prufrock is aware that the individual is responsible for his own deliverance from self and the abyss that underlies it, but Prufrock's self-enclosed mind, like the minds of the personae in "Rhapsody" and "Preludes," remains trapped in its own unreality. He has a vague notion of the Absolute toward which he strains, and his impulse to action, his desire for self-abandonment and surrender, is further thwarted by a will that is paralyzed by the false counsel of the rational mind. At the end of the "tedious argument" between the spiritual and rational selves, the will of Prufrock, like the will of the quester of *The Waste Land*, must make, if self is ever to be delivered from self, "The awful daring of a moment's surrender."

The deceptive surface patterns of these early poems collectively reveal an underlying sensibility in the process of defining, affirming, and exercising the personal intellectual-emotional center that excites it. In effect, Eliot's sensibility enacts an artistic and philosophical dialogue with the symbolist idealism of Laforgue, just as Laforgue's enacts a dialogue with the scientific positivism of his own age. The creative energy of Eliot's anti-romantic sensibility is primarily intellectual and is directed against the lunar enemies of the Absolute, against the demons of egoistic sentimentalism that lead one into intellectual and spiritual darkness. In some poems the imagination mutes the youthful shrillness of the poet's voice by keeping an aura of humor, whimsicality, absurdity, and mockery over the actions of the masked dandies, gallants, and marionettes who serve as his personae. The poet also disguises the intent and tone of the poems with appropriately ironic titles: "Nocturne," "Humouresque," "Rhapsody," "Suite," "Love Song," "Conversation Galante." When the poetic voice is directed against the external lunar symbol of the Laforguean Unconscious, the symbolic irony is dressed in Laforguean clothes and masks, but when it voices the realities underlying the lunar illusion that the Inner Light leads man toward self-fulfillment, when it portrays the effects of romantic premises on the benumbed individual consciousness, the frivolity gives way to dejection, the symbolic irony to imagistic realism.[25]

At the center of that intellectual temperament, however, is a deep-seated spiritual impulse, and though it knows already not to follow the Inner Light, that impulse is continually frustrated by the limits of the rational self. Beginning with these early poems—and from "Prufrock" to "Gerontion" to the persona in *The Waste Land* to the penitent in *Ash-Wednesday* to *Four Quartets*—the nature, causes, and effects of spiritual frustration become the primary preoccupations of Eliot's personae, as central as the spiritual quest itself. At the close of the Laforguean period in 1911, the nature of the Absolute remains undefined, but in those poems Eliot initiates his long reaction against what Hulme called the "spilt religion" of romanticism. It was perhaps inevitable that when the undergraduate Laforguean poet became a graduate student of philosophy he would immerse himself in the Absolute of F. H. Bradley. When he began to write again in 1915, the sensibility behind his unfocused tragic vision continued to direct itself into parody, caricature, and satire, notably of such "guardians" of modernism as Arnold and Emerson ("Matthew and Waldo"), who in Eliot's poem "Cousin Nancy" are mocked as leaders of "The army of unalterable law," a line aptly borrowed from Meredith's "Lucifer in Starlight." Such Goliaths of the romantic faith had clearly become the intellectual and poetic targets of Eliot's "mad poetics."

Eliot's classical convictions remained buried in the ironic substratum of the Laforguean poems, but by 1916, following his exposure to the philosophy of Hulme and the completion of his dissertation on Bradley, the philosophical quandary over the nature of the Absolute was over. By the time he began his literary reviews in London, he had achieved sufficient critical distance from Laforgue to begin analyzing his earlier poetic engagement with him. Now preoccupied with metaphysical poetry and the relation of thought and feeling, Eliot had come to see that Laforgue suffered from a dissociation of thought and feeling much more advanced than that of Donne. As assistant editor of the *Egoist,* he began to use Laforgue as a critical criterion, comparing his sensibility to that of such contemporary poets as Marianne Moore: "Even in Laforgue, there are unassimilated fragments of metaphysics and, on the other hand, of sentiment floating about. I will not assert that Miss Moore is as interesting in herself as Laforgue, but the fusion of thought and feeling is perhaps more complete." Soon after giving his final Extension lecture, Eliot confessed to a London audience:

> I am no longer of the opinion that Laforgue, at the stage which he had reached
> at his death, was a great poet; I can see sentimentalism, absorption in himself,
> lack of balance. But in Laforgue there was a young man who was generally in-
> telligent, critical, interested in art, science and philosophy, and always himself:
> that is, every mental occupation had its own precise emotional state, which
> Laforgue was quick to discover and curious to analyse.[26]

Eliot could identify Laforgue's skill in finding the emotional equivalent for ideas, the crucial skill that Eliot had recently redefined as the "objective correlative," and he would soon associate him with the metaphysical poets for having "the same essential quality of transmuting ideas into sensations, of transforming an observation into a state of mind" (*SE* 290). Not until he gave his Clark Lectures at Cambridge in 1926, however, could he fully characterize the dissociated romantic mind that he had engaged in his early poetry.[27]

In those lectures, Eliot traces not only the dissociation of sensibility but the "disintegration of the intellect" in European poetry by exploring the harmony of philosophical, religious, and personal emotion in Dante, the dissociation evident in Donne, and the tortuous stress and tension manifest in Laforgue. Eliot portrays Laforgue as a poet haunted by the need to live some philosophy, even the despairing, romanticist abstractions of Schopenhauer and of Hartmann's *Philosophy of the Unconscious*. In Laforgue, says Eliot, "we have the *entertainment* of German philosophical systems which are too abstract and skeletonised for the warm adherence of flesh and blood which is full belief, but which are powerful enough to disturb and afflict his personal emotions" (*VMP* 295). While Laforgue succeeds in giving the nearest verse realization of the philosophy, his mind is caught up in a "continuous war" between personal feelings and philosophical ideas. The philosophies of the nineteenth century, Eliot explains,

> whether of Kant, or Fichte, or Hegel, of Schopenhauer, or James, or Bradley or
> Russell, are corrupted by feeling; the poetry of the nineteenth century, whether
> of Wordsworth, or Shelley, or Tennyson or Browning, is corrupted by thought.
> In this confusion a man like Laforgue was destroyed; for the philosophy which
> he endeavoured to feel was a philosophy already muddled by feeling—for what
> is more emotional than the philosophy of Schopenhauer or Hartmann?—his
> feelings required quite another system of thought. (*VMP* 221–2)

Eliot thus brings the classical solution to Laforgue's romantic confusion: what the moonstruck sentimentalist dreaming about the *jeune fille* at the piano needs, says Eliot, is some *Vita Nuova* "to justify, dignify and integrate his sentiments toward the *jeune fille* in a system of the universe" (*VMP* 216) or, as he later rephrased it, "some way of salvation in which the mind and the feelings, the soul and the body, shall cooperate towards fulness of life. . . . It was not Miss Leah Lee, the pretty English governess, or post-Kantian pseudo-Buddhism that could do the trick" (*VMP* 285).[28] He had said as much, in so many words, in 1909.

It is thus clear that the poetic and philosophical mind of the American poet who encountered Hulme in 1916 was already classical in temperament and spiritual in quest; Hulme confirmed and deepened it all with Original Sin. In his poetry Eliot had already begun to record the arrival of his demons as the intellectual soul began its arduous struggle with the rational will. The demon of sentimentalism came to be supplanted by the demon of mechanism, by "the demon of doubt which is inseparable from the spirit of belief," by the "devil of the stairs" that the penitent in *Ash-Wednesday* looks back upon, and finally by the ubiquitous "demon of the absolute," the false counsellor who prevents the will from crossing the vast gap between flesh and Word. These were real demons of the spiritual intellect, but even in 1910 Eliot had begun to feel a more visceral presence, a darker angel that had only begun to stir and cast its mental shadow. It would accompany him from Boston to London, where, as he moved away from Laforgue toward a new encounter with Baudelaire, the playful young ironist would soon be driven to a more savage form of the comic mode.

THE SAVAGE COMEDIAN

Apples of ashes, golden bright;
Waters of bitterness, how sweet!
O banquet of a foul delight,
Prepared by thee, dark Paraclete!

Eliot has never enjoyed a public reputation as a comic poet or as an obscene poet, but his new friends in London in 1915 were well acquainted with the lusty characters who peopled his bawdy ballads and limericks. Eliot playfully interspersed the narrative of his letters to Conrad Aiken with stanzas on the escapades of King Bolo and his Big Black Kween, "that airy fairy hairy-'un, who led the dance on Golder's Green with Cardinal Bessarion."[1] He sent poems entitled "The Triumph of Bullshit" and "Ballade pour la grosse Lulu" to Wyndham Lewis, and he wrote to Pound from Merton College, Oxford, that Lewis's "puritanical principles seem to bar my way to Publicity. . . . I understand that Priapism, Narcissism etc. are not approved of, and even so innocent a rhyme as '. . . pulled her stockings off / With a frightful cry of "Hauptbahnhof!' is considered decadent" (L1 86). Lewis, who saw the poems as "excellent bits of scholarly ribaldry," jokingly told Pound that he wanted to print them in his periodical *Blast* but would uphold his "naif determination to have no 'Words Ending in -Uck, -Unt, and -Ugger!'"[2]

There is much in Eliot's juvenile graffiti that is vulgar and coarsely humorous. That said, it is of interest that the impulse to sexual caricature was accompanied by an equally strong impulse to poems of spiritual martyrdom. It is of even greater interest that the bawdy element not only survived his twenty-fifth year but, with the appearance of Sweeney in 1918, became one of the most serious and personal elements of his art. Between 1915 and 1925, as he read deeply in comedy, myth, and ritual, Eliot created around Sweeney a comically sordid poetic landscape of brothels, lowlifes, and exotic types: Doris, Mrs. Turner, Mrs. Porter, Fresca, Grishkin, Rachel, and others. Collectively, they inhabit the phantasmagoria through which Eliot expresses his moral convictions about a world governed by vanity, fear, and lust.

Eliot wrote many of his bawdy poems prior to his marriage to Vivien in June 1915; however, he was to "keep his hand in" for many years.[3] The early Columbo and Bolo poems were written simultaneously with several religious poems that reflect the "debates" and conflicts of body and soul—"The Death of Saint Narcissus," "The Love Song of Saint Sebastian," "The Burnt Dancer," and others. But the sexual-spiritual torment evident in these poems was soon to be intensified by the sexual-spiritual nightmare that followed his marriage to Vivien. From the outset, Eliot's precipitous marriage also placed him in a rather humorless financial plight, somewhat relieved by Bertrand Russell's generosity in taking the couple into his London flat for several months. Grateful for his mentor's personal and professional assistance, Eliot published in 1916 a caricature of Russell at a Harvard garden party, "Mr. Apollinax," prophetically portraying the notorious philanderer as "Priapus in the shrubbery" and experimenting with a hint of animal caricature in the description of Professor and Mrs. Channing-Cheetah, a technique that would flower in the Sweeney poems.

Two years of marital difficulty and poetic dryness were to elapse before Sweeney appeared among Eliot's new quatrain poems of 1918. Where did he come from, this apeneck brothel browser? What prompted Eliot to shift his focus from martyr to whoremonger, to displace the tragic and spiritual with the comic and carnal? What is the relationship of the Sweeney poems of 1918 and 1919 to The Waste Land, where Sweeney makes a cameo appearance in "The Fire Sermon," and to Sweeney Agonistes, where Eliot's mythic figure reenacts an ancient ritual of death and resurrection? These are some of the questions that press upon a group of modernist poems that have troubled critics for the past seventy years.

Pound and Lewis knew the witty practical joker in Eliot, but they did not know in 1915 that he was already a serious student of the comic spirit. He had studied Aristophanes at Harvard, and he kept Bekker's five-volume edition close at hand.[4] During his year abroad in Paris in 1910–11, when he came under the influence of Bergson's writings, Eliot read Laughter: An Essay on the Meaning of the Comic (1903), a book-length study in which Bergson develops his belief in the moral function of comedy. Bergson explores the comic through his belief that the vital spirit (élan vital) must constantly combat the tendency to sink into the mechanical. The attitudes and gestures of the human body—automatism, inelasticity, "petrified movements," habits contracted and maintained—all, he says, are "laughable in exact proportion as that body reminds us of a mere machine." "Any incident is comic," he argues, "that calls our attention to the physical in a person, when it is the moral side that is concerned"; physical and spiritual defects may be seen as "overtones" of each other.[5]

Bergson's analysis of the comic pervades the quatrain poems, but Eliot subsequently encountered a more arresting discussion of the comic poet in

Baudelaire's essay "On the Essence of Laughter," originally published in 1855. Baudelaire argues that laughter, which is satanic and based on pride and the individual's feeling of superiority over other beings, is the experience of contradictory feelings—of infinite greatness in relation to beasts and of infinite wretchedness in relation to absolute being. Baudelaire distinguishes what he calls the "absolute comic," whose work "has a mysterious, a durable, an eternal element," even as the work is "destined to show men their own moral and physical ugliness."[6] The absolute comic is the superior artist, one who is receptive to absolute ideas and who brings those ideas to bear on the moral degradation of fallen humanity. In playing with the ideas of pride and superiority in his audience, the absolute comic works with laughter that is provoked by the grotesque, which carries the audience beyond its feelings of superiority over other people to its feelings of superiority over nature. In depicting the human slide toward the bestial, the absolute comic reveals not only the guttering moral consciousness that separates men from beasts but the horror of man's separation from absolute being. The absolute comic further demonstrates a "permanent dualism, the capacity of being both himself and someone else at the same time."

Eliot seized upon Baudelaire's definition of the absolute comic, and with it he was directed by Baudelaire to its most ferocious practitioners in England. "To find the ferocious and ultra-ferocious comic," wrote Baudelaire, in a passage quoted by Eliot, "we must cross the Channel and pay a visit to the misty kingdoms of the spleen," where the distinguishing mark of the comic is violence.[7] As he began to write the Sweeney poems in 1918, Eliot immersed himself in the savage and violent tradition of English comedy, from Christopher Marlowe and Ben Jonson to Charles Dickens, thence to the most contemporary manifestation of the ferocious comic in England—his bawdy friend Wyndham Lewis.

Eliot was in fact teaching in his night classes for adults the work of Marlowe, Jonson, and Dickens, and reviewing the work of Lewis, while he was writing his quatrain poems and accompanying workshop criticism. In his essays on Marlowe and Jonson in 1918 and 1919, Eliot identifies in his masters the techniques of caricature that inform his own work. He focuses on *The Jew of Malta* to characterize Marlowe's genius for achieving serious moral thought through caricature, seeing him in effect as an absolute comic. Arguing that in Elizabethan drama "the more farcical comedy was the more serious," Eliot holds that the play should be read as a farce. "I say farce," he writes, drawing directly upon Baudelaire, "but with the enfeebled humour of our times the word is a misnomer; it is the farce of the old English humour, the terribly serious, even savage comic humour, the humour which spent its last breath in the decadent genius of Dickens." Marlowe's style, Eliot continues, "secures its emphasis by always hesitating on the edge of caricature at the right moment" (*SE* 124)—a technique that Eliot employs repeatedly in the Sweeney poems, as when Rachel Rabinovitch "Tears at the grapes with murderous paws."

Eliot continued to explore the comic techniques of *The Jew of Malta* by comparing it with Jonson's *Volpone,* where the vice-ridden characters are all linked to the appropriate animal (Volpone the Fox, Mosca the Fly, Voltore the

Vulture, etc.). Jonson's "type of personality," Eliot observes, "found its relief in something falling under the category of burlesque or farce" (*SE* 158). In examining Jonson's comic methods of achieving moral seriousness, Eliot praises his mastery of grotesque caricature: "It is a great caricature, which is beautiful, and a great humour, which is serious." Jonson was also an absolute comic for Eliot, and he wrote admiringly in a valuable essay, "The Romantic Englishman, the Comic Spirit, and the Future of Criticism," that Jonson's drama is therefore "a criticism of humanity far more serious than its conscious moral judgments. 'Volpone' does not merely show that wickedness is punished; it criticizes humanity by intensifying wickedness. How we are reassured about ourselves when we make the acquaintance of such a person on the stage!"[8]

This lost art of serious English caricature, Eliot had discovered, could now be found anew in the fiction of Wyndham Lewis, whose novel *Tarr* had been serialized in the *Egoist* in 1916–17, when Eliot was assistant editor. When the book was published in 1918, Eliot reviewed it on several occasions. "Mr. Lewis's humour is near to Dickens," he observes, "but on the right side, for it is not too remote from Ben Jonson." In language that found its way into "Sweeney Erect," Eliot declares that *"Tarr* is a commentary upon a part of modern civilization: now it is like our civilization criticized, our acrobatics animadverted upon adversely, by an oran-outang of genius, Tarzan of the apes." Eliot identifies in Lewis those aspects of savage humor that were most important to his own work, singling out, for example, Lewis's mastery of humiliation, which Eliot described as "one of the most important elements in human life, and one little exploited."[9] He subsequently praised *Tarr* for possessing "an element of that British humour, so serious and savage, to which Baudelaire once devoted a short study."[10] Lewis was Eliot's single visible ally; and in connecting himself and Lewis to Baudelaire on the one hand and to Dickens, Jonson, and Marlowe on the other, Eliot felt that they had revived the absolute comic in England. Each was, to use Lewis's title, "A Soldier of Humour."[11]

Thus, in his criticism leading up to *The Waste Land,* Eliot clearly sought to prepare a favorable climate for the ferocious English humor of which he had become both proponent and practitioner. Indeed, we should begin to see that the early thrust of Eliot's literary modernism was in the revival of this comic mode. Ironically, as Eliot began his experiments against an enfeebled humor, his modern audience misread his comic signs. But now the questions press again: what happened in Eliot's personal life to turn the bawdy balladeer into a savage comedian in 1918? What emotional relief, as he described it in Jonson, did his type of personality seek in turning to the comic quatrains? The intellectual, almost evangelical interest in comic theory did not in itself lead him to the new mode; rather, the poems grew out of an urgent need to find an artistic form for the preoccupations of a deeply wounded sensibility. A distinctive feature of humor, Eliot writes in discussing *Tarr,* is "the instinctive attempt of a sensitive mind to protect beauty against ugliness; and to protect itself against stupidity."[12] What ugliness and stupidity, we want to know, motivates these difficult, stripped-down poems of sexual grotesques involved in adulterous and other illicit encounters, with constant allusions to lechery, cuckoldry, and betrayal? Perhaps we shall never

know the full story, but we now know the bitter truth of a long-rumored situation, Bertrand Russell's sexual affair with Vivien Eliot.

Ever since the secrets of the Russell archives were opened eighteen years
ago, critics have been slow to respond to the revelation that Russell, who had repeatedly denied any intimate relation with Vivien in memoirs, admits to sleeping
with her in his private letters.[13] Russell's most recent biographer, Ray Monk, has
now scoured the evidence to show that the affair lasted from the summer of 1915
to 1919, with sexual intimacy commencing by 1916, if not earlier. In September
1916, a year into his affair with Vivien, Russell met and began an affair with a
young aristocratic actress, Lady Constance Malleson, whose stage and intimate
name was Colette O'Niel. As he shifted his affections to Colette, he decided to
tell her from the outset about his "very intimate" relation with Vivien, giving her
"the same justification for the affair that he had given Ottoline when it started:
that his affection was good for Vivien, and therefore good for Eliot, whom she
would punish if Russell stopped giving her affection."[14] Two months later, in yet
a further justification of the intimacy, he wrote to Ottoline that Vivien "was useful to me, & there was nothing really bad in the whole affair I think. I should
have gone all to pieces a year ago without some interest of that kind."[15] As the
affair ran its on-again, off-again course over the next two years, the evidence at
hand indicates that Eliot gradually learned of the double betrayal, probably no
later than December 1917, or early in 1918, when Russell shared a cottage that
Vivien let in Marlow. As will be seen, it was there that Eliot suffered a horrific
spiritual dispossession. It was there that he began drafting "Whispers of Immortality," writing ironically in a canceled passage of the seduction of "wives of
men" by "Sons of God," prompting Pound's question, "what angel hath cuck-
woled thee" (*IMH* 369):

Our sighs pursue the vanishd shade
And breathe a sanctified amen,
And yet the Sons of God descend
To entertain the wives of men.

And when the Female Soul departs
The Sons of Men turn up their eyes.
The Sons of God embrace the Grave—
The Sons of God are very wise. (*IMH* 368)

When Eliot began to draft his quatrain poems in 1917–18 his playful bawdy had
taken a significant turn; the subdued vision of sexual humanity that had plagued
him as a younger poet had become even more terribly darkened and activated by
Russell's lustful betrayal and Vivien's adulterous desire. To cope with the humiliation, to protect himself from the moral ugliness and stupidity, Eliot turned savagely to the sexual caricature of Sweeney and his friends. In so doing, he gradually created a personal myth of sexual betrayal, psychological retribution, and
moral regeneration. We begin with "Sweeney Erect" and its epigraph from Beaumont and Fletcher.

In assigning *The Maid's Tragedy* to his night class of Extension students in 1918, Eliot told them that the gifts of Beaumont and Fletcher as dramatists were "on the whole better exhibited in the scene than in the complete play" (see p. 48). Little did those students know how much one scene meant to him—the scene that provides the epigraph for "Sweeney Erect," the betrayed Aspatia's bitter lament of her desertion by her lover for the king's mistress. "But man— / Oh, that beast, man! " she cries (2.2), asking her waiting women to be sad with her as she recounts stories of lost heroines. She asks to see one woman's needlework of Ariadne and Theseus, who abandoned Ariadne in the Cyclades, on the waste shores of Naxos. "You have a full wind and a false heart, Theseus," she says to the picture, and then more bitterly, "You shall not go so," vengefully commanding the woman to make the scene one of fear and disaster for Theseus. Wholly distraught, Aspatia complains that the colors are not dull and pale enough to show the depths of Ariadne's misery and orders the woman to rework the mythic portrayal. "Do it by me," she exclaims. "Do it again by me, the lost Aspatia" (lines 65–6). Eliot thus prefaces "Sweeney Erect" with a reference to Aspatia at the height of her hysterical state, deeply upsetting her waiting women ("Dear madam!" one exclaims [line 79]). His misquoted epigraph is taken from the conclusion of Aspatia's frantic identification with Ariadne:

> And the trees about me,
> Let them be dry and leafless; let the rocks
> Groan with continual surges; and behind me
> Make all a desolation. Look, look, wenches,
> A miserable life of this poor picture! (lines 74–7)[16]

"Sweeney Erect" begins with the poet's recasting of Aspatia's hysterical imperatives in the first two stanzas—Paint me Ariadne, deserted on Naxos; Display me the "perjured sails" of Theseus, departing—as though the poet would, like Aspatia, harshly rework the betrayal. But the summoning of Ariadne's pathos is suddenly, in a jarring shift of myth and style, deflated and displaced by sheet-covered lovers, with only their feet and hands protruding for dawn's searching light. It is as though the poet, in his abrupt redirection of the poem, cannot continue the pathetic mode and is forced to shift to burlesque, dissolving his original impulse in lowlife comedy. The descent of the mythic dimension is swift: if not Ariadne and Theseus, then perhaps Nausicaa and Polypheme? No, all the way down to Doris and Sweeney. Sweeney's prehensile arm, arched over Doris, erupts from the sheets in a "Gesture of orang-outang" as he rises in steam from their torrid undercover rendezvous. Torpid, tousled, and detumescent, he becomes a great gaping yawn, an "oval O cropped out with teeth," and immediately begins his post-erectile performance, his aubade, as it were. A violent scissor-kick jack-knifes him from the supine to the prone in so ungainly a manner, in such exaggerated clumsiness, that he desperately pushes the bedstead for support and, with a Marlovian touch, "claws" at the pillow slip to regain his balance. Newly and safely erect, our brothel comedian continues the morning entertainment with his madcap ablutions, in the pink. Sweeney, who "Knows the female temperament," prepares to shave, lathering not just his cheeks but his whole face, setting the comic mood for Doris's awakening, allowing no room for post-coital *tristesse*. Her laughter, we may imagine, is spontaneous and delighted, recalling her later reminiscence in *Sweeney Agonistes:* "He's like a fellow once I knew. / *He* could make you laugh." Even the narrator, as absolute comic, joins the fun; so grotesque is the silhouette of broadbottomed Sweeney at his toilet that the pedantic intruder cannot resist a double-edged gibe at Emerson's noble depiction of man as the shaper of history. Eliot's own unequivocal attitude toward Emerson surfaced in a review that preceded the poem: "Neither Emerson nor any of the others was a real observer of the moral life."[17]

For his *pièce de résistance* Sweeney begins toying with his razor, testing its sharpness on the hairs of his leg, an acrobatic gyration that elicits a shriek of animal laughter; indeed, Sweeney's Chaplinesque, music-hall pantomime throws Doris into a paroxysm of uncontrollable laughter, making her clutch breathlessly at her aching, bursting sides. (She recalls the canceled passage on Fresca's entertainment in *The Waste Land:* "The Russians thrilled her to hysteric fits" [*WLF* 26]). In her seizurelike extremity, Doris is appropriately caricatured as "The epileptic on the bed." The riotous laughter brings the house down, however, and Doris's room is quickly crowded upon by the alarmed "ladies of the corridor." When they discover that they have mistaken hilarity for violence, their solicitude turns sharply to indignation and high-minded propriety. And if Madam Turner is personally perturbed and professionally concerned, Doris is nonchalant and wholly unrepentant in dismissing them. She soon returns, happily spent, washed, and toweled, to her sometime fancy man Sweeney, "padding" like a lioness, bountifully toting those old restoratives, those creature comforts, "sal volatile / And a glass of brandy neat." The poet's caricatures of their movements—Sweeney's orangutang gesture and his "clawing," Doris's hyenalike shrieks and her "padding"—are individually comical, but collectively they viciously imprint the bestial on Sweeney's and Doris's actions, implying at poem's end that they will now curl up in their lair with no moral disturbance, with no disquieting metaphysic to trouble their animal coupling, however illicit.

This brothel burlesque is, however, so skillfully amusing on the surface that we forget its tragic origins—forget to recall Aspatia at the crucial moment of misunderstanding in the corridor. In the awkward uncertainty about Doris's hysteria, the tragic and the burlesque intersect, and it is here that we sense the poet's comic debasement of Aspatia's grief in a personal myth. Whereas Aspatia, decrying the bestiality of man, rises to hysteria in her grief, Doris, laughing violently at the grotesque antics of Sweeney, rises merely to hysterics. The figures of Aspatia and Doris come together as their separate cries reach a similar pitch, and the parallels force the reader to recognize the sexual bestiality and moral blindness common to both the tragic and the comic action. Eliot's comic creations seem blissfully unaware of their moral natures in this poem, but the absolute comic is aware of them; he is also painfully unforgetful of Aspatia, whose betrayal was enacted by a lustful king and his mistress who facilitated a convenient sexual arrangement at Aspatia's expense. The poet himself is not amused by Doris and Sweeney, whom Bergson would view as sexual machines. Eliot's personal voice is unmistakable; this is Aspatia's poem, written for her with great empathy.[18]

After Eliot had collected his quatrain poems for a limited edition entitled *Ara Vos Prec,* he wrote to his brother about them on 15 February 1920: "Some of the new poems, the Sweeney ones, especially 'Among the Nightingales' and 'Burbank' are intensely serious, and I think these two are among the best that I have ever done. But even here I am considered by the ordinary Newspaper critic as a Wit or satirist, and in America I suppose I shall be thought merely disgusting" (*L1* 363).[19] This rare volume contained a unique printing of "Sweeney Among the Nightingales," which included a second epigraph from an anonymous Elizabethan play, *The Raigne of King Edward the Third.*[20] In the play, King Edward becomes infatuated with the virtuous Countess of Salisbury while her husband is away at war. In contemplating her beautiful features, he compares her voice to the music of the nightingale. His second thought about the comparison provides the epigraph: "And why should I speake of the nightingale? / The nightingale sings of adulterate wrong" (2.2.109–10). The amorous king thinks it too self-satirical to conceive of his desire as adulterous, and he rationalizes semantically that to be virtuous with such a lady would be sinful, and to be sinful with her would be virtuous.

The epigraph was printed in bold block capitals, typographically disproportionate to the title and text. However appropriate for the poem, it seems to be deliberately, intemperately emblazoned on the page, as if to catch a guilty eye. Eliot inexplicably stripped the epigraph before the poem reappeared the next year in the first American edition of his work, but in the textual history of the poem, it remains a telling emblem of mind during composition.[21] The succeeding action of the play, which traces the countess's unyielding constancy before the lecherous king, illuminates Eliot's ironic personal attraction to the play. When the king begs her to lend her body to him "to sport with all," she eloquently refuses to relinquish the bower of her "intellectual soule": "If I should leave her house, my Lord, to thee, / I kill my poore soule and my poore soule me." When she learns of his further plots to seduce her, she takes up a knife, swearing to kill the husband sleeping in her bosom. Only then does the king awaken from his lust and bow to her fidelity and moral integrity. "Arise," he commands her,

> and be my fault thy honors fame,
> Which after ages shall enrich thee with.
> I am awakened from this idle dreame. (2.2.197–9)

For Eliot, however, the sexual nightmare continued.

The other, retained epigraph comes from the *Agamemnon* of Aeschylus—the moment when, shortly after his return to Argos from Troy with his unwilling concubine, Cassandra, Agamemnon is brutally slain by his wife, Clytemnestra, who acts in adulterous league with her lover, Aegisthus. Entrapping him in the folds of his robe while he bathes, she slays the king with an axe as he cries out, "Alas, I am struck a mortal blow!" This epigraph and the allusions to Agamemnon's death in the final stanza provide a crucial tragic frame for Eliot's low comedy.

We find Sweeney in a brothel again, on a stormy, threatening night, presumably the object of ribald teasing by the nightingales. Laughing in compound caricature, his simian gestures and the changing coloration of his face make him a figure of protean animal shapes—ape, zebra, giraffe. The narrator, an absolute comic contemplating the epigraph's tragedy, tries to envelop his own comic scene in portent. But the ominous atmosphere, in which Death and the Raven seem to await entry, is laughably deflated by the image of Sweeney guarding the hornèd gates of pleasure—a debunked image from the *Aeneid* by way of Dryden that Eliot reworked in a fragment of *The Waste Land*: "the human engine waits . . . To spring to pleasure through the horn or ivory gates" (*WLF* 43). But the sexual machines in this brothel are run down. Though Sweeney is the object of sexual solicitation by the two conspiring ladies, he is curiously indifferent to their automatic advances. When the mechanical approach of the woman in the Spanish cape results in a clumsy, boisterous pratfall, the seduction falls into burlesque. Her slatternly fall triggers nothing more than a bored yawn and an unerotic tug on a sagging stocking. Sweeney, who has meanwhile fallen out of laughter into a languid silence, responds only to her infectious yawn and collapses into a sluggish sprawl. So apathetic are the bodily appetites of this "silent vertebrate" that he comically contracts into a concentrated ball of refusal when the waiter offers fruit.[22]

This first assault having been aborted in boredom, the ravenous Russian, Rachel *née* Rabinovitch, seizes on the hothouse grapes to make her move on Sweeney. The exaggerated dramatization of her adulterous appetite, tearing at the grapes with "murderous paws," takes her to the bestial edge of caricature. She turns her ferocious feline devouring into a more aggressive sexual advance, but heavy-eyed Sweeney, who suspects entrapment, declines her move with a gesture of fatigue and removes himself from the sexual game of chess. Once outside, leaning through the window, he becomes a nonparticipating guest, but with the heavy-scented wisteria wrapped about his golden grin he still evokes the image of "Priapus in the shrubbery." He feigns good humor, but what, we wonder, has happened to his libidinous ways? He may be spent, but he also seems preoccupied, even disturbed, his weariness as much mental as physical, his grin forced. Does Sweeney have that "sense of foreboding" that Eliot claimed, according to F. O. Matthiessen, the poem was written to show?[23] We leave him looking in as his host, presumably Mrs. Porter, admits another customer and the nightingales resume their seductive song of adulterate wrong.

The portentous voice that earlier acquiesced to the more insistent description of sexual intrigue now resumes authority over the banal scene. Adopting again a constellational perspective, the absolute comic narrator makes the ironic observation that the siren songs of the nightingales are near another human community, the convent of the Sacred Heart, where the chaste brides of Christ sublimate desire in devotion. The observation itself charts the moral distance between brothel and convent, nightingale and nun, and the narrator continues to elevate the perspective with a more distant, more mythical association of

Sweeney's nightingales with the nightingales of the "bloody wood." In 1958, Eliot explained that "The wood I had in mind was the grove of the Furies at Colonus; I called it 'bloody' because of the blood of Agamemnon in Argos."[24] This striking revelation almost forty years after the fact explains why the allusions of the final stanza have been so unyielding. In perhaps the clearest example of the modernist technique of dislocating and conflating myths, Eliot purposefully fused scenes from Sophocles' *Oedipus at Colonus* and Aeschylus's *Agamemnon,* borrowing the nightingales from Sophocles for Agamemnon's death scene. "It was a simple matter," Eliot continued, "to bring the dead Agamemnon into the open air, and to transfer the nightingales from one place to another." Singing above the dead Agamemnon, wrapped in his blood-stained robe/shroud, the nightingales in this very personal, seemingly vindictive poem, defecate on the sinful king, their "liquid siftings" staining the shroud already dishonored by Clytemnestra's adultery. But their song also awakens the Furies, the All-Seeing Ones, and *that* is the borrowed association that bears upon the poem. Indeed, the sense of foreboding that weighs upon Sweeney's libido, unconsciously felt by Sweeney but strongly perceived by the absolute comic, is a sense that the Furies, the inflexible agents of retribution who pursue men into atonement, are now at hand. The nightingales follow Sweeney into *The Waste Land,* where the song that cries "'Jug jug' to dirty ears" again signals the arousal of the Furies, whose pursuit, we shall see, has wreaked a terrible metamorphosis upon the protagonist of *Sweeney Agonistes.*

At the time he wrote "Sweeney Among the Nightingales," Eliot was absorbed by what he called "the phantom-psychology" of Aeschylus, Sophocles, and Shakespeare,[25] a psychology that was to inform Eliot's work beyond *The Family Reunion,* and in the Sweeney poems he begins to trace the psychological transformation of promiscuous characters possessed by moral agents. Human beings may tend, comically and tragically, toward the mechanical and bestial, but to Eliot human beings cannot escape the horrible consequences of sensual abandonment. He knew that sexual tragedy—its special moral imbalance and lack of restraint—brings the greatest spiritual horror, unleashes the hound of heaven, the dark angel, the Furies, the hoo-ha-ha's. So pursued, Sweeney becomes a study in the phantom-psychology of illicit sexuality, as do other characters in *The Waste Land*.

The savage comedian is in his blackest humor in "A Game of Chess," in his portrait of an anonymous lady in her baroque boudoir, a Cupid's bower of cloying sensual objects and images, none more visually graphic than a painting above the mantel of the terrible metamorphosis of Philomel into the nightingale, "As though a window gave upon the sylvan scene." The painting gives inviolable voice to her mythic violation and transformation, and suggests that, with always a new Tereus as hoopoe, it is a violation that, banally, "still the world pursues." On the walls hang other scenes of passion and seduction, "other withered stumps of time," from which "staring forms" (including Dido and Cleopatra) lean out, silently indicting the lady in her own sexual intrigue. By firelight she brushes out her hair into "fiery points" that glow into unspoken words, accusatory words of Philomela's severed tongue, knowing words that would be "savagely still," awaiting eventual retribution. The mental savagery of the stillness frightens the lady into a dislocated dialogue with a phantom voice, which tells her to wait with him for "a knock upon the door." The savage voice knows who come to knock: the All-Seeing Ones have found her out.

Eliot attempts to develop the agon between the sensual and the spiritual further in his seventy-line portrait of Fresca, an excised passage that served as an opening prelude to Sweeney's brief appearance in "The Fire Sermon," named after Buddha's urging of his followers to divest themselves of the fire of passion and thereby become "delivered from the depravities." Fresca, languidly dreaming of "pleasant rapes" in her boudoir, has not yet undergone her inevitable transformation into a Mary Magdalene, is herself unaware of the dark angel lingering in the sexual urge, but the absolute comic narrator identifies the treacherous chemistry of her desire: "The same eternal and consuming itch / Can make a martyr, or plain simple bitch" (*WLF* 26). The presence of a spiritual ache latent in sexual desire is nowhere better expressed than in "Whispers of Immortality," where Eliot summons the sexual metaphysics of John Donne, who knew that "No contact possible to flesh / Allayed the fever of the bone." In contemplating Fresca's sexual reveries and anxieties, the narrator hears at his back, or at her back, not time's wingèd chariot, as does Marvell's artful seducer, but the haunting "chuckle" of death. This chuckle, he knows, brings more than a *carpe diem* awareness of mortality; it brings a horrific awareness of the void that underlies illicit sexuality.

The Waste Land quester, musing on the rat-infested, infertile land, then hears behind his back the blaring horns and motors that herald Sweeney's annual return to Mrs. Porter in the spring. Since the earlier poems, Sweeney and Mrs. Porter have become such personal mythic figures in Eliot's imagination that they can make their appearance in the poem without introduction, casually displacing Actaeon and Diana in a mythic parade of passion. Heard in the fanfare are lines from a bawdy music-hall ballad:

> O the moon shone bright on Mrs. Porter
> And on her daughter
> They wash their feet in soda water

Yet Sweeney and Mrs. Porter are but fleeting figures in the phantasmagoria of this section, this "cauldron of unholy loves,"[26] where the montage of images and allusions will not hold in the quester's mind, flooded as it is with associative fragments of high and low passion, constancy, and betrayal. As Sweeney and Mrs. Porter fade out of the disturbed procession, the unstilled wail of the ravished nightingale marks their departure and summons the Furies, who will drive them toward their ritual deaths.

Even in this brief scene in "The Fire Sermon," we can see that Eliot had already discovered a ritual frame for the moral regeneration of Sweeney and his wayward friends. Since 1916 he had been reading the Cambridge anthropologists, all of whom were making the case that comedy and tragedy had their origins in ancient fertility rituals. As an absolute comic, Eliot had become particularly interested in F. M. Cornford's *Origins of Attic Comedy*, published in 1914, which argues that a phallic fertility ritual of death and resurrection underlies the development of comedy and that elements of this ritual provide the framework for the plays of Aristophanes. Meticulously following Cornford's reconstruction of the Aristophanic plot formula, with its strong sexual element, Eliot turned immediately from *The Waste Land* to fully ritualize Sweeney's annual visit to Mrs. Porter, making them adversaries in an agon of life and death, making her murder, resurrection, and marriage to Sweeney the modern lowbrow equivalent of an ancient classical drama.

Beginning in 1923, *Sweeney Agonistes* went through a succession of titles, subtitles, epigraphs, and scenarios.[27] The earliest title, "Pereira; or, The Marriage of Life and Death, a Dream," not only defines the agon of the play; it points to the dreamlike state of being which Doris has entered in the prologue and which Sweeney tries to describe in the agon. Doris has come home with "a terrible chill." "I *think* it's only a chill," Dusty tells Pereira on the telephone, but we discover that she suffers from a vague apprehension and fear not unlike Sweeney's in "Sweeney Among the Nightingales." Superstitiously cutting a deck of cards, she turns up the two of spades—the coffin, a ritual symbol of death. "I'm sure it's mine," she says frantically. "I dreamt of weddings all last night." She thereby forecasts the ritual death, resurrection, and marriage that she must soon undergo. As the epigraph from Aeschylus's *Choephoroi* now implies ("You don't see them, you don't—but I see them: they are hunting me down, I must move on") the Furies are aswarm in her consciousness.

When the agon begins, we discover that Sweeney's purgation and metamorphosis have already taken place, and in the ritual drama he appears symbolically as a risen god or king to deliver Doris and Mrs. Porter from their death-in-life. He engages in flirtatious but threatening banter with Doris about the manner of her death—her ritual cooking—preparatory to the sacramental eating of her flesh on a "cannibal isle," where her rebirth will take place. (The scene evokes Aristophanes' *Knights,* where the Sausage-seller cooks Demos in a rite of ritual boiling and resurrection). "You wouldn't eat me! " exclaims Doris. "Yes I'd eat you!" Sweeney savagely replies, "In a nice little . . . missionary stew." Sweeney then begins to remind Doris of the transformation of consciousness that takes place on that isle of regeneration, a recognition that there is nothing at all in life but "Birth, and copulation, and death." Sweeney, who has evidently slain her before, gives her a hint of his own horrific transformation:

I've been born, and once is enough.
You dont remember, but I remember,
Once is enough.

His subsequent story of a man who once did a girl in, and of the innate desire of any man to do a girl in, is told by way of analogy to reveal a dispossessed state of mind. "I've gotta use words when I talk to you," he says in frustration, knowing how horribly inexpressible is a mind that is neither dead nor alive, that no longer has any "joint" with the ordinary plane of reality. Eliot's savage intention, he says, was to present Sweeney as a character "whose sensibility and intelligence should

be on the plane of the most sensitive and intelligent members of the audience."
While his speeches are addressed to the other characters in the play, who are
"material, literal minded and visionless," those characters are conscious of being
overheard by the sensitive audience. "There was to be an understanding between
[Sweeney] and a small number of the audience," Eliot explains, "while the rest of
the audience would share the responses of the other characters in the play"
(UPUC 153). The chorus, chanting "The Terrors of the Night," makes the shared
sensibility concrete by chuckling the phantom laugh that signals the arrival of
the hoo-ha's: "You've had a cream of a nightmare dream and you've got the hoo-
ha's coming to you."

The "Fragment of an Agon" stops abruptly with the insistent "Knock
Knock Knock" (the same "knock upon the door" awaited in "A Game of
Chess"), but we now know from Eliot's synopsis and extant scenarios that the
play would follow the Aristophanic formula.[28] In the scene to follow, Mrs. Porter
makes her riotous entrance, singing a bawdy refrain from the ballad of Casey
Jones: "And the neighbors knew by the shrieks and the groans / That the man at
the throttle was Casey Jones." Sweeney, a reborn Casey Jones who, as a canceled
epigraph relates, "In the red light district . . . found his fame," begins the agon
as a principle of Life in argument with Mrs. Porter, a principle of Death in the
form of sexual sin. As he symbolically slays her, the murder is interrupted by a
number of intruders, including Pereria, the degenerate landlord who threatens
the girls with eviction. Sweeney defeats Pereria in theological argument, casting
him out as unworthy of living a better life and revealing to him that he has become Pereria's landlord, the "Superior Landlord" of the revised title. Mrs. Porter's
resurrection, which signals the successful expulsion of death and the induction of
new life, is followed by a marriage and feast, with Sweeney the Cook scrambling
the eggs for a wedding breakfast of life and death. "It may not be too fanciful,"
one critic has observed, "to see in the fictional severance and reunion an image of
the spiritual condition and the spiritual destiny of Eliot and his wife, as Eliot perceived them."[29]

In the hymeneal procession that ends the scenario of the play, Sweeney
would be held up as l'homme moyen spirituel, the triumphant representative of the
Life principle. As such, he has come a long way from making Doris laugh in
"Sweeney Erect," from his apprehension of the Furies in "Sweeney Among the
Nightingales," from his ponderous bathtub ruminations on the flesh and the
Word in "Mr. Eliot's Sunday Morning Service." For Eliot, the Aristophanic ritual
thus became his experimental model for comic purgation, for the dramatization
of what we can now see as the Sweeney myth, the "enforcèd ceremony" of his
savage art.[30] And in retrospect, the menacing aspects of the earlier poems—
Sweeney's razor, for example—suggest that those poems may have been conceived as experiments with ritual scenes.

Eliot tinkered with Sweeney Agonistes for productions in the 1930s, but he finally abandoned any intention of completing it—perhaps because the human
drama that motivated it had ended and the comedian had lost his ferocity, perhaps because his marriage itself had died, not to be reborn. On 8 April 1936 Eliot
wrote to Paul Elmer More that it "has always pleased me that you had a special

liking for *Sweeney Agonistes:* I think myself that it is the most *original* thing that I have done." Nonetheless, Eliot explains, "It is useless to speculate whether, if circumstances had permitted my finishing that play at the time, it would have been equally good as a whole; the only thing that is certain is that twelve years have made too great a difference in me for me to touch it now" (Princeton).

The poems that comprise *Ash-Wednesday* had turned his poetry back to another sexual-spiritual dilemma, and with the announcement of his conversion in 1928, he was ironically cast into the role of public martyr. By the time Vivien was committed to Northumberland House by her brother and doctors in the summer of 1938, Eliot had learned to live alone with his own guilt over a broken marriage.[31] Even so, the playful side of Eliot had not been broken, the music-hall side and the O'Possum side. After his separation from Vivien, he continued to send Bolo stanzas, light verse, and songs to his friends on the odd occasion. On 5 January 1935, regretful that he had been unable to join her on the New Year, he sent Virginia Woolf "one of my songs" for New Year's celebration with champagne (Berg):

> I don't want any Wurzburger—
>   I'd sooner drink gasoline.
> I don't care to tarnish
> My throat with such varnish:
>   It's allright to oil up a sewing-machine.
> I don't care for Budweiser,
> And Anhauser-Busch I decline:
> The platform I stand on
>   Is Moet & Chandon—
> The bubbles that blow off the troubles for mine![32]

One song brought a momentary gaiety of mood that summoned others, including the New Year chorus of an Australian miner's song. "I have another good song," he concluded the letter, "it goes":

> I met you first at Spring St.
>   And then upon my word
> I thought I'd known you all my life
>   When we reached 23d.
> I won your heart at Haarlem,
>   At the Bronx you murmured Yes:
> We lost no time
> On that ride sublime
>   On the Subway *Express.*

"And several more," he confessed as he ran out of space, and we may imagine that he could have gone on singing remembered songs all evening.

In the remaining years of this darkening decade the comic and horrific sides of Eliot's temperament continued to play in counterpoint. By 1939 Sweeney's

Furies, "the sleepless hunters," had taken possession of Harry in *The Family Reunion* (*"You* don't see them, but I see them, / And they see me"), and yet within months there appeared not only *Old Possum's Book of Practical Cats* but Eliot's contribution to a pamphlet of playful doggerel, twenty-five copies of which were printed strictly for private circulation. Entitled *Noctes Binanianae,* it contains, the subtitle says, "Certain Voluntary and Satyrical Verses and Compliments as were lately Exchang'd between some of the Choicest Wits of the Age . . . now printed without castration after the most correct copies."[33] The Latinate construction originated from the gathering place of the authors—John Hayward's London flat, 22 Bina Gardens—where in high conviviality "Possum" (or "Elephant," Eliot), "Coot" (Geoffrey Faber), "Whale" (Frank Morley), and "Tarantula" (John Hayward) exchanged their versified badinage. This late collection of poetical repartee on the eve of war reminds us that Eliot was not, by temperament, a savage comedian. In his bawdy, lighthearted moods, his more natural moods perhaps, he would beg us, as "Possum," as Tom, not always to take him so seriously.

IN THE MUSIC HALLS

I can't sing a bit, I can't shout;
　　But I go through my songs with a birr;
And I always contrive to bring out
　　The meaning that tickles you, sir.

They were written for me; they're the rage;
　　They're the plainest, the wildest, the slyest;
For I find on the music-hall stage,
　　That that kind of song goes the highest.

So I give it them hot, with a glance
　　Like the crack of a whip—oh, it stings!
And a still, fiery smile, and a dance
　　That indicates naughtiest things.

—John Davidson, "In a Music-Hall" (1891)

So sings Lily Dale, one of six performers portrayed in John Davidson's poem "In a Music-Hall" (1891), where the poet's lost soul is stung into recovery by song and wink, gesture and glance. Lily is followed on stage by Selene Eden, who consciously employs the "conquering mystery" of her art to engage "The aching senses of the throng." Then Julian Aragon takes his devilish comic turn:

Ha, ha, ha! ho, ho, ho! hee, hee, hique!
I'm the famous Californian Comique!
　　I'm as supple as a willow,
　　And as graceful as a billow,
I'm handsome, and I'm strong, and I've got cheek.

Cheek's nothing; no, by Jingo! I'm obscene!
My gestures, not my words, say what I mean
　　And the simple and the good,

> They would hiss me if they could,
> But I conquer all volition where I'm seen.
>
> I twist, contort, distort, and rage and rustle;
> I constrain my every limb and muscle.
>> I'm limber, I'm Antaean,
>> I chant the devil's paean,
> I fill the stage with rich infernal bustle.

How well Davidson understood the mysterious art of the performers—their extraordinary control over the audience, their uncanny ability to release aching senses in diabolical laughter. And yet Davidson, soon dead, was but one of scores of English artists to be drawn to the gas-lit throng, to those rancid and hot public halls of the 1890s. "Unto us they belong," sang Ernest Dowson, who took refuge from disappointment in the halls.

> Unto us they belong,
> Us the bitter and gay
> Wine and woman and song.

The strange enchantment was epitomized not so much by Walter Sickert's painting of Marie Lloyd in the Old Oxford Music Hall, but by its appearance in the most avant-garde monthly of the decade—the *Yellow Book*.[1] "While for Sickert the music-hall was a workshop," wrote William Rothenstein, "for the rest of us it was a pleasant dissipation. The Empire Promenade was the orthodox place to go. . . . At the Empire, or the Tivoli, or the Oxford, one would meet Arthur Symons, Ernest Dowson, Herbert Horne, Selwyn Image, Beardsley, or Max. While we others amused ourselves, playing with fireworks, Dowson meant deliberately to hurt himself."[2] Max Beerbohm, a regular at the Pavilion and the old Tivoli, found lasting beatitude in those unhallowed halls, caught up as he was by "the dear old magic of the unity of . . . song after song, good, bad, and indifferent, but all fusing with another and cumulatively instilling a sense of deep beatitude—a strange sweet foretaste of Nirvana."[3] "They supply a gap in the national history," wrote an intrigued Kipling, whose *Barrack-Room Ballads* (1892) was inspired by songs and patter heard in Gatti's Music Hall, "and people haven't yet realised how much they had to do with the national life."[4] Artists and writers were thus driven to capture or explain the mesmeric effect of the music-hall phenomenon. "Maybe it was the drabness of ordinary life that made the music-halls so attractive," Rothenstein speculated.[5] Yeats, discussing Davidson's "In a Music-Hall" for American readers, took pains to point out that his friend Symons was "a scholar in music halls as another man might be a Greek scholar or an authority on the age of Chaucer. He has studied them for purposes of literature and remained himself, if I understand him rightly, quite apart from their glitter and din."[6] But Yeats did not read his friend rightly, for Symons, obsessed with the elusive mystery of the halls, saw his completion as an artist dependent upon a complete identification with the performers. "My life is like a music-hall," he wrote,

> Where, in the impotence of rage,
> Chained by enchantment to my stall,
> I see myself upon the stage
> Dance to amuse a music-hall.[7]

The poet's abiding envy of the performer was to remain part of the unsifted residue of the 1890s until a young American arrived in London in August 1914. Ironically, T. S. Eliot was to become the last inheritor of the music-hall mystery, the poet-detective who would crack its comic code, the dramatist who would see in its bizarre comedians the possibility of reviving poetic drama in the modern world.

I

When Eliot first arrived in London in August 1914 he was already steeped in the songs of American vaudeville and minstrel shows, and in Boston he had frequented the Grand Opera House for performances of melodrama. Before going up to Merton College, Oxford, he read Wyndham Lewis's vorticist publication *Blast,* which had bestowed its blessings on several music-hall entertainers—George Robey, George Mozart, and Harry Weldon—and Eliot took to them at once. In April 1915 he wrote to his American cousin Eleanor Hinkley that in his spare time from his Oxford studies he had "been to a few music halls" (*L1* 97). Indeed, he had become a habitué, the new Arthur Symons of the halls, and he rapidly became familiar with the stars: particularly George Robey, famous for his turn as "The Prehistoric Man"; the risqué Marie Lloyd, reigning queen of the halls since the 1890s; and the great grotesques, Little Tich, the four-foot dwarf who danced in three-foot boots, and Nellie Wallace, the "Dame" of pantomime, famous for her daring caricatures of femininity as the Widow Twankey, both of whose acts Eliot saw as "an orgy of parody of the human race" (*SE* 457). Among his literary friends, Eliot's music-hall peregrinations had earned him the nickname Captain Eliot.

One of Eliot's familiar haunts after taking up residence in London was the Old Oxford Music Hall. In August 1917 the Oxford, taken over by new management, booked in a musical comedy, *The Better 'Ole,* by two wartime officer-comedians, Captain Bruce Bairnsfather and Captain Arthur Eliot. T. S. Eliot, the assistant editor of the *Egoist,* criticized the popular production under pseudonym in the December issue, where he asked sardonically if Wyndham Lewis's objection to the ubiquitous English Grin was not really "a slur upon the cheery philosophy of our brave boys in the trenches, which has been so happily caught by the witty pen of Capt. Bairnsfather?"[8] By March 1918, as the production headed towards eight hundred performances in an eighteen-month run, Eliot felt obliged to publish in the *Egoist,* over announcements of Joyce's *Ulysses* and Lewis's *Tarr,* that the coauthor of *The Better 'Ole,* Arthur Eliot, was not, "roughly speaking, a member of my family."[9] Of more amusing and significant interest is the fact that he wrote the letter from an imaginary province, "Little Tichester," the seat of Eliot's music-hall imagination.

Eliot's public denial of any association with Arthur Eliot was not so light-hearted as it may seem. He had an instinctive dislike of musical comedy and deplored the fact that it had shouldered music hall out of the Oxford. He was, in fact, soon to publicly dissociate himself from the Bairnsfather-Eliot brand of humor. Behind the scenes he had found an intriguing affinity between music-hall humor, which had its origins in Elizabethan inns, and what he termed the "savage humour" of Elizabethan drama. Writing on the plays of Christopher Marlowe, he argued that *The Jew of Malta* is a more accessible play if it is read not as a tragedy but as a farce, the farce of the old English humor: "It has nothing in common with . . . Captain Bairnsfather or *Punch*. It is the humor of that very serious (but very different) play, *Volpone*" (*SE* 123). The humor of Marlowe and Jonson is, in short, humor with a moral sting—the sting mastered by Davidson's Lily Dale. And this, to Eliot, was what the music hall had kept alive—the capacity to use laughter as a sword—and he saw its comedians as unconscious moral agents. From this point of view Eliot had already begun to experiment with the techniques of music-hall humor in his Sweeney poems, which he described as his most serious to date, and it would seem that the Prehistoric Man—a virtual Polyphemus—in George Robey's notorious turn was the prototype for Eliot's own comic savage, Sweeney. Further, it would seem that Sweeney's post-coital pantomime in "Sweeney Erect," where his antics have Doris laughing epileptically on the bed, is modeled on a comic turn, just as it would seem that the music-hall ballad of Mrs. Porter, heard in *The Waste Land* ("O the moon shone bright on Mrs. Porter") provided the surname for Sweeney's brothel-keeper.

Thus, when asked to begin writing a series of articles and "London Letters" for the *Dial* in America, Eliot seized the opportunity to explore his thoughts on music-hall and Elizabethan drama. In his first article, "The Possibility of a Poetic Drama" (1920), he observed that most attempts to resurrect the poetic drama have aimed at the wrong audience, at that small segment of society that wants poetry. But the Elizabethan drama, he explained, "was aimed at a public which wanted *entertainment* of a crude sort, but would *stand* a good deal of poetry." The problem for the contemporary dramatist, as Eliot saw it, was to take an existing form of popular entertainment "and subject it to the process which would leave it a form of art." And to Eliot the material for a new poetic drama was unquestionably to be found in the music-halls. With no space to develop his argument, and in anticipation of a horde of hecklers, he concluded the essay with his bold suggestion:

> Perhaps the music-hall comedian is the best material. I am aware that this is a dangerous suggestion to make. For every person who is likely to consider it seriously there are a dozen toymakers who would leap to tickle aesthetic society into one more quiver and giggle of art debauch. Very few treat art seriously. There are those who treat it solemnly, and will continue to write poetic pastiches of Euripides and Shakespeare; and there are others who treat it as a joke. (*SW* 58)

Eliot had no intention of letting readers of the *Dial* fail to take him seriously. In his first "London Letter" of March 1921, he promised serious discussions of the music-hall and theatrical scene while drawing attention to the "excellent bill" of comedians at the London Palladium—Marie Lloyd, Little Tich, George Mozart, and Ernie Lotinga—one of Eliot's new favorites, a master of mime. Their presence at the Palladium, an unlikely neoclassical sanctuary for music-hall performers, whose halls were rapidly going over to revue and cinema, "provokes," Eliot wrote, "an important chapter in the Extinction of the Music Hall, the corruption of the Theatre Public, and the incapacity of the British public to appreciate Miss Ethel Levey." Though Eliot thought revue comedians were generally unworthy of the music-hall, Levey—known for her trademark dance, the Grizzly Bear (which Eliot offered to teach to Virginia Woolf)—had recently captured his dramatic interest, and I will return to her.[10] "All of these problems are part of my plan," he promised, including discussion of a new production of Ben Jonson's *Volpone* and the deplorable state of Shakespearean acting in England.

That production of *Volpone* by the Phoenix Society conveniently focused Eliot's mind on the relation of music-hall and Elizabethan drama once again.[11] Asked by Wyndham Lewis to contribute to his new journal, *Tyro,* Eliot argued in his essay "The Romantic Englishman, the Comic Spirit, and the Function of Criticism" that the Englishman's myth of himself, his romantic ideal, has become "pitiably diminished" in the theatre since the seventeenth century, that even the myth of the once virile, politically potent John Bull has degenerated into the feeble cartoons of *Punch,* into "a John Bull composed of Podsnap and Bottom-ley."[12] "It is only perhaps in the music halls," Eliot affirms, that we can find a "partial realization" of the old English myth today. Little Tich, George Robey, Nellie Wallace, Marie Lloyd, George Mozart, George Graves, Ernie Lotinga—all the named favorites that inhabit Eliot's imagination—make possible for him the reconstruction of a vital myth for the modern English stage. Like the characters in Jonson's *Volpone,* the characters in their comic turns let the Englishman see himself as "more admirable, more forceful, more villainous, more comical, more despicable" than he actually is. In these mythic turns, says Eliot, the music-hall comedians "effect the Comic Purgation."

> The romantic Englishman, feeling in himself the possibility of being funny as these people, is purged of unsatisfied desire, transcends himself, and unconsciously lives the myth, seeing life in the light of imagination. What is sometimes called "vulgarity" is therefore one thing that has not been vulgarised.

The performer creates the myth by an imaginative transformation and exaggeration of reality, and while his character elicits the audience's sympathy, approval, or contempt, he unconsciously criticizes the moral weakness of that audience. "The audience do not realize," Eliot explains, "that the performance of Little Tich is a compliment, and a criticism, of themselves. Neither could they appreciate the compliment, or swallow the criticism, implied by the persons whom Jonson put on the stage." Eliot, clearly working out his own dramaturgy in the essay, had, like Little Tich and George Robey, like Marlowe and Jonson, already imagined his mythic character, Sweeney, into being. Eliot's problem was not only how to get him from the poetry to the stage, but how to create an audience for him when modern dramatists, playgoers, and critics were afraid of the savage myth.

In his next "London Letter" Eliot told his American readers that the production of *Volpone* was "the most important theatrical event of the year in London. . . . [I]t brought the great English drama to life as no contemporary performance of Shakespeare has done."[13] But as he lamented the fact that Shakespeare's great characters had been reduced to personal roles for the actor-managers, he took heart in observing that "the continued popularity of Shakespeare perhaps has this meaning, that the appetite for poetic drama, and for a peculiarly English comedy or farce, has never disappeared; and that a native popular drama, if it existed, would be nearer to Shakespeare than to Ibsen or Chekhov." In contemplating the possibility of a popular poetic drama, Eliot believed that its success would depend upon the recovery of that peculiarly violent English humor, "the old English ferocity," as he described it, the "comique féroce et très-féroce" observed by Baudelaire.[14] This was to be the humor of a play that was already in his imagination, *Sweeney Agonistes,* a ferocious humor that was still visible in the North of England, particularly in Lancashire, where the music halls had flourished and where most of the famous stars, including Little Tich, George Robey, Marie Lloyd, and Nellie Wallace had originated.

"Lancashire wit is mordant, ferocious, and personal," Eliot wrote. "The fierce talent of Nellie Wallace (who also has a Lancashire accent) holds the most boisterous music-hall in complete subjection."[15] "I have seen Nellie Wallace interrupted by jeering or hostile comment from a boxful of Eastenders; I have seen her, hardly pausing in her act, make some quick retort that silenced her tormenters for the rest of the evening" (*SE* 456–7). Here was material for a new poetic drama, and though Eliot thought that revue comedians were inferior to music-hall comedians, he nonetheless brought to the attention of his readers "our best revue comedienne," Ethel Levey, an American-born actress who had never had quite the appreciation that Eliot thought she deserved:

> Her type is quite different from that of Marie Lloyd or Nellie Wallace. She is the most aloof and impersonal of personalities; indifferent, rather than contemptuous, towards that audience; her appearance and movement are of an extremely modern type of beauty. Hers is not broad farce, but a fascinating inhuman grotesquerie; she plays for herself rather than for the audience. Her art requires a setting which (in this country at least) it has never had. It is not a comedy of mirth.

In the type of Ethel Levey, Eliot had found a stage presence for yet another of his modern poetic characters—Doris Dorrance. Already he had begun to transform the elements of ferocity and indifference into what would become an Aristophanic melodrama.

The collapse of Eliot's emotional health in the summer of 1921 broke the momentum of his dramatic formulations; moreover, *The Waste Land* was heavy on his mind. Ordered to rest for three months, he still carried images and sounds of the music halls to Margate and then to Lausanne, where he drafted most of the poem.[16] In the canceled opening section, a train of lowbrows in fancy dress—Silk Hat Harry (evidently modeled on a favorite character of George Graves), Myrtle, Trixie, Stella, Gus Krutzsch, and others sing fragments of vaudeville and music-hall songs, and in the second section, "A Game of Chess," the phantom interlocutor answers the frantic questions of the neurasthenic woman with that irreverent music-hall ditty, "O O O O that Shakespeherian Rag— / It's so elegant / So intelligent," further intensifying her dislocation from reality.[17]

On his way back to London, Eliot intentionally stopped over in Paris to see the famous Mistinguett, the Marie Lloyd of the French music hall, at the Casino de Paris, where he experienced his "first and most welcome reminder of London." While he admired her versatility and uniqueness as an actress, he was struck, as he subsequently wrote to his American readers, by another startling quality:

> in herself she played a part which I thought would have been better understood and liked by an English music hall audience than it was at the Casino de Paris. I thought of Marie Lloyd again; and wondered again why that directness, frankness and ferocious humour which survive in her, and in Nellie Wallace and George Robey and a few others, should be extinct, should be odious to the British public, in precisely those forms of art in which they are most needed, and which, in fact, they used to flourish.

The form of art in which this nearly extinct humor was needed, of course, was the poetic drama, which was Eliot's abiding preoccupation even as Ezra Pound put his blue pencil to the draft of *The Waste Land*. As the poem took its final form in 1922, Eliot found the financial support for his new periodical, the *Criterion*. For the first issue in October, which would contain the first printing of *The Waste Land*, Eliot intended that his friend John Rodker should prepare a special rubric on the music halls, evidently in preparation for future articles on his dramatic theory, but Rodker disappointed him. That disappointment paled, however, when on the eve of publication occurred one of the cultural disappointments of the decade—the death of Marie Lloyd at the age of fifty-two.

Eliot mourned his music-hall idol in the pages of the *Dial*, describing her death as "the most important event which I have had to chronicle in these pages." Indeed, he felt and registered the shock of her death as a personal, national, and historical loss. For seven years she had fueled his creative imagination and had unknowingly served as a collaborator for his theory of art. She had achieved as a popular performer what he wished to achieve as an artist in search of popular forms—the elevation of crude material to the level of art. She had made a virtue of vulgarity, and in exchange for the sympathy of her lower-class audiences she gave a kind of moral expression to their lives. "My own chief point," Eliot emphasized, "is that I consider her superiority over other performers to be in a way a moral superiority." But most important, in the bawdy laughter and moral ferocity of her comic turns Marie Lloyd had disclosed to Eliot the mysterious principle of dramatic art that had so intrigued and eluded Symons

Marie Lloyd, Queen of the Halls

Little Tich in the Big
Boot Dance

Nellie Wallace in a pratfall

Ethel Levey in the Grizzly Bear Dance

Mistinguett at the Casino de Paris

George Robey as the Prehistoric Man

George Graves as Baron Popoff

George Mozart as Idle Jack

Ernie Lotinga

Ernie Lotinga as Private Jimmy Josser

Athene Seyler as Lady Fidget in *The Country Wife*

Léonide Massine dancing the
farucca in *Le Chapeau Tricorne*

Massine in Picasso's costume for
Le Chapeau Tricorne

Massine as the Chinese
Conjuror in *Parade*

The Can-Can in
La Boutique Fantasque

Lydia Sokolova as the Chosen Virgin in *Le Sacre du Printemps*

and other poets of the 1890s—the necessity of collaboration.[18] "The working-man who went to the music-hall," Eliot wrote, "and saw Marie Lloyd and joined in the chorus was himself performing part of the act; he was engaged in that collaboration of the audience with the artist which is necessary in all art and most obviously in dramatic art" (*SE* 458). Eliot never forgot it—indeed, he would later realize that the possibility of a modern poetic drama depended more on the discovery of music-hall collaboration than on the recovery of the old English ferocity. Not long after Marie Lloyd's death—in the early months of 1923—Eliot returned to *Sweeney Agonistes*.

II

Were the Sweeney poems already in Eliot's mind as fragments of a ritual drama even as they were written in 1918–19? Soon after their collective appearance in *Ara Vos Prec* in February 1920 he wrote "The Possibility of a Poetic Drama," the last essay to be included in *The Sacred Wood*. Already mixed in his imagination with studies of primitivism, myth, and ritual was the "mythic method" absorbed from reading chapters of Joyce's *Ulysses* as they came into the *Little Review*. On 25 September 1920, a few weeks after meeting Joyce in Paris, and just days after mentioning *The Waste Land* to his mother for the first time, Eliot visited Virginia Woolf to talk about caricature and poetic drama. They both struggled with the definitions:

> He told me he was more interested in people than in anything. . . . His turn is for caricature. In trying to define his meaning ("I don't mean satire") we foundered. He wants to write a verse play in which the 4 characters of Sweeny [*sic*] act the parts. A personal upheaval of some kind came after Prufrock, & turned him aside from his inclination—to develop in the manner of Henry James. Now he wants to describe externals. Joyce gives internals. His novel Ulysses, presents the life of man in 16 incidents, all taking place (I think) in one day. This, so far as he has seen it, is extremely brilliant, he says.[19]

The composition of *The Waste Land* took precedence over *Sweeney Agonistes* for the following year, but Eliot continued to plan the play all the while. On 24 January 1922, in the midst of their final editing of the poem, he wrote to Pound: "I would have sent Aeschyle before but have been in bed with flu. . . . Trying to read Aristophane" (*L1* 504). He soon settled on Aristophanes for the classical frame of *Sweeney Agonistes* and on Aeschylus for the epigraph.[20] "As for *The Waste Land*," he wrote to Richard Aldington later in the year, "that is a thing of the past so far as I am concerned and I am now feeling toward a new form and style" (*L1* 596). When the critic Jacob Isaacs met Eliot for the first time at Sidney Schiff's house early in 1923 he found Eliot feeling his way; the topic of discussion was printed in Isaac's memory: "It was Aristophanes."[21] On 26 April Eliot wrote to John Quinn that the play was "more ambitious than anything I have ever done yet."[22]

By 1923 Eliot was wholly preoccupied with the development of a new poetic drama, and though it was the music-hall comedian who had initially sparked his dramatic imagination, he had since discovered performers and techniques in other forms of popular entertainment—as varied as the circus, the ballet, modern music, and mime—and amalgamated them into a new dramaturgy. He was now in full reaction against the realistic drama and acting inherited from the nineteenth century and committed to his own concept of symbolic drama, to a total theatre where gesture, movement, rhythm, and detachment are essential attributes of the actor.

The pieces began to coalesce after Sergei Diaghilev brought the Ballet Russes back to London in September 1918 for the first time since the war began. Ironically, the only venue available was the Coliseum, Sir Oswald Stoll's palace for music hall and variety, and Diaghilev had to endure seeing his productions sandwiched between the various turns and acts. The company's success, which owed much to the choreography of Léonide Massine, eventually brought a transfer to the Alhambra on 30 April 1919. The Eliots got tickets for 13 May, when they saw *Le Carnaval, Le Oiseau de Feu,* and *Les Femmes de Bonne Humeur.* Enraptured by the dancing of Massine and Lydia Lopokova, Eliot returned on 22 July with the Sitwells, who had earlier befriended Diaghilev, Massine, and Lopokova, to see the two dancers in the toyshop ballet *La Boutique Fantasque,* marked by their shockingly mischievous Can-Can. The program included the London premiere of *Le Chapeau Tricorne,* choreographed by Massine to Manuel de Falla's syncopated music and Pablo Picasso's cubist scenery and costumes. The production resulted in an astonishing synthesis of contemporary idioms and classical techniques. The brevity and simplicity of Picasso's backcloth, wrote Cyril Beaumont, the Sitwell's inveterate ballet-watching friend, "was acclaimed by painters as a masterpiece" and did much to establish Picasso's reputation in London.[23] Falla's music, "invested with a rare impish humour, . . . offered a mocking comment on the characters of various personages and the nature of certain incidents in the ballet." Massine, who "danced like one possessed," dominated the ballet as the Miller, dancing his intensified version of the Spanish folk dance the *farucca:*

> Few . . . will have forgotten the colour and bravura with which he invested his Farruca, the slow snap of the fingers followed by the pulsating thump of his feet, then the flickering movement of his hands held horizontally before him, palms facing and almost touching his breast. All at once this gave place to a new movement in which his feet chopped the ground faster and faster until he suddenly dropped to the ground on his hands, and as quickly leapt to his feet and stopped dead, his efforts greeted with thunderous applause.

Eliot returned the following evening to see *Papillons* and *Prince Igor.* In all these performances he was struck by Diaghilev's transposition of popular forms into classical dance, by his startling success in creating a truly modern ballet; he immediately saw a parallel between Diaghilev's experiments in ballet and his own in poetic drama. In the autumn, in his most important public lecture to date, "Modern Tendencies in Poetry," he elaborated the parallel:

I have some very kind things to say of the ballet, but I am compelled to speak of it first in this unpleasant connection. For the ballet, with the immense and important development it has recently had, has certainly lost some of the formal beauty of the older ballet, which depended more on pure technical excellence of dancing. It has become a tremendous appeal to the senses, without any emotion whatever.

This leads me back to the poet. . . . The ballet has done this much good. It has made us aware that we *can* pass an evening in a theatre and have some intense experience, even if it is not a purely artistic one. We are not going to accept, after that, being bored for three hours under the pretence of the art of the drama; whether it be a social play, a comedy, or the poor old "poetic drama."[24]

The choreographer and the dancer had shown the poet that, in the modern renewal of traditional forms, technical artistry and formal purity must make room for both artistic intensity and popular entertainment, a hallmark of Elizabethan drama. As Eliot had said of Hardy's instinct in staging *The Dynasts,* "to get a poetic vision on to the stage was more important than neat blank verse."[25] And when John Middleton Murry published his verse play *Cinnamon and Angelica* (1920), Eliot took the occasion to observe that though Murry "has studied blank verse with great care . . . he is not held down by the necessity of *entertaining* an audience cruder than himself; the emotional structure is the only structure." To Eliot, the poetic vision of the entertaining dramatist moves unsullied through different levels of emotion in the play:

The poetic drama cannot avoid all audience. In the middle of a rowdy seventeenth-century playhouse pit the thought of Shakespeare, the feeling and the shuddering personal experience of Shakespeare moved solitary and unsoiled; solitary and free as the thought of Spinoza in his study or Montaigne in his tower.[26]

Thus, when Massine and Lopokova danced the Can-Can in *La Boutique Fantasque,* the critic Beaumont, steeped in classical ballet, was appalled that "there were some gestures by Massine—particularly when he slipped to the ground and his partner whirled her leg over his head—which, to say the least, were inelegant."[27] But the unexpecting audience loved it, and such ungainly gestures and unorthodox turns in the ballet were grist for Eliot's theatrical mill: they opened the way in Eliot's imagination for Sweeney and his crude companions to inhabit poetic drama. More immediately, Lopokova may have inspired Eliot's portrait of Fresca in another canceled passage of *The Waste Land:* "Fresca's arrived (the Muses Nine declare) / To be a sort of can-can salonnière" (*WLF* 27).

Eliot now moved back and forth between the music halls and the concert halls for his material, and he must have been electrified to see the artistic fusion of the two in Massine's role as the Chinese Conjurer in Jean Cocteau's one-act ballet *Parade* when the company returned in November 1919.[28] Beaumont again witnessed the combination of Cocteau's acrobatic text, Erik Satie's music, Picasso's scenery, and Massine's choreography:

At the time *Parade* was first produced the circus and music-hall were favoured vehicles of artistic expression, and *Parade* was a ballet fashioned from such elements. The ballet satirized a number of well-known types and the dances were based on the movements and gestures associated with such characters. . . . The best dance was undoubtedly that of the Chinese Conjurer, in which Massine wittily parodied the movements associated with pseudo-Oriental conjurers of the music-hall stage.[29]

As Massine himself testified, "*Parade* was not so much a satire on popular art as an attempt to translate it into a totally new form. It is true that we utilized certain elements of contemporary show-business—ragtime music, jazz, the cinema, billboard, advertising, circus and music-hall techniques—but we took only their salient features, adapting them to our own ends." In his own fusion of the popular and the classical, Massine had entertained his London audience with the very sense of caricature that Eliot labored to define and resuscitate.[30] As a performer, Massine, like Ethel Levey, had an uncanny ability to *transmit* intense dramatic emotion, both comic and tragic. In Levey and Massine, Eliot discerned the impersonal attributes of his ideal actor, but he looked in vain for comparable qualities on the modern stage. After seeing Massine, he turned to the Phoenix Society's production of *The Duchess of Malfi,* which he saw on 23 November 1919, to discuss the difficulties that beset the poetic dramatist. "The problem for anyone who wants to write a verse play," he wrote, "would be to make some intense effect carry across to the stalls and gallery, to convey a dominant tone. To obtain, with verse, an effect as immediate and direct as that of the best ballet." To Eliot, the possibility of achieving such an effect is prevented by modern actors, whose training in "interpretation" ensures their inadequacy for poetic drama: "For poetry is something which the actor cannot improve or 'interpret'; there is no such thing as the interpretation of poetry; poetry can only be transmitted; in consequence, the ideal actor for a poetic drama is the actor *with no personal vanity. . . .* [T]he training that any contemporary actor has received is apt to make him devote more attention to himself than to such a person as John Webster."[31] Though Eliot's theory of poetic drama was weighted with the realities of the London stage, where the modern play was still made for the actor, he continued to prepare the way in his prose.

As he worked on *The Waste Land,* Eliot turned his personal preoccupations with poetic drama into hints about general developments for his "London Letters" in the *Dial.* In July 1921, in anticipation of attending Diaghilev's recently opened ballet and hearing Stravinsky's music, he told his American readers that Diaghilev's previous productions in London had been greeted "as the dawn of an art of the theatre" and that "the ballet will probably be one of the influences forming a new drama, if a new drama ever comes." To Eliot, Diaghilev's ballet, in comparison to the earlier ballet of Nijinsky, was "more sophisticated, but also more simplified, and simplifies more; and what is needed of art is a simplification of current life into something rich and strange."[32] That summer Diaghilev's short-lived revival of Stravinsky's *Le Sacre du Printemps,* choreographed by Massine and danced with Lydia Sokalova, struck deep chords for Eliot's poem and play. Stravinsky's music sounded for Eliot the discordant pageant of horns and motors to which Sweeney and Mrs. Porter would soon march in *The Waste Land,* on their way to reenacting a primitive ritual in *Sweeney Agonistes.* Eliot recorded the effect for his American readers:

> The spirit of the music was modern, and the spirit of the ballet was primitive ceremony. The Vegetation Rite upon which the ballet is founded remained, in spite of the music, a pageant of primitive culture. . . . Whether Strawinsky's [sic] music be permanent or ephemeral I do not know; but it did seem to transform the rhythm of the steppes into the scream of the motor horn, the rattle of machinery, the grind of wheels, the beating of iron and steel, the roar of the underground railway, and the other barbaric cries of modern life; and to transform these despairing noises into music.[33]

At the height of his London success, Diaghilev determined to mount a revival of one of the most famous of classical ballets, *La Belle au Bois Dormant (The Sleeping Princess),* scored by Tchaikovsky, but in February 1922 the extravagant production failed midway through a planned six-month run. Diaghilev returned to Paris, embittered and in debt, and his company of great dancers began to split up.[34] Massine, who had left Diaghilev months earlier after a dispute, formed a small troupe of his own from the remnants and returned to Covent Garden in April for a modest program that included *Ragtime,* a parody danced to Stravinsky's music. Eliot, in attendance, found Massine "more brilliant and beautiful than ever," and when Mary Hutchinson (who met Massine through the Sitwells) offered to arrange a meeting with Massine after he began a series of *divertissements* at the Coliseum, Eliot was ecstatic: "I want to meet him more than ever, and he is a genius" (L1 523). After they eventually met on 22 June, Eliot wrote to thank her for the evening: "I liked Massine very much indeed—with no disappointment—and hope that I shall see him again. He was much as I expected him to be. I enjoyed the whole evening and thought it perfect. . . . Do you think Massine liked me? and would he come and see me, do you think?" (L1 529–30). There is no record of their discussion, or of a further meeting, but Massine was at the center of Eliot's mind as he put *The Waste Land* behind him and turned to *Sweeney Agonistes.*

III

The death of Sarah Bernhardt on 26 March 1923 brought the nineteenth-century French theatre to a formal close, much as Marie Lloyd's death signaled the demise of the music halls, and in paying tribute to Bernhardt in "Dramatis Personae" Eliot marked the transition by pointing to the "chaos" of the modern stage and forecasting a new drama. He took his cue from one of Cocteau's "professional secrets":

> Le cirque, le music-hall, le cinématographe et ces entreprises qui, depuis Serge de Diaghilew, mettent de puissants vehicules aux mains des jeunes, autant de

forces qui conspirent, sans même connaître leur entente, contre ce que le théâtre
est devenu, savoir: un vieil album de photographies.

"Such statements," Eliot declared, "will shortly be incontestable" (*Cr* 1:303).[35] As
a conscious ally of Cocteau, he sought out those performers in Paris (or in London) who emanated both a special sense of their time and an individuated
rhythm—Rastelli at the circus,[36] Mistinguett in the music hall, Chaplin in the
film—and for certain effects even Cocteau's friends the Guitrys, whose fashionable boulevard farces Eliot had deprecated for years. When Seymour Hicks
adapted one of their most popular plays, *Faisons un rêve*, for the London stage as
Sleeping Partners in 1918, Eliot wrote of the production:

> We may still, no doubt, take a certain pleasure in the Guitrys, especially if we
> have the prudence to see them in London rather than in Paris. They will always
> be interesting here if only because they demonstrate the extraordinary clumsi-
> ness of English actors who imitate them. . . . If there must be telephoning
> on the stage, Lucien and Sacha Guitry know how to do it better than anybody
> . . . but the spectacle of Seymour Hicks telephoning for months on end is
> enough to discredit the use of that instrument altogether. (*Cr* 1:304)[37]

It is apparent, as Eliot worked out the scenes of *Sweeney Agonistes,* that his calcu-
lated decision to give Doris the telephone was inspired by the Guitrys, surely by
the hilarious telephone soliloquy, to which he refers here, in the second act.[38]

Eliot had begun to infuse all sorts of popular arts into *Sweeney Agonistes,* in-
tending to make it a composite of several cultural levels of entertainment, like
Elizabethan drama. It would have the telephone from a Guitry melodrama; it
would have Lincoln Snow, a blackface musician with his banjo from the American minstrel show; it would have Milton Swartz from Jewish jazz; it would have
rapid cross talk from the music halls,[39] gestures and mime from modern dance
and ballet. Indeed, in one scenario Eliot planned to include a three-minute ballet
in the play—like the Massine-Lopokova Can-Can—just as he would do in his
pageant play *The Rock*. Moreover, in his directions for an American production of
Sweeney Agonistes, Eliot advised the director that the action "should be stylized as
in the Noh drama," that the characters *"ought* to wear masks," and that he had
"intended the whole play to be accompanied by light drum taps to accentuate
the beats (esp. The chorus, which ought to have a noise like a street drill)."[40] All
this was to be orchestrated into a modern rhythm, like Stravinsky's music, making
a new symbolic drama, a new dramatic ritual.

Eliot had come to believe that the drama, not only in its ancient origins but
in the present day, is a ritual and that "the failure of the contemporary stage to
satisfy the craving for ritual is one of the reasons why it is not a living art" (*Cr*
1:305–6). To Eliot, ritual is essentially a dance, but a dance also contains poetry
and music, and their common element is rhythm. "It is the rhythm," he says, "so
utterly absent from modern drama . . . which makes Massine and Charlie
Chaplin the great actors that they are, and which makes the juggling of Rastelli
more cathartic than a performance of *A Doll's House*."[41]

Thus, though the physical type for Sweeney was drawn from the music halls, his style of acting was taken from Massine. Eliot had found only one actor, Ion Swinley of the Phoenix Society, whose style of acting was sufficiently abstract and simplified to play Sweeney, but he lacked an essential quality:

> Mr. Swinley, I feel, with his masklike beauty, belongs to this unrealised stage; at the same moment I regret that he has not had the training in movement and gesture—the only training in movement and gesture—the training of ballet. For his physical type is not dissimilar to that of Leonid [*sic*] Massine, who seems to me the greatest actor that we have in London. Massine, the most completely unhuman, impersonal, abstract, belongs to the future stage. (*Cr* 1:305)[42]

While other actors use the conventional gestures of the ordinary stage, they are only able to *express* emotion. The abstract gesture of Massine, on the other hand, "*symbolises* emotion," and that was the quality required for the successful actor of Sweeney in Eliot's symbolic drama.

Eliot continued to frequent the declining halls through the 1920s, using them as a point of reference in his reviews of drama and of another popular form that had captured his critical interest—modern dance. In April 1924, following the Phoenix Society's revival of Wycherley's *Country Wife*, Eliot regretted that in the general acclaim for the production the role of Lady Fidget as played by Athene Seyler had gone unnoticed. Describing Seyler as "probably the finest living actress of comedy in England," Eliot again linked the Elizabethan drama and the music hall by applauding her extraordinary ability to elicit a ferocious humor in this and other roles. Seyler's "personality," Eliot wrote,

> commands the scene whenever she appears. She played the part of Lady Fidget with a cold ferocity, a pure and undefiled detachment which makes her worthy to rank in that supreme class which includes Marie Lloyd and Nellie Wallace. Miss Seyler has also a gift of expression and gesture; beautiful hands, and knows how to use them; distinctions extremely uncommon amongst the usual suburban manners of the comedy stage. (*Cr* 2:234)

Eliot's corresponding interest in comic gesture had come from his ongoing study of modern dance, particularly in Diaghilev's ballets as danced by Massine, and there, as in the music-hall turns, he was intrigued not only by what could be borrowed from each modern art for a modern poetic drama but by the particular relationship of each performer to the audience. In a double review entitled "The Ballet" (1925), Eliot remarked of Tyra de Kleen's *Mudras: The Ritual Hand Poses of the Buddha Priests and Shiva Priests,* "I believe that the ballet could *borrow* a great deal from the beautiful and varied movements of the hands exhibited in this book" (*Cr* 3:443). In the accompanying review of Cecil Sharp's historical study of European dancing, *The Dance,* Eliot complained that Sharp "had never really understood the modern ballet (such as that of Diaghilev)" and that in his prejudice against "acrobatic virtuosity" he had never analyzed the difference between

dancing and acrobatics. To make the distinctions for Sharp, Eliot turned once
again to the music halls:

> The difference between acrobatics and dancing may be observed in any music-
> hall: it is a difference of total effect, of the faculty to which the performer ap-
> peals. The acrobat, however bad or good, appeals to the mind rather than to the
> senses. . . . There are acrobats, such as Rastelli, whose juggling appeals to our
> sense of beauty of form; but this is an added gift. The primary appeal of acro-
> batics is to the mind. In *dancing,* the physical skill is ancillary to another effect.
> You must have the skill or you cannot produce this effect; but the appreciation
> of skill is for the trained critic alone, not for the general audience. (*Cr* 3:442)

This abiding interest in detachment, gesture, and modes of appeal to mind and
emotion was, of course, part of the formulation of a dramatic theory in which
playwright and actors, who often play characters that are vehicles for emotions
they do not understand, work to lead the audience beyond the dramatic, past the
surface action and emotion, to a plane of spiritual action and emotion that tran-
scends them, a plane where the distinctions of individuality meet, a plane that
dramatic action in the ordinary sense cannot make perceptible.

IV

By the end of the 1920s Eliot had made the music-hall comedian his paradigm
for discussing the nature of the poet and the social function of poetry. When we
know his early formulations about the art of the performers, his later offhand
references to that art pose no difficulty, as in "A Dialogue on Dramatic Poetry"
(1928), when one of the conversants tosses into the dialogue the observation that
Ernie Lotinga's use of bawdy humor "is a tribute to, an acknowledgment of conventional British morality" (*SE* 50).[43] We understand clearly, when, in the introduction to *The Use of Poetry and the Use of Criticism* (1933) we encounter Eliot's
throwaway assertion, after Walter Pater, that "the poet aspires to the condition of
the music-hall comedian"—and in the conclusion, where we read: "Every poet
would like to think that he had some direct social utility. . . . All the better,
then, if he could have at least the satisfaction of having a part to play in society as
worthy as that of the music-hall comedian" (*UPUC* 32, 154). We take delight,
too, in discovering that the cockney workmen in Eliot's pageant play *The Rock*
(1934) are fans of George Robey, who is "on the 'alls" and "does the comic
turn," and in hearing their foreman Ethelbert sing in celebration of their church
a music-hall song that his wife says "was wrote for you special" before their marriage thirty years earlier, *"At Trinity Church I Met My Doom"*:[44]

> When I was a lad what 'ad almost no sense
>   Then a gentle flirtation was all my delight;
> And I'd often go seeking' for ex-pe-ri-ence
>   Along the New Cut of a Saturday night.

It was on a May evenin' I'll never forget
> That I found the reward of my diligent search;
And I made a decision I never regret,
> Which led to a weddin' at Trinity Church.[45]

Further, in Eliot's BBC broadcast "The Need for Poetic Drama" (1936), published after the production of *Murder in the Cathedral*, we nod knowingly when he declares that poetic drama has developed to its present stage because dramatists now realize

> that the actor should be in an intimacy of relation to the audience which had
> for a long time been the secret of the music-hall comedian. . . . When we
> see a great music-hall comedian on the stage, such as George Robey or Ernie
> Lotinga, we feel that he is conscious of his audience, that a great deal of the ef-
> fect depends upon a sympathy set up between actor and audience.[46]

In *The Cocktail Party: A Comedy* (1950), the Unidentified Guest, later identified as Sir Henry Harcourt-Reilly, downs two gin and waters and then merrily sings a refrain of "One Eyed Riley" as he exits the first scene: *"Tooryooly toory-iley, / What's the matter with One Eyed Riley?"* (*CPP* 365).[47] The director of the play, E. Martin Browne, was immediately struck by the effect of the song, "the first indication of a streak of unexpected gaiety in the character of the psychiatrist. . . . I was not surprised that Eliot, who particularly relished an oblique stroke of humour, should have been tempted to use 'One Eyed Riley' as his title."[48] That was indeed the title of the first draft, a title misleadingly too Cyclopean for the intended fusion of the classical and the contemporary in the play. Eliot subsequently explained the parallel with the *Alcestis:*

> But those who were at first disturbed by the eccentric behaviour of my un-
> known guest, and his apparently intemperate habits and tendency to burst into
> song, have found some consolation after I have called their attention to the be-
> haviour of Heracles in Euripides' play.[49]

Though *Sweeney Agonistes* was unfinished, Eliot's aim in his major plays was to correlate the ancient with the modern, the serious with the trivial, the refined with the crude: Aristophanes with Sweeney and Doris, Aeschylus with Harry, Euripides with Reilly. What he had admired in Shakespeare, especially in the savage humor of *Antony and Cleopatra,* was the ability to bring about "a fusion of sordidness and magnificence . . . into one and the same thing."[50] He had admired it in Marlowe's *Dido Queen of Carthage,* where the Grecian soldiers seized Cassandra "And swung her howling in the empty air," leaving her "sprawling in the streets" (*SE* 124), just as he had admired it in the comic turns of Marie Lloyd and Ernie Lotinga, in the pratfalls of Nellie Wallace, in the Can-Can of Léonide Massine and Lydia Lopokova, artists who knew that the effective placement of the sordid enhanced the magnificent, that serious effects could be achieved by something not unlike caricature.

V

From the "Shakespeherian Rag" to "One-Eyed Riley," songs made popular in music hall and vaudeville continuously made their way into Eliot's poetry and plays, even as an epigraph for his Clark Lectures on metaphysical poetry: "I want someone to treat me rough. / Give me a cabman" (*VMP* 40).[51] The recognition of these popular lyrics restores a lost dimension of the works, as does the recognition in *The Elder Statesman* (1959) that Mrs. Carghill, jilted by Lord Claverton in their youths, was then a revue comedienne, Maisie Mountjoy (created in the image of Ethel Levey), who now hums her old hit tune "It's Not Too Late for You to Love Me." Indeed, Eliot himself hummed and sang music-hall and other popular songs all his life. His friend Mary Trevelyan recorded in her unpublished memoir "how Eliot would sing tunelessly in a harsh low voice on the way home after dinner: music hall songs of his youth, or Negro Spirituals" (*TSE* 445). Valerie Eliot attests that he had an astounding repertoire of "music-hall ditties,"[52] including one that he frequently sang while being shaved, singing made hazardous because he would not stay still:

My name is Tough
And I live in Tough Alley
And the further down you go
The tougher it gets,
And I live in the last house.
I am so tough my spit bounces!

Visiting Pound in Venice after Eliot's death, she was shocked when Pound himself suddenly began reciting the lyrics during a meal, remembering them from Eliot. V. S. Pritchett, expressing his lack of surprise after hearing that Eliot's second marriage had mellowed him, said of his friend in an interview: "Even so, the admirer of comedian George Robey and the English music hall, the singer of 'The One-Eyed Riley,' could hardly have been impregnable to geniality."[53]

Thus, we can now begin to see that Eliot's mind was as steeped in popular culture as it was in literary culture, that his poems and plays draw deeply on both traditions, and that most of his major works represent a commingling of popular and classical forms refined into something rich and strange.[54] Much more could be made of all this, of course, but the bell has rung in the music-hall lounge, and I hear the barman's insistent cry, "HURRY UP PLEASE ITS TIME."

THE HORRIFIC MOMENT

Thou art the whisper in the gloom,
The hinting tone, the haunting laugh:
Thou art the adorner of my tomb,
The minstrel of mine epitaph.

R ecollections?" mused Pound in his brief eulogy to Eliot, "let some thesis-
writer have the satisfaction of 'discovering' whether it was in 1920 or '21 that
I went from Excideuil to meet a rucksacked Eliot. Days of walking—conversation? . . . Who is there now for me to share a joke with?"[1] How curious that
their brief walking tour of southern France should surface as Pound's choice recollection after fifty years of friendship. Did he know that the trip was no joking
matter, that Eliot had undergone a horrifying emotional experience that triggered
the composition of *The Waste Land?* It was Eliot's first holiday from London since
the previous summer at Marlow, where he drafted "Whispers of Immortality," and
the thesis-writers have now discovered that the two set foot from Excideuil on
their tour of the Dordogne on 15 August 1919.[2] In Canto 29 Pound recalls their
visit to the castle ruins in Excideuil, where Eliot ("Arnaut"), observing "the wave
pattern cut in the stone" of the spire of St. Thomas, deliberately "shocked" Pound
by exclaiming, "I am afraid of the life after death."[3] The next day Eliot sent a post-
card to Lytton Strachey, writing that though London was extraordinarily difficult,
in his wandering of the Corrèze he was happy—it provided "a complete relief
from London" (*L1* 327). Shortly thereafter they wandered into the town of
Périgueux to visit the famous Basilique Saint-Front. Pound had been there before,
in the summer of 1912, recording his disturbing vision in "Provincia Deserta"
(1915):

I have walked
     into Perigord,
I have seen the torch-flames, high-leaping,
Painting the front of that church;
Heard, under the dark, whirling laughter.
I have looked back over the stream
     and seen the high building,
Seen the long minarets, the white shafts.

It was here, Eliot reveals eleven years later, that his fragile happiness was shattered by yet another spiritual crisis. In an unpublished letter of 9 August 1930 to his friend and confessor, William Force Stead, whose new volume of verse, *The House on the Wold,* had just appeared, Eliot wrote that the despairing title poem "expresses feelings that I know but have never seen so well expressed. This sense of dispossession by the dead I have known twice, at Marlow and at Périgueux" (Yale).

Eliot attempted to characterize this dispossession in every mode of his writing—in his poetry ("the way of dispossession" in *Four Quartets),* in his essays on other poets (Baudelaire's "looking into the Shadow"), and in his drama (Harry's experience of "that sense of separation, / Of isolation unredeemable, irrevocable," Reilly's fear of "the final desolation / Of solitude in the phantasmal world / Of imagination, shuffling memories and desires" [*CPP* 330, 419]). And on at least one occasion he slipped into personal experience:

> There are moments, perhaps not known to everyone, when a man may be nearly crushed by the terrible awareness of his isolation from every other human being; and I pity him if he finds himself only alone with himself and his meanness and futility, alone without God. It is after these moments, alone *with* God and aware of our worthiness, but for Grace, of nothing but damnation, that we turn with most thankfulness and appreciation to the awareness of our *membership:* for we appreciate and are thankful for nothing fully until we see where it begins and where it ends.[4]

Such moments of isolation were not new to Eliot in 1918–19, and the admitted experiences at Marlow and Périgueux open a window for looking deeper into his artistic sensibility. Indeed, we can begin to see that much of his career was motivated by his attempt to escape from and gain artistic control over the dispossessing horrors attendant upon "personality," that the relation between personal horror and impersonal art was one of his foremost preoccupations as poet and critic. From the outset of his career he ransacked literature for evidence of controlled horror. His critical essays abound with the discovery of horrific visions of life, and his poetry is a virtual repository of horrific epigraphs and allusions that are there to objectify and intensify the personal moments of spiritual terror in the poem. Eliot took the horrific way to the beatific, and he discovered as artist-critic that the horror of life is often inexpressible, that it can be too intense for even the most objective correlative, that even tragedy cannot adequately contain it.

We now know that in 1910–11 Eliot went through a period of emotional-spiritual upheaval, and in an early poem entitled "Silence" (1910) he records an ecstatic visionary experience. Though the moment of peace and stillness occurs in a continually dissolving world, it also occurs in a context of spiritual terror, and the stillness and the peace are for Eliot indistinguishable from the terror inspired by his sense of the void:

> You may say what you will,
> At such peace I am terrified.
> There is nothing else beside. (*IMH* 18)

There is a close connection in Eliot's poetry between the rare moments of ecstasy and the recurring moments of horror, but from the beginning the ecstasy is lodged in the memory as a stay against horrors that are most frequently released by desire. "Memory!" he cries in "Rhapsody on a Windy Night," but in that poem the mind that futilely shakes its memory, "As a madman shakes a dead geranium," is overwhelmed by images of the sordid, the horrid. In "Preludes" the "thousand sordid images" that inhabit the soul prevent the mind from realizing "The notion of some infinitely gentle / Infinitely suffering thing." Prufrock, who emerges as a persona in the same turbulent period, has lived familiarly in a world of desire and ritualized action, but his growing consciousness of age and loss of physical attractiveness have been accompanied by dark visions and darker re-visions that terrify him as they rise upon his consciousness. He knows that he will soon be left alone; after a life of sensual distraction he lives in terror of self-revelation. In alluding to the revealing parable of the wealthy Dives and the beggar Lazarus, he faces with horror and would, like Lazarus, "tell you all" of what Abraham calls "a great chasm" between those in human torment and those in Abraham's bosom.[5] The emotional substratum of terror and paralysis is so overwhelming that his "question" remains horribly inexpressible, his spiritual anguish intimated but unresolved. Students often wonder how Eliot at twenty-two could have so successfully created Prufrock's ageing consciousness. Eliot explains in "Cyril Tourneur" (1930): "We are apt to expect of youth only a fragmentary view of life. . . . But occasionally the intensity of the vision of its own ecstasies or horrors, combined with a mastery of word and rhythm, may give to a juvenile work a universality which is beyond the author's knowledge of life to give, and to which mature men and women can respond" (*SE* 189).

By the time he began his critical writings and Extension lecturing in 1916, Eliot had already gathered his masters of horror, intrigued by their ability to control and project the horrific moments of their protagonists—among them Sophocles' Oedipus, Aeschylus's Orestes, Dante's Ugolino, Marlowe's Faustus, Shakespeare's Hamlet, Webster's Duchess, Dostoyevsky's Raskolnikov—and as he began to study the horror of tragedy he brought their weight to bear upon his criticism of moderns and contemporaries. In his review of H. C. Duffin's *Thomas Hardy: A Study of the Wessex Novels* (1916), Eliot says disdainfully that the slaughter of Sue Bridehead's children in *Jude the Obscure* is "a horror nearer to Cyril Tourneur than to Sophocles, and hints at a faint infection of decadence."[6] In his

Extension classes he compared Hardy's conception of tragedy to Greek tragedy, later revealing the nature of that comparison in his discussion of Seneca and Elizabethan horror:

> It is no more reasonable to make Seneca responsible for this aspect of Eliza-
> bethan drama than it is to connect Æschylus or Sophocles with *Jude the Obscure*.
> I am not sure that the latter association has not been made, though no one sup-
> poses that Hardy prepared himself by close application to the study of Greek
> drama. (*SE* 84)

As will be seen, Hardy was to serve as a foil for Eliot's discussion of tragedy and horror for the next eighteen years. Similarly, he usually found the horror in Poe's work to be based more on the immaterial and ghostly than on the spiritual, and the horrific atmosphere in Balzac, he concluded, is no more than "the highest possible development of the atmosphere of Mrs. Radcliffe."[7]

By contrast, Eliot was quick to identify and sympathize with fellow writers whose attempts to represent significant visions of horror fell on an uncomprehending public, as in his review of Edith Wharton's *Summer* (1917), where he describes the scene of the county fair at Nettleton as "one of unrelieved horror. This novel will certainly be considered 'disgusting' in America; it is certain that not one reader in a thousand will apprehend the author's point of view."[8] Thus, in assigning *The Duchess of Malfy* in his Extension course, he focused his students' attention on Webster's "skill in dealing with horror" (see p. 48). In Webster's ability to find objects and situations for extreme states of mind and feeling, Eliot had already found a model for his earliest critical principle, the "objective correlative," unnamed until further developed in "Hamlet and His Problems" two years later. By then he had already applauded in James and Hawthorne the skillful relation between their "deeper psychology" and their "sense for situation." It was the skill that Tourneur lacked in *The Revenger's Tragedy*, where he could not control the personal horror: "The cynicism, the loathing and disgust of humanity . . . are immature in the respect that they exceed the object. Their objective equivalents are characters . . . which seem merely to be spectres projected from the poet's inner world of nightmare, some horror beyond words" (*SE* 190). Eliot similarly accused Shakespeare of exceeding his object in *Hamlet*, but when we look closely at this famous essay we see that Eliot was more preoccupied with Shakespeare's obscure private motive than with the fact of artistic failure: "under compulsion of what experience he attempted to express the inexpressibly horrible, we cannot ever know" (*SE* 146). Eliot brooded over Shakespeare's personal horror, turning repeatedly to the consciousness beneath the work: "It is not only the external history of Shakespeare's life that is deficient," he wrote. "It is that internal history . . . that internal crisis over which our imagination is tempted to brood too long, that we shall never know."[9] Eliot believed that Shakespeare and his other masters of horror worked over the thin ice of a profound spiritual awareness and terror. And he learned from Dante, his "spiritual leader," that confronting the personal negativism that is the source of that terror was for all those masters an essential of the creative process: "The contemplation of the horrid or sordid or disgusting, by an artist, is the necessary and negative aspect of the impulse toward the pursuit of beauty. . . . The negative is the more importunate" (*SW* 143).

Thus, on the surface, the detached critic coolly developed a poetics of horror while his own dark angel did its "subtle violence." The path of the poet from 1914 to 1918 is strewn with the detritus of visionary fragments and bawdy ballads, where martyrs and whoremongers tug at his consciousness, the exhausting battle of flesh and spirit evident in the strain between Saint Sebastian and Sweeney. It was in a state of both spiritual and physical exhaustion that Eliot, working in the bank and giving Extension lectures, agreed that he and Vivien should share a cottage in the country with Russell.

In 1916–17 Russell conducted his circle of affairs with Ottoline, Vivien, and Colette with but few moral misgivings, breaking off from one to take up again with another. In September 1917, in a fit of jealousy over Colette's new relation with Maurice Elvey, Russell turned again to Vivien after a nine-month break, even when Colette tried to assure him that Elvey "is not my lover in the sense that you are the lover of Ottoline and Mrs E." Together again, Russell and Vivien now made plans to take a cottage somewhere in the country after the Eliots returned from a summer holiday in Bosham. Russell and Vivien would occupy the cottage during the week; Eliot would stay in the London flat to work at the bank and join them on weekends. On 30 October Russell wrote to Colette that though he had intended to keep the renewed relationship with Vivien on friendly terms "(except perhaps on very rare occasions)," he found that she "was very glad that I had come back, & very kind, & wanting much more than friendship. I thought I could manage it—I led her to expect more if we got a cottage—at last I spent a night with her."[10]

In this deceptive state of affairs, the threesome thus took a five-year lease on a house in Marlow during the first week of December. On New Year's Day 1918 Russell wrote to Colette to assure her that he was not in love with Vivien, and to keep the doors open he professed:

> I do not care if I have a physical relation with her or not. But I am happy in talking to her and going about with her. She has a very unselfish affection for me, and but for her I don't know how I should have lived through the unhappiness of these last months. I am intensely grateful to her, and I expect that she will be an essential part of my life for some time to come. But I don't know yet whether that will be so. (p. 515)

The intimate arrangement of what Russell called his "Marlow plan," which included some philosophical stimulation from Eliot, was rudely interrupted in April 1918, after he had been prosecuted under the Defence of the Realm Act and made to begin serving a six-month sentence in Brixton prison for making prejudicial statements against the Government over the German peace offer. From prison he informed Eliot, who was assiduously trying to get an officer's commission in the U.S. Navy, that he would have to stop paying his share of the Marlow house. Meanwhile, Eliot paid a personal visit to Colette for an undisclosed purpose, possibly to broach her knowledge of Vivien's relations with Russell.[11]

After Russell was released from prison in September, he began to see Vivien again, but in late November he informed Colette, who was preparing to abort a pregnancy by Elvey (the abortion to be paid for by Russell), that he had told Vivien over dinner that he would not be seeing her "for a considerable time." To recover from all the emotional strain, he went to Ottoline in Garsington. By mid-January 1919 he was back in touch with Vivien, but by this time she had decided that she disliked "fading intimacies" and wanted a complete break. Russell continued to write to her, however, insisting that his affection for her was more than that of "a roving seducer." As Robert Bell recounts, Eliot was deeply upset that Russell continued to write to Vivien, who had suffered a nervous collapse, and he expressly forbade her to answer Russell's letters. "In what must have been a very delicate and mortifying gesture," writes Bell, "Eliot instructed Russell to cease and desist."[12] Even so, it would be several months before Russell reclaimed the last of his possessions from Marlow.

During the dark days at Marlow Eliot began to live out a Jacobean nightmare of sexual mortality and experienced a spiritual devastation that would recur within months at Périgueux. As we shall see, he later wrote to Ottoline that Russell had committed acts of evil and that the "spectacle of Bertie" had been a significant factor in his eventual conversion. Eliot's perception of Russell's calculating lust, Vivien's vicious infidelity, and the eternal consequence of their betrayal brought on a horrific moment, a recurring phantasma that would thereafter suffuse the fabric of his work with sounds and scenes of sexual betrayal and violence:

> Twit twit twit
> Jug jug jug jug jug jug
> So rudely forc'd.
> Tereu

After he finally separated from Vivien, Eliot wrote to Paul Elmer More on 18 May 1933 that the past eighteen years had been a nightmare, "like a bad Dostoevski novel" (Princeton).

Even at Marlow Eliot called upon Webster and Donne, masters of the tension between sex and death, to help him confront the darker "metaphysics" of desire in "Whispers of Immortality." The central figure of the poem is the voluptuous, musk-scented Grishkin: bosomy, exotic paragon of sexual allurement, around whom circulate like seraphim the "Abstract Entities"—Love, Desire, Passion, Bliss, Fidelity—awaiting those who seek her charms, whispering the illusion that sexuality is divine. But Webster, Donne, Eliot, and their "lot" hear disturbing whispers that beneath sexual desire lies the terrible chuckle of death, as in *The Waste Land,* where the pursuer of a coy mistress hears behind his back not Time's winged chariot but "the rattle of the bones, and chuckle spread from ear to ear." Webster, and particularly Donne, fear not death but the all-encompassing fear of that fear—a spiritual terror brought on and intensified by the compulsions of flesh. Webster cannot help seeing, beneath the desirous breasts and lips, the dry-ribbed skeleton, reclining in a mocking pose of seduction and grinning at the surrender of mind and body to lust. Similarly, Donne found "no substitute for sense; / To seize and clutch and penetrate"; that is, to seduce or even rape the mind, making it tighten its fantasies of "lusts and luxuries" into a horrible vision of the fathomless mortality that underlies illicit sexuality. "Expert beyond experience," Donne knew, as Eliot says Beyle and Flaubert knew, "the awful separation between potential passion and any actualization possible in life."[13] Baudelaire knew it as well, but not Whitman: "Whitman had the ordinary desires of the flesh; for him there was no chasm between the real and the ideal, such as opened before the horrified eyes of Baudelaire."[14] Eliot had described, echoing Brutus in *Julius Caesar,* the horrific mechanism of mind in a catalogue of chasms in "The Hollow Men":

> Between the idea
> And the reality
> Between the motion
> And the act
> Falls the Shadow

This is the darkest umbral image of the Holy Spirit, a vision of destructive power from which the mind recoils in horror.[15] Eliot's later description of Ferdinand and the Cardinal in Webster's *Duchess of Malfy* defines both the tension and the shared metaphysics of the poem: they are men "divided between irresistible passions and unescapable nightmares, forced to act wickedly and yet in terror of damnation."[16]

When Eliot returned to London from Périgueux and southern France on 31 August 1919, Vivien wrote in her diary: "Tom came home. . . . Very nice at first, depressed in evening" (Bodleian). In the next few months the "heap of broken images" that had been in accumulation since 1910 began to coalesce under the intensity of those moments in Marlow and Périgueux. On 5 November he wrote to his mother that when he completed an essay "Ben Jonson," where he argues that the major artist must have the "third dimension," that the surface objects must have "a network of tentacular roots reaching down to the deepest terrors and desires" (*SE* 155), he hoped to get started on "a poem that I have in mind" (*L1* 344), and on 18 December he told her that his New Year's resolution was "to write a long poem I have had on my mind for a long time" (*L1* 351). As he moved toward the composition of *The Waste Land,* his mental stress increased, and before the poem was published he wrote to John Quinn that when he became too tired or worried he recognized "all the old symptoms ready to appear, with half a chance, and find myself under the continuous strain of trying to suppress a vague but intensely acute horror and apprehension" (*L1* 573).

As he dealt with his own horrors he turned again to those of Dostoyevsky, who had made a profound impression on him while he was writing "Prufrock," analyzing Dostoyevsky's techniques for portraying the mind *in extremis*: "Dostoyevsky's point of departure is always a human brain in a human environment and the 'aura' is simply the continuation of the quotidian experience of the brain into seldom explored extremities of torture. Because most people are too unconscious of their own suffering to suffer much, this continuation appears fantastic."[17] His controlled use of epilepsy and hysteria, Eliot declared, is part of his genius as a writer, his gift "for utilizing his weaknesses; so that epilepsy and hysteria cease to be the defects of an individual and become—as a fundamental weakness can, given the ability to face it and study it—the entrance to a genuine and personal universe."[18] It remained for Eliot to describe in Baudelaire the essential world of good and evil in which genuine ecstasy and horror reside. Baudelaire, a "deformed Dante" whose revolting portrait of the *hypocrite lecteur's* human soul informs the "Unreal" phantasmagoria of *The Waste Land*, had become Eliot's modern spiritual leader: "More than any poet of his time, Baudelaire was aware of what most mattered: the problem of good and evil."[19] Out of the experience of the visionary and phantasmal planes comes a recognition of the reality of good and evil, a reality that informs the sensibilities (and the "moral interest") of Hawthorne and James, Baudelaire and Dostoyevsky. It does not inform the sensibilities of Shaw, or Anatole France, or Thomas Hardy, believed Eliot, and consequently the horrific and the phantasmal in their works fail to throb "with the agony of spiritual life."[20] Isolated from a world of good and evil, horror exists merely as "atmosphere."

Marking his essays with signposts back to the disturbed workshop, Eliot gathered from his masters the horrific moments for *The Waste Land*, where the paralyzed memory of ecstasy is overwhelmed by voices of desire fraught with horror. In the original epigraph from Conrad ("somewhat elucidative," he argued with Pound over its cancellation) he included the emotional source of Kurtz's horrific cry—the moment, in the face of death, in which he relives his life "in every detail of desire, temptation, and surrender" and perceives the eternality of damnation. Throughout the drafts he incorporated one horrific vision after another, as in "Elegy," where, alluding to Poe's "Ligeia," he "saw sepulchral gates flung wide / Reveal (as in a tale by Poe) / The features of the injured bride!" and where God's "flames of ~~horror~~ . . . desire . . . Approach me with consuming heat" (*WLF* 117).[21] The original focus of "Death by Water" was the fisherman's vision of the three seductive sirens who sang "A song that charmed my senses, while I was / Frightened beyond fear, horrified past horror" (*WLF* 59), but many such visions were canceled, not at Pound's insistence but through Eliot's own determination to keep the emotion of the poem "coldly independent of the author, of the audience, there and forever like Shakespeare's and Aeschylus's emotions."[22] In the finished poem we experience the cold intensity of that horror beyond horror in part through the mounting allusive moments, from that of Kurtz to that of Ugolino, who awakens in the Tower of Hunger to discover that his innocent sons are being sealed into the place forever: "and down below I heard them nailing up the door of the horrible tower."[23]

The mental state that these and other maddened allusions effect in the poem is further reflected in the critical writings that followed its publication. He wrote in the introduction to Valéry's *Le Serpent* (1924) that he found in Valéry's *La Pythie* not a philosophy but "a poetic statement of a definite and unique state of the soul dispossessed."[24] And he was so deeply moved by Una Ellis-Fermor's study of Marlowe's Faustus, in whom he saw his own mental extremity, that he quoted her analysis at length in his review and incorporated the passage into "Shakespeare and the Stoicism of Seneca" (1927). It struck at the heart of his poem:

> Faustus becomes a sentient nucleus of nerves at the mercy of that terror which leaves him only the power to suffer and exclaim against his suffering. The mind, upon the verge of dissolution, is given over to pure fear, absorbed by the inexpressible horror of the doom before it. A strange spiritual alchemy is at work; the soul itself disintegrates under our eyes. Marlowe follows Faustus further across the borderline between consciousness and dissolution than do any of his contemporaries. . . . He penetrates deeply into the experience of a mind isolated from the past, absorbed in the realization of its own destruction.[25]

Marlowe, Eliot wrote in admiration of Ellis-Fermor's analysis, could not only "conceive the proud hero, as Tamburlaine, but also the hero who has reached that point of horror at which even pride is abandoned" (*SE* 133).

"What is *The Waste Land* about?" asked E. M. Forster in an early and neglected discussion, "T. S. Eliot and His Difficulties" (1929). "It is a poem of horror. . . . And the horror is so intense that the poet has an inhibition and is unable to state it openly."[26] Forster's distinctions about horrific experience serve to illuminate Eliot's own discussions about the heroes of horror:

> In respect to the horror that they find in life, men can be divided into three classes. In the first class are those who have not suffered often or acutely; in the second, those [including Dostoyevsky and Blake] who have escaped through horror into a further vision; in the third, those who continue to suffer. . . . Mr. Eliot, their equal in sensitiveness, distinct from them in fate, belongs to the third.

After *The Waste Land*, Eliot turned to a study of horror in Seneca's tragedies (soon choosing for the epigraph of "Marina" that terrible moment in the *Hercules Furens* when Hercules awakens to the realization that in his madness he has slain his wife and children). Eliot holds that the extent to which Seneca is responsible for the horrors that disfigure Elizabethan drama is overestimated, arguing, on the one hand, that though the reader may not like the horrors he cannot "wholly deplore anything which brings information about the soul," and on the other, that "the genius of no other race could have manipulated the tragedy of horror into the magnificent farce of Marlowe, or the magnificent nightmare of Webster." Though Seneca may have given them license, the Elizabethan taste for horror is a "phenomenon of interest" because it is inherent in the people and the age. What is of import is that Eliot holds two of his familiar tragedies of horror—those of Dante's Ugolino and Sophocles' Oedipus—as a "moral measure" against the general tragedy of the Elizabethan age. In these two tragedies, he argues, "in the end, the mind seems to triumph" (*SE* 79). That is, using Forster's distinction, they complete what is in effect a tragedy of the soul and move through horror into a further vision. And though Eliot's early protagonists are arrested in a hell of suffering, there is hope of vision in that suffering. "I am Arnold, who weeps and goes singing," Eliot translates in "Dante" (1929), from canto 26 in the *Purgatorio* where the lustful are purged in flame. "I see in thought all the past folly. And I see with joy the day for which I hope, before me" (*SE* 256). This central passage on Arnaut Daniel, where ecstasy is anticipated through suffering, provides not only the original epigraph of "Prufrock" but the titles for *Ara Vos Prec* and "Som de l'escalina" and the final lines for "Exequy" and *The Waste Land*. Like Arnaut, Eliot's suffering personae move through the horrid, the sordid, and the disgusting, but there is never a "decadent" or Hardyesque interest in extreme emotion for its own sake. There is never, as Eliot says of Charles Williams's horror stories, "an exploitation of the supernatural for the sake of an immediate shudder."[27]

Eliot continued his study of horror through the 1930s, often reexamining authors from earlier discussions and enlarging the panoply of masters. He came to admit that Cyril Tourneur's "place as a great poet" resides in *The Revenger's Tragedy*, "in which a horror of life, singular in his own or any age, finds exactly the right words and the right rhythms" (*SE* 192). In *The Changeling* Thomas Middleton wrote "one tragedy which more than any play except those of Shakespeare has a profound and permanent moral value and horror" (*SE* 170), and in *'Tis Pity She's a Whore* Eliot finds John Ford, at the moment of Annabella's avowed incestuous love, "double-stressing the horror, which from that moment he will never allow you to forget; but if he did not stress the horror he would be the more culpable" (*SE* 197). Like Chapman, Dostoyevsky, and Dante, they are capable of living on several planes at once: "the essential advantage for a poet," Eliot wrote apropos of Arnold's comment on Burns, "is not, to have a beautiful world with which to deal: it is to be able to see beneath both beauty and ugliness; to see the boredom, and the horror, and the glory" (*UPUC* 106).[28] To Eliot, these authors are always in a world of good and evil, and their aim and achievement is to keep the different planes of reality intersecting, finding voices for each. To Eliot, this is where Hardy falls short as an artist. "I do not object to horror," he wrote in *After Strange Gods* (1934), turning with irony to Hardy's use of horror in *Barbara of the House of Grebe*:

> *Œdipus Rex* is a most horrible plot from which the last drop of horror is extracted by the dramatist; and among Hardy's contemporaries, Conrad's *Heart of Darkness* and James's *Turn of the Screw* are tales of horror. But there is horror in the real world; and in these works of Sophocles, Conrad and James we are in a world of Good and Evil. In *Barbara of the House of Grebe* we are introduced into a world of pure Evil. The tale would seem to have been written solely to provide a satisfaction for some morbid emotion. (*ASG* 57–8)

Hawthorne and James, like Conrad and Dostoyevsky, may be indifferent to religious dogma, Eliot said in his 1933 Harvard course on contemporary English literature, but their works reveal an "exceptional awareness of spiritual reality," a "profound sensitiveness to good and evil," and an extraordinary power to convey horror (Houghton). When they present evil, one shudders in what Eliot calls "genuine aesthetic horror" (*SE* 79). As Eliot wrote to Paul Elmer More on 2 June 1930, not even religious belief brings release from spiritual terror:

> To me religion has brought at least the perception of something above morals, and therefore extremely terrifying; it has brought me not happiness but a sense of something above happiness and therefore more terrifying than ordinary pain and misery; the very dark night and the desert. To me, the phrase "to be damned for the glory of God" is sense and not paradox; I had far rather walk, as I do, in daily terror of eternity, than feel that this was only a children's game in which all the contestants would get equally worthless prizes in the end. And I don't know whether this is to be labelled "Classicism" or "Romanticism": I only think that I have got hold of the tip of the tail of something quite real, more real than morals or than sweetness and light and culture. (Harries 142)

In his experience and study of "inexpressible horror," Eliot had come to believe in the 1930s that tragedy was not only an impermanent intellectual abstraction but inadequate as a form for much horrific experience. He wrote in "From Dryden to Coleridge" (1934): "For to those who have experienced the full horror of life, tragedy is still inadequate. Sophocles felt more of it than he could express, when he wrote *Oedipus the King*; Shakespeare, when he wrote *Hamlet*. . . . In the end, horror and laughter may be one—only when horror and laughter have become as horrible and laughable as they can be."[29] It seems that *Sweeney Agonistes*, departing in the first epigraph from the moment when Orestes describes the Furies, was an early, if unsuccessful, attempt to fuse horror and laughter and break the limits of horrific expression, at least for "a small number of the audience" (*UPUC* 153). Jacob Isaacs recalls that when the play was produced by the Group Theatre,

> Mr. Eliot, it seems to me, was trying to see whether tragic feelings could be expressed, not through the obvious medium of tragedy, but through the medium of farce. The performance, which I remember very well, and which I believe somewhat puzzled Mr. Eliot, while preserving the farce, completely blurred the tragedy which is perfectly clear in the text.[30]

Lost in the farce was a world of desire and action where Sweeney is certain of but one reality beyond "Birth, and copulation, and death"—a spiritual terror—its onset described by the comic chorus as the hoo-ha's: "You've had a cream of a nightmare dream and you've got the hoo-ha's coming to you." Only divestment of desire, Eliot implies through the second epigraph from St. John of the Cross, can lead one from the horror of the hoo-ha's to the ecstasy of divine union. Eliot's later plays, for whatever external tragic action they lack, also attempt to dramatize the internal lives of those who live in desperation on the edge of horror, tormented by the involuntary persistence of "lusts and luxuries" and a sense of depravity that cannot be transcended. "You can't understand me," says Harry:

> It's not being alone
> That is the horror—to be alone with the horror.
> What matters is the filthiness. I can clean my skin,
> Purify my life, void my mind,
> But always the filthiness, that lies a little deeper . . . (*CPP* 327)

For thirty years the thrust of Eliot's criticism had been to redefine the drama of the soul—the dispossessed protagonist, in a world of good and evil, desire and action, moving through horror and suffering toward beatitude—but in the early 1940s, as the preoccupation with horror subsided, he wrote in "The Duchess of Malfy," in disillusionment with the moral decadence of a mechanistic world: "In a world without meaning there can still be horror, but not tragedy"—not in a world where right and wrong, and the soul and its destiny, are no longer the most important things.[31] In his own life, however, the intersection of the timeless and the horrific moment had come. In the "white light" of this "new world," as he describes it in *Burnt Norton*, the nature of the old world is made explicit, "under-stood / In the completion of its partial ecstasy, / The resolution of its partial hor-ror." With this completion and resolution, the memory—no longer mixed with desire and horror—releases the past visionary moments that now sustain the poet in "the waste sad time / Stretching before and after." In his new world, so close and so far from the old, Eliot's horrible darkness, like Harry's, had become his divine light, his furies his "bright angels."

FIRST-RATE BLASPHEMY

I fight thee, in the Holy Name!
Yet, what thou dost, is what God saith:
Tempter! Should I escape thy flame,
Thou wilt have helped my soul from Death:

W hen T. S. Eliot first discovered Baudelaire and the Symbolists in 1907–8, he found assurance that in French symbolist poetry there existed a truly "modern" poetic language and that there were similar unexplored possibilities of language and imagery in English poetry. The aesthetic presence of Baudelaire is evident throughout Eliot's early poetry, but when he returned to a fuller study of Baudelaire's poetry and prose in 1919 his interest had clearly shifted to the moral and spiritual plane.[1] Underlying the Baudelairean imagery and allusions in *The Waste Land* is Eliot's deeper and more pervasive interest in Baudelaire as a waste-land "saint," as the first desert father of the reaction against romanticism, and in the early 1920s Baudelaire succeeded even Dante as the central figure through whom Eliot defined the spiritual difficulties and moral responsibilities of the modern poet.

Of greater consequence than the early poetic influence of Baudelaire on Eliot is Eliot's subsequent *use* of Baudelaire in developing his theory for the moral valuation of literature. In his reengagement with Baudelaire's sensibility from 1919 to 1935, Eliot labored to define in Baudelaire and his "decadent" followers the manifestation of a morbid spiritual condition that he saw as characteristic of the most profound religious quests in modern literature. He eventually delimited the moral center of his theory not, as traditionally supposed, in the "heresy" of Blake and the "orthodoxy" of Dante, but in his absorbing interest in the "blasphemy" of Baudelaire. In the process of redefining modern blasphemy as his pivotal concept, he made concerted attempts to find a coherent terminology capable of accurately reflecting his moral presuppositions and attitudes. But both the intent and the chronology of his resultant Christian idiom have been misunderstood, if not abused. Eliot further made important distinctions between moral and aesthetic criticism and between "religious" and other forms of imaginative literature, but most of these distinctions have been lost to critical discussion. Consequently, while Eliot's audience has generally adhered to the principles of his aesthetic criticism, since the 1930s it has largely looked unapologetically upon the moral criticism as an anachronistic dead end. This chapter, through a focus on Eliot's gradual articulation of Baudelairean blasphemy, seeks to bring critical coherence to the systematic development of Eliot's elusive moral theory.

Eliot's initial discovery of Baudelaire coincided with the beginning of his long philosophical inquiry into the nature of the Absolute. After 1908, in an attempt to escape the "dissolvent" scepticism that had grown out of his Unitarian background, Eliot explored and abandoned the metaphysics of modern philosophers from Bergson to Bradley before turning, in 1916, to the postulates of T. E. Hulme. As we have seen, Hulme's "religious attitude," which sees man's nature as imperfect, limited, and endowed with Original Sin, became the metaphysical basis for the formulation of Eliot's broad classical point of view. Through Hulme's Pascalian theory of discontinuity, which asserts absolute "gaps" between vital phenomena and religious values, and which makes unnecessary any reconciliation between science and religion, Eliot found a way of freeing his spiritual impulses from the paralyzing forces of scientific rationalism. But for years thereafter Eliot's journey toward "The awful daring of a moment's surrender" was constantly impeded by doubt, despair, dispossession. To Eliot, so thin was the line between scepticism and faith that he eventually saw the collective demons of doubt as "inseparable" from the spirit of modern belief, which he believed to have been in constant mutation since the Renaissance and which he began to redefine in relation to the corrosive forces of his own age.

In 1916 Eliot also began the struggle to reconcile scepticism in the intellectual and artistic world with the moralist role he had already begun to ascribe to the poet-critic. And yet as he structured his intellectual conservatism on what was to him the "fact" of Original Sin and sought intellectual allies to support an anti-romantic revolution of ideas in politics, religion, and literature, he found that of the Hulmean humanists who maintained the necessity of the religious attitude, most were sceptics similarly engaged in the struggle with mechanism. This struggle, as Hulme described it, "stands in the way of any idealist or religious interpretation of the universe" and "is a necessary stage through which all the saints must and should pass" (*CWTEH* 143). With these modern saints, many of whom could not themselves cross over the threshold of belief, Eliot had great sympathy, and because of the intensity of their spiritual struggles he afforded them high positions in his "absolute" literary-spiritual hierarchy.[2] To these sceptical Christian humanists, in his view, the tentative concepts of orthodoxy and heresy, as he redefined them between 1916 and 1927, did not aptly apply. They were not heretics, nor were they orthodox. They were "first-rate" blasphemers.

I

Preliminary to a discussion of Eliot's description of Baudelaire and modern blasphemy a clarification is needed of the misleading attitudes that have developed toward the intent of Eliot's moral criticism. Too many of Eliot's critics still see his notorious employment of the terms "orthodoxy" and "heresy" in *After Strange Gods* (1934) as the unwarrantable transformation of dogmatic religious beliefs into criteria for literary judgment following his so-called lapse into religion in 1927. But in fact Eliot had been experimenting with the terms for eighteen years in an attempt to find a more precise critical terminology to displace the vagueness and imprecision of "romantic" and "classical," terms that inadequately expressed the absolute moral assumptions underlying his critical attitude. He quite probably got the ecclesiastical terminology from Hulme, who in January 1916 had defined the Rousseauistic "humanist attitude," which sees man as fundamentally good and capable of infinite perfectibility, as "a heresy, a mistaken adoption of false conceptions" (*CWTEH* 450).[3] Hulme's association of orthodoxy and heresy with the religious and humanist attitudes and with the philosophical, political, and literary ramifications of each is precisely the sense behind Eliot's adoption of the terms,[4] the rationale for which he later explained in *After Strange Gods*:

> The concepts of *romantic* and *classic* are both more limited in scope and less definite in meaning. Accordingly they do not carry with them the implication of absolute value which those who have defended one against the other would give them: it is only in particular contexts that they can be contrasted in this way, and there are always values more important than any that either of these terms can adequately represent. (*ASG* 30)

Eliot first employed the terms "orthodoxy" and "heresy" in a review in July 1916 of Clement Webb's *Group Theories of Religion and Religion of the Individual*, writing that this work "represents the resistance of the orthodoxy, the brains, and the scholarship of Oxford to a new heresy in religion."[5] Eliot's primary critical focus in his early reviews was on the religious or humanist sensibility underlying or informing a writer's work, and Charles Gardner's *William Blake the Man* (1919) gave him an opportunity to portray Blake's sensibility in the *Athenaeum* in February 1920.[6] As he had made no prior theoretical explanations or critical distinctions for his preferred terms, Eliot cautiously chose to label Blake's sensibility "eccentric" rather than heretical, a caution he exercised for seven years. In 1920 he also began to discourage further critical use of "romantic" and "classic," primarily because of the cross-purpose arguments to which these diffusive terms inevitably led, suggesting that "it would perhaps be beneficial if we employed both terms as little as possible, if we even forgot these terms altogether, and looked steadily for the intelligence and sensibility which each work of art contains."[7] In his early essays and reviews Eliot was looking for what he later called "orthodoxy of sensibility," that is, a Hulmean view of life based on a tragic, religious attitude and a sense of objective, absolute moral values. In April 1920 Eliot established Dante, with his "saner attitude toward the mystery of life," as his initial model of orthodoxy, and in *The Sacred Wood* (1920) he placed the essay on Dante in juxtaposition to the essay on Blake, who, to Eliot, "did not see enough," and "became too much occupied with ideas," ideas about "supernatural territories" that "illustrate the crankiness, the eccentricity, which frequently affects writers outside of the Latin traditions" (*SW* 132–3). In "Blake" and in his earlier essay on Yeats entitled "A Foreign Mind" (1919),[8] the eccentricity, or heresy, grows out of the poet's apparent ignorance or denial of humanity's imperfect nature and soul, an ignorance or denial resulting from a combination of the delusive philosophical "climate" of the post-Enlightenment age and what Eliot calls, after Paul Elmer More, "the demon of the absolute . . . the spirit of heresy in all things."[9]

The demon of the Absolute is the embodiment of the natural human tendency to shrink before a too harsh dualism of flesh and spirit. The resultant "demonic possession" of the self by the self leads the poet, in pride and isolation, to assume the role of God *manqué*, to exaggerate the value or truth of the personal insights, visions, and philosophy with which he fabricates a morally relative universe dislocated from the realities of existence. "Romanticism," Eliot had written in his 1916 syllabus, "stands for *excess* in any direction. It splits up into two directions: escape from the world of fact, and devotion to brute fact" (see p. 27) To Eliot, it is not that the visions themselves of Blake and Yeats are too remote from the world, but that they base their visions on the supposed divinity of the imagination. In 1919 Eliot further defined romanticism as "a short cut to the strangeness without the reality," a short cut that "leads its disciples only back upon themselves" (*SW* 26). And in "A Foreign Mind," implicitly using Hulme's "religious attitude" as the basis of reality, Eliot characterized the "dream" of Yeats as "a qualification or continuation of himself. . . . His remoteness is not an escape from the world, for he is innocent of any world to escape from. . . . His mind is, in fact, extreme in egoism." To dramatize the deceptive heretical nature of Yeats's egoism, Eliot drew from Edward Gibbon the analogue of the fifth-century group of heretical philosophers who held that the visible Jesus, the son of God, was a "phantasm" who assumed the shape of man:

> He was not really incarnate, but divinely deceived the world; and controversy foamed about the question whether such a doctrine did not impeach divinity with the sin of lying. Mr. Yeats might be such a fantastic avatar; supported by adepts and narthekophorei, controversy might rage again about the question whether Mr. Yeats really feels and thinks, or whether the deception, if it is the case, is derogatory to his divinity. As with the fantastic God, we do not see his thought or his feeling grow out of human experience.

What these early review-essays show is that from 1916 the charge of heresy is based on an author's romantic self-consciousness and on his self-redemptive view of life, not on his departure from religious belief and dogma. But while Eliot deplored the "remoteness" of Blake and the early Yeats, his moral criticism was nearly always accompanied and tempered by praise of the aesthetic qualities of their work—of the "verbal beauty" of Yeats, "who is always the artist," of the "genius and inspiration" of Blake, whose work cannot be ignored "as poetry." This is also true of his later criticism of Lawrence, who was both the most "gifted" and perceptive of his contemporaries and "an almost perfect example of the heretic" (*ASG* 38). Eliot seldom criticized from a moral standpoint authors for whose artistic ability he did not hold a large measure of respect, but his dichotomy between aesthetic and moral criticism goes unrecognized by those critics who, unprepared for the sudden shifts from one plane to the other, attack the allegedly inconsistent, contradictory nature of his critical judgments. But one of Eliot's discussants in "A Dialogue on Dramatic Poetry" (1928) affirms:

> You can never draw the line between aesthetic criticism and moral and social criticism; you cannot draw a line between criticism and metaphysics; you start with literary criticism, and however rigorous an aesthete you may be, you are over the frontier into something else sooner or later. The best you can do is to accept these conditions and know what you are doing when you do it. And, on the other hand, you must know how and when to retrace your steps. You must be very nimble. I may begin by moral criticism of Shakespeare and pass over into aesthetic criticism, or vice versa. (*SE* 55)[10]

Thus, Eliot's concept of heresy, which was clearly intact from the outset of his critical career, did not affect his capacity for aesthetic judgment, even though his criticism became increasingly weighted toward moral observations. The intent was not to restrict the imaginative possibilities of art or to prescribe dogmas as touchstones in order to ensure the moral "safety" of art; the intent was, following Hulme, to dissociate and isolate "the part of them in which they resemble all the great poets, and the part in which they differ and which gives them their character as romantics" (*CWTEH* 65).

II

Even as Eliot established Dante as his personal orthodox ideal he realized that Dante was too remote for emulation and could not be separated from the lost, disintegrated culture that had formerly provided for a unity of thought and feeling. By 1920, certainly by the publication of "Dante as a 'Spiritual Leader,' " Eliot had immersed himself in Baudelaire, who quickly became for Eliot the modern counterpart to Dante and enabled him to accommodate his moral criticism to the difficulty of belief in an increasingly fragmented world. In the spiritual anguish of Baudelaire, whose reputation as a satanist ironically still prevailed, Eliot discovered the nineteenth-century antipode to romantic heresy, and in Baudelaire's denunciation of the ideas of progress and humanitarianism in the *Journaux Intimes* he rediscovered a "lesson" he had already learned. As he stated in his first essay on Baudelaire in 1921, "All first-rate poetry is occupied with morality: this is the lesson of Baudelaire."[11] Deeply concerned with the problem of good and evil, Baudelaire, like Hulme and Eliot, had also perceived that "La vraie civilisation n'est pas dans le gaz, ni dans la vapeur, ni dans les tables tournantes. Elle est dans la diminution des traces du péché originel." The concept of Original Sin is the necessary foundation for a consistent, coherent structure of objective moral values. In contrast, says Eliot,

> Romanticism endeavoured to form another morals—Rousseau, Byron, Goethe, Poe were moralists. But they have not sufficient coherence; not only was the foundation of Rousseau rotten, his structure was chaotic and inconsistent. Baudelaire, a deformed Dante . . . aimed, with more intellect *plus* intensity to arrive at a point of view toward good and evil.

Eliot's recognition of the anti-romantic, essentially Christian attitude underlying Baudelaire's frustrated spiritual struggles gave new impetus and direction to the conceptual development of his moral criticism, and in the following months Baudelaire was at the center of Eliot's critical and creative preoccupations. In "Andrew Marvell" (March 1921) Baudelaire appears as "the inventor of an attitude, a system of feeling or of morals" (*SE* 292), and in "The Metaphysical Poets" (October 1921) Baudelaire and Racine are identified as "the greatest two psychologists, the most curious explorers of the human soul" (*SE* 290). When Eliot returned to *The Waste Land* in November 1921 he approached it through Baudelaire's "Fourmillante cité, cité pleine de rêves," but it was Baudelaire's real moral world within the "Unreal" poetic world that most interested Eliot, and it was primarily as moralist that Baudelaire was to figure in Eliot's future criticism. As Eliot was to remark in his review of Peter Quennell's *Baudelaire and the Symbolists* (1930), "any adequate criticism of Baudelaire must inevitably lead the critic outside of *literary* criticism. . . . [He] is not merely, or in my opinion even primarily the *artist*; and if I compared him with anyone in his own century . . . I should place him with men who are important first because they are human prototypes of new experience, and only second because they are poets" (*Cr* 4: 358).

In Eliot's early sense of the terms, Baudelaire's sensibility was not heretical but orthodox, though the inerasable associations of the latter term made its critical use undesirable; consequently, Eliot began to give it both an historical and a religious dimension and used it reservedly, usually in relation to Dante, though occasionally "orthodox" appears when "orthodoxy of sensibility" is meant.[12] When in the mid-1920s Baudelaire reappeared in Eliot's criticism, it was not as an orthodox but as a "metaphysical" poet, a more flexible term that Eliot defined outside its limited seventeenth-century context to reflect, in part, the orthodoxy of sensibility in poets from Dante to the present. His first definitions emerged in "Note sur Mallarmé et Poe" (1926), published only in French and written during the composition of his Clark Lectures on the nature of metaphysical poetry.[13] In essence, the visionary or hallucinative poetry of the metaphysical poets, who have "la passion de speculation métaphysique," is anchored in a tragic sense of reality; they do not, Eliot explains, jump abruptly into a vague, nebulous dream world or expect its base to descend from the heights like Jacob's ladder: "c'est le monde réel qui est par eux agrandi et continué." To be admitted to the worlds of Rimbaud or Blake, says Eliot, one must patiently submit to a complete reorganization of his sense of reality, whereas with Donne, Mallarmé, Poe, and Baudelaire "nous sommes dans un monde où tout le matériel, toutes les données, nous sont parfaitement familières; seulement par chacun de ces poètes notre sensibilité est prolongée."[14] Whatever philosophical system they use, in which they may or may not believe, the individual moral world that they create is "un monde qui comprend le développement de la passion humaine la plus grave."

Though the experiment with the term "metaphysical" was temporary, it fostered further critical distinctions that were crucial to Eliot's moral criticism. Eliot realized that his initial definition of metaphysical poetry was too broad, focused as it was on the reassociation of thought and feeling, for metaphysical poets with orthodoxy of sensibility are concerned with different spheres of value. Poets such as Donne, Mallarmé, and Poe are primarily concerned not, like Dante and Lucretius, with the truth of the philosophical systems they use in their poetry but with their value in exploring the relation between ideas and emotions. In his third Clark Lecture, Eliot distinguished these two modes of metaphysical poetry: "There are . . . essentially two ways in which poetry can add to human experience. One is by perceiving and recording accurately the world—of both sense and feeling—as given at any moment; the other by extending the frontiers of this world" (*VMP* 95). Poets of the worldly or temporal mode (he names Homer, Catullus, Chaucer) are "non-religious" in the sense that they are primarily concerned with human emotions, feelings, and objects, with ideas in themselves, with expanding the human sensibility and the reality of the visible, created world, whereas poets who explore a "wider and loftier world" are "religious" in the sense that they are also concerned with perceiving and exploring the absolute values of a higher spiritual reality, with expanding the human soul. Among the poets who have proceeded to this latter expansion of reality, says Eliot, "I place Dante first absolutely, and Baudelaire first in recent times" (*VMP* 95).

Poetry of the worldly mode is generally outside the periphery of Eliot's moral criticism, while poetry of the religious mode, which includes Blake and Lawrence as well as Dante and Baudelaire, constitutes its central concern. Many poets participate to some extent in both modes, but when they do they must successfully fuse them, and the critic must be able to see when there is merely a confusion. It is the "impure" poetry of confusion, between what Hulme called things human and things divine, that receives the moral focus of Eliot's criticism. However, it is important to see that the moral theory, based on orthodoxy of sensibility, is constructed to recognize, on the one hand, the imaginative importance of those worldly poets who, in their explorations of the real world and in their hallucinative dream worlds, seek permanent human values in personal and impersonal experience, and on the other hand to praise the religious significance of those sceptical and "blasphemous" poets, such as Baudelaire, who solitarily seek absolute religious values beyond the flux of human experience. To further clarify his definition of a religious poet, in 1930 Eliot made a "convenient distinction" between "religious" and "devotional" poets: "I call 'religious' what is inspired by religious feeling of some kind; and 'devotional' which is directly about some subject connected with revealed religion. The latter term is, therefore, the most restricted."[15] And in "Religion and Literature" (1935), Eliot distinguished further between the "general" religious awareness of poets such as Dante and Baudelaire and the more "limited" awareness of Christian devotional poets such as Vaughan and Southwell, who

> are not great religious poets in the sense in which Dante, or Corneille, or Racine, even in those of their plays which do not touch upon Christian themes, are great Christian religious poets. Or even in the sense in which Villon and Baudelaire, with all their imperfections and delinquencies, are Christian poets. (*SE* 391)

In Eliot's criticism, the traditional ideas of orthodox and devotional literature are secondary to literature infused with intense religious feeling and awareness, however frustrated and diseased the experience and vision might be. The appropriate term for that condition, "first-rate blasphemy," was in the making.

III

In "The Mysticism of Blake" (1927), a review of six books by or about Blake, Eliot finally labeled Blake a heretic in print.[16] Blake's commentators, Eliot observed,

> have told us that Blake was completely alone, and that he was deficient in humility, or exceeding in pride. Now Isolation is not conducive to correct thinking; and Pride (or lack of Humility) is, we know, one of the chief theological sins. Blake is philosophically an autodidact amateur; theologically, a heretic.

When Richard Aldington, his interest sparked by the review, wrote to offer his own comments on Blake, Eliot replied: "In re philosophy—anyway I agree and applaud everything you say about Wm Blake. Blake is a chapter in the History of Heresy (my great unwritten work in 15 vols. 4to)."[17] Eliot was already applying the principles of the unwritten history in his reviews, beginning with a trio of "heresiarchs," Machiavelli, Montaigne, and Hobbes:

> It is characteristic of all these men that their ideas are often right and sometimes profound; but that they are always one-sided and imperfect. Hobbes, like Machiavelli and Montaigne, did not invent errors; he merely forced certain ideas as far as they can be made to go; his great weakness was lack of balance.[18]

He then moved on to another unbalanced figure of the Renaissance, Descartes, whose sixth Meditation he had already characterized in his Clark Lectures as the sort of "crude and stupid piece of reasoning . . . which gave rise to the whole of the pseudo-science of epistemology which has haunted the nightmares of the last three hundred years" (*VMP* 81). There Eliot had argued that Cartesian dualism "marks the real abyss between classic scholastic philosophy and all philosophy since," that it signals the shift from ontology to psychology, from a classical interest in Being to a new romantic self-consciousness : "Instead of ideas as meanings, as references to an outside world, you have suddenly a new world coming into existence, inside your own mind and therefore by the usual implication inside your own head. Mankind suddenly retires inside its several skulls" (*VMP* 80).[19] Descartes, Eliot now argued in his review of Jacques Maritain's *Three Reformers* (1928), "remains the great typical figure of modern 'heresy' in the generalized sense of that word":

> Whatever the aberrations of individual philosophers of the Middle Ages . . . still the Greek philosophy of Plato and Aristotle had maintained its influence towards balanced wisdom, had prevented human thought from flying to peripheral extremes. In the simple, lucid and persuasive writings of Descartes the various elements are, so to speak, released from each other, so that you need only to press one aspect of his philosophy or another to produce the extremes of materialism and idealism, rationalism and blind faith.[20]

Strongly aware of the nature of heresy and the dissociative forces of rationalism since the Renaissance, Eliot struggled to define a modern *sensibility* that reflected his own difficult spiritual struggle, his own blasphemous poetry.[21] On 3 August 1929, over two years after his conversion, Eliot wrote to his friend Paul Elmer More:

> What I should like to see is the creation of a new type of intellectual, combining the intellectual and the devotional—a new species which cannot be created hurriedly. I don't like either the purely intellectual Christian or the purely emotional Christian—both forms of snobism [*sic*]. The co-ordination of thought and feeling—without either debauchery or repression—seems to me what is needed. Most critics appear to think that my catholicism is merely an escape or an evasion, certainly a defeat. I acknowledge the difficulty of a positive Christianity nowadays; and I can only say the dangers pointed out, and my own weaknesses, have been apparent to me long before my critics noticed them.[22]

Between 1927 and 1934, parallel with his gradual employment of heresy and orthodoxy, Eliot began to redefine yet another theological term, first by asserting the "feeble" nature of blasphemy in the modern world. In his review of Charles Homer Haskins's *Renaissance of the Twelfth Century* (1927), Eliot was intrigued by Haskins's account of the "irreligious or sacrilegious" lyrics of the goliardic poets. "No one," Eliot says of Haskins in his chapter on Latin poetry,

> has more clearly, in a few pages, exposed the twelfth century anomaly—and yet the essential congruity—of the finest religious verse and the most brilliant blasphemous verse. To the present generation of versifiers, so deficient in devotion, and so feeble in blasphemy, the twelfth century might offer an edifying subject of study.[23]

For the next seven years Eliot studied and experimented with the term, finally declaring in "Personality and Demonic Possession," delivered at the University of Virginia in 1933: "I think that there is an interesting subject of investigation, for the student of traditions, in the history of Blasphemy, and the anomalous position of that term in the modern world."[24] As he reinterpreted the meaning of blasphemy, he incorporated it into his Christian idiom as a new critical concept for describing those sceptical writers who are at once primarily orthodox in sensibility and, in a Christian sense, partially heretical or blasphemous in thought but whose moral imaginations significantly reflect the darkest spiritual realities of the intellectual soul in search of God. Just as modern heresy is a present romantic reality in Eliot's criticism, traditional orthodoxy is a lost classical ideal, and few, if any, of the European and American authors who receive Eliot's critical attention, with the exception of Dante, are orthodox in the Christian sense of the term. Because of the "unfavorable environment" for belief, Eliot did not believe that perfect orthodoxy was possible or even desirable at the present time. "It is a very different thing," he states, "to be a classical author in a classical age, and to maintain classical ideals in a romantic age" (ASG 34–5), and in the present age an author cannot be orthodox except in sensibility and "in tendency." And at the same time, says Eliot, blasphemy "is a very different thing in the modern world from what it would be in an 'age of faith'" (ASG 52). For the renewal and continuance of the "Latin traditions" in the present and in "the dark ages before us," Eliot ironically turns to those authors who are capable of "first-rate blasphemy, which is one of the rarest things in literature, for it requires both literary genius and profound faith, joined in a mind in a peculiar and unusual state of spiritual sickness" (ASG 52).

Eliot first employs the term in "Shakespeare and the Stoicism of Seneca" (1927), in which he compares Marlowe's "mature" attitude toward the hero with that of his contemporaries, whose Elizabethan individualism was fused with a stoical attitude that Eliot sees as antithetical to Marlowe's implicit Christian sense of humility. In the essay, Eliot describes Marlowe as "the most thoughtful, the most blasphemous (and therefore, probably, the most Christian) of his contemporaries" (SE 133). Eliot's paradoxical association of "the most blasphemous" with "the most Christian" stems from Marlowe's maintenance of a religious attitude in that "period of dissolution and chaos . . . [when] any emotional attitude which seems to give a man something firm, even if it be only the attitude of 'I am myself alone', is eagerly taken up" (SE 132). In such an unfavorable period, says Eliot, a religious attitude is extremely rare and important, and blasphemy, rather than being a sign of doubt, is a sign of spiritual life. As one of Eliot's discussants states in "A Dialogue on Dramatic Poetry," "The attitude of Restoration drama towards morality is like the attitude of the Blasphemer towards Religion. It is only the irreligious who are shocked by blasphemy. Blasphemy is a sign of Faith. Imagine Mr. Shaw blaspheming! He could not" (SE 45). Eliot would fully expand the concept in After Strange Gods:

> One can conceive of blasphemy as doing moral harm to feeble or perverse souls; at the same time one must recognise that the modern environment is so

unfavorable to faith that it produces fewer and fewer individuals capable of being injured by blasphemy. One would expect, therefore, that (whatever it may have been at other times) blasphemy would be less employed by the Forces of Evil than at any other time in the last two thousand years. Where blasphemy might once have been a sign of spiritual corruption, it might now be taken as a symptom that the soul is still alive, or even that it is recovering animation: for the perception of Good and Evil—whatever choice we make—is the first requisite of spiritual life. We should do well, therefore, to look elsewhere than to the blasphemer, in the traditional sense, for the most fruitful operations of the Evil Spirit today. (*ASG* 52–3)

As Eliot looked to the heretics for the intrusion of the "demonic" into modern literature, he looked to the blasphemers for the infusion of the religious dimension, and as Lawrence, "un démoniaque, un démoniaque simple et naturel muni d'un évangile,"[25] became his perfect example of the heretic, Baudelaire became his perfect example of the blasphemer.

In 1922 Eliot had called Baudelaire "a deformed Dante," but in spite of his limitations and imperfections Baudelaire is the only poet likened to Dante in Eliot's criticism. Though Eliot considers Baudelaire a lesser poet than Dante, the essential disparities are the effects of a different time and place rather than of sensibility. The Christian system of thought that was "complet et conscient" for Dante had become "fragmentaire ou simple objet de recherche" for Baudelaire,[26] but though Baudelaire's culture had distorted his vision it had not deluded his mind. In spite of the preoccupations of his romantic age, "an age of . . . scientific progress, humanitarianism and revolutions which improved nothing, an age of progressive degradation" (*SE* 427), Baudelaire renovated and struggled to maintain a religious attitude toward absolute value, good and evil, sin and redemption. And in Eliot's second essay on Baudelaire, originally entitled "Poet and Saint . . ." (1927), Eliot sees beneath the satanic phantasmagoria an incessant though unsuccessful struggle for spiritual life, and he defends Baudelaire's "profound attitude toward life," his preoccupation with religious values, his sense of sin and suffering, and the sense of humility that came from "looking into the Shadow"(*FLA* 90). To Eliot, Baudelaire is not only a personal guide but a "saint" of his time:

> The important fact about Baudelaire is that he was essentially a Christian, born out of his due time, and a classicist, born out of his due time. In . . . his sensibility, he is near to Dante and not without sympathy with Tertullian. But Baudelaire was not an aesthetic or a political Christian; his tendency to "ritual" . . . springs from no attachment to the outward forms of Christianity, but from the instincts of a soul that was *naturaliter* Christian. And being the kind of Christian that he was, born when he was, he had to discover Christianity for himself. In this pursuit he was alone in the solitude which is only known to saints. To him the notion of Original Sin came spontaneously, and the need for prayer. . . . And Baudelaire came to attain the greatest, the most difficult, of the Christian virtues, the virtue of humility. (*FLA* 97–9)

Moreover, in his poetry Baudelaire was, like Dante, constantly striving to depersonalize and sublimate human emotions and passions: "no man was ever less the dupe of passions than Baudelaire; he was engaged in an attempt to explain, to justify, to make something of them, an enterprise which puts him almost on a level with the author of the 'Vita Nuova' " (FLA 90). Baudelaire's orthodoxy of sensibility and his capacity for depersonalization and sublimation govern his explorations of the human soul and guide them toward a significant expansion of reality. In these important regards Baudelaire is the most nearly orthodox poet the romantic age has to offer. The material of his poetry is spiritual suffering and beautitude, but as Eliot states in "Baudelaire" (1930), his soul was capable only of suffering, and in his inability to transcend this suffering Baudelaire, like Marlowe's Faustus, turned to a morbid study of his soul, and in this he was "wholly unlike Dante." Baudelaire's suffering leads to a deformed, "dim" and "wishy-washy" notion of beatitude, but it nonetheless "implies the possibility of a positive state of beatitude" (SE 423). To keep his descriptions of the spiritual affinity between the two poets in perspective, Eliot continually delineates the relativity of that affinity; hence, in many important respects, such as in the relations of man and woman and in the difficult task of adjusting "the bestial to the human and the human to the supernatural, Baudelaire is a bungler compared with Dante" (SE 428). He is orthodox only in sensibility because there remains a great deal of romantic detritus in his ideas. In his inability to sufficiently remove much of his work from its origins in "Byronic Paternity and Satanic Fraternity," he manifests an imperfect, vague, and romantic conception of the good and of Love. "The complement," says Eliot,

> and the correction to the Journaux Intimes, so far as they deal with the relations
> of man and woman, is the Vita Nuova, and the Divine Comedy. But—I cannot
> assert it too strongly—Baudelaire's view of life, such as it is, is objectively appre-
> hensible, that is to say, his idiosyncrasies can partly explain his view of life, but
> they cannot explain it away. And this view of life is one which has grandeur and
> which exhibits heroism; it was an evangel to his time and to ours. (SE 430)

With his recovery of the "historical sense" and "the religious comprehension," Baudelaire began "the insurgence of something which can hardly be called classicism, but which may decently be called Counter-Romanticism" (Cr 4: 357). But though he was far in advance of the point of view of his time he "was very much of it, very largely partook of its limited merits, faults and fashions. . . . He was universal, and at the same time confined by a fashion which he himself did most to create" (SE 419). To Eliot, the fashions of Baudelaire were the inevitable tendencies of a classical poet in a romantic age: "Inevitably the offspring of romanticism, and by his nature the first counter-romantic, he could, like anyone else, only work with the materials which were there" (SE 424). The fashionable material was blasphemous diabolism, but, Eliot explains, Baudelaire was concerned "not with demons, black masses, and romantic blasphemy, but with the real problem of good and evil. It is hardly more than an accident of time that he uses the current imagery and vocabulary of blasphemy" (SE 378). Baudelaire did indulge in some of the more satanic and occult forms of decadent Catholicism, but underneath the "romantic blasphemy," which was mostly a pose in reaction to bourgeois morality, is the "genuine" blasphemer:

> When Baudelaire's Satanism is dissociated from its less creditable paraphernalia, it amounts to a dim intuition of a part, but a very important part, of Christianity. . . . Genuine blasphemy, genuine in spirit and not purely verbal, is the product of partial belief, and is as impossible to the complete atheist as to the perfect Christian. It is a way of affirming belief. This state of partial belief is manifest throughout the *Journaux Intimes*. What is significant about Baudelaire is his theological innocence. He is discovering Christianity for himself. . . . He is beginning, in a way, at the beginning; and, being a discoverer, is not altogether certain what he is exploring and to what it leads; he might almost be said to be making again, as one man, the effort of scores of generations. . . . His business was not to practise Christianity, but—what was much more important for his time—to assert its *necessity*. (SE 421-2)

Baudelaire's "state of partial belief" is an important variety of belief in the modern world. To Eliot, as to Baudelaire,

> the recognition of the reality of Sin is a New Life; and the possibility of damnation is so immense a relief in a world of electoral reform, plebiscites, sex reform and dress reform, that damnation itself is an immediate form of salvation—of salvation from the ennui of modern life, because it at last gives some significance to living. (SE 427)

Though the protean forms of mechanism and romanticism frustrate their quests and misshape their visions, the blasphemers unconsciously keep Christian humanism and tradition alive in a heterodox and humanitarian age.

The historical matrix out of which Eliot redefined his concept of modern blasphemy is located in the spiritual malaise and morbidness that had spread over symbolist and decadent writers in late-nineteenth-century France and England. Even prior to 1916, when he taught a course dealing with the Catholic literary revival in France, Eliot had been absorbed by the recurrence of the blasphemous impulse in the works of numerous French and English authors.[27] With Baudelaire as the father of them all, this unique religious phenomenon occurs as a pre-conversion experience that manifests itself widely in the works of such authors as Léon Bloy, Villiers de l'Isle Adam, Barbey d'Aurevilly, J. K. Huysmans, Oscar Wilde, Lionel Johnson, Francis Thompson, Ernest Dowson, and a host of others, most of whom eventually converted or returned to the Catholic church. In the works of many of these authors, there is a general pattern underlying their spiritual autobiographies. Out of disgust with materialism and conventional religious values, their sensibilities fall into a rebellion that often takes the form of occultism, satanism, and "romantic blasphemy." Then, out of a desire to extend the boundaries of emotional and religious experience, they begin an aesthetic and spiritual escape into the self. The delight in perverse and artificial sensations is followed by an introspective religious quest that leads ultimately to morbid psychological explorations of the self and soul. The resultant "spiritual sickness" is characterized by disillusionment and a hopeless sense of abandonment and separation from grace. It leads to a sadistic, blasphemous impulse, which Des Esseintes effectively describes in Huysmans's À *Rebours* (1884): "This strange and ill-defined condition cannot in fact arise in the mind of an unbeliever. It . . . consists first and foremost in a sacrilegious manifestation, in a moral rebellion, in a spiritual debauch, in a wholly idealistic, wholly Christian aberration."[28] Following the realization that the religion of art and the self is incapable of providing answers to the ultimate problems of existence, there begins a turning outward from the self until the blasphemy is supplanted by a cry for faith. "Lord, take pity on the Christian who doubts," cries Des Esseintes at the close of the novel, "on the unbeliever who would fain believe, on the galley-slave of life who puts out to sea alone, in the night, beneath a firmament no longer lit by the consoling beacon fires of the ancient hope!"

The pattern is not always completed. As Eliot states in "Spleen" (1910), many are arrested "On the doorstep of the Absolute" (*CPP* 603), but the reflection of the state of mind in the art is recognizable as a stage in the progress of the soul. For the modern poet-saint, the blasphemy, the acedia, the paralysis, the anguish, the despair, and the doubt are a necessary prelude to modern belief. It is then, as the penitent begins the journey out of the self toward faith, that he begins the struggle with mechanism, rationalism, and the demon of the Absolute. It is this stage that marks the beginning of the spiritual struggle in *Ash-Wednesday*.

When Eliot's concepts of orthodoxy, heresy, and blasphemy are removed from their general theological associations, as Eliot intended, they may be used to distinguish more precisely among the artists from Dante to Blake to Baudelaire in his literary-spiritual hierarchy. The most valuable term is blasphemy, for it prevents certain unorthodox classical writers from being automatically, falsely identified with the romantics, the heretics. Moreover, blasphemy focuses on their spiritual struggle and moral awareness without confusing them with orthodox belief and doctrine, places their quest in a historical and traditional perspective, distinguishes them from "worldly" or nonreligious poets, and sets them above Christian devotional poets in terms of their greater religious awareness. With their moral interest and sense of good and evil, numerous authors besides Baudelaire and his immediate followers are most accurately seen and elevated as valuable blasphemers in Eliot's critical prose. The essential strain common to both Hawthorne and James, says Eliot, was "their indifference to religious dogma at the same time as their exceptional awareness of spiritual reality," their "profound sensitiveness to good and evil," and their extraordinary power to convey horror.[29] Included are Dostoyevsky and Conrad, who, with their "essential moral preoccupation," had unusual perceptions of "Evil," which "cannot even be perceived but by a few."[30] Eliot sees James Joyce, whose blasphemous mind is "penetrated with Christian feeling," as "the most ethically orthodox of the more eminent writers of my time" (*ASG* 38). As Eliot wrote to More, shortly after that volume appeared, "It is quite possible that I overestimate Joyce . . . or use him as a stick to bat the others with. . . . And if I condemned him, it would not be *with* Lawrence and Hardy, but in quite another *giro*" (Princeton).[31] Though Baudelaire is chief among the poets who exhibit "first-rate blasphemy," Eliot's broad concept of the term embraces all those modern poets who are "essentially" Christian.[32] Whatever their attitudes toward the "outward forms" of Christianity—ritual, dogma, doctrine, orthodox belief—their profound though "sick" spiritual awareness gives significant expression to the major passions and scepticism of every man as they attempt to realize absolute values in a doubt-ridden world.

IV

In his obscenity trial of 1857 Baudelaire was acquitted of blasphemy by a French court; ironically, he stands approvingly accused in Eliot's criticism, for in the modern world blasphemy becomes a substitute for and ultimately a step toward orthodoxy.[33] In the early 1930s, with his concepts and models clearly formulated and identified—an historical orthodoxy (Dante), modern blasphemy (Baudelaire), modern heresy (Blake, Lawrence), and a more broadly used "orthodoxy of sensibility" (Dante, Baudelaire, Mallarmé, Poe)—Eliot was ready to publicly initiate a long-hinted-at critical system that could make clear and viable distinctions among the moral worlds of Dante, Baudelaire, and Blake, as against the purely (or impurely) imaginative worlds of Mallarmé and Poe. In the preface to *For Lancelot Andrewes* (1928), Eliot announced the preparation of a volume entitled *The Principles of Modern Heresy,* though it never appeared, and in "Experiment in Criticism" (1929), which describes the difficulty of using terms such as "metaphysical," "classicism," and "romanticism," he had called for an "experiment in criticism of a new kind, which will consist largely in a logical and dialectical study of the terms used. My own interest in these problems has been fostered partly by dissatisfaction with the meaning of my own statements in criticism, and partly by dissatisfaction with the terminology of the Humanists."[34] When Eliot finally presented the terms in his Page-Barbour Lectures at the University of Virginia in 1933, the surrounding conditions were disastrous. In these three brief lectures Eliot assumed "the role of moralist" to try to convert to his critical principles those who have "never . . . applied moral principles to literature quite explicitly" (*ASG* 12–13). Though orthodoxy, heresy, and blasphemy as critical concepts are clearly discernible in the lectures, they were discussed in a cultural-religious context that was misleading to his critical audience. Further, the Page-Barbour Foundation required that the lectures be published as originally delivered and not as part of a subsequently expanded book on the same subject. Eliot knew that the lectures needed qualification and expansion; he wrote about them to More on 7 November 1933:

> Again, an unsatisfactory piece of work. A good subject, I think: fundamentally a criticism of the lack of moral criteria—at bottom of course religious criteria— in the criticism of modern literature. But the treatment is very sketchy, and I cannot do anything satisfactory to myself in the time. . . . I hope that the

book will not let me in for a great deal of controversy—not merely that Hardy is condemned—or that Lawrence appears as a *suppôt de Satan*—but that on a fundamental matter like this I seem to take up an isolated position, and dissociate myself from most of my contemporaries, including Yeats, Richards, Read. (Princeton)

In his apologetic preface, Eliot asks the reader's patience

when he finds that some ideas are put forward without a full account of their history or of their activities, and that others are set down in an absolute way without qualifications. I am aware that my assertion of the obsolescence of Blasphemy might thus be subject to stricture: but if I had developed the refinements and limitations that present themselves to the mind of the Christian enquirer, I should have needed at least the space of one whole lecture; and what I was concerned to do was merely to explain that the charge of blasphemy was *not* one of those that I wished to prefer against modern literature. (*ASG* 12)

Nonetheless, most of his potential converts defected, regretful that he had made "no greater progress in Christianity than to advance from witch-hunting to heresy-hunting."[35] In dismay, Eliot had the volume placed permanently out of print, and his eighteen-year experiment came abruptly to an end.

After 1934 the principles of Eliot's moral criticism continued to pervade several essays, but in "Religion and Literature" (1935) Eliot reaffirmed his long-held critical proposition for essentially the last time: "Literary criticism should be completed by criticism from a definite ethical and theological standpoint" (*SE* 343); however, the arduously defined terms had been dropped.[36] As the moral criticism gradually gave way to dramatic interests and cultural criticism, the prominence of Baudelaire, who had served Eliot not only as a modern Dante and model of modern blasphemy but as the spiritual pilgrim through whom he objectified and defined the nature of his own spiritual struggles, gradually began to diminish. As I will show, by the mid-1930s Eliot would begin to look back upon the aesthetic and moral arguments of "Classicism vs. Romanticism" as an abandoned struggle of "literary politics," and his interest in the saintly blasphemy of Baudelaire would shift to the achieved spiritual wisdom of George Herbert, who, with Baudelaire and others, would become a vital element of Eliot's "familiar compound ghost."

Eliot's moral criticism must no longer be seen as a post-conversion indulgence in the application of Anglo-Catholic religious beliefs to literature. Between 1916 and 1934 Eliot made the first sustained attempt in English literature to construct a logical, dialectical, and categorical critical *system* for the moral valuation of "truth" and "greatness" in literature, qualities which, as he says, "cannot be determined solely by literary standards; though we must remember that whether it is literature or not can be determined only by literary standards" (*SE* 388).[37] Admittedly, Eliot often talked more as a Christian than as a critic and occasionally subordinated his impersonal critical principles to his personal religious feelings, especially in the numerous essays and addresses that were directed to specifically Christian audiences, but his critical system was nonetheless objective in theory. Moral criticism of right and wrong visions of life inevitably encounters opposition and repudiation, especially when, in a romantic and relativist age, that criticism is countercultural and absolutist, but though Eliot's critical audience has generally failed to comprehend the nature of his abandoned experiment, it is time to look back upon the high seriousness of that experiment with a new disinterest.

"ALL ABOARD FOR NATCHEZ, CAIRO AND ST. LOUIS"

The Journey of the Exile in *Ash-Wednesday*

The second Death, that never dies,
That cannot die, when time is dead:
Live Death, wherein the last soul cries,
Eternally uncomforted.

How odd that a conductor's final call for a rail journey to St. Louis should have provided the original title for the early drafts of "Perch' io non spero," the opening section of *Ash-Wednesday* (1930).[1] Eliot had recently delighted in hearing this familiar call of his youth on an immensely popular phonograph record of 1927, "The Two Black Crows," by the American blackface vaudeville team known as Moran and Mack.[2] "Their phonograph records sell prodigiously," reported the *New Republic* in March 1928, "their first disc being more popular, it is claimed, than any other ever made. They are quoted more freely than any other personages today. Everywhere one hears people making foolish attempts to imitate Mr. Mack, pathetic efforts to recapture the mood of serenity into which his voice and manner had insinuated them."[3] Eliot owned their first disc and likely attended a performance during their sensationally successful, fourteen-week run in London in 1927. He certainly became one of their imitators, foisting Moran's rendition of the conductor's call on his London friends. "What struck us," wrote I. A. Richards, in describing Eliot's formal demeanor, dress, and conduct at the time, was that they "went along with delighted and highly critical immersion in records of 'The Two Black Crows', especially of a record involving 'All aboard for St. Louis.' I don't know how often we were patiently taught how to say this right. I do know very well that I have never got it right."[4]

For all the lighthearted mimicry among friends, there was a personal somberness in Eliot's private inscription of the boarding call on his manuscript:

"Ballata: All Aboard for Natchez, Cairo and St. Louis," below which he penned "Perch' io non spero," the opening utterance of Cavalcanti's own "Ballata: *In Exile at Sarzana*":

> Because I think not ever to return,
>   Ballad, to Tuscany,—
>   Go therefore thou for me
>   Straight to my lady's face,
>   Who, of her noble grace,
>   Shall show thee courtesy.[5]

At the beginning of his poem, Eliot identifies deeply with the exiled poet who, grieving in his heart and conscious of approaching death, commends his soul to his ballad, bidding it speak "Of my dead mind" unto that distant lady

> Who is so calm and bright
> It shall be deep delight
> To feel her presence there.
> And thou, Soul, worship her
> Still in her purity.

Turning and truncating Cavalcanti's phrase—"Because I do not hope to turn again,"—Eliot, in his own emotional and spiritual exile in London, abandons all hope of returning to his own Tuscany and to the lady held in memory there. His modern ballata, *Ash-Wednesday*, makes the journey in his place, recounting the anguish of a soul whose love poem laments the impossibility of a merely human love.

It comes as no surprise that Eliot alludes to the poetry of his fellow exiles, Cavalcanti and Dante, in starting his ballata, for the thrust of his 1926 Clark Lectures on the varieties of metaphysical poetry had been to show the distinct relation of human and divine love in the poetry of Dante and the *trecentisti* in contrast to the confused relations of succeeding poets and periods, when not only a dissociation of sensibility but a "disintegration of the intellect" had set in. The effort of Dante and his contemporaries, Eliot had argued, "was to enlarge the boundary of human love so as to make it a stage in the progress of the divine" (*VMP 166*). The primary epigraph for his lectures was taken from the *Vita Nuova*, section 18, that affecting scene in which one of a number of noble ladies, in pity for Dante's unrequited love of Beatrice, asks him to what end does he love his lady, to which he replies: "Ladies, the end and aim of my Love was but the salutation of that lady of whom I conceive that we are speaking; wherein alone I found that beatitude which is the goal of desire." Eliot then concluded his third lecture, "Donne and the *Trecento*," by quoting the passage as an example of a higher, more worthy form of love than one finds in Donne's "Extasie." Dante's expression of love for Beatrice, Eliot holds, is "the contemplation of absolute beauty and goodness partially revealed through a limited though delightful human object" (*VMP* 114).[6] Eliot actually inaugurated his poetic sequence with a Dantean poem published separately as "Salutation" (later to become part 2), focusing initially on his own beloved "Lady," whose goodness and loveliness and honor of the Virgin make all who view her "shine with brightness." Eliot's adoration, like Dante's, was to become a stage in his struggle to move beyond desire toward a perception of beatitude.

Eliot was thus steeped in the love poetry of the *trecentisti*, particularly in the *Vita Nuova*, as he began *Ash-Wednesday*, and certain essays concomitant to the developing poem serve to gloss his absorption of Dante's method into his own. Following the publication of "Salutation" and "Perch' io non spero," Eliot reviewed *The New Beatrice* by Gretia Baldwin (1928), criticizing the author for denying the presence of the personal in the allegory of the *Vita Nuova* and arguing that "with Dante there is always a foundation of personal human feeling":

> What Miss Baldwin, like many interpreters of the 'Vita Nuova' does not seem
> to allow is that it may be both personal and allegorical; to some readers, at least,
> the peculiar intensity of the document is due to just this union which commentators are anxious to deny. . . . Though the form of the 'Vita Nuova' be
> shaped by convention, though it is in no way autobiographical in the modern
> sense, the book is obviously based on human passion; and without this basis it
> would have been merely a curiosity of literature, not an immortal work.[7]

In his essay "Dante" (1929), written concurrently with the composition of the poem, Eliot affirmed his belief that the *Vita Nuova* "could only have been written around a personal experience" (*SE* 273), subsequently writing to More about the essay: "My only contribution is possibly a few hints about the Vita Nuova, which seems to me a work of capital importance for the discipline of the emotions; and my last short poem 'Ash Wednesday' is really a first attempt at a sketchy application of the philosophy of the Vita Nuova to modern life" (Harries 141).

It is thus unfortunate that *Ash-Wednesday* is so often presented merely as Eliot's "conversion poem," when it is in fact an extraordinary love poem of great personal intensity and spiritual discipline. It forms a crucial nexus in Eliot's poetry: it draws upon the paralysis of will in "Prufrock" and "Gerontion," upon the admixture of memory and desire in *The Waste Land*, upon the dream-crossed twilight of "The Hollow Men"; it looks toward the white light of *Burnt Norton* and the meaningful prayer of *Little Gidding*. The six parts constitute a complex stylistic moment in a continuous spiritual journey, and yet, after almost seventy years of reading and explicating, critics still leave it in exasperation.[8] Eliot was himself exasperated by the initial critical responses to the poem, writing to his friend and confessor William Force Stead: "Some damned fool of a Cambridge paper referred to it as devotional poetry, which rather misses the point" (Yale). It is neither a devotional poem nor a poem of conversion; it represents the beginning of an exile's arduous lenten journey from a life of tormented human love toward the prayerful hope of finding, like Dante, a *vita nuova* in divine Love. Shortly after the poem appeared, Eliot wrote to Stead of

> a theory I have nourished for a long time, that between the usual subjects of
> poetry and "devotional" verse there is a very important field still very unex-

plored by modern poets—the experience of man in search of God, and trying to explain to himself his intenser human feelings in terms of the divine goal. I have tried to do something of that in "Ash-Wednesday." (Yale)

Readers who encounter *Ash-Wednesday* in any edition of Eliot's *Collected Poems* are not aware that in its first printing the poem was dedicated "To My Wife" (not *"For* My Wife"). It was a puzzling gesture, especially in light of his emotional and moral estrangement from her, stemming from the sexual betrayal with Bertrand Russell over a decade earlier. A permanent separation was on the horizon. Complicating the dedication was Eliot's recent renewal, concurrent with his conversion, of his relationship with his first love, Emily Hale, who was to become, as Lyndall Gordon forcefully argues, imaginatively transfigured into the Lady of *Ash-Wednesday*. Though Gordon sees the dedication as "a placatory gesture, no more, for the poem looks away from her towards a promised land" (*TSE* 294), part of the poem is addressed to his wife, particularly part I, even if it was not "for" her. Though some critics still resist any attempt to relate the personal and the poetic in Eliot's poetry, the more we understand about his paradoxical theory of impersonality the more we know that with Eliot, as with Dante, "there is always a foundation of personal human feeling" in the poetry, and that the critic's job of work, following Eliot's own critical practice, is to resurrect the depersonalized voice in the poem, to reconnect "the man who suffers and the mind which creates" (*SE* 18), to measure the pressure of the life on the poem. The accumulation of biographical and bibliographical facts finally enables us to bring the poem down from a high level of spiritual abstraction, and from an impersonal, overly intellectualized explication of allusions, to a comprehension of the personal emotions and memories that are deeply seated in the poem.

Eliot once again models his exiled persona partly on the purgatorial figure of Arnaut Daniel, the Provençal poet pointed out to Dante and Virgil by Guido Guinicelli from among his lustful companions in *Purgatorio* 26. In his essay "Dante," Eliot asserted that the souls in purgatory "deliberately and consciously" accept the torment of purgative flame: "The souls in purgatory suffer because they *wish to suffer*, for purgation. . . . In their suffering is hope." To underscore the assertion, Eliot quotes and translates the "superb verses" of Arnaut:

"Ieu sui Arnaut, que plor e vau cantan;
   consiros vei la passada folor,
   e vei jausen lo jorn, qu' esper, denan.
Ara vos prec, per aquella valor
   que vos guida al som de l'escalina,
   sovegna vos a temps de ma dolor."
POI S' ASCOSE NEL FOCO CHE GLI AFFINA.

"I am Arnold, who weeps and goes singing. I see in thought all the past folly. And I see with joy the day for which I hope, before me. And so I pray you, by that Virtue which leads you to the topmost of the stair—be mindful in due time of my pain." Then dived he back into that fire which refines them.
(*SE* 256)

So defining is this passage for the purgatorial journey of the exile in *Ash-Wednesday* that in an early draft (King's) Eliot not only named two parts of the poem from it (part 2, "Jausen Lo Jorn", retitled from "Salutation"; part 3, "Som De L'Escalina") but worked and enjambed other phrases into the poetic narrative (part 4, "Sovegna vos la passada folor," now "Sovegna vos"; "Poi s' ascose nel foco and / After this our exile," concluding lines, Dante's now deleted). Part 4 was itself entitled "Vestita Di Color Di Fiamma," from that succeeding moment in *Purgatorio* 30 when Beatrice appears before Dante "in colour of living flame," just as she appeared to him for the first time many years before, described in the opening passages of the *Vita Nuova*. It was in this working draft that Eliot shifted the opening of *Ash-Wednesday* from "Salutation" to "Perch' io non spero," from the persona's response to his Lady's "salutation" to the penitential, first-person voice of Arnaut, the voice closest to his own. In the allusions to Arnaut's suffering and Dante's adoration, Eliot counterpoints the themes of purgation and sublimation before temporarily resolving the tension in part 5, here entitled "La Sua Voluntade," from canto 3 of the *Paradiso*, when Piccarda informs Dante of the nature of blessedness: "la sua volontade è nostra pace" ("Our peace in His will"). At this stage of the poem, a year into composition, the five-part draft was untitled.[9] The five informative section titles were eventually removed, and a full year would pass before Eliot could substantially revise parts 4 and 5 and complete the journey with part 6.

The decision about arrangement, and the eventual title, may have followed Eliot's emotionally unguarded letter earlier in the year to Paul Elmer More—deliberately dated "Shrove Tuesday" (20 February) and evidently the day of Eliot's first confession—a letter in which he observes that those people for whom religion seems unnecessary appear "to be unconscious of any void—the void that I find in the middle of all human happiness and all human relations, and which there is only one thing to fill. I am one whom this sense of void tends to drive towards asceticism or sensuality, and only Christianity helps to reconcile me to life, which is otherwise disgusting" (Harries 141). The following day Eliot would have been anointed and admonished: "Remember man, that thou art ashes, and to ashes thou shalt return." In a state of extreme mortification, he may have determined to situate the developing poem in the symbolism of this day, a day commemorating Christ's forty days in the wilderness, a day when asceticism prevails over sensuality, a day that begins a lenten journey that holds out the faint hope of Easter. On 15 March 1928, three weeks into Lent, Eliot confided to Stead that he had made his first confession, "and feel as if I had crossed a very wide and deep river: whether I get much farther or not, I feel very certain that I shall not cross back, and *that* in itelf gives one a very extraordinary sense of surrender and gain."[10]

I

The somber persona who begins to speak on Ash Wednesday is already in an advanced state of mortification, having wilfully and utterly divested himself of temporal desire. Fully aware of cause and consequence in his accepted condition, he is free from all illusions of human "power" or "glory" or knowledge. What he knows is the severity of his spiritual exile—from the timeless Garden of divine grace into a desert of actual time and place. He has decidedly renounced that which is most desirable to him, the "blessèd face" and "voice" of a Lady. Paradoxically, he has found liberation in deprivation, and joy in suffering, for though he has renounced all hope of trying to turn again to a lost life, he now has the hope of constructing "something" new, "something / Upon which to rejoice," a *vita nuova*. The only thing that obstructs his progress is his memory of an unexpiated past.

Not until the fourth section do we realize that the persona's dramatic monologue is addressed to an *other*—another lady who occupies a persistent place in his painful memory. His inability to repress her image provokes the first prayer of the poem, "to God to have mercy upon us," upon the persona and the obscure object of a failed love, both of whom are complicit in the failure. In his continued prayer, "that I may forget / These matters that with myself I too much discuss / Too much explain," lies the real emotional center of part 1, a complex of guilt, remorse, and contrition over his part in "matters" that have become Prufrockian in their tedious and overwhelming persistence in his mind. But because he can no longer turn or hope to right the wrong, like Cavalcanti in exile he enjoins his ballata to carry his missive of regret and repentance to her:

> Let these words answer
> For what is done, not to be done again
> May the judgement not be too heavy upon us

And so we comprehend, at far remove from the "matters" but close to the emotions of failure, how the poem is initially addressed "To My Wife." She, too, must stand in judgment, but the poet judges only himself in attempting to empty his memory. His compassionate invocation is to be taught how "to care and not to care" at once, and how to "sit still," without expectation. Even the surrounding air is "Smaller and dryer than the will," which must undergo greater dessication and diminution for the penitent to make further spiritual progress. As Arnaut ends his self-revelation with a plea to Dante to pray for his soul, Eliot's persona utters the end of the Salve Regina, imploring the Virgin to pray for "us sinners," who include the two estranged selves among her Son's many transgressors. "Holy Mary Mary Mother of God" he addressed her directly in an early draft (Houghton), "Pray for us now and at the hour of our death." Part 1 thus concludes with this the first of several recurring prayers from liturgical rites and penitential psalms. Still impeded by the memory and the will, the persona, who has revealed the triangle of feminine objects in his consciousness, implicitly retreats into the refining fire.

II

In recent years we have learned much more about the personal matters that underlie and inform *Ash-Wednesday*—Vivien's affair with Bertrand Russell, Eliot's emotional separation from them, and the gradual rekindling of his love for Emily

Hale, initiated no later than September 1923, less than a year after the publication of *The Waste Land,* when he sent her an inscribed copy of another Arnaut-inspired volume of poems, *Ara Vos Prec* (1919).[11] His inscription, written "with the author's humble compliments" and greatly indicative of his unhappiness, is taken from Dante's encounter (*Inferno* 25) with Brunetto Latini, author of *Il Tesoro* (*The Treasure*). When Latini realizes that he has fallen behind his group, he races off to catch them, calling back to Dante in lines that Eliot knew and printed well:

SIETI RACOMMENDATO
IL MIO TESORO
NELLO QUAL VIVO ANCOR
E NON PIU CHIEGGIO
POI SI REVOLSE

"May my 'Tesoro' be entrusted to you, my Tesoro in which I am still living. And I do not ask more than this." Then he turned around . . .

The act of sending such an inscribed book to Emily Hale reveals an old and painful longing to turn again, to revive a dormant love, to extricate himself from a hellish marriage, to return from exile.[12] But that desired love, it seems, had already become highly idealized, and we may have seen evidence of the process in "La Figlia Che Piange," in the girl who "turned away, but with the autumn weather / Compelled my imagination many days," and in the similar figure of the hyacinth girl, in whose presence the persona has a visionary moment, "Looking into the heart of light, the silence." The first hint of Eliot's commitment that any renewed relationship would remain unconsummated appears in the second epigraph to *Sweeney Agonistes,* the unfinished but concluding part of Eliot's Sweeney myth, which, as argued earlier, Eliot develops as a personal myth of sexual betrayal, psychological retribution, and moral regeneration in response to Vivien's and Russell's behavior. The epigraph, as noted earlier, is from St. John of the Cross, *Ascent of Mount Carmel* (book 1, chapter 4): "Hence the soul cannot be possessed of the divine union, until it has divested itself of the love of created beings." When Eliot's friend Bonamy Dobrée, who was "revolted" by the epigraph, wrote to Eliot to tell him that he regarded it "with horror," Eliot replied:

The doctrine that in order to arrive at the love of God one must divest oneself of the love of created beings was thus expressed by St. John of the Cross, you know: i.e. a man who was writing primarily not for you and me, but for people seriously engaged in pursuing the Way of Contemplation. It is only to be read in relation to that Way: i.e. merely to kill one's human affections will get one nowhere, it would be only to become rather more a completely living corpse than most people are. But the doctrine is fundamentally true, I believe. Or to put your belief in your own way, that only through the love of created beings can we approach the love of God, that I believe to be UNTRUE. . . . I don't think that ordinary human affections are capable of leading us to the love of God, but rather that the love of God is capable of informing, intensifying and elevating our human affections, which otherwise have little to distinguish them from the "natural" affections of animals.[13]

By the time Eliot began *Ash-Wednesday* he was a committed follower of St. John and the way of contemplation, a way that necessitates moving through the dark night of sense and desire, and purging the memory and the will, in order to attain the divine union. The poem is in part the personal drama of a soul struggling with desire, memory, and will while pursuing the way, as part 1 has begun to reveal.

In part 2, the exiled persona addresses his Lady, a Beatrice-like figure whose desirous face and voice he has previously renounced. In the earliest, untitled draft of the poem, sent to Stead, and in the first printing of the poem, there were two conjoined epigraphs, the first from Ezekiel, "The hand of the LORD was upon me," the second from *Purgatorio* 24, "e vo significando" ("he dictates within me").[14] The former alludes directly to the Lord's spiritual transportation of the exiled prophet to the valley of dry bones, in verses that provide Eliot with much of the narrative structure, phrasing and imagery of the poem (Ezekiel 37:1–7):

> The hand of the LORD was upon me, and carried me out in the spirit of the LORD, and set me down in the midst of the valley which was full of bones.
>
> And caused me to pass by them round about: and behold there were very many in the open valley; and, lo, they were very dry.
>
> And he said unto me, Son of man, can these bones live? And I answered, O Lord GOD, thou knowest.
>
> Again he said unto me, Prophesy upon these bones, and say unto them, O ye dry bones, hear the word of the LORD.
>
> Thus saith the Lord GOD unto these bones; Behold, I will cause breath to enter into you, and ye shall live:
>
> And I will lay sinews upon you, and will bring up flesh upon you, and cover you with skin, and put breath in you, and ye shall live; and ye shall know that I *am* the LORD.
>
> So I prophesied as I was commanded, and as I prophesied, there was a noise, and behold a shaking, and the bones came together, bone to his bone.

Ezekiel's voice folds into Dante's, heard when Bonagiunta da Lucca asks him if he is the inventor of the "sweet new style" in the *Vita Nuova,* citing the opening line of the canzone in section 19, "Ladies that have intelligence of Love." Dante replies (*Purgatorio* 24, 52–54): "Io mi son un che, quando / amor mi spira, noto, ed a quel modo / che ditta dentro, vo significando" ("I am one who, when Love inspires me take note, and go setting it forth after the fashion he dictates within me").[15] In part 2, Love dictates that the poet sublimate his Lady's love through the first of a series of dream-visions.

At the beginning of part 2, the poet addresses his Lady in the aftermath of a dream-vision, describing for her in his "dissembled" state the organ-devouring leopards, the metaphorical agents of his violent sensual evisceration in the valley of dry bones. And yet, though the senses are removed and the bones are dry, the memory lingers. Seeking only to forget and to be forgotten, he freely proffers his deeds "to oblivion," his love "to the posterity of the desert and the fruit of the gourd." His Lady, no longer an object of physical desire, has become a figure of spiritual purity, one who "honours the Virgin in meditation" and who soon withdraws "In a white gown, to contemplation, in a white gown," guiding him toward a state of beatitude. His plea is for the utter annihilation of memory so that he may follow her, "Thus devoted, concentrated in purpose." As he meditates upon his "Lady of silences," she becomes identified in vision with the Virgin, the beginning of her sublimation. In devotion, his dry bones sing to her from the desert floor a personal litany of her intercessory powers as Rose and Mother of the divine Garden. Eliot initiates the litany through a borrowed line that he elsewhere calls the "pure poetry" of Ecclesiastes, the bones "chirping / With the burden of the grasshopper."[16] He reveres the Lady as his "Rose of memory," his "Rose of forgetfulness," through whom his memory of natural objects may be raised to the supernatural and transformed in divine union. "Grace to the Mother," he wrote in the first printed version, "For the end of remembering / End of forgetting." Through her intercession, the exile in the desert may find entrance to the Garden where not only "all loves end" but "all love ends," the Garden whose opened gates bring the "End of the endless journey to no end / Conclusion of all that / Is inconclusible." In his litany, in his prayer for release and transcendence, the personal dilemma behind the prayer forcibly breaks through the liturgical form as an imperative invocation:

> Terminate torment
> Of love unsatisfied
> The greater torment
> Of love satisfied

At the close of the litany, the bones fall back from their song-prayer, happily "scattered and shining," enjoying "the blessing of sand," and for the first time "Forgetting themselves and each other, united / In the quiet of the desert," waiting for the spirit of God to breathe life into them. In the aftermath of visionary sublimation, a progression has occurred, a blessing has been bestowed, a respite has been granted. In context of Ezekiel's borrowed vision, hope has been restored, for God has shown him that His spirit can make living souls of dry bones and end their exile from Israel: "And shall put my spirit in you, and ye shall live, and I shall place you in your own land" (Ezekiel 37:14). We see now the appropriateness of Eliot's substitute title from Arnaut, "Jausen Lo Jorn," "with joy the day," a muted joy borne of Arnaut's hope in suffering: "And I see with joy the day for which I hope, before me."

On 10 April 1928, two days after Easter and almost a year now after his formal conversion, Eliot wrote to Stead, who was fully apprised of Eliot's personal problems, to tell him of the difficulty of his spiritual journey in relation to his personal life:

> If Easter is a season of hope, it is also a season when one wants to be given hope. . . . I do not expect myself to make great progress at present, only to "keep my soul alive" by prayer and regular devotions. Whether I shall get farther, I do not know. . . . I do not know whether my circumstances excuse my going no farther or not. . . . I feel that nothing could be too ascetic, too violent, for my own needs (Yale).

In March, in the throes of Lent and in evidence of how ascetic he wished to be, Eliot had taken a vow of celibacy.

III

In part 3, Arnaut's vision of a virtuous ascent of the spiritual stair toward divine union "al som de l'escalina" has become displaced by a nightmare struggle on treacherous stairs inhabited by grotesque faces.[17] These include the "deceitful face of hope and of despair" worn by the devil of the stairs, a demon of sensuality whom the penitent sees engaged in violent struggle with the "same shape" of himself. As he leaves them twisting and turning in the "fetid air," the stairs become "dark, / Damp, jagged," and though the faces have disappeared, he uses faces as analogues for the stairs—"an old man's mouth drivelling, beyond repair," and "the toothed gullet of an agèd shark"—stark images of mouths exhausted and ruined by lifetimes of appetency.

The vivid struggles with despair and appetency, however, are not so great as the struggle with memory, especially the persistence of bitter memories that stop the mind in its ascent. On the third stair the penitent suddenly sees "The broad-backed figure," a figure known to him, a figure now in the image of Pan, playing on his "antique flute." He is seen through a window that is "bellied," not only like a fruited fig but like the amorous Pan, who enchants not only the Maytime but a woman, whose "blown hair is sweet, brown hair over the mouth blown, / Lilac and brown hair." His presence again recalls the figure of "Priapus in the shrubbery," Eliot's earlier image of Bertrand Russell, with his "centaur's hoofs" and "pointed ears," in "Mr. Apollinax," even before his seduction of Vivien.[18] Here, Pan's sensual music and his enchanted lady are an utter "Distraction," relentless in the penitent's nightmare of memory. Pan will return with his flute in part 4, but as the faces and music temporarily fade the penitent knows that he must receive intercessory strength, "strength beyond hope and despair," to reach the topmost of the stair. Struggling with despair and desire, and under the heavy weight of memory, it is an exhausting climb. The persona finally takes up the distracting flute as metaphor of his morbid melody, playing in the poem only phrases of the "stops and steps of the mind" on the jagged stairway to Eucharist. Here, on the bottommost of the stairs, his mind dampened and darkened by sensuous images and carnal memories, he can utter and repeat only fragments of the communicant's prayer before receiving the sacred Host: "Lord, I am not worthy that thou shouldst come under my roof; but speak the word only and my soul will be healed." The vivid, deeply disturbing dream, the darkest in the poem, leaves him with an overwhelming sense of humility.

IV

The humbled voice of the persona suddenly becomes audible in a dramatic shift of tone in part 4, where we hear him praising his Lady in the midst of a catalogue of defining clauses that describe her movement and actions, "Who walked between the violet and the violet." She is again portrayed as a Beatrice figure who moves gracefully and speaks graciously among the others, "in Mary's colour." She has appeared before him after a long absence, in a "white light," much as Beatrice appeared before Dante in the Earthly Paradise, "vestita di color di fiamma" (*Purgatorio* 30), which Eliot took as his temporary title. Dante's vision of Beatrice—his spirit after so many years "trembling in her presence," his feeling of "the hidden power that went out from her, the great strength of the old love," his running like a frightened child to his mother to say to Virgil, "I know the tokens of the ancient flame"—this, to Eliot, is one of the most powerful passages, one revealing "the greatest *personal* intensity," in the *Divine Comedy*: "And in the dialogue that follows," says Eliot of Beatrice's chastisement of Dante for the unfulfilled promises of his youth and the unworthiness of his manhood, "we see the passionate conflict of the old feelings with the new; the effort and triumph of a new renunciation, greater than renunciation at the grave, because a renunciation of feelings that persist beyond the grave" (*SE* 263). The meeting of Dante and Beatrice becomes an analogue for his own experience in part 4 of *Ash-Wednesday*, where his persona, in a heightened emotional state, celebrates his Lady's return to him and praises her restorative powers in making a garden of his desert. Overwhelmed by her presence, he suddenly utters in Arnaut's plaintive voice, "Sovegna vos"—"Be mindful"—of the pain, the past folly.

His spirit lifts again, however, to praise her power to cleanse and renew the sordid years between her last and present appearance. "Here are the years that walk between," he exclaims as he envisions a pageant of years headed by Pan, a pageant "bearing / Away the fiddles and the flutes," those instruments of betrayal and misery, restoring "Through a bright cloud of tears" the wasted years, restoring with a new verse Dante's "ancient rhyme." His Lady's imperatives resound, like Beatrice's, to redeem in penitence the lost time and the "unread vision," to move from the lower dream of desire to the "higher dream" of beatitude. As the purged and restored years pass in review before them, the "jeweled unicorns," leading a brilliant cortège in the visionary pageant, carry away in "the gilded hearse" the dead years of his life and memory.

His Lady of silences, the "silent sister," now appears in a garden between the yew trees, and though "the garden god," Pan, stands in front of her, she has made his flute "breathless" at last. There she "bent her head" in recognition of the persona and silently "signed" him, giving him the longed-for "salutation" wherein he knows at last "that beatitude which is the goal of desire" (*VMP* 116). It is the visionary climax of *Ash-Wednesday*. At that moment the garden comes to life; the fountain springs up and the bird sings down to him the resounding imperative of his dream-vision, "Redeem the time, redeem the dream." For the penitent, the dream of the bestowed salutation is taken as "The token of the word unheard," unspoken until the divine spirit shakes from the evergreen yew in the graveyard garden "a thousand whispers" of the dead, the whispered promise of eternal life breaking from the yew's golden tip. Though Dante's description of Arnaut diving back into the refining fire broke through here in the draft, "Poi s'ascose nel foco," the deleted image now defers to the voice of the exile in prayer, uttering to the Virgin a broken fragment of the prayer's concluding cry to her: "And after this our exile show unto us the blessed fruit of thy womb, Jesus."

V

In the aftermath of his token experience of "the word unheard," the persona enters into a meditation on the nature and presence of the divine Word in the "unstilled world." Originally entitled "La Sua Voluntade" and containing much of the last twenty-five lines of part 6, the section was revised to expand the meditation on the silent Word but also to pay further homage to the intercessory power of the silent Lady. As the biblical voice of a compassionate God recurs, "O my people, what have I done unto thee" (Micah 4), the persona now revokes his earlier renunciation of her blessèd face and voice, realizing that there is "No place of grace for those who avoid the face / No time to rejoice for those who walk among noise and deny the voice." The dream-vision of the "veiled sister" between the yew trees returns, the figure of "the garden god" with his flute now vanished. As she again becomes identified in vision with the Virgin, his interrogative invocations implore her to pray for all who walk in darkness, for all the "banished children of Eve" at the garden gate. Finally, he entreats her to affirm before the world the presence of "the garden in the desert" as she ascends, like the mortal Virgin, "spitting from the mouth the withered apple-seed." In the manner and tradition of Dante and the *trecentisti*, the sublimation of love is complete, the renounced face of the "donna e laggiu" (the lady down there) having become the adored face of the "donna e lassu" (the lady up there)—all part of the effort to expand the boundary of human love in the progress toward the divine.

VI

In part 6 we find the persona slowly awakening from his long dream journey into the "dreamcrossed twilight" of the material world, "wavering" once again "between the profit and the loss" that Phlebas before him had forgotten only in death. The exile has dreamed himself to a New England shore, home among the goldenrods and granite again. Looking through "the wide window towards the granite shore" upon white sails and unbroken wings flying seaward, he feels the gradual resurgence of desire and the senses—"(Bless me father)," he says parenthetically and penitentially, not wishing to wish "these things." "Because" the exile did not hope to turn again, he began his spiritual journey; "Although" he does not hope to turn again, he must return to the ordinary world, through the ivory gates, from true dreams to false dreams. While the "lost heart" quickens and rejoices as the emptied senses are filled with the sights and sounds, the smells and tastes of sea, bird, and flower, the "weak spirit quickens to rebel" against the unwanted displacement of supernatural voices and visionary images. The "blind eye," reopening on a world of false dreams, begins to create "empty forms" from the maddened surface of things. The painful descent from the spiritual to the material is "a time of tension," and when the quickened voices shaken from the yew-tree in part 4 begin to drift away, the rebelling spirit demands, "Let the other yew be shaken and reply." As the dream-vision ends in the necessitous acceptance of return to painful personal "matters," the persona makes a final invocation to his beloved intercessor, who is at once "Blessed sister, holy mother, spirit of . . . the garden," reiterating the prayers with which he initiated his journey, prayers uttered in the unbearable torment of a satisfied human love:

> Suffer us not to mock ourselves with falsehood
> Teach us to care and not to care
> Teach us to sit still

On his journey he has been informed, like Dante, "in words," says Eliot, "which even those who know no Dante know: *la sua voluntate è nostra pace*" (*SE* 265), "Our peace in His will." As he sits among the familiar granite rocks, a place of possible grace, he utters to her, his "spirit of the river, spirit of the sea," the cry of the exile: "Suffer me not to be separated." Greatly humbled and in great spiritual exhaustion, the weak spirit turns at last directly to the Lord, completing his broken cry with a fragment of the most plaintive of psalms (102), "And let my cry come unto Thee."

The journey of the exile begins but does not end in *Ash-Wednesday*. In August 1929, when the poem was nearing final form, Eliot wrote to More about the growing criticism of his conversion as an escape and a defeat: "it is rather trying to be supposed to have settled oneself in an easy chair, when one has just begun a long journey afoot."[19] He had only begun to walk and wait in darkness. Later, in *The Family Reunion,* he would have Harry recount to Mary the horror of "That sudden comprehension of the death of hope" and the folly of "The instinct to return to the point of departure / And start again as if nothing had happened" (*CPP* 308). Certainly the hand of John of the Cross and the way of contemplation and detachment were to become crucial to the poet-penitent's journey afoot through the darkness to the divine goal.

When Emily Hale arrived in London to visit Eliot in the summer of 1930, only weeks after the publication of the poem, she could not have known that his love for her had already been expanded beyond desire, that *Ash-Wednesday*, though dedicated to his wife, was in fact a modern *Vita Nuova* for her. With their companionship renewed, with the separation from Vivien pending, with annual meetings before them, it must have seemed, to Emily at least, that he could turn again. She was to be loved, but not to be a lover, or a wife. He could best explain the reality to her in his poetry. "What might have been," he wrote to her in *Burnt Norton*, after their visit there in 1934,

> is an abstraction
> Remaining a perpetual possibility
> Only in a world of speculation.
> What might have been and what has been
> Point to one end, which is always present.
> Footfalls echo in the memory
> Down the passage which we did not take
> Towards the door we never opened
> Into the rose-garden. My words echo
> Thus, in your mind.

It takes all four quartets to conclude *Ash-Wednesday* and end the exile's journey in "the crowned knot of fire." The *Four Quartets*, too, constitute a great love poem, of human love lived beyond desire. They are enriched when read again through *Ash-Wednesday*, a poem of the greatest personal intensity in the search for divine love, a poem worthy of his master's ancient rhyme.

THE IGNATIAN INTERLUDE

Dark Angel, with thine aching lust!
Of two defeats, of two despairs:
Less dread, a change to drifting dust,
Than thine eternity of cares.

Eliot and Ignatius? Most students of Eliot would be at a loss to describe any familiar relationship. Though Eliot found his way to Ignatius through John Donne, there is no mention of Ignatius in Eliot's prose before he wrote his Clark Lectures on metaphysical poetry in 1925–26. He knew from Isaak Walton's *Life* that Donne was brought up an English Catholic under Jesuit influence (two uncles were eminent Jesuits) and that his mother was a recusant until her death. "I had my first breeding and conversation," wrote Donne, "with men of a suppressed and afflicted religion, accustomed to the despite of death and hungry of an imagined martyrdom."[1] Though Eliot began studying Donne in 1906, and writing on him in 1917, he seems not to have explored Donne's Jesuit background or picked up a copy of Ignatius's *Spiritual Exercises* (1548) until he began preparing his Clark Lectures. Eliot knew, of course, that after Donne passed from the Roman to the Anglican church, he attacked the Jesuits generally in *Pseudo-Martyr* (1610) and satirized Ignatius particularly in *Ignatius His Conclave* (1611). In his lectures Eliot was himself a severe critic of Ignatius and the *Spiritual Exercises*, but when a Jesuit in the audience reproved him for his incautious remarks, Eliot was embarrassed into a serious study of the *Exercises*. It was one of the most unsettling checkings in his intellectual life: over the next seven years he would work through a cycle of visions and revisions of Ignatius as a mystic, and he would become absorbed in working out the effect of Ignatius's method on seventeenth-century mysticism, particularly on Donne. In the process he discovered, on the one hand, how deeply Donne was indebted to Ignatius for the structure and imagery of his poems and sermons, and on the other how limited was Donne as a mystic and philosophical poet. Eliot's encounter with Ignatius led him not only to conclude his participation in the classic-romantic controversy but to divorce himself from Donne's sensibility as he prepared himself for the final phase of his poetic career.

In preparing his Clark Lectures, Eliot was more interested in the role of the Society of Jesus in the seventeenth century than in Ignatius himself. His critical attitude toward the Society had been shaped by his extensive reading of Elizabethan literature and by works as far apart as Blaise Pascal's attacks on Jesuit casuistry in *Provincial Letters* (1656–57) and Remy de Gourmont's in *The Velvet Path* (1902). He was sympathetic to biographical and historical studies that emphasized the militaristic, political, and literary aspects of the Society, and he had probably read such highly colored studies as Francis Thompson's *Saint Ignatius Loyola* (1909).[2] As he laid out his lectures in the autumn of 1925 he had already planned to treat the Society's influence in the Counter-Reformation; unexpectly, he found needed authority for his treatment in Mario Praz's *Secentismo e Marinismo in Inghiltera*, which he received for review from the *Times Literary Supplement*. Immediately upon completing the book on 23 November, he wrote to Praz to compliment him and to express his envy that Praz had "forestalled" him on several points, including "your insistence on the importance of the Society of Jesus at that time" (MS VE). In his review, Eliot suggested that "as an Italian" Praz

> is perhaps better fitted than most of our English critics to appreciate the enormous influence during the first half of the seventeenth century of the Society of Jesus. This influence was exerted upon English poetry in two ways: indirectly through the vast quantity of Jesuit poetry and *belles-lettres* then produced—much of which Crashaw, for one, certainly read. The Jesuits of that time were perhaps the most intelligent body of politicians that has ever existed; it speaks ill for the intelligence of later political and religious bodies . . . that no similar attempt to capture the human mind through poetry and *belles-lettres* has ever been made.[3]

Eliot accepted Praz's authority and demonstration of Jesuit literary influence without further investigation; he was to reserve the thrust of his own criticism for the effects of Jesuitism on a change in religion and mysticism, a change that Praz had also observed. "No one is more aware than [Praz]," Eliot wrote in his review,

> of the world of difference between the religion of the seventeenth century and that of the thirteenth. It is the difference between psychology and metaphysics. Here Signor Praz is able to supply what has been a conspicuous defect of English criticism of Donne: a comparison between Donne and the metaphysical poets of the age of Dante. This is a point upon which he touches lightly, and which we wish he might examine in greater detail.

Eliot was of course using the review to set up his own detailed examination of Dante and Donne in the Clark Lectures, where he would also identify Ignatius and the Jesuits with the psychological transformations that took place in the religion and mysticism of the sixteenth and seventeenth centuries.

In his earliest critical reviews Eliot was captivated by the poetic sensibility of Donne, in whose poetry emotion and object "preserve exactly their proper proportions."[4] By 1921 the "unification of sensiblity" evident in Donne had become the chief criterion of Eliot's criticism in "The Metaphysical Poets," where he first described the "dissociation of sensibility" that followed Donne in the seventeenth century. By 1925, however, Eliot's view of Donne's sensibility had radically changed. Following his closer study of the resemblances and differences between Dante and Donne, Eliot changed his theory of dissociation of sensibility after Donne to a theory of "disintegration of intellect" after Dante, implicating Donne in the decline. In his Clark Lectures, Eliot was now to argue that Donne's poetry shows a "tendency towards dissolution" (*VMP* 76), and his untested hypothesis was that "the Jesuits had a great deal to do with it: their fine distinctions and discussions of conduct and casuistry tend in the direction of a certain self-consciousness which had not been conspicuous in the world before" (*VMP* 80). Eliot had become interested in the various forces, particularly in Spanish mysticism of the sixteenth century, that gradually brought about a "diversion," as he called it, "of human inquiry from ontology to psychology" (*VMP* 79). Accordingly, he now saw Donne's mind riven by the medieval "ontologism" of the Calvinists and the Counter-Reformation "psychologism" of the Jesuits. He portrayed Donne as "part Jesuit and part Calvinist" and suggested that "a profound examination of the doctrines of both sects . . . might, if it did not kill the experimentor, throw some light on Donne's mind" (*VMP* 149). Eliot had not yet made that profound examination, but he proceeded to develop his lectures on the premise that under Jesuit influence Donne takes a psychological rather than an ontological attitude toward objects, ideas, and emotions in his poetry.

Eliot proceeds from the observation that behind the poetry of Dante and the *trecento* stands not only the scholastic philosophy of Aquinas but the mysticism of Richard of St. Victor, author of a twelfth-century mystical treatise *De Gratia Contemplationis*, known as the *Benjamin Major*. After illustrating the austere emotional discipline of the the *Benjamin Major*, Eliot sets out to contrast it with the emotional laxity of Ignatius Loyola's *Spiritual Exercises*. To this end he cites "a rare and interesting work," Herrmann Müller's *Les Origines de la Compagnie de Jésus* (Paris: Librairie Fischbacher, 1898), which argues that the *Spiritual Exercises* were in fact based on Mohammedan practices. The study had been ignored in previous histories, except for a dismissive citation in Thomas J. Campbell's massive study *The Jesuits 1534–1921* (1921), where Müller is mentioned for his "entirely novel theory" that the *Exercises* is, as he says, "an amalgam of Islamic gnosticism and militant Catholicism." "Strange to say," remarks Campbell, himself a Jesuit, "Müller feels aggrieved that the Jesuits do not accept this very illogical theory, which he insists has nothing discreditable or dishonoring in it."[5] Eliot, however, was intrigued by the claim, and in supporting it refers to Müller twice as his only authority, clearly aiming to keep in question the spiritual purity of the

Exercises. Though from the outset he praises Ignatius as an "extraordinary" man and saint, he portrays him as a thoroughgoing romantic, "a sort of Don Quixote" (*VMP* 76), arguing that he is as much a psychologist as Descartes, as much a romanticist as Rousseau. To dramatize his point, Eliot read from what he thought was a copy of the *Spiritual Exercises*, but which was instead an inauthentic director's manual based on them. Contrasting Ignatius with Richard of St. Victor, he unknowingly quoted the anonymous director's own, non-Ignatian contemplation on death in *Manresa: Or the Spiritual Exercises of St. Ignatius, for General Use* (1881):

> Contemplate—(1) Your apartment faintly lighted by the last rays of day, or the feeble light of a lamp; your bed which you will never leave except to be laid in your coffin; all the objects which surround you and seem to say, You leave us for ever! (2) The persons who will surround you: your servants, sad and silent; a weeping family, bidding you a last adieu; the minister of religion, praying near you and suggesting pious affections to you. (3) Yourself stretched on a bed of pain, losing by degrees your senses and the free use of your faculties, struggling violently against death, which comes to tear your soul from the body and drag it before the tribunal of God. (4) At your side the devils, who redouble their efforts to destroy you; your good angel, who assists you for the last time with his holy inspirations.[6]

Having reiterated Müller's thesis that the *Exercises* are based on Mohammedan practices, Eliot questions his audience, as he rests his case, "Is this not a spiritual haschisch, a drugging of the emotions, rather than, as with Richard of St. Victor, an intellectual preparation for spiritual contemplation?" (*VMP* 106)

By chance, an American Jesuit was in the audience—Father Francis Joseph Yealey, S.J. (1888–1977), from the St. Stanislaw Seminary in Florissant, Missouri. Father Yealey was writing his doctoral dissertation on Emerson at Christ's College, Cambridge, and attended all of Eliot's lectures. On 13 March 1926, four days after the series concluded, Yealey wrote to Eliot to correct and politely reprove him for the untoward comparison of Ignatius with Richard of St. Victor. Yealey pointed out that Eliot's quotation of "a certain meditation on death" does not occur in the authentic Latin version of the *Spiritual Exercises*. He explained that the exercises were designed to be developed by a spiritual director, who was free to add other meditations without making clear the relation of the additions to the text of Ignatius. "I think you will find," Yealey continued,

> St. Ignatius' own thought as austere and straightforward in its way as that of Richard of St. Victor. May I add that I did not think your comparison especially happy? Richard's treatise on contemplation is analytical and discursive. The Exercises, besides dealing primarily with the different though related business of asceticism, are not a treatise at all but a series of fairly obvious working-principles whose virtue is supposed to lie partly in their arrangement and partly in being assimilated in the most intimate and practical manner possible by personal effort.

> Let me thank you heartily for the great pleasure and stimulation I had from
> your lectures. (MS VE)

Yealey's was an important correction, one that Eliot would eventually note on his
typescript. Moreover, in addition to the admonishment and thanks, Yealey sent
Eliot a copy of *The Text of the Spiritual Exercises* (4th ed. rev.), translated by John
Morris and others from the original Spanish (London: Burns, Oates & Washbourne, 1923). It was a brilliant gift, one that would jolt Eliot into reading and
studying the *Exercises* closely in the coming months. But his present view of Ignatius as being outside the Aristotelian-Victorine-Dantesque tradition surfaced
again a fortnight later in his monthly "Commentary" for the *Criterion* (April
1926), where, responding to a discussion of "the Roman inheritance" and the
continuity of "Authority and Tradition" in western Europe, he writes that the
idea of a common culture based on that inheritance and continuity "is an idea
which comprehends Hooker and Laud as much as (or to some of us more than)
it implies St. Ignatius or Cardinal Newman" (*Cr* 4 222).

Shortly after the completion of his lectures Eliot received for review *The
Book of Robert Southwell* by Christobel M. Hood (1926). Had he received it earlier, he certainly would have included Southwell in his treatment of the baroque
sensibility.[7] Eliot, who appears not to have read Southwell's verse before preparing his lectures, now found it "of great interest" to learn that Southwell
(1562–1595; beatified 1926), a member of a prosperous family in Norfolk, had
been sent as a boy to Douai and then to Paris to be educated by Jesuits, that he
had been admitted to the Society of Jesus in Rome in 1578, that he was sent to
join the English Mission in 1586, that he was arrested and confined in the Tower
in 1592, and that three years later he was hanged as a martyr, "solely as a Jesuit
priest occupied in priestly functions in defiance of the law."[8] In discovering
Southwell's devotional poems, Eliot observes that

> anyone acquainted with Signor Praz's important "Secentismo e Marinismo in
> Inghilterra" is likely to suspect that Southwell had more than a slight knowledge
> of the Italian poetry, and the Jesuit poetry, both Latin and Italian, of his time.
> . . . [A] fuller knowledge of his literary origins would bear testimony to the
> power of a mode of taste then sweeping over Europe, though as yet less notice-
> able in England, which came to be called baroque.

Though Eliot finds the verse to be "never first rate," the "by-product" of a Jesuit
who "is primarily the priest as man of action," he tentatively affords Southwell an
early place in an important movement of sensibility. In Southwell's verse, Eliot
perceives once again

> that fusion or confusion of feeling of human and divine, that transposition of
> human sentiment to divine objects which characterizes the religious verse of
> the sixteenth and seventeenth centuries, in contrast to that of the thirteenth
> century, in which the distinctions of feeling towards human objects and divine
> objects are preserved.

Eliot found the Jesuit-trained English poet to be an intriguing forerunner of metaphysical poetry and declared that "the whole of his verse should be studied by those who are interested in the poetry of the generation which followed his." Eliot planned to revise and enlarge his lectures as a book to be entitled *The School of Donne*, and it was now clear to him not only that he would have to place Southwell before Donne in the historical synthesis but that he would have to reach a fuller understanding of Ignatian meditation.

By summer's end Eliot appears to have read enough of the unadulterated text of *Spiritual Exercises* to temper his earlier views. He certainly had Ignatius on his mind, evidenced in his essay on "Lancelot Andrewes," which appeared in September 1926. There he pays special attention to Andrewes's *Preces Privatae* in Canon F. E. Brightman's edition (1903); Eliot quotes at length from Brightman's "interesting introduction" on the structure of the prayers. In Brightman's "excellent piece of criticism" Eliot finds a hint that Andrewes's prayers "should take for Anglicans a place beside the Exercises of St. Ignatius and the works of St. François de Sales" (*FLA* 22). Brightman does not mention the two saints, but in his elaboration of the "careful structure" and "strict plan" of the *Preces*, and in his characterization of the prayers as "things in which he 'habitually exercises himself day and night,'" Eliot was obviously struck by the Ignatian analogies.[9] His serious study of the *Spiritual Exercises* had also led him to St. François de Sales, the primary interpreter of the *Exercises* and chief commentator on Ignatian spirituality, which greatly informs the spiritual doctrine in the twelve books of de Sales's *Treatise on the Love of God*. A new, more respectful attitude toward the *Exercises* is suddenly and unexpectedly evident here; Father Yealey's letter and textual gift had clearly led Eliot into studied reconsideration of his earlier views. Further, Eliot had begun to describe the Jesuit influence on Donne in a less romantic and psychological light, observing that

> Donne many times betrays the consequences of early Jesuit influence and of his later studies in Jesuit literature; in his cunning knowledge of the weaknesses of the human heart, his understanding of human sin, his skill in coaxing and persuading the attention of the variable human mind to Divine objects, and in a kind of smiling tolerance among his menaces of damnation. (*FLA* 31)

It should be remembered that when Eliot began his reconsideration of Ignatius and the *Spiritual Exercises* he was undergoing his own conversion to the Anglican church, culminating in his baptism on 29 June 1927. Moreover, he was not only writing the Ariel poems (1927–31) and the fragments of *Ash-Wednesday* (1930), poems that record the arduous personal aftermath of conversion, but fighting a continuous battle over the nature of classicism and romanticism with John Middleton Murry, begun in the pages of the *Adelphi* and the *Criterion* in 1923. One aspect of the debate was the relation of Catholicism and classicism, and by the time Eliot wrote his Clark Lectures the Catholicism–classicism argument had expanded to include their diametrical views of the Society of Jesus. "That Jesuitism is a phenomenon typically of the Renaissance is a fact upon which I insist," Eliot declared:

It represents a very important point of disagreement between Mr. Middleton Murry and myself. Mr. Murry holds the opinion that Jesuitism is identical with Christianity, and that Christianity—Roman Christianity—is identical with classicism, and it is on these grounds that he has advised me to take a spiritual director. I cannot help thinking that a little study of the history, constitution and practices of the Society of Jesus would show him that it has nothing to do with classicism, but is on the contrary, what I, if not he, would call Romantic, and excessively Romantic. The fact that the Society of Jesus is of Spanish origin is an indication that it is outside of the Graeco-Roman classical tradition. (*VMP* 75–6)

In a two-part essay entitled "The 'Classical' Revival," published while the lectures were in progress, Murry had declared that the "self-torturing and utter nihilism" of *The Waste Land* contradicts and renders sterile the kind of "Catholic classicism" that Eliot professes.[10] "He is," wrote Murry, "essentially, an unregenerate and incomplete romantic," and he suggested that Eliot might become a classicist by joining the Catholic church.[11] When Murry's *Life of Jesus* (1926) appeared a few months later, Eliot reviewed it harshly in the *Criterion*, cleverly but caustically turning the romantic tables on Murry, making him out to be a closet Unitarian (the childhood religion that Eliot had abandoned) and a would-be Jesuit. Accusing Murry of preaching "the familiar gospel of Rousseau: the denial of Original Sin," Eliot points to the Unitarian and Jesuitical principles underlying Murry's agnostic and casuistic portrayal of Jesus: "Mr. Murry has great gifts; gifts which would have led him, as a member of the Society of Jesus, to eminence, power and peace of mind . . . Mr. Murry is, doctrinally, inclined to Unitarianism, and, emotionally, inclined to Jesuit Catholicism of the seventeenth century" (*Cr* 5: 255, 257–8).

As Eliot studied the *Exercises,* his expressed attitude toward Ignatius began to change even if his attitude towards Jesuitism did not. In June 1928 he evoked Ignatius in confrontation with another *bête noir* of romanticism, F. L. Lucas, whose view of the Renaissance Eliot found particularly repellent.

Mr. Lucas has a liking for the Renaissance which is as much fanciful as imaginative, and which is like nothing so much as it is like the Elizabethan's imaginative view of Italy and Spain. The Elizabethan imagination which made a composite bogey of Machiavelli and St. Ignatius seems to me but little more confused than that of Mr. Lucas who talks about the Renaissance breeding "men free from the repressions, the cringings, the conformities of the centuries of superstition." (*Cr* 7:445)

Eliot alludes particularly to Donne's satire of Ignatius and Machiavelli in *Ignatius His Conclave*, which Eliot was evidently reading for John Hayward's new edition of Donne's poetry and prose, which appeared in January 1929.[12] Donne's satanic satire of Ignatius and Machiavelli was the culmination of many such "bogey" portraits that had made them stock figures of Elizabethan drama. Eliot had recently written his defense of Machiavelli, who "has been the torment of Jesuits and Calvinists, the idol of Napoleons and Nietzsches . . . and the exemplar of a Mussolini or a Lenin" (*FLA* 49). To Eliot, Machiavelli was "a man who accepted in his own fashion the orthodox view of original sin" (*FLA* 62); he was neither a fanatic ("he merely told the truth about humanity") nor a romantic ("What Machiavelli did not see about human nature is the myth of human goodness which for liberal thought replaces the belief in Divine Grace") (*FLA* 63–4).

Eliot was not tempted to write a similar defense of Ignatius, but he obviously felt that Ignatius had been unreasonably abused, especially by Donne, if not by himself. In the year following his baptism, Eliot held Ignatius in critical suspension in his mind as he struggled to make spiritual progress through prayer and regular devotions under the guidance of Father Francis Underhill, though he would draw further conviction for his determined path from Ignatius's own vow of chastity in pursuit of mystical union. On 10 April 1928 he wrote to his friend Stead that he felt the need for "the most severe, as Underhill would say, the most Latin, kind of discipline, Ignatian or other" (Yale). By the end of 1929, when Eliot was writing "Religion without Humanism," a rather dramatic change had occurred in his public attitude toward Ignatius. In the essay, in which he deplores the lack of intellectual and emotional discipline in humanism, he had come to admit Ignatius (with a parenthetical qualification) into a select company of disciplined mystics:

> There is much chatter about mysticism: for the modern world the word means some spattering indulgence of emotion, instead of the most terrible concentration and askesis. But it takes perhaps a lifetime merely to realise that men like the forest sages, and the desert sages, and finally the Victorines and John of the Cross and (in his fashion) Ignatius really *mean what they say*. Only those have the right to talk of discipline who have looked into the Abyss. The need of the modern world is the discipline and training of the emotions; which neither the intellectual training of philosophy or science, nor the wisdom of humanism, nor the negative instruction of psychology can give.[13]

Meanwhile, Father Yealey had come back into Eliot's life. In October 1927 Yealey submitted his doctoral dissertation, "Emerson and the Romantic Revival," to the secretary of the Faculty Board of English, E. M. W. Tillyard, who asked Eliot to serve as outside examiner. Eliot replied on 27 October that he would be delighted to serve, provided that "the Board realises that I am not at all an authority on Roman Catholic dogma, or even on Emerson, so that my opinion would not in any case be a highly specialised one" (King's). Eliot received the manuscript and went through it immediately, writing to Tillyard on 31 October: "I have read your Jesuit's dissertation on Emerson and I think it ought to be accepted beyond doubt" (King's). Eliot submitted his two-page report on 7 November and returned the dissertation, but when Professor Oliver Elton criticized the study, resulting in a two-year deferral, Eliot informed Tillyard on 28 February 1928 that he agreed with Elton's criticism (King's).[14] The extent of Eliot's continued involvement with Yealey's dissertation is unknown; Yealey successfully revised the dissertation and eventually received his doctorate from Cambridge by proxy in November 1929.

After receiving Yealey's admonishment in March 1926, Eliot mentally noted the correction, put the letter away, and turned to the *Spiritual Exercises*. In one of his later revisions of the Clark Lectures, probably in mid-1929 but well after beginning his intensive study of Ignatius, Eliot recalled Yealey's letter with the familiarity of their extended relationship and wrote in the margin, below the quotation from the unauthorized edition of *Spiritual Exercises*: "Father Yealey S.J. has notified me that the passage I quoted is probably not by Ignatius, but added much later. I had used it because of the remarkable similarity of imagery to that of Donne" (*VMP* 105n). That this was Eliot's original intention in quoting the passage is doubtful: the tone betrays such a conscious motive. But during the three-year period in which he steeped himself in the *Spiritual Exercises* and carried on periodic revisions of the lectures, he would have discovered the motive he now ascribes. Indeed, his fascination with the similarity of the imagery of Ignatius and Donne surfaces for the first time in "The Prose of the Preacher: The Sermons of Donne" (1929), where he points to Donne's Jesuit upbringing and argues that "his command of the terrors of death and damnation in other passages shows him a student of the Ignatian method; and I think he shows his training here too, in winning his auditors by sympathy and understanding, and suddenly pulling them up at the end."[15] Eliot then quotes a passage from one of Donne's late sermons (80, 1626) that allegedly reflects the imagery of Ignatius:

> I throw myself down in my chamber, and I call in, and invite God, and His Angels thither, and when they are there, I neglect God and His Angels, for the noise of a fly, for the rattling of a coach, for the whining of a door; I talk on, in the same posture of praying; eyes lifted up; knees bowed down; as though I prayed to God; and if God, or His Angels should ask me, when I thought last of God in that prayer, I cannot tell: Sometimes I find that I had forgot what I was about, but when I began to forget it, I cannot tell. A memory of yesterday's pleasures, a fear of to-morrow's dangers, a straw under my knee, a noise in mine ear, a light in mine eye, an anything, a nothing, a fancy, a chimaera in my brain, troubles me in my prayer.[16]

Eliot had long been puzzled by the fact that Donne reveals very few literary influences on his work. Like Walton before him, Eliot had come to believe that Donne's poetic imagination "was fed chiefly on works of theology and law. In his verse, he is a theologian and a lawyer; and in his theology, he is very much a poet." In his Clark Lectures Eliot had expressed dismay over the seemingly indiscriminate, hodge-podge nature of Donne's theological readings, but in studying the *Spiritual Exercises* he began to see that Donne's imagination was steeped in Ignatius. It was a new and startling revelation for Eliot, and it led him to a radical reappraisal of Spanish influences on seventeenth-century English poets.

That appraisal came less than a year later in "Thinking in Verse: A Survey of Early Seventeenth-Century Poetry," originally given as a BBC broadcast on 7 March 1930.[17] In a wide-ranging discussion of seventeenth-century verse, Eliot points again to significant changes in religious sensibility from the thirteenth to the seventeenth centuries, particularly to a decline in the quality of mysticism— from the "intellectual and international" mysticism of the Victorines to the "sensual and erotic" mysticism of the Spanish mystics. He again points out the admirable role of the Jesuits in the Counter-Reformation, that of winning a divided Europe back to the faith by appealing to intellectual and artistic interests. The result of these activities, he declares, was that the poetry of Europe was colored by "the Spanish imagination" of St. Theresa and St. Ignatius. There is nothing new in Eliot's talk to this point; indeed, it is mainly a summary of ideas in his Clark Lectures. But as the historical synthesis unfolds, he begins to include the observations of his recent reading, first declaring that the initial influence of Theresa and Ignatius in English poetry appears "in the work of that curious poet Robert Southwell." He then explains that during the "outburst of mysticism" that produced Theresa, the most influential of the Spanish mystics, Spain also produced Ignatius, "a man of a very different type, a great saint and a very great man indeed." If Eliot still saw Ignatius as a great man, he no longer saw him as a mystic. In presenting Ignatius to an audience for the second time in four years, Eliot searched for and found a more modern counterpart than Don Quixote for comparison. "For force of character," wrote Eliot,

> there is only one man in contemporary Europe to whom I can compare him, and I do so without the slightest disrespect to the saint: I can only compare him to Lenin. He had a similar intense ruthlessness, though in a better cause. And I make the comparison to Lenin chiefly to emphasise his difference from St. Theresa and St. John. He was no mystic; he was an administrator, a warrior, a born ruler of men; with that fanaticism which brings small men to perdition, and great men to immortality. In the ordinary acceptance of chancelleries and cabinets he was no politician; and therefore, he was one of the greatest politicians of all.

This striking comparison, which emphasizes the secular rather than the spiritual strengths of Ignatius, would have had an even stronger effect then than now: Lenin, succeeded by Stalin, had been dead but six years. However appropriate the comparison, it was employed as a preface to his equally severe comparisons for the *Spiritual Exercises*:

> Now, if you read and study the *Spiritual Exercises*, you will find a stock of images which reminds you, and by no mere coincidence, of Donne. Donne, as I shall try to show, was no mystic. And neither was St. Ignatius. Mysticism is a gift of grace; you will never become a mystic unless you have the gift. The *Exercises* are not aimed at making mystics. . . . They are a very practical handbook, like the late Lieut. Muller's handbook of physical exercises, to enable anybody to extend the intellectual conviction of the Faith to imaginative conviction. A similar method might be used by an historian, so steeped in Greek history as to see Thermopylae as he has seen events in his own life, in order to make his readers realise those events. So St. Ignatius works on the imagination, to make us re-

alise the Passion as he realised it. But this is not mysticism; it is merely confirmation of Christian Faith. And we shall find the visual imagery of St. Ignatius in
Donne, whose childhood was passed under Jesuit influence.[18]

Eliot's recognition of Donne's debt to Ignatius had the effect of altering and
clearing his mind about both men—all his previous doubts, qualifications, and
reservations about their status as mystics had been confirmed. Eliot had never
himself referred to Donne as a mystic, but he was now prepared to confront the
critical habit of discussing him as a mystic. Further, Eliot had come to see the
Spiritual Exercises as little more than an image-rich handbook for "anybody"
seeking imaginative realization of faith. Certainly he had lost all faith in the *Exercises* as a spiritual document based on intellectual and emotional discipline. He
had come to a new understanding of the ways in which the two major strands of
the "Spanish imagination" had influenced seventeenth-century poetry, and he
concluded his talk by expressing his wish "to keep two things separate. Donne is
more affected by Ignatius; Crashaw more by Theresa."

The gradual diminishment of Donne's importance to Eliot was hastened by
his study of Ignatius, and by the mid-1930s both had essentially disappeared
from the center of Eliot's critical consciousness. He was already working on his
last major essay on Donne, "Donne in Our Time" (1931), in which he expressed
his belief that "Donne's poetry is a concern of the present and the recent past,
rather than of the future."[19] A decade removed from the "The Metaphysical
Poets," he was now certain that Donne's unified sensibility was dissociated after
all:

> In Donne, there is a manifest fissure between thought and sensibility, a chasm
> which in his poetry he bridged in his own way, which was not the way of me-
> diaeval poetry. His learning is just information suffused with emotion, or com-
> bined with emotion not essentially relevant to it. In the poetry of Dante . . .
> there is always the assumption of an ideal unity in experience, the faith in an ul-
> timate rationalisation and harmonisation of experience, the subsumption of the
> lower under the higher, an ordering of the world more or less Aristotelian. But
> perhaps one reason why Donne has appealed so powerfully to the recent time is
> that there is in his poetry hardly any attempt at organisation; rather a puzzled
> and humorous shuffling of the pieces; and we are inclined to read our own
> more conscious awareness of the apparent irrelevance and unrelatedness of
> things into the mind of Donne.[20]

Ignatius is not mentioned; Donne is singularly portrayed as "the antithesis of the
scholastic, of the mystic and of the philosophical system maker." In any event,
Eliot's astute recognition of the Ignatius-Donne relationship preceded recognition by the academic community by almost twenty years.[21]

When in January 1933 Eliot turned to abbreviate his eight Clark Lectures for
his three Turnbull Lectures, he revised his description of Donne's intellectual
background to say that there was "a great deal of Jesuitism in it; and I do not
think that anyone who has ever examined the origins and constitution of that

remarkable order can fail to notice its great difference from any of the orders founded in the Middle Ages, or any of the more modern orders founded on their model" (*VMP* 259). He also clarified more distinctly the distance and the difference between Dante and Donne. While Dante had the philosophy of Aquinas and the mysticism of the Victorines behind him, for Donne "there was a mixture of mediaeval philosophy . . . and the visual imaginative method of St. Ignatius—in whose *Exercises* any student of Donne must saturate himself" (*VMP* 292).

Weeks later, in his penultimate Norton Lecture, "The Modern Mind" (17 March 1933), Eliot again took issue with another romanticist, his friend and antagonist I. A. Richards. Eliot presents Richards as a familiar "type" of modern mind, not only in his Arnoldian declaration in *Science and Poetry* (1926) that "poetry is capable of saving us" but in his five-point "recipe," as Eliot calls it, for the spiritual meditation of a poem in *Practical Criticism* (1929). Eliot quotes from Richards's proposed scheme a passage that "throws some light upon his theological ideas":

> Something like a technique or ritual for heightening sincerity might well be worked out. When our response to a poem after our best efforts remains uncertain, when we are unsure whether the feelings it excites come from a deep source in our experience, whether our liking or disliking is genuine, is *ours*, or an accident of fashion, a response to surface details or to essentials, we may perhaps help ourselves by considering it in a frame of feelings whose sincerity is beyond our questioning. Sit by the fire (with eyes shut and fingers pressed firmly upon the eyeballs) and consider with as full "realisation" as possible— (*UPUC* 131)[22]

Eliot was appalled at Richards's Ignatius-like "frame of feelings" and characterized the whole proposal as "nothing less than a regimen of Spiritual Exercises" (*UPUC* 132). He then addressed each of Richards's five points in turn, declaring that

> his modern substitute for the *Exercises* of St. Ignatius is an appeal to our feelings, and I am only trying to set down how they affect mine. To me Mr. Richards's five points only express a modern emotional attitude which I cannot share, and which finds its most sentimental expression in [Bertrand Russell's] *A Free Man's Worship*. (*UPUC* 134)[23]

Eliot had come full circle with Ignatius and the *Spiritual Exercises* since 1926. After a concerted effort, he found it impossible to come to temperamental or intellectual terms with the the Ignatian method of the *Spiritual Exercises*, much less with the psychological structures and emotional appeals of its modern counterparts. In bringing the *Spiritual Exercises* analogously into the company of *Practical Criticism* and *A Free Man's Worship*, Eliot laid them to rest in his mind; he never mentioned them or Ignatius in his criticism again. The ontological and psychological assumptions were irreconcilable: Ignatius, Murry, Lucas, Richards, and

Russell were not mystics; they were, to Eliot, in addition to being revolutionists, theologians, philosophers, psychologists, and critics, essentially and undeniably romantics, ultimately heretics.

By 1933 the decade of the fierce classic-romantic wars was coming to an end for Eliot. To say that he had exhausted his interest in Ignatius is not to say, however, that his mind had not been colored by "the Spanish imagination." By the mid-1930s Donne and Ignatius, and Crashaw and Theresa, had gradually been displaced in Eliot's mind by an English contemplative, George Herbert, and a Spanish mystic, St. John of the Cross. These two had become his companions, Herbert's *The Temple* and St. John's *Ascent of Mount Carmel* his handbooks, as he moved into *Four Quartets*. As he embarked on that poetic and philosophical journey, the receding of Donne and Ignatius, and the rising of Herbert and St. John in Eliot's consciousness, marked a crucial transition in his own search for a unified sensibility.

"IF I THINK, AGAIN, OF THIS PLACE"

The Way to *Little Gidding*

Do what thou wilt, thou shalt not so,
Dark Angel! triumph over me:
Lonely, unto the Lone I go;
Divine, to the Divinity.

Eliot did not just happen upon Little Gidding; it was a symbolic place of mind long before his pilgrimage to the chapel in 1936, well before he began to write the poem in 1941. Even as he wrote the renunciatory fragments of *Ash-Wednesday* in the aftermath of his conversion, his mind was fixed on the Anglican example of Nicholas Ferrar, whose stark renunciation of worldly preferments and whose friendships with George Herbert and Richard Crashaw had struck Eliot's imagination. Early in the 1920s he was familiar with Walton's portrayal of the devotional community in his *Life of Herbert*. When he read Mario Praz's account in *Secentismo e Marinismo in Inghilterra* (1925) of Crashaw's relation to Ferrar and his remarkable niece Mary Collett, he was moved to write: "The section of Signor Praz's book which deals with . . . Crashaw's connexion with the retreat of Little Gidding and with the misfortunes of Peterhouse makes extremely good reading."[1] If he was not as yet familiar with J. H. Shorthouse's detailed description of religious life at Little Gidding in *John Inglesant* (1881), he was soon to be so, for he added the 1927 edition to his library. By the time of his baptism and confirmation in that year, Eliot already saw Little Gidding as a distant paradigm of the contemplative life, founded as it was on a mystical devotional spirit that he would embrace with increasing intensity. During the next decade, as he prepared for his fated visit, he did indeed think again and again of "this place" and its people. Eliot, like Herbert, was touched and led to Little Gidding by the "genius" of Ferrar, but the drama of the pentecostal journey to both place and poem lies in Eliot's rediscovery of Herbert in the 1930s.

The thrust of this chapter emerges from the neglected fact that Herbert became a crucial figure to Eliot in an intense personal drama—the collapse of his marriage to Vivien Eliot and the resumption of his relationship with Emily Hale. This tension in his personal life was further complicated by the austere religious commitments—including the vow of celibacy—made in the aftermath of his conversion; in Herbert (and in St. John of the Cross) Eliot found a way of working out the conflict between personal and religious emotion in a new mode of contemplative poetry—*Four Quartets*. Further, it was through Herbert that Eliot rediscovered the English mystical tradition, and in making that tradition an integral part of his own contemplative life he made Herbert and the fourteenth-century English mystics the guiding spirits of *Little Gidding*. As new biographical and bibliographical material reveals, and as a fresh reading of the poem confirms, Herbert did indeed show Eliot the way to *Little Gidding*. For the rest of his life Eliot continued to acknowledge the impact of *The Temple* on his poetic consciousness and to include Herbert among the final handful of poets to whom he paid his greatest homage.

I

Throughout the 1920s Herbert remained a "devotional poet" of minor interest to Eliot in comparison to Donne and Crashaw, who were the primary objects of his inquiry into the relation of thought and feeling. At the end of the decade Eliot still looked upon Herbert as the mild-mannered poet of the domestic vicarage, and though his admiration of Donne's verse was still intact he had become sharply critical of Crashaw's religious wandering. However much he admired the devotional verse of the seventeenth century, at the time of his conversion in 1927 Eliot had not found a patron poet in Herbert or in any other poet of the Anglican communion; he had to look to the Continent, to Baudelaire, to find the nature of his spiritual struggle exemplified in poetry. In May, the month before his baptism in Finstock Church, he wrote that Baudelaire, in his isolated discovery of Christianity, "was alone in the solitude which is only known to saints. To him the notion of Original Sin came spontaneously; and the need for prayer. . . . And Baudelaire came to attain the greatest, the most difficult, of the Christian virtues, the virtue of humility" (*FLA* 98–9). Eliot had himself come the purgative way of his patron saint, John of the Cross, and of Baudelaire—a way based on the reality of sin, the necessity of prayer, and the achievement of humility. For the next three years Eliot would praise the spiritual heroism of Baudelaire's attitude toward life, writing in "Baudelaire" (1930) that "such suffering as Baudelaire's implies the possibility of a positive state of beatitude" (*SE* 423). The concomitant importance of St. John to Eliot's spiritual life and the depth of Eliot's immersion in *The Ascent of Mount Carmel* were only hinted at in the epigraph to "Fragment of a Prologue," the first section of *Sweeney Agonistes*: "Hence the soul cannot be possessed of the divine union, until it has divested itself of the love of created beings" (*CPP* 115). Accompanied to the Anglo-Catholic church by a French poet and a Spanish mystic, Eliot had nonetheless begun his search for their counterparts on English soil.

When Eliot resumed his comparative study of Donne, Crashaw, and Herbert in "The Devotional Poets of the Seventeenth Century" (1930), he appeared not to have altered his estimation of Crashaw and Herbert as devotional poets. The religious feeling in Herbert's poetry, he observed, "is easy for the English mind, whether Anglican or Dissenting," whereas in Crashaw "we encounter a fine English poet who is at the same time a little alien."[2] Donne remains the superior poet, and in comparing the two Eliot was moved to remark that Walton "perhaps overdoes it" in portraying Herbert's reputation for saintliness. Herbert would seem to be completely divorced from Eliot's critical consciousness, and yet a complexity in the poet had begun to intrigue him, evidenced in his unexpected reassessment of the "simplicity" of Herbert's verse. He discussed Herbert's "Prayer (I)," ostensibly to show Donne's influence on the conceits, but primarily to point to Herbert's genius for simplifying intense emotion in his devotional verse. "There remains his personal quality," he concluded, "and the necessity for saturating oneself in his verse to get it."

During the next two years Eliot's immersion in Herbert's verse led to a dramatic transformation, indeed reversal, of his previous attitude toward Herbert as an Anglican poet and priest. In "George Herbert," published as part of a series in the *Spectator* entitled "Studies in Sanctity," he criticized not only the "false setting" in which Herbert has been represented in anthologies and popular editions but his own participation in the conventional view.[3] Having moved beyond the anthology pieces himself, and having read industriously in *The Temple*, Eliot expressed his astonishment at the "spiritual stamina" of the work, at its extraordinary sincerity, at the inextricability of Herbert's religious vocation from his poetic talent. "Throughout there is brain work," he wrote with conviction, "and a very high level of intensity; his poetry is definitely an *oeuvre*, to be studied entire. And our gradual appreciation of the poetry gives us a new impression of the man."

In penetrating the complex architecture of *The Temple*, Eliot had discovered the "personal quality" that had eluded him—Herbert's unique consciousness of sin, prayer, and humility and his profound sense of purgation in the pursuit of beatitude. In his newfound recognition of the intensity of Herbert's spiritual struggle, Eliot cautiously associated him with St. John of the Cross, not to compare Herbert's spiritual accomplishment but to suggest that "no lower theme could have evoked his genius." Herbert's balance of emotion and intellect led Eliot to describe him as "an anatomist of feeling and a trained theologian," and he quoted from "The Pearl" to show that Herbert's mind "is working continually both on the mysteries of faith and the motives of the heart": "I know the wayes of Learning," Herbert begins his address to the Holy Spirit, and yet in spite of his knowledge of the human ways of Learning, Honour, and Pleasure, achieved by attributes that lead only to prideful separation from the Holy Spirit, he cries in each refrain, finally aware that the "silk twist" of grace is the only requirement for divine union, "And yet I love thee." Eliot's essay was thus more than a retraction and correction of old attitudes; it was a proclamation of his spiritual identity with Herbert as penitent and poet. Herbert's poetry, he wrote, "expresses the slow, sometimes almost despairing and always agonizing toil of the proud and passionate man of the world toward spiritual life; a toil and agony which must always be the same, for the similar temperament, to the end of the world." Herbert not only displaced Baudelaire at the side of St. John; he displaced Donne at the center of Eliot's consciousness. It was a remarkable admission and conclusion: "I never feel that the great Dean of St. Paul's, with his mastery of the spoken word, his success and applause to the end, quite conquered his natural pride of mind; Herbert, the vicar of Bemerton, in his shorter life went much farther on the road of humility."[4]

Eliot had come to view Herbert's poems as Herbert humbly described them when, on his deathbed, he sent the unpublished manuscript to Ferrar, as "a picture of the many spiritual conflicts that have passed betwixt God and my soul, before I could subject mine to the will of Jesus my Master: in whose service I have now found perfect freedom."[5] The week after his essay on Herbert appeared, in March 1932, Eliot revealed in a BBC talk the essentials of his spiritual life. They read like a litany of the Christian values that had inspired both Ferrar and Herbert: "values which I must maintain or perish," he declared, "the belief, for instance in holy living and holy dying, in sanctity, chastity, humility, austerity."[6] Thus, Eliot must have been delighted as editor to receive T. O. Beachcroft's study "Nicholas Ferrar and George Herbert," which he would publish in the *Criterion* for October.

Beachcroft's article was a timely confirmation and extension of Eliot's own reading of Herbert. Tracing Ferrar's influence on the personal life and religious poetry of Herbert, Beachcroft argued the complexity of Herbert's verse, asserting that his so-called saintliness and simplicity constituted "a protracted struggle of the intellect and will."[7] The essay was an invitation to the further study of Herbert's mystical faculty, which Eliot was later to apprehend in English mystics of the fourteenth century.

Just as Beachcroft's essay appeared, Eliot sailed to America for the academic year at Harvard, leaving behind his estranged wife Vivien, in what would become a permanent separation. As Lyndall Gordon has movingly shown, Eliot was on the threshold of "the gravest moral crisis of his life" (*TSE* 284). In March 1928, after bringing Vivien back to London from the Sanatorium de la Malmaison in Paris, he had taken the vow of celibacy. That act of detachment had become a significant aspect of his spiritual progress; it freed him to make a total commitment to the Holy Spirit. In 1930, however, that commitment was greatly complicated by Emily Hale's arrival in London and the renewal of their relationship after sixteen years. He would soon see her again in America, and yet again after his return to England. The clash of his determined drive for purity and the unexpected renewal of an old desire brought on an intense personal and moral dilemma—greatly aggravated by his impending separation from Vivien. Ever since he had learned of her affair with Russell, he had found her morally repugnant. On 14 March 1933 he wrote to Ottoline Morrell from Harvard about Russell and Vivien:

Bertie, because at first I admired him so much, is one of my lost illusions. He has done Evil, without being big enough or conscious enough to Be evil. I owe him this, that the spectacle of Bertie was one contributing influence to my conversion. Of course he had no good influence on Vivienne. He excited her mentally, made her read books and become a kind of pacifist, and no doubt was flattered because he thought he was influencing her. . . . Unfortunately she found him unattractive.[8]

He then addressed the permanent separation: "For my part, I should prefer never to see her again; for hers, I do not believe that it can be good for any woman to live with a man to whom she is morally, in the larger sense, unpleasant, as well as physically indifferent" (Texas).

It is not yet known how long after the Russell affair Eliot entered into correspondence with Emily Hale, but by 1923, as already mentioned, he was sending her copies of his books with telling inscriptions of his hellish situation.[9] From 1927 to 1930, during the composition of the *Ash-Wednesday* poems, Eliot sent numerous inscribed copies of his works to her, including *Journey of the Magi* (1927), inscribed less than a month after his conversion.[10] Their eventual reunion in the summer of 1930 clearly revitalized Eliot's emotional life, but he had nonetheless committed himself to the purgative way. The persistent theme of regret, always coloured by the presence of imaginary children in the garden, was struck in part I of "Landscapes"—"New Hampshire," an autobiographical poem written after their visit together in June 1933, twenty years after their love began:

> Children's voices in the orchard
>
> . . .
>
> Twenty years and the spring is over;
> To-day grieves, to-morrow grieves,
> Cover me over, light-in-leaves. (*CPP* 138)

In part 3 of this sequence, "Usk," a poem that looks forward to *Little Gidding*, Eliot would reveal the conflicting voice of his spirit as he contemplated a ruined chapel in the Welsh landscape:

> Seek only there
> Where the grey light meets the green air
> The hermit's chapel, the pilgrim's prayer. (*CPP* 140)

After he returned to England, and in the midst of this growing crisis, Eliot immersed himself in Herbert once again. When he visited Pikes Farm in the winter of 1934 his friend Frank Morley recorded:

> I recall one crisp wintry night . . . when, out of doors, we happened to be talking about Herbert. It made me think, erroneously, he might be thinking of an essay, and I asked him. "Not yet," said Tom, or something to the effect that he had marked many passages in Herbert but, or so I gathered, had not felt ready to write about him."[11]

But Eliot had already written his essay; he was now thinking of Herbert's treatment of "the mysteries of faith and the motives of the heart," the subject of a poem that would be precipitated by his visit to Burnt Norton with Emily Hale in September 1934.

The dilemma posed by his love for Emily Hale—to find happiness in a new marriage or in a kind of spiritual martyrdom, in attachment or detachment—had been irrevocably resolved in Eliot's mind months before he began to write *Burnt Norton*. Shortly after beginning *Murder in the Cathedral* in December 1934, he contributed to *Time and Tide* an untitled essay on "Liberty" under the weekly heading "Notes on the Way." In the course of the essay he moved from political liberty to moral liberty, from the meaning of liberty to "a paradox of liberty," as stated by St. John of the Cross in a passage that was now at the center of Eliot's spiritual consciousness:

> *To follow Christ is to deny self; this is not that other course which is nothing but to seek oneself in God, which is the very opposite of love. For to seek self in God is to seek for comfort and refreshment from God. But to seek God in Himself is not only to be willing to be deprived of this thing and of that for God, but to incline ourselves to will and choose for Christ's sake whatever is most disagreeable, whether proceeding from God or from this world; this is to love God.[12]*

Eliot moved from liberty to liberation, and from liberation to the "last word" on free will, as stated by Dante in the *Paradiso* (canto 3, line 85) and translated by Eliot at the end of *Ash-Wednesday*: "la sua volontate è nostra pace" ("Our peace in His will"). Ultimately concerned with the individual's freedom to choose his own salvation or damnation, he wrote out of his concern with the small amount of "real freedom" in the lives of most people. It moved him to a startling assertion: "Our obligation, certainly, is to love—to love *without desire* (for the latter is to seek oneself in the beloved object, see St. John of the Cross quoted above)—or I might say to love beyond desire—for such love is not effected by the mere quenching of desire." Here, before the first quartet was composed, is an almost verbatim statement in prose of the primary theme of detachment in part 3 of *Little Gidding*:

> liberation—not less of love but expanding
> Of love beyond desire, and so liberation
> From the future as well as the past.

Again, he rested the rationale of his statement on the words of St. John:

> *The soul, by resigning itself to the divine light, that is, by removing every spot and stain of the creature, which is to keep the will perfectly united to the will of God—for to love Him is to labour to detach ourselves from, and to divest ourselves of, everything which is not God's for God's sake—becomes immediately enlightened by, and transformed in, God.[13]*

Eliot's essay on liberty was determined by his own resolve to sublimate human love in divine contemplation. Thus, *Burnt Norton* possessed from the beginning what he felt *Little Gidding* was lacking in its first draft: "some acute personal reminiscence (never to be explicated, of course, but to give power from well below the surface)" (*CFQ* 67). From that substratum the opening of *Burnt Norton* expresses a deeply personal conversation with Emily Hale; it reads as a love poem of great regret, expressed with an emotional resignation that is relieved only by a timeless intersection in the rose garden. It is a poem of painful human loss—of what might have been, of the laughter of hidden children, of "the waste sad time / Stretching before and after"—all this in conflict with a greater call toward the possibility of beatitude through deprivation and solitude.

During this period of moral struggle and poetic formulation, Eliot associated himself with the Society of the Sacred Mission at Kelham, an Anglican religious community. Visiting the Society periodically from 1931 to the outbreak of war, he became not a saint but an advanced student of contemplative life through study, devotion, and solitude. Kelham was a place of spiritual retreat for Eliot, and it became, in effect, his Little Gidding. There he befriended Brother George Every, himself a poet and playwright, and early in 1936 Every asked Eliot to criticize the manuscript of his verse play *Stalemate—The King at Little Gidding* (unpublished). The play focuses on Charles I's third visit to Little Gidding in May 1646 when, in the company of his chaplain, he sought refuge in the dark of night after the battle of Naseby—the "king at nightfall" in Eliot's poem. On 13 March Eliot wrote to Every about the merits and faults of the play, criticising the lack of action and the uneven verse but encouraging him to persevere.[14] Helen Gardner suggests that "it was Mr. Every's play that linked fire with Little Gidding in his mind" (*CFQ* 63), but the fire in Eliot's mind came from his pentecostal experience there, and from the poetry of George Herbert.

Eliot's long-delayed pilgrimage to Little Gidding had now become imperative, and so arrangements were made. On Saturday, 23 May, he went up to Cambridge to spend the weekend with John Maynard Keynes, who took him to guest night at King's College and to lunch on Sunday. On Monday afternoon, the 25th, after participating in a *viva voce* that morning, Eliot motored over to Little Gidding in the company of the eminent Pascal scholar Hugh Fraser Stewart and his wife Jessie. It had been a miserably wet May, and though the white May blossoms were in full bloom on the hawthorns, the forecast was for more unsettled weather, cloudy and cold with occasional rain. However, when Eliot later mentioned his visit in a letter to Emily Hale's aunt, Mrs. Edith Perkins, he described it as the "only really lovely day" in May that he could remember (*CFQ* 35). It was, indeed, a day of "Midwinter spring."

The symbolic coincidence that his visit took place in the week leading to Whitsunday would not have escaped him as he stood before the "dull facade" of the restored chapel and the weathered tomb of Nicholas Ferrar. He knew from Walton and others that it was on Whitsun eve of 1625, during the plague, that Ferrar persuaded his family to leave London for Little Gidding; he knew that during the week before Whitsun of 1626 Ferrar fasted and prayed, waiting for the descent of the Holy Spirit, before going to Archbishop Laud on Trinity Sunday to take the deacon's orders that would enable him to conduct services for his community. Over the entrance to the chapel is the stone slab from the original front, chiseled with words chosen by Ferrar: "THIS IS NONE OTHER BUT THE HOUSE

OF GOD AND THE GATE OF HEAVEN." Eliot's pentecostal poem, when it came, would record not only the private "glow" that he experienced there, but his communication in prayer with the dead of Little Gidding.

Similar moments of illumination occurred in swift succession—at the Dry Salvages in the late summer of 1936 and at East Coker in August 1937. Meanwhile, in the years before the composition of the three quartets, a wealth of new information appeared on Little Gidding. When Bernard Blackstone's "Discord at Little Gidding" appeared in *TLS*, the public learned of the strident personality and "singularly unpleasant" behavior of John Ferrar's wife, Bathsheba, who would make her way into Eliot's poem among those "not wholly commendable."[15] When A. L. Maycock, the Cambridge author and librarian, published his *Nicholas Ferrar of Little Gidding* (1938), Eliot had Blackstone review it for the *Criterion* in October. Maycock's book, wrote Blackstone, erases myths and distorted views of Ferrar and lays the groundwork for a much-needed scholarly study. Later in the year, Blackstone brought out the materials for such a study in his *Ferrar Papers*, declaring Ferrar to be "in singleness of vision and completeness of achievement . . . the most original genius in the church during the vital period of her post-Reformation history."[16] Eliot had the volume reviewed by another Kelham friend, Charles Smyth, who praised Blackstone's sense of the spiritual complexity of Ferrar's writings: "we should not wish to quarrel with the statement that 'the restraint, the quiet dignity, and the objectivity of Ferrar's writings proceed rather from a continuous inner tension than from habitual serenity' " (*Cr* 18:369). Eliot thus encouraged and witnessed in his own periodical a critical elevation of Ferrar similar to Beachcroft's earlier revaluation of Herbert. Elaborations of his own knowledge and experience of Little Gidding were appearing at every turn, and when his friend Charles Williams published *The Descent of the Dove: A Short History of the Holy Spirit in the Church* (1939), Eliot expressed relief in his review that Williams had given St. John of the Cross "his due place."[17] But he would have found further satisfaction in the special importance that Williams gave to the *via negativa* of the fourteenth-century English mystics, particularly Dame Julian of Norwich and the anonymous author of *The Cloud of Unknowing*, authors who had become integral to Eliot's study of Herbert.

Eliot had not found such satisfaction in the recent writings of his friend Paul Elmer More, who had made his own way into the Anglican church concurrently with Eliot. In fact, when More traced the stages of his spiritual progress in "Marginalia" (1936), in which he describes at length "how deeply my own philosophy of life was moulded . . . by *John Inglesant*,"[18] Eliot wrote to More on 11 January 1937 that his spiritual biography was "oddly, even grotesquely, more like my own, so far as I can see, than that of any human being I have known" (*Harries* 136). Earlier in their correspondence, however, Eliot had been frankly critical of More's view of St. John of the Cross in *The Catholic Faith* (1931). Writing on 17 February 1932, he argued that "you are overbold in your criticism of one who is crowned with so much authority" (*Harries* 144). When, shortly before More's death, Eliot wrote an article on him for the *Princeton Alumni Weekly*, he renewed the criticism: More "seems to me to fail to appreciate the greatness of St. John of the Cross."[19] But in More's *Anglicanism* (1935) Eliot had come to see a more significant failing: "he seems to me more Anglican than the Anglicans, and to write as if the English Church began with Hooker. . . . He does not give recognition to the probable importance of the mystics of the fourteenth century—of Richard Rolle and Julian of Norwich for instance—as late as the time of Lancelot Andrewes and George Herbert."

Eliot had first studied the English mystics at Harvard in Evelyn Underhill's *Mysticism* (1911), in which she discussed Rolle, Dame Julian, Walter Hilton, and the author of *The Cloud of Unknowing*. As he renewed his reading of them in the 1930s, he had Beachcroft review F. M. M. Comper's *Life and Lyrics of Richard Rolle* in the *Criterion* (January 1934). They were all so much in his consciousness when writing *The Family Reunion* (1939) that he had Agatha say to Harry, as he goes off to follow the Eumenides:

Accident is design
And design is accident
In a cloud of unknowing. (*CPP* 337)

Eliot believed with Underhill and others that Andrewes, Herbert, and Ferrar were steeped in the *via negativa* of these mystics and that a knowledge of their works was necessary to penetrate much seventeenth-century theology. Eliot steeped himself in their manuals of contemplative life, and when the first draft of *Little Gidding* stalled in 1941 it was these English mystics whom Eliot summoned for help.

In consciously linking himself to them through the seventeenth century, he became the direct descendant of the English devotional tradition. Of greater consequence, in identifying himself with them through St. John and Herbert, he placed himself specifically in a more ancient tradition that he wished to revive— that of the contemplative poet. In this tradition lay the foundation of what Eliot had described to William Force Stead as his theory that the modern poet had only begun to explore "the experience of man in search of God, and trying to explain to himself his intenser human feelings in terms of the divine goal" (see p. 151). Eliot professed that this had been his aim in *Ash-Wednesday*; it was his aim in *Four Quartets* as well, and his models for the undertaking were Herbert, St. John, and the English mystics.

Prior to composing his last three quartets Eliot wrote a lecture on George Herbert that has escaped most eyes. On 25 May 1938, at the behest of the dean of Salisbury, E. L. Henderson, Eliot gave to the Friends of the Cathedral in the chapter house his lecture "George Herbert." The body of the lecture, called a "Brilliant Lecture" on "A Tough Man in a Tough Age" (a headline taken from the text), was printed in the report of the local paper, the *Salisbury and Winchester Journal*. After his introductory remarks on Herbert's local associations, Eliot told the audience that his greater familiarity with Herbert's works and his greater maturity of mind and sensibility had led him "to concede to Herbert as a religious poet a pre-eminence among his contemporaries and followers. I am, therefore, at the stage of asking for a revision of his reputation; feeling, as I do, that he has been not so much critically as implicitly underrated."[20]

In the address Eliot describes Herbert variously as "the most intellectual of all our religious poets," as "a man of his time, for whom sin was very real, and the promises of death very terrible," and as a man who "happened to be something very near a saint." He affirms Herbert's superiority not only to Donne, in whom "something of the particular and private sinner . . . remains, as a kind of sediment, even in his most religious verse," but to Vaughan and Traherne, whose occasional "mystical flashes" cannot stand up to Herbert's "steady intellectual light." Writing without his earlier caution in comparison, Eliot now asserts that "the only poetry I can think of which belongs to quite the same class as Herbert—as expression of purity and intensity of religious feeling, and . . . for literary excellence—is St. John of the Cross." With this association of the poet and the contemplative now significantly in place, he goes on to characterize the presence of Herbert's personal voice in his impersonal poems:

> What impresses me as the peculiar quality of Herbert's poetry is that while familiarity with it makes us feel that we have got to know a particular, unique man, we know him only in his poetry and not through his poetry. We cannot, as with Donne, read his poetry as a kind of cypher which will yield clues to a peculiarly interesting personality behind poetry [sic]. What is relevant is all there, and we do not ask to know more of him than what is conveyed in his utterance of his meditations on the highest spiritual mysteries. Within his limits, therefore, he achieves the greatest universality in his art; he remains as the human soul contemplating the divine.

In urging his listeners to return to Herbert's text, Eliot asks them to see him as "a man of great intellectual gifts and great psychological insight: and to regard devotional verse like his, not as a pleasant by-path of poetry, but as the highest, if not the most comprehensive that a poet can attempt." Eliot's praise of Herbert in this 1938 lecture confirms what his 1932 essay had strongly suggested, that Herbert's achievement as a meditative poet in *The Temple* had become Eliot's aim in *Four Quartets*. Lecturing coincidentally on the second anniversary of his visit to Little Gidding, Eliot concluded with a reading of Herbert's "Whitsunday," chosen, he says, "for its sublimity of content and its technical mastery":

> Listen sweet Dove unto my song,
> And spread thy golden wings in me;
> Hatching my tender heart so long,
> Till it get wing, and flie away with thee.
>
> Where is that fire which once descended
> On thy Apostles? thou didst then
> Keep open house, richly attended,
> Feasting all comers by twelve chosen men.
> . . . .
> Lord, though we change, thou art the same;
> The same sweet God of love and light:

Restore this day, for thy great name,
Unto his ancient and miraculous right.

Herbert's invocation of the descending fire had become a permanent image in Eliot's imagination, an image enriched by the sublimity of his own pentecostal experience at Little Gidding. And yet the worldly fires remained: in July 1938, after Emily Hale had returned for her annual summer visit, Vivien was certified and committed to Northumberland House. This event would only compound Eliot's desire to atone for abandoning her. Emily returned the following summer, but the onset of war was not only to hasten her departure; it was to bring her years of separation and despondency. As Lyndall Gordon observes, "At some point she must have come to terms with the fact that, so long as Vivienne lived, Eliot would not marry" (*TSE* 406). After her late-summer departure in 1939, Eliot, sharing a flat with Eric Cheetham, vicar of St. Stephen's Church, enrolled at the Air-Raid Wardens' Post in Kensington and returned not only to a life of disciplined prayer but to the *Quartets*.

II

Even as Eliot wrote and published *East Coker* and *The Dry Salvages*, the Cambridge critic Muriel Bradbrook had sensed the presence of Herbert in Eliot's later poetry, and even before the appearance of *Little Gidding* she had published "The Liturgical Tradition in English Verse: Herbert and Eliot" (1942). Bradbrook argued astutely that "Herbert's successes throw light on Eliot's difficulties and help to an understanding of what he has achieved."[21] Eliot himself felt the anxiety of influence as he composed the poems, writing to Anne Ridler on 10 March 1941, as he turned to the first draft of *Little Gidding*, that his intention in part 4 of *East Coker* had been "to avoid a pastiche of George Herbert or Crashaw—it would be folly to try" (*CFQ* 109). In the half-century since the publication of *Four Quartets*, however, critics have hardly touched what a few have occasionally intuited. David Ward, writing on *Little Gidding* in *T. S. Eliot between Two Worlds* (1973), asserts: "One is reminded strongly of the devotional poems of George Herbert"; but Ward concludes that Eliot's technique "is radically different from Herbert's practice" and that "Eliot lacks Herbert's confidence."[22] In *T. S. Eliot: The Longer Poems* (1976), Derek Traversi remarks only in passing that "the spirit of Herbert is indeed present in the poem,"[23] but only in Ronald Bush's *T. S. Eliot* (1984), do we find a brief but substantial hint that Eliot "anticipated" *Little Gidding* in his remarks on Herbert.[24]

Though it is beyond the scope of this discussion to initiate a comparative study of their verse techniques, a reconsideration of *Little Gidding* does show how pervasively the "spirit" of Herbert informs the poem. That spirit, however, guides as much as it informs, for in his fusion of the personal and the mystical Herbert served Eliot immeasurably as a spiritual architect of *Four Quartets*. His poetry inspired in Eliot a modern form of meditative verse and showed him how to explore personal emotions in terms of the divine goal. Shortly after the publication of *Four Quartets*, Eliot took pains, in "What Is Minor Poetry?" (1944), to characterize *The Temple* "as something more than a number of religious poems by one author," describing the work in terms that characterize *Four Quartets* in general and *Little Gidding* in particular:

> What has at first the appearance of a succession of beautiful but separate lyrics, comes to reveal itself as a continued religious meditation with an intellectual framework; and the book as a whole discloses to us the Anglican devotional spirit of the first half of the seventeenth century. What is more, we get to understand Herbert better, and feel rewarded for the trouble, if we know something about . . . the English mystical writers of the fourteenth century. (*OPP* 45–6)

In *Little Gidding*, where the pressure of sin on Eliot's own devotional spirit emerges as a primary theme, Herbert and the English mystics join Nicholas Ferrar and St. John of the Cross as the presiding spirits of the poem. Behind them stand the shadowy figures of Emily Hale and Vivien Eliot.

"Winter scene. May," wrote Eliot in his preliminary sketch of the poem (*CFQ* 157). How familiarly and appropriately his eventual portrayal of that "Midwinter spring" draws on Herbert's "The Flower," which Eliot later described as a poem in which "we hear the note of serenity, almost of beatitude, and of thankfulness for God's blessings" (*GH* 25). Herbert likens the Lord's visitation to his "shrivel'd heart" to that sudden moment in May when the "late-past frosts" humbly pay tribute to the freshly budding flowers, and he compares his spiritual transformation to the physical change in nature:

> Grief melts away
> Like snow in May,
> As if there were no such cold thing.

Though sin and pride have brought God's wrath ("What frost to that?") and the death of previous springtime rebirths, the poem celebrates the return, once again, of the Holy Spirit to the penitent-poet:

> And now in age I bud again,
> After so many deaths I live and write;
> I once more smell the dew and rain,
> And relish versing: O my onely light,
> It cannot be
> That I am he
> On whom thy tempests fell all night.

"I cannot resist the thought," Eliot later wrote,

> that in this . . . stanza—itself a miracle of phrasing—the imagery, so apposite to express the achievement of faith which it records, is taken from the experi-

ence of the man of delicate physical health who had known much illness. It is on this note of joy in convalescence of the spirit in surrender to God, that the life of discipline of this haughty and irascible Herbert finds conclusion: *In His will is our peace. (GH 26)*

But Herbert's joy significantly gives way to humility before the "Lord of love," to the recognition that "we are but flowers that glide" between deaths, that we are dependent upon grace, that those who would be any greater "Forfeit their Paradise by their pride."

Eliot's poem, too, analogically portrays a divine visitation to his dormant, darkened soul at Little Gidding through the silent transition from winter to spring. Like the soul, the frost-frozen landscape creates an illusion of perpetual suspension, only to become "sodden" with the day's slow thawing. The solar fire that flames the ice and creates a blinding glare suddenly becomes a pentecostal fire, an intense "glow" that rekindles the "dumb spirit" and warms the "soul's sap." At that moment of beatitude the natural world of Little Gidding is wholly transformed by the supernatural: poet and hedgerow are lifted out of sense and time; for "an hour," flower blossoms revert to snow blossoms in an unfading world free from the progressive "scheme of generation." If this intense glow occurs at zero spring, the astounded poet is moved to ask in an extension of the season-soul analogy, "Where is the summer, the unimaginable / Zero summer?" Where is the full inward fire, the blinding glare, of the Holy Spirit? That terrifying, "incandescent" descent is richly imagined in part 4 of the poem.

The lyrical re-creation of his visionary experience at Little Gidding leads the poet to a subjunctive and impersonal meditation on the sameness of the experience for all contemplatives who gravitate toward this holy place, past the pigsty and other mundane objects to the "dull facade" of the chapel and Ferrar's tombstone. "For wherever a saint has dwelt," Eliot had written in *Murder in the Cathedral*, as though he were thinking of Little Gidding, "There is holy ground, and the sanctity shall not depart from it / Though armies trample over it, though sightseers come with guide-books looking over it" (*CPP* 281–2). In the second and third verse paragraphs of part 1 Eliot does indeed celebrate the place, the discipline and the prayer of "the Protestant-Saint" Nicholas Ferrar. There are "other places" of other saints, named by Eliot elsewhere and alluded to in *Murder in the Cathedral* and in earlier quartets—those "at the sea jaws," St. Columba at Iona and St. Cuthbert at Lindisfarne; "over a dark lake," St. Kevin at Glendalough; "in a desert," the Egyptian St. Anthony and the hermits of Thebes; "or a city," St. Anthony at Padua—but Ferrar's Little Gidding, "the nearest," affirms the promise of Pentecost: the presence and accessibility of the Holy Spirit in the world, "Now and in England."

As Eliot evokes the present and the past of Little Gidding, he remains wrapped in the subjunctive contemplation of a future communicant: "If you came this way . . . It would always be the same: you would have to put off sense and notion." At whatever time or season, for whatever refuge, each penitent must follow the purgative way to Little Gidding, must arrive in humility and without expectation to engage in the mystery of prayer: like Ferrar, who came in renunciation; like Charles, who came as a "broken king"; like Herbert, who came continuously in spirit, counseling Ferrar on his nightly prayer vigils, or "night-watches," and trying in vain to exchange his parish in Bemerton for a smaller one near Little Gidding before he died; like Crashaw, who attended Ferrar's night watches and continued them in the chapel at Peterhouse; like Eliot, who came three centuries later just before Pentecost.

Suddenly the narrative shifts from the subjunctive to the indicative mood, as if the poet were impatient of the communicant's sense of purpose: "You are not here to verify," he is instructed, "You are here to kneel / Where prayer has been valid." The achievement of humility, the poet implies, is inextricable from the efficacy of prayer, both of which are the hallmarks of Little Gidding. His declaration of the power of prayer on this hallowed ground, and his attempt to suggest the complexity of prayer as "more / Than an order of words," reverberate with Herbert's "Prayer (I)," in which nothing less than a string of conceits can suggest the range and reach of prayer for "something understood," and with "Prayer (II)," in which prayer has become not only "an easie quick accesse" to the Lord and a weapon against the destructive power of sin but the one human necessity:

> I value prayer so,
>   That were I to leave all but one,
> Wealth, fame, endowments, vertues, all should go;
> I and deare prayer would together dwell,
> And quickly gain, for each inch lost, an ell.

Eliot's meditation on Little Gidding as a personal and historical place of "the intersection of the timeless moment" is governed by a realization in *The Dry Salvages*, that after the "hints and guesses" of a timeless world "the rest / Is prayer, observance, discipline, thought and action" (*CPP* 190). The discipline of contemplative prayer, the fixing of the human upon the divine will, is "right action," a way to divine communion. In that communion the Holy Spirit bestows upon the poet, as upon the Apostles at Pentecost, the tongues of flame of the dead, who speak in fire the language of redemption—purgation, prayer, and purification. The tongues here unfolded remain persistent voices in the poem.

In each quartet the eternal stillness of a divine pattern of reality is set against the endless movement of a temporal pattern, a pattern characterized by action and appetency, desire and knowledge, hope and despair, and, in *Little Gidding*, sin and error. At the beginning of part 2 Eliot turns from the intersection of the timeless at Little Gidding to its movement in time, bounded as it is by earth, air, fire, and water. Eliot reportedly told a friend that this section of the poem "came out of" his fire-watching experience during the Blitz, that the bombing debris "would slowly descend and cover one's sleeves and coat with a fine white ash."[25] Even allowing that description, however, the fragmented London scene is no more than a projection upon Little Gidding, for the lyric is built upon Eliot's rich familiarity with the history and place of Little Gidding. The succession of images in the first stanza—roses, story, house, wall, wainscot, and mouse—allude to both the manor house and the chapel as they were first restored and inhabited by the

Ferrars: the abundant rose gardens, trellises, and cut-flowers that beautified them; the oak wainscoting deftly installed in them; the storybooks read in the great chamber of the house by members of the "Little Academy," the family study circle that met daily to read stories and dialogues based on the lives of saints. In depicting the continuous dissolution of Little Gidding, the dust of its objects now "suspended" and "inbreathed," Eliot draws on Herbert's heavy consciousness of dust, perhaps directly on what he called the "striking effect" (*GH* 28) of lines in Herbert's "The Church Floore": "Sometimes Death, puffing at the doore, / Blows all the dust about the floore."

Eliot's lyric begins and ends with allusions to the "burnt roses" and the "marred foundations" of the chapel, which was plundered, wrecked, and partially burned by a Puritan soldiery in 1646, leaving Ferrar's faithful brother, John, an ageing man, standing in the ashes to record the destruction. In time, the objects of Little Gidding—its roses, readers, house, and chapel—become, like the superimposed objects of London in the Blitz, ash of fire, dust of air, particles of earth and water, substances that mock human pride and the illusion that time can be conquered without grace. "Where is there an end of it?" the poet had asked of the "soundless wailing" and the "silent withering" in *The Dry Salvages*. "There is no end of it," he answers there and here, no end to the pattern of hope and despair until the death of air, no end to the "vanity of toil" until the death of earth and water and fire.

The allusions to the pillaging of Little Gidding during the Civil War thus precipitate the poet's psychological dislocation to Kensington during the Blitz. His removal from the place of beatitude to the "three districts" of bombardment is governed by a series of ironic declensions: vision becomes hallucination; Ferrar's night watches become Eliot's fire watches; the descent of the Dove in tongues of flame becomes the destructive dive of "the dark dove with the flickering tongue"; the auditory communion with the dead of Little Gidding becomes an automatized dialogue with the compound ghost of masterful writers—the central figure of whom we know to be Yeats. Eliot's intention, as he later explained, "was the same as with my allusions to Dante in *The Waste Land*: to present to the mind of the reader a parallel, by means of contrast, between the Inferno and the Purgatorio, which Dante visited and a hallucinated scene after an air-raid" (*TCC* 128). The phantasmal encounter of the poet and his composite master is based on a fusion of *Inferno* 15, where Dante meets the shade of Brunetto Latini, and *Purgatorio* 26, where he encounters the shades of Guido Cavalcanti and Arnaut Daniel. But, as Eliot explained to John Hayward, "I wished the effect of the whole to be Purgatorial which is much more appropriate" (*CFQ* 176). The parallel between Dante's and Eliot's encounters with their dead masters lies in the purgatorial realization that the poet cannot seek redemption or immortality in art, and in the further recognition of the evanescence of poetic fame. "You taught me how man makes himself eternal," Dante says to Brunetto, but Brunetto, damned for his lust, answers about his writing: "I am prepared for Fortune as she wills . . . He listens well who notes it." So the shade of Yeats, who to Eliot became the greatest writer of the century but who also followed the religion of art, now urges that they be forgiven their "thought and theory" and admonishes his companion about the illusion of poetic permanence: "last year's words belong to last year's language / And next year's words await another voice." The composite voice speaks, like Guido and Arnaut, from the refining fire, and as Eliot explained the parallel to Hayward, "the people who talk to him [Dante] at that point are represented as not wanting to waste time in conversation but wishing to dive back into the fire to accomplish their expiation" (*CFQ* 196). Dante swears his lasting devotion to his poetic father, Guido, and proclaims the sublimity and permanence of his art: "Your sweet ditties, which so long as modern use shall last, will make their very ink precious." But Guido, mindful of the transience of literary glory, quickly points to "a better craftsman," Arnaut Daniel, and before disappearing into the fire he petitions not Dante's praise but his prayers for those in a world "where power to sin is no more ours."

Dante would make for Arnaut "a grateful place for his name," but the thankful Arnaut replies, before he returns to the refining fire, "be mindful in due time of my pain." Eliot's ghostly poet, momentarily removed from the purgatorial flames, is similarly mindful not of their common art but of the poet's mortal decline from that art. He recounts only "the gifts reserved for age," the ironic "crown" of the poet's kingly effort in language—expiration of sense, impotence of rage, laceration of laughter, shame of motives, consciousness of harm inflicted, persistence of humiliation.[26] Before he fades like Hamlet's ghost, Eliot's ghost, aware that neither art nor fame lend peace to the artist, echoes Arnaut's awareness of the necessity of purgation:

> From wrong to wrong the exasperated spirit
> Proceeds, unless restored by that refining fire
> Where you must move in measure like a dancer.

It is a timely admonition for a poet engaged, like Herbert and St. John, in the poetic contemplation of divine love.

It is the more ironic that the most discernible voice of the shade is that of Yeats, whom Eliot had criticized severely during his lifetime for his romantic, self-redemptive view of art and reality. But as Yeats's and Dante's shades testify, art provides no protection from sin and error, no possible means of redemption, and all suffer remorse for their intellectual pride. The insistent voice of the encounter, that the poet must achieve humility in his art as in his life, is strongly informed by the voice and verse of Herbert, who in such a poem as "Jordan (II)" describes how he "bustled" in fascination with "my lines of heav'nly joyes," how in pride "did I weave my self into the sense," only to hear an imagined friend "Whisper, *How wide is all this long pretence!*" After the war, when, at Emily Hale's request, Eliot gave a lecture, "On Poetry," to the 1947 class of Concord Academy, he said it again in prose: "I am sure that for a poet humility is the most essential virtue."[27]

The poet departs the disfigured streets of Kensington and returns in part 3 to the mental locale of Little Gidding, where he turns over three "conditions" of mind like multiple flowers in a hedgerow. Here the poem moves toward a dramatic moment as the poet brings his "intenser human feelings" to bear on his divine goal. In the early drafts Eliot had sought to infuse an "acute personal reminiscence" into part 2, but his attempts to do so were canceled. That reminiscence occurs here, in the spiritual liberation of the desiring self from painful memories that are expressed obliquely as abstract states of mind, "never to be explicated": his attachment to Emily Hale and his human love for her; his detachment from her in contemplation of the Holy Spirit; and, "growing between them," his indifference to Vivien. This is the triangular complex, the tormenting matrix of memory, that underrides the *Four Quartets*. But now comes the dramatic declaration that the memory, which imprisons the self in its fixation on things and persons, may be transformed in contemplative prayer from a human to a spiritual knowledge of things and persons. "This is the use of memory," he declares in affirmation of that primary faculty of the soul described by the English mystics and by St. John, who chart the purging and purification of memory in advancement toward divine union: "For liberation—not less of love but expanding Of love beyond desire, and so liberation / From the future as well as the past." "See," he points in climactic release at the moment of transformation:

> now they vanish,
> The faces and places, with the self which, as it could, loved them,
> To become renewed, transfigured, in another pattern.

The "unflowering," death-in-life condition of indifference is not to be slighted in the poet's personal search for spiritual liberation. Detachment from desire is painful in itself and demands disciplined self-denial; simultaneous detachment from indifference, from a total absence of feeling toward another object whose reality is as intense as its opposite, disturbs and hinders the mind in concentration. Thus the doubly difficult aim of the contemplative poet is to transcend desire on the one hand and indifference on the other through spiritual knowledge of both objects. The spiritual man, explains St. John, "attains to liberty of spirit" in detachment. "He acquires also in this detachment from creatures a clear comprehension of them, so as to understand perfectly the truths that relate to them, both naturally and supernaturally. For this reason his joy in them is widely different from his who is attached to them, and far nobler."[28] As St. John makes clear, detachment from the beloved object leads not to indifference but to serene exaltation ("Detachment & attachment only a hair's width apart" Eliot wrote on the draft [*CFQ* 197]). Eliot thus employs a political analogue to distinguish states of detachment and indifference: a patriot, in the ordinary process of mature detachment from self-interest, may in time find his "own field of action" to be "of little importance," but he is "never indifferent," never so acutely removed from his object. For Eliot, unflowering indifference is a motive for, not a result of, liberation.

The juxtaposition of spiritual liberation and political liberty prompts a momentary reflection that anticipates the redefinition of history in part 5: "History may be servitude, / History may be freedom." Whatever the historical extremes of political being, there is no individual liberty without the liberation of the soul. It was a central theme of his earlier essay on liberty:

> To me, the notion of *liberty* is meaningless without the further notion of *libera-*
> *tion*. One lives, not to be free, but to be freed. And to be *freed from* is meaningless
> unless one has some notion of what one is to be *freed for*. . . . If human souls
> are not ultimately important, or if they are not equally important, then liberty
> does not matter. . . . I do not think that the political idea of *liberty* can subsist
> quite apart from the religious idea of *liberation*. Mere political liberty cannot be
> permanently interesting; unless we have some notion of the purpose and desti-
> nation of the individual, which makes it necessary that he should be free to ful-
> fill this purpose and destination.[29]

For Eliot, who in part 3 meditates his spiritual liberation between the historical
fluctuations of servitude and freedom, the only human liberty consists in the salvation of the individual soul, in liberation from sin in contemplative prayer.

As the mind moves over the painful footfalls and spiritual ecstasies of the
memory, a voice obtrudes, as once it did upon a predecessor in prayer, the anchoress of Norwich, Dame Julian, who in asking the Lord of the reality of sin
heard from him the necessity of sin: "Sin is Behovable." This voice from her
fourteenth "shewing," assuring her that "all shall be well" through prayer and the
grace of the Holy Spirit, frames the poet's return to the personages of Little Gidding. It was a late but significant addition to the draft, as was the allusion to *The
Cloud of Unknowing* in part 5. As Eliot wrote to Hayward on 2 September 1942,
he wanted to "give greater historical depth to the poem by allusions to the other
great period, i.e. the 14th century" (*CFQ* 70). Though he remarked that he
"might have dragged in Richard Rolle and Walter Hilton" if he knew them better and if he did not think that he would be "overdoing it," their mystical presence is nonetheless felt in the contemplative reach for what they both call "the
fire of love." As Eliot reaches deeper into history—deeper into the English mystical tradition—for moments of revelation in solitude, those lifted moments become continuous with Eliot's present, "Now and in England." "It seems, as one
becomes older," he had written in *The Dry Salvages*, "That the past has another
pattern, and ceases to be a mere sequence"(*CPP* 186). In *Little Gidding* that other
pattern of timeless moments prevails; it collapses historical sequence and binds
Dame Julian and Ferrar and Herbert and Eliot together on another plane of
reality as he begins to think, "again, of this place."

Eliot recalls the inhabitants and visitants of Little Gidding before and after
the Civil War—including those of a "peculiar genius," the Anglican poet Herbert, dead before the war, and the Royalist poet Crashaw, Anglican turned
Catholic—all of whom were touched by the spiritual genius of Ferrar and by a
"common genius" for prayer and devotion. He thinks again of the encirclement
of Little Gidding by Puritan forces, of Charles's final visit, of his execution with
Laud, Strafford, and others, and even of Milton, who, though he died "blind and
quiet" after justifying the ways of God to men, had gone blind writing tracts in
defense of the execution. Poet and politician, deacon and penitent, Puritan and
Royalist, victor and defeated, all are removed in the communality of death from
their impure fields of action. In recollection of these separate struggles for political and religious liberty, the poet is driven to ask, "Why should we celebrate /

These dead men more than the dying?" What is celebrated is not the divided group of dead men but the symbolic place of the defeated men, Little Gidding, a place where motives have been purified in prayer, a place where grace has been bestowed. Desecrated as it was during the bitter religious conflict of the Civil War, Little Gidding remains, in war-torn England, a symbol of liberation in the loss of liberty, of salvation in the midst of defeat. At one with Eliot's voice is the Voice from Dame Julian:

> And all shall be well and
> All manner of thing shall be well
> By the purification of the motive
> In the ground of our beseeching.

The purpose of repeating Dame Julian's revelation he wrote, was "to escape any suggestion of historical sentimentality about the seventeenth century by this reiterated reference to the fourteenth century and therefore to get more bearing on the present than would be possible if the relation was merely between the present and one particular period of the past."[30] The bearing on the present is the immediacy of her belief that the reality and necessity of sin are made well by the reality and necessity of prayer. "Beseeching," she writes of contemplative prayer, "is a true, gracious, lasting will of the soul, oned and fastened into the will of our Lord by the sweet inward work of the Holy Ghost."[31]

Tormented by the irreconcilable conflict between human desire and divine love, the poet envisions in part 4 the awesome moment, the "Zero summer" of the Holy Spirit's pentecostal descent before the Apostles, the blinding fire striking spiritual terror as the tongues of flame speak the language of redemption and declare that grace is "the one discharge from sin and error." In the temporal world of desire and movement, of hope and despair, the "only hope" lies in redemption from the consuming fire of desire by the consuming fire of the Holy Spirit.

Dame Julian, who sought "oftentimes to learn what was our Lord's meaning," was answered in "ghostly understanding" in her sixteenth revelation: "*Learn it well: Love was His meaning. Who shewed it thee? Love. What shewed He thee? Love.*" The poet, seeking to understand the involuntary persistence of desire, also hears that ghostly voice: "Who then devised the torment? Love." "Desire itself is movement," he had written in *Burnt Norton*:

> Not in itself desirable;
> Love is itself unmoving,
> Only the cause and end of movement. (*CPP* 175)

Like Hercules upon his self-made pyre—his great strength useless to remove the "intolerable shirt of flame," his mortal body burned to release his soul to Olympus—the poet would mount the pyre of purgation in great relief from the pyre of desire.

Dame Julian concludes her *Revelations* with a meditation on beginning and ending: "In our making we had beginning; but the love wherein He made us was in Him from without beginning. And all this shall we see in God, without end." Eliot draws upon her ending to consider the nature of "any action," including poetry. Like contemplative poets before him, particularly Herbert in numerous poems, Eliot turns to reflect upon his craft of words in relation to his quest for the Word. Indeed, it would appear that Herbert's lyrics on the relation of poetic language and divine love determined this recurring pattern of the quartets. Eliot's words and lines, like all human actions, are in constant movement, beginning and ending, and as every poem becomes "an epitaph" to an action, so every action ends beneath "an illegible stone"—the words of all epitaphs erased in time. Humble in his "devotional" poetry, and caught up as he is among the paradoxes of beginnings and endings, the poet moves assertively toward the final paradox of belief: the end "is where we start from," he had said in opening the section, but death "is where we start."

The relation of the dying (that is, the living) and the dead takes command of the poet's consciousness as he suddenly reverts to the visionary moment of part 3, where he had pointed ("See, now they vanish") only to the transformation of personal memory and self in a timeless pattern of reality. Uttering the same soft imperatives, he points once again to the rebirth of the dying and the dead in an expanded vision of redemption and eternal union: "See, they depart, and we go with them. . . . See, they return, and bring us with them." Eliot's visionary moment is one with a pattern of timeless moments in time, moments of eternal life symbolized in the rose and the yew-tree. His moment "in a secluded chapel," gradually unfolded in the poem, unites him with hermit and anchoress, poet and saint, beloved and estranged, in an eternal present. The poet who had experienced a horrific "dispossession by the dead" at Marlow and Périgueux is finally repossessed by the dead at Little Gidding. For the poet, liberated at that moment from what he had called in "Gerontion" the "contrived corridors" of history, "History is now and England." The voice of one contemplative, the author of *The Cloud of Unknowing*, speaks to all who would answer the call to the difficult life of the spirit. His last resounding phrase closes this moment of beatitude: "What weary wretched heart and sleeping in sloth, is that, the which is not wakened with the drawing of this love and the voice of this calling?"[32] For Eliot, the calling was irresistible.

The spiritual and historical transformation of self and its objects at Little Gidding leads to the momentary serenity and reconciliation of the poet's final address. On an abstract level he speaks for a universal "We" but on a personal level for an intimate "we," the "we" at the beginning of *Burnt Norton*. In "A Note on War Poetry," published a month after the appearance of *Little Gidding*, Eliot concluded in a throwaway afterthought to his major poem that

> the abstract conception
>
> Of private experience at its greatest intensity
> Becoming universal, which we call "poetry,"
> May be affirmed in verse. (*CPP* 202)

At the close of *Little Gidding*, the pressure of intense experience releases the poem from abstraction, releases a succession of private images recalled from earlier poems—the "remembered gate"; the "voice of the hidden waterfall," which was meant, Eliot wrote to Hayward, "to tie up New Hampshire and Burnt Norton" (*CFQ* 29); the recurring image of imaginary "children in the appletree"; the "stillness" in which the children were "half-heard" between waves at the Dry Salvages; a line repeated from the rose garden in *Burnt Norton*—"Quick now, here, now, always." But in this extraordinary poem of prayer, love, and transcendence—the completion of Eliot's *Vita Nuova*—the poet speaks to his beloved beyond desire, in detached love, all too aware that the "condition of complete simplicity" demanded of him has in human terms cost "not less than everything." His voice thus gives way yet again to the consoling voice that spoke to Dame Julian in prayer, "And all shall be well and / All manner of thing shall be well." Renunciation of desire, assures the author of *The Cloud of Unknowing*, will "at the last help thee to knit a ghostly knot of burning love betwixt thee and thy God, in ghostly onehead and accordance of will." Whatever the visionary source of "the crowned knot of fire," for Eliot too the ghostly knot is knit through continuous self-denial and purgation. At the poem's end the relentless "tongues of flame" are not yet infolded, and the fire of desire and the rose of divine love are not yet one. Like the ubiquitous figure of his art, Arnaut, who sees with joy the day for which he hopes before him, Eliot turns away, back into that refining fire: "sovegna vos a temps de ma dolor."

III

As each quartet was published, Eliot sent an inscribed copy to Emily Hale, and he continued to send her inscribed copies of his work as late as 1959, but detachment was never to descend to attachment, even after Vivien's death in 1947. When they met in America later that year, Eliot convinced Emily that he loved her, "but," as she wrote, "apparently not in the way usual to men less gifted i.e. with complete love thro' a married relationship" (*TSE* 412). Had he tried to say as much in *Little Gidding*? Prior to speaking to her in 1947, he had joined A. L. Maycock in founding the Friends of Little Gidding. That symbolic and practical act was meant to reawaken interest in Little Gidding as a place of holiness three hundred years after the Puritan plundering, but it also renewed his commitment to "the voice of this Calling." Meanwhile, in admiration of a poetry that explores the mysteries of faith and the motives of the heart, Eliot had again turned his attention to the correction of Herbert's status as a "minor" poet.

On 26 September 1944, several weeks before the publication of *Four Quartets* in England, Eliot delivered his address "What Is Minor Poetry?" Using Herbert as his primary poet for comparison, and defining a major poet as "one the whole of whose work we ought to read, in order fully to appreciate any part of it," he argues that in *The Temple* "there is something we get from the whole book, which is more than a sum of its parts. . . . So in the end, I, for one, cannot admit that Herbert can be called a 'minor' poet: for it is not of a few favourite poems that I am reminded when I think of him, but of the whole work" (*OPP* 45–6). Fully saturated in what he had earlier called the "personal element" and the "spiritual stamina" of Herbert's work, Eliot had become Herbert's champion in his criticism. At one point in the mid-1930s, when he curiously labeled Herbert a minor poet in "Religion and Literature" (1935), he had been shy of revealing Herbert's importance to his own work. But when he included that essay in the second American edition of *Selected Essays* (1950), he added a note to his earlier remarks, reaffirming his judgment in "What Is Minor Poetry": "I stated with some emphasis my opinion that Herbert is a major, not a minor poet. I agree with my later opinion" (*SE* 391).

In succeeding years Herbert grew in stature from a major poet to a great poet in Eliot's mind, one of a shrinking number in his reading life. "I turn more often the pages of . . . George Herbert than those of Donne," he wrote in "To Criticize the Critic" (1961): "what has best responded to my need in middle and later age is different from the nourishment I needed in my youth" (*TCC* 22–3). In that same year, at a luncheon given by Bonamy Dobrée for Herbert Read and Frank Morley, Dobrée mentioned that Eliot had promised him an unspecified essay for the British Council pamphlets. "I suggested," Morley recalled, "try him on George Herbert. Read's electrometer woke. 'Would he do it?' asked Bonamy. 'Try him,' suggested Read. Bonamy tried him, and by then Tom felt ready."[33]

Eliot's pamphlet *George Herbert* (*GH*), published in 1962, is in part a synthesis of his uncollected and unpublished essays on Herbert during the previous thirty years, a formal act of homage to the poet who led him through the 1930s to the quartets and whose poetry had been a mainstay of his later years. Though he quotes extensively from individual poems in praise of their technical mastery and metrical virtuosity, and though he praises Herbert for "a resourcefulness of invention which seems inexhaustible, and for which I know no parallel in English poetry" (*GH* 31), his emphasis is on "the *content* of the poems which make up *The Temple*" (*GH* 19). In "The Collar" and other poems, writes Eliot in definition of his affinity for Herbert, "we can find ample evidence of his spiritual struggles, of self-examination and self-criticism, and of the cost at which he acquired godliness" (*GH* 13). As in his earlier essays, he describes *The Temple* as if he were describing *Four Quartets*, "as a coherent sequence of poems setting down the fluctuations of emotion between despair and bliss, between agitation and serenity, and the discipline of suffering which leads to peace of spirit" (*GH* 23). Appropriately, he concludes the essay by quoting in full the poem with which Herbert concluded *The Temple*, "Love III." In the poem, which to Eliot "indicates the serenity finally attained by this proud and humble man" (*GH* 34), Love repeatedly summons the hungry poet, who is hesitant in his unworthiness, "Guiltie of dust and sinne." The final lines could serve as an epigraph for *Little Gidding*: "You must sit down, sayes Love, and taste my meat: / So I did sit and eat."

George Herbert was to be Eliot's last major essay. On 29 May 1963, following the fiftieth-anniversary commemorative performance of *Le Sacre du Printemps* in London, Igor Stravinsky visited Eliot and his wife Valerie, who in 1957 brought Eliot the human love and happiness that he had long denied himself, and who later revealed that "sometimes he thought of himself as a minor George Herbert."[34] At this meeting Eliot told Stravinsky "that the best parts of his new essay on George Herbert were the quotations, and he regretted that he had not had a 'sense of his audience' while writing it. . . . 'Herbert is a great poet,' [Eliot] went on, 'and one of a very few I can read again and again.'"[35] Stravinsky, whose *Le Sacre du Printemps* had influenced the composition of *The Waste Land*, had recently completed his setting of part 4 of *Little Gidding*, entitled *Anthem (the dove descending breaks the air) for Chorus a cappella* (1962). Less than two years later, at the memorial service for Eliot on 4 February 1965, the Westminster Abbey Choir filled the church with Eliot's lyrics and Stravinsky's music. As Eliot would have approved, and as his wife, who shared his love of Herbert, arranged, the congregation then stood and joined the choir in singing one of Eliot's favorite hymns, Herbert's "Praise (II)," one that Eliot thought was, "like all the rest of his work, personal" (*GH* 33):

> King of glory, King of peace,
>> I will love thee:
> And that love may never cease,
>> I will move thee.
> Thou hast granted my request,
>> Thou hast heard me;
> Thou didst note my working breast,
>> Thou hast spared me.
>
> Wherefore with my utmost art
>> I will sing thee,
> And the cream of all my heart
>> I will bring thee.
> Though my sins against me cried,
>> Thou didst clear me;
> And alone, when they replied,
>> Thou didst hear me.
>
> Seven whole days, not one in seven,
>> I will praise thee;
> In my heart, though not in heaven,
>> I can raise thee;
> Small it is, in this poor sort
>> To enrol thee:
> E'en eternity's too short
>> To extol thee. (*The English Hymnal*, no. 424)

APPENDIX

American Publishers and the
Transmission of T. S. Eliot's Prose

T S. Eliot's presence and influence as a critic have been so monumental in our experience of modernist literature that we have never thought to question the stability and reliability of his texts, or the solidity and permanence of his critical canon. His volumes of prose, particularly *The Sacred Wood*, *Selected Essays*, and *The Use of Poetry and the Use of Criticism*, are so central to Eliot studies and to the discussion of modernism that we have had little cause to turn our attention to the construction, production and transmission of the English and American editions of his work between 1917 and 1965. The general assumption has been that the American-born Eliot, as an English editor and publisher, must always have been in full control of the selection and publication of his own prose collections. We would be astonished to discover otherwise, that American publishers actually initiated most of the major collections, that some American editions of Eliot's prose became corrupted without his knowledge, and that we continue to use these editions for scholarly purposes unaware of their unreliable textual character. But as the archives of publishers of modernist authors begin to open, and as more materials related to the production and transmission of modernist texts become available, we can begin to see that Eliot's prose was as vulnerable to the anarchic state of international publishing as that of any of his contemporaries. His volumes, too, show the effects and consequences of unjust copyright laws, ungoverned editorial practices, and the breakdown of communication between English and American publishers. With some new archival materials at hand, this study aims to begin a reconstruction of the history and socialization of Eliot's primary texts in America. If their separate histories make an urgent case for new critical editions of his prose, they also deepen our perception of the complex relation of author, editor, and publisher and show Eliot in a lifetime struggle to shape and reshape his canon for the marketplace.

I

The Sacred Wood has been Eliot's most stable volume of prose since it was finally published in London by Methuen in 1920, followed by the second edition in 1928. It is a collection that we take for granted, as though Eliot surely and methodically gathered the essays together at a strategic time in his career. Though much of its contents were subsequently collected again in *Selected Essays,* the volume retains its integrity and remains in print as one of the most important prose collections in modern literature. However, it could have been, and almost was, a much less coherent and influential collection, and we now have access to materials that show how unfocused and unstable were its early versions as they progressed, passing through the hands of several American publishers and intermediaries, toward a major, seemingly settled volume.

Eliot's early articles and reviews were driven not by critical impulse but by financial necessity after he married and decided to remain in London. Through Bertrand Russell's connections he found remuneration by writing short reviews for the *International Journal of Ethics* and the *New Statesman*, where one of his first significant literary reviews, "Reflections on *vers libre,*" appeared in 1917 (only to remain in neglect there for many years). Just as Ezra Pound conducted the publication of *Prufrock* in 1917, so he orchestrated Eliot's first appearance between boards as a critic, and it is now more amusing than ironic that *Ezra Pound: His Metric and Poetry* was published anonymously and only in America, where it too languished for years. It was strategically designed to appear with the publication of Pound's *Lustra*, and Pound prescribed anonymity for Eliot primarily to preclude charges of logrolling. As he explained to John Quinn, who made the arrangements with Pound's publisher, Alfred Knopf, "I want to boom Eliot and one can't have too obvious a ping-pong match at that sort of thing" (*L1* xxiii).[1]

As Eliot moved from Poundian anonymity toward critical notoriety in his subsequent reviews for the *Egoist*, the *Little Review,* and the *Athenaeum*, his first attempted collection after the publication of *Prufrock* was a miscellany of prose and poetry that he sent to Alfred Knopf in America at John Quinn's behest. Eliot was motivated not by pride of prose but by anxiety about convincing his parents that he had not made a mess of his life. "It is not the book I should have liked," he wrote to Quinn in September 1918. "I should prefer to keep the prose and verse apart; and the former, I fear, bears marks of haste in the writing in many places. But it is time I had a volume in America. . . . I hope you will not find the book a wholly journalistic compilation" (*L1* 245). Eliot was not proud of the collection, and we would like to see the 1918 contents page, for he had not yet written any of the major essays that would appear in *The Sacred Wood*. When

Knopf rejected the manuscript in January 1919, on grounds that since Pound's *Pavannes and Divisions* was not selling he could not take a chance on Eliot, Quinn offered it unsuccessfully to other American houses—Boni and Liveright rejected it in June, John Lane Company in August—until he finally returned it to Eliot, who had been adding and deleting essays at every turn. The death of his father earlier in the year had lessened Eliot's anxiety about publishing in America, but in any case no American publisher was prepared to take a collection of essays from a totally unknown author. Had a publisher acquiesced to Quinn's persistence, the contents of the latest gathering in July 1919 would have included "Eeldrop and Appleplex," "A Romantic Patrician" (Eliot's review of George Wyndham's *Essays in Romantic Literature*), "A Sceptical Patrician" (his review of *The Education of Henry Adams*), "The New Elizabethans and the Old" (a review of a book on poets who had been killed in the war), and "American Literature" (a review of *A History of American Literature,* vol. 2, edited by William P. Trent and others). The selection was governed by his estimate of American interests rather than his own critical concerns. "I wish that I were anywhere near satisfied with the book," he wrote to Quinn (*L1* 313).

When he received the returned manuscript from Quinn he removed the poems and gave them to John Rodker with some new poems for publication at the Ovid Press as *Ara Vos Prec*. The new poems had been accompanied by three important and now canonical essays—"'Rhetoric' and Poetic Drama," "Some Notes on the Blank Verse of Christopher Marlowe," "Hamlet and His Problems"—and Eliot was greatly relieved to have the earlier prose pieces returned. "Some of it I shall probably use," he wrote to Quinn on 5 November 1919, "some of it I shall certainly suppress; I do not want to use any of it without thorough revision" (*L1* 343). Eliot then combined the unsuppressed essays, only one of which ("A Romantic Patrician") would make it to *The Sacred Wood*, with some of the *Egoist* articles that Harriet Weaver had recently encouraged him to collect, and this newly cobbled volume was actually announced by the Egoist Press as *The Art of Poetry* in December 1919.[2] *The Art of Poetry* was to be built up around a lecture that Eliot considered his most important to date, "Modern Tendencies in Poetry," but the director of the Arts League of Service, which had sponsored the lecture, whisked it off to India for publication in the first number of *Shama'a*, effectively removing it from circulation. When the English publisher Richard Cobden-Sanderson approached Eliot about collecting his *Athenaeum* essays, Eliot wrote to his brother that he now envisaged not one but possibly two volumes of prose in the spring of 1920 (*L1* 331).

Though the contents of Eliot's prose collection still fluctuated with every vanishing promise and possibility, he had nonetheless begun to feel the cumulative influential effect of his reviews, almost a hundred in number, on contemporary criticism. "I really think," he wrote immodestly to his mother, "that I have far more *influence* on English letters than any other American has ever had unless it be Henry James" (*L1* 280). In the autumn of 1919 he seemed to discover his unique critical voice, and the "heresies" (*L1* 327) that he called his essays and reviews took on a new critical force.

While Eliot was conscious of his public image as a critic, his friend Richard

Aldington was the one poet-critic who did not believe that Eliot's poetry was superior to his prose. He disliked Eliot's poetry altogether, in fact, but at the same time he openly proclaimed that Eliot was "the only modern writer of prose criticism in English" (*L1* 321). Aldington, who regularly reviewed French literature for *TLS*, took him to meet the editor, Bruce Richmond, who had read Eliot's articles in the *Athenaeum* and requested the meeting. "The result of our first meeting," wrote Eliot, who was assigned to write on Elizabethan and Jacobean poetry, particularly dramatic poetry, "was my leading article on Ben Jonson; and nearly all of my essays on the drama of that period—perhaps all of my best ones—started as suggestions by Richmond."[3] "Ben Jonson" (13 November 1919) was followed by "Philip Massinger" (27 May 1920), and Richmond's commissions and editing pushed Eliot's prose to a new plateau. "For Bruce Richmond we wanted to do our best," wrote Eliot, who frequently acknowledged his debt: "Good literary criticism requires good editors as well as good critics, and Bruce Richmond was a great editor: fortunate those critics who wrote for him."[4]

Richmond's appointment of Eliot in the autumn of 1919, and the challenge he presented to him in Elizabethan literature, were crucial factors not only in the reshaping of *The Sacred Wood* but in determining the primary focus of Eliot's criticism. In rapid succession came "Ben Jonson," "Tradition and the Individual Talent," "Swinburne as Poet," "William Blake," "Euripides and Professor Murray." Not until March 1920 did he take time to contact Algernon Methuen, who had approached him months earlier about a possible collection, and on the 26th he wrote to Quinn: "I am gradually putting a prose book together—I think much more solid than the first attempt; and there is a good possibility of getting a good publisher to take it here"(*L1* 378). As he contracted successfully with Methuen he published "Dante as a 'Spiritual Leader'" and "Philip Massinger," displacing lesser essays, and he raced against his submission deadline to write "The Perfect Critic," "The Possibility of a Poetic Drama" and the introduction (chiefly on Matthew Arnold). In nine months he had written the essays that would form the permanent nucleus of his critical canon and change the course of academic criticism for the next fifty years. Fortunately for Eliot, and for his readers, five publishers had backed away from the earlier versions before Methuen published *The Sacred Wood* in November 1920. It now had a literary rather than an American focus: "Taken together," declares the dust jacket of the various essays, "they form a study of past Poetry which will assist in the appraisement of the present."

It is curious that Eliot finally went to Methuen with his prose, wary as he was of the English publishing establishment and committed as he was to small alternative houses for his poetry—the Egoist Press, the Ovid Press, the Hogarth Press. He had looked upon the establishment as a monolithic, almost impenetrable barrier, writing to his mother that he had warned an American Jewish friend "that getting recognised in English letters is like breaking open a safe—for an American, and that only about three had ever done it"(*L1* 392). But even after the volume appeared he eschewed the enhancement of his image as a critic lest it discolor his image as a poet. When André Gide wrote to compliment him on his new essays, he replied, "If you know me only through *The Sacred Wood*, I should like to send you my poems, which are at least superior to my prose writings!" (*L1*

495). In fact, he began to cultivate an indifference toward his prose, frequently making disparaging remarks about it, as though it was not and never could be representative of his best work. "Candidly," he wrote to Sydney Schiff, "I don't think that prose ought to be paid at the same rate as verse" (L1 332), and he made the decision to publish *The Waste Land* in the first number of the *Criterion* "because I thought it wiser not to appear myself as a prose essayist in the early numbers" (L1 572). He was to maintain this distance from his prose throughout his career, and it may have allowed for the liberties that publishers would eventually take with it.

One of the American publishers, Alfred Knopf, then came forward to take the English sheets of *The Sacred Wood* for a small American edition of 365 copies, published in February 1921. Thanks to the fact that Knopf chose to import English sheets and thereby forego the option of acquiring the American copyright, it was the last time that Eliot would enjoy identical texts in the English and American editions of his prose.

II

After the publication of *The Sacred Wood*, the next three reviews that Eliot wrote for Bruce Richmond, all in 1921, more than justified the *TLS* appointment— "Andrew Marvell," "John Dryden," and "The Metaphysical Poets." These were also permanent additions to his canon, and through the agency of Virginia and Leonard Woolf they were to enjoy a collected life of their own, published as *Homage to John Dryden* at the Hogarth Press in 1924. The Woolfs had published a small edition of Eliot's *Poems* in 1919, followed by the first English edition of *The Waste Land* in 1923, and Eliot believed that no one in England really paid attention to his poems until the Woolfs took him up. We are only now beginning to learn just how important this scarce collection of essays was to the notice of Eliot's prose in England. Lytton Strachey and John Middleton Murry had favourably reviewed *The Sacred Wood* in England, as had Conrad Aiken and Marianne Moore in America, but overall the reviews were "mixed" and the impact of the volume was still very modest, especially in America, where his mother characterized the reviews as "savage" (L1 419n). But when *Homage to John Dryden* circulated among F. R. Leavis, I. A. Richards, E. M. W. Tillyard, Basil Willey, and others in the new Cambridge School of English, the effect was enormous. Leavis has testified that

> *The Sacred Wood* . . . had very little influence or attention before the Hogarth Press brought out *Homage to John Dryden*. . . . It was with the publication in this form of those essays . . . that Eliot became the important contemporary critic. It was the impact of this slender new collection that sent one back to *The Sacred Wood* and confirmed with decisive practical effect one's sense of the stimulus to be got from that rare thing, a fine intelligence in literary criticism.[5]

The volume was instrumental in Eliot's appointment as Clark Lecturer at Cambridge in 1925, an unlikely appointment that enabled him to develop his theory of metaphysical poetry, the theory that he apologized for having abandoned in his dispirited preface to *Homage to John Dryden* (*VMP* 4–5). The stimulated interest in *The Sacred Wood* led to the second edition in May 1928, with Eliot's important new preface. Knopf declined to import English sheets for an American issue, evidently because the first edition had moved slowly and was still in print; nonetheless, the critical principles in the volume were soon to form the basis of the New Criticism in the American academy: "the problem appearing in these essays," Eliot wrote in his new preface, "which gives them what coherence they have, is the problem of the integrity of poetry, with the repeated assertion that when we are considering poetry we must consider it primarily as poetry and not another thing" (*SW* x).

Eliot also indicated that he had recently passed on "to another problem not touched upon in this book: that of the relation of poetry to the spiritual and social life of its time and of other times" (*SW* x). He was of course pointing to his new volume of prose, *For Lancelot Andrewes*, which would appear in November 1928 with his famous declaration that the point of view behind the essays was "classicist in literature, royalist in politics, and anglo-catholic in religion."[6] Five of these eight extra-literary essays would go forward to *Selected Essays*, together with the three in *Homage to John Dryden*, nine from *The Sacred Wood*, and fourteen others collected for the first time. Many of these suffered significant alterations and deletions in transit, particularly the great essay "Dante" (1929), which lost the preface, the epigraph from the *Vita Nuova*, the dedication to Charles Maurras, and the unidentified quotation from Maurras's own study, *Le Conseil de Dante* (1920).[7] Scholars who persist in working only from the collected trade editions, and who fail to return to the essays in their original form and format, will do so at their peril until we have standard critical editions of Eliot's prose in place.

III

The English and American editions of *Selected Essays 1917–1932* were published simultaneously by Faber and Faber and by Harcourt Brace on 15 September 1932, just as Eliot sailed to America for the first time since leaving eighteen years earlier. But contrary to all expectation, the Harcourt Brace archives show that this famous collection was initiated neither by Eliot nor by Faber and Faber. It was in fact the brainwave of two young editors at Harcourt Brace—Ray Everitt and Charles Pearce, who acted with the encouragement and support of Donald Brace.[8] On 24 February 1930 Everitt wrote to Frank Morley of Faber and Faber, saying that "Two or three of us here have followed T. S. Eliot for some time, and we find our interest in his work deepening." Everitt asked for Morley's assistance in publishing a "definitive edition" of Eliot's essays, including "a number of old ones specially corrected with new ones added—a book which would define his critical position." Everitt hoped that Morley would approach Eliot about the proposal, and suggested that Brace could discuss it with Eliot on his spring visit to London. "Don't you think," he asked in conclusion, "that a definitive edition of Eliot's essays would be a timely and important publication?" Morley passed the letter on to Eliot and urged Brace to come in when he arrived: "I do not not think it impossible that something could come of it and if something did I think it would be good"(HBA).

Nothing did come of it, however, for a full year, and Everitt, meanwhile, left the firm. Undeterred, on 3 March 1931 Pearce sent a new proposal directly to Eliot, enclosing two lists of essays (both missing from files)—one in chronological order, the other grouped under several headings—and offering to handle all editing, proofreading, and copyright matters for him. Eliot replied on 12 March that he liked the proposal "very well" and was "flattered" by Pearce's detailed attention:

> I think your suggestions for contents and arrangement are on the whole excellent. I should have a few suggestions of detail to make; for instance, there are two or three long essays which you probably have not seen and which I should like to include, possibly instead of a few of those in your collection. The first question, however, to discuss, is one of copyrights. (HBA)

Morley, preparing to sail for America the next day, arranged to meet with Pearce in New York on 2 April, at Eliot's request. Pearce apparently failed to make a strong impression on Morley; almost five months later, on 25 August, Morley, having mislaid Pearce's letters to him and Eliot, was forced to write to Alfred Harcourt for Pearce's name and copies of the correspondence "to make sure that we all have the same idea about the volume." He disclosed that Eliot had been going through his essays and making selections, and that Morley himself was negotiating with Methuen for permission to include essays from *The Sacred Wood*.

Five months later, on 12 January 1932, Morley finally sent Donald Brace two copies of Eliot's provisional table of contents for consideration, noting that the length ran to 145,000 words and that Eliot had come up with no title other than *Selected Essays*: "We are busily collecting the material—the trouble is that Eliot has found difficulty in finding some of it and I hope to be able to write more fully by next mail. . . . Three or four of the essays are either unfinished or need polishing, and I am prodding Eliot daily." After a year of mulling, searching, and selecting, Eliot expanded Pearce's groups from five to eight. The result was the first organization of his canon, for which he used abbreviated and misremembered titles, some of which were to stick. The list included some unfinished or unwritten pieces that were dropped or abandoned in the following months:

Selected Essays by T. S. Eliot

I

Tradition and the Individual Talent
The Function of Criticism

VIII

Arnold and Pater
Bradley
Marie Lloyd
Humanism of I. B.
Second Thoughts
Charles Whibley

Pearce informed Brace that eight of the essays were entirely new to him, and on 9 February 1932 Morley wrote to Brace to account for them:

> The chief problem here is that some of the essays have not actually been completed yet, that is why . . . Pearce hasn't seen them. The essay on Herbert is being completed for next week's issue of the Times Literary Supplement;[9] Ford is due for completion before the end of this month;[10] What Time is It? is in the same state;[11] A Note on John Marston has been written but we have talked over one or two alterations;[12] Heywood and Tourneur have appeared in the Times Literary Supplement; Charles Whibley is completed—none of these appeared in America. Marie Lloyd, in a different form, appeared in a London Letter to the Dial some time back.[13]

Pearce made a strong appeal to add "Donne in Our Time."[14] Eliot considered but eventually refused the request as he reshaped the contents under the eye of Morley, who wrote to Brace on 22 April: "Studying the text intensively I am more than ever impressed with its permanent value." Pearce, however, received a different note on the contents from an unidentified in-house colleague: "Isn't it rather a pity that Eliot is so *English* in this collection? Only Dante crosses the Channel. I wish he had included some of the *Criterion* essays on foreign writers & thinkers!" By 27 April, when Morley sent Brace the last batch of galleys, all corrected by Eliot, "The Idea of a Literary Review" and "What Time Is It?" had been dropped from section 1; sections 2 and 3 were conflated, deleting "The Possibility of a Poetic Drama" and "A Note on Marston"; "Herbert" was cut from section 5; "Baudelaire" and, at the last minute, "Wilkie Collins and Dickens" were added to what was now section 7. By 5 May Brace had the galleys in hand; only proofs for the prelims and a new contents page inclusive of dates were outstanding as Brace and Pearce worked on the American copyright and permission problems.

Eliot had every reason to express his concern to Pearce about copyrights at the beginning of the project. He was at once uncertain of the copyright status of his essays and prose collections and fully aware of the isolationist stance of American copyright law, which he had described in the *Criterion* (July 1927) as "a matter which touches closely anyone who publishes a book, or even a periodical article in Great Britain." As a strong supporter of the movement for copyright reform, he told his readers that "the present American Copyright Law is a flagrant injustice to British and still more to Irish writers, and one of the first particulars to which 'International Intellectual Co-operation' should be directed" (Cr 6:3). He was deeply conscious of the effects of the Chace law of 1891, which contained a notorious clause requiring books to be printed in the United States in order to secure American rights. In the *Criterion* for November 1927 he quoted a reply from a sympathetic American editor about the dilemma:

> I also note your opinion of the American copyright law, and I wish I could send word that there was hope of passing a new bill this year. . . . The famous manufacturing clause [of the Chace law] which kept us out of the International Copyright Union was a concession to the printing unions which was finally made in order to get any bill passed. The unions did not at that time have leaders who could see far enough ahead to realize what a mistaken demand theirs was. (Cr 6:387)

What Pearce discovered in this shortsighted climate was that when Knopf imported English sheets for the American issue of *The Sacred Wood* he thereby lost the opportunity to obtain the American copyright. Further, Knopf had declined to import sheets of the second edition in 1928, and Pearce believed that the volume was now out of print in America, unaware that Knopf had in fact imported five hundred second-edition sheets for an American issue in 1930.[15] On his side, Morley discovered that Methuen had also failed to acquire the American copyright and that Eliot and Harcourt Brace were thus free to include the eight essays. In his negotiated agreement with Methuen, Morley arranged that Harcourt Brace need pay them nothing for the right to reproduce the material in America. And though the three essays in *Homage to John Dryden* had been copyrighted in America in 1928, when they were included in the Doubleday Doran publication of *The Hogarth Essays*, it was permissible to include them in Eliot's new collection because they originally appeared in England in 1924. Other American copyright holders of Eliot's essays—*Hound and Horn*, Oxford University Press (New York), and others—were sent formal letters requesting permission to reprint, and in the end all permissions were granted without any payment of fees.

Such accommodation for permissions did not, however, mean that the individual essays in the American edition of *Selected Essays* were now protected. Morley wrote to Eliot from New York on 3 October 1932, shortly after publication and after receipt of the first request to reprint an extract from an essay in the volume,

> Since the greater part of the contents of *Selected Essays* is not protected by copyright here, these people could legally take extracts without asking for permission. As a matter of fact, however, they will for the most part not realize this and will ask us. It is our regular practice to be rather strict in the matter of granting permission and to require fees, at least whenever the use is in a publication issued for profit. (HBA)

Eliot accordingly authorized Brace to handle requests in this manner, expressing his hope that there would not be many requests for entire essays.[16]

Morley had done everything in his power to ensure that the texts of the two editions would be identical, but American editorial requirements and practices were to conspire against this. He wrote to Brace on 17 May: "My supplementary table of contents should have been received by now. There is nothing else to add to the material, which even unto preliminaries is a complete duplicate of ours, but I will send you a page proof to check up by as soon as it comes in in the course of a few days" (HBA). The set of page proofs from the English edition was forwarded on 14 June, "embodying some further corrections passim. This completes the material for the book" (HBA). Brace replied on 29 June that the book could now be completed rapidly, and he successfully urged Morley to agree upon a mutual publication date of 15 September.[17]

The errors in both editions of *Selected Essays 1917–1932* began in the dated title—there were no essays earlier than 1919—and in the misdating of seven separate essays on the contents page. These were Eliot's unchecked errors of memory, and though all were eventually corrected in the third English edition (1951), two essays remain misdated in the current American edition—"The Humanism of Irving Babbitt" (1928, not 1927) and "Second Thoughts about Humanism" (1929, not 1928).[18] The Harcourt Brace contents page, moreover, survives as a congeries of editorial oversights and liberties, and it is clear that in spite of the fact that revised proofs of the contents were sent, a version of Eliot's provisional, abbreviated contents page remained on the editor's desk: the special punctuation of "Rhetoric" in " 'Rhetoric' and Poetic Drama" remains missing; the erroneous "The Elizabethan Dramatists" prevails over "Four Elizabethan Dramatists." "Hamlet," however, has been restored by the editors to its original title, "Hamlet and His Problems," in *The Sacred Wood*—this title appears in no English edition of *Selected Essays* but persists in the current American edition. Though "Christopher Marlowe" is correctly expanded from "Marlowe" on the contents page, the corresponding correction failed: it remains "Marlowe" in the text and running title.

The persistent editorial problems of the American edition of *Selected Essays* began, of course, when Harcourt Brace was compelled to set the text from Faber and Faber's corrected galleys. Complying with American copyright law, Harcourt Brace completely redesigned the book, with different binding, type, typography, page layout, pagination, punctuation, and so forth.[19] When we go to the Gallup bibliography before initiating any scholarship, we find the reassuring statement: "Contents as in the English first edition;" but Gallup's descriptive method was "based upon that adopted by the American Library Association," which is not concerned to describe textual variations (*Gallup* 48, 11). Quite apart from American punctuation conventions, and not to mention differences in line spacing and indentation, there is a gamut of unauthorized emendations to run, emendations that Pearce and Brace doubtless felt they were free and correct to make at the time. For example, in what was to become a habitual practice with American publishers of Eliot's texts, his own habit of modernizing the spellings of Elizabethan titles was rejected and the old spellings were restored, as on the first page of "Thomas Middleton," where the title words *Chess, Girl,* and *Gypsy* are altered to *Chesse, Girle* and *Gipsie* (p. 140). And in a passage from "Shakespeare and the Stoicism of Seneca" the seemingly benign emendation of a capital letter results in the greater error of dropped italics: "It is *equally* great poetry" (p. 137) has become "it is equally great poetry" (p. 117). These and other inconsistencies continue to differentiate the two texts in their current editions.

More serious problems lay in the future, but Harcourt Brace did have Eliot's American interests at heart. On the same day they published *Selected Essays,* they took advantage of being Eliot's new American publisher to bring out the first American edition of *Poems 1909–1925*, seven years after the English edition of 1925. Up to then, American readers had only Knopf's small edition of *Poems* (1920)—the American version of *Ara Vos Prec*—and Boni & Liveright's *The Waste Land*, both of which were out of print, and Knopf had affirmed that *Poems* would not be reprinted. Thus, when Harcourt Brace announced the forthcoming publication of *Selected Essays*, their offices were flooded with inquiries as to why they had no *Selected Poems*. Brace reported to Morley on 24 June that "Harvard Co-op thinks they will have much more call for the Poems than the Essays, and several other booksellers inquire about the Poems and complain of the fact that no edition is available for them." To meet the anticipated immediate demand, Morley acceded to Brace's request to import five hundred sheets of *Poems 1909–25*. Thus, when Eliot arrived in Boston on 26 September the new Harcourt Brace editions of his poetry and prose were reaching the shops. On 18 October Brace cabled for 250 additional sheets of poems, increased the order to 500, and then sent for another 500 on 19 December: "From the 500 sheets received this month, all but 147 have been sold in three days because of orders waiting for them. I think we shall be ready for this third lot of 500 by the time it can reach here" (HBA).[20] Eliot's presence at Harvard and his Norton Lectures doubtless enhanced sales; however, due to the ten-year publishing vacuum for his poems and the generally weak marketing of his works in America, he was to remain unrecognized as a native son by some of the press, evidenced in the Chicago *Daily Tribune*, which hailed him as an "English Lion" and as "the greatest living English poet" after he had returned to London.[21]

Despite their attempts to serve Eliot's interests in America, Harcourt Brace unknowingly got into editorial trouble by being unmindful or unapprised of what Faber and Faber were doing to *Selected Essays* in England. In October 1934 Faber lifted from the first edition the contents of section 3 on Elizabethan literature, added Eliot's new *TLS* essay "John Marston," and published the collection separately in the Faber Library series as *Elizabethan Essays*. Later in the same month, Faber published the second English edition, revised and enlarged, of *Selected Essays*—enlarged by reincorporating the whole of *Elizabethan Essays* into section 3. There was no corresponding second edition by Harcourt Brace, and so for the next seventeen years English readers enjoyed a revised text and a bonus essay in *Selected Essays*.[22]

Meanwhile, *For Lancelot Andrewes* had gone out of print, leaving Eliot no appropriate vehicle for his new essays on religious and social topics, including "Religion and Literature," "The *Pensées* of Pascal," "Modern Education and the Classics" and "In Memoriam." He removed three essays from the contents of *For Lancelot Andrewes* and combined the remainder with his new essays in a revised edition entitled *Essays Ancient and Modern* (1936). Once again Eliot's distant atti-

tude toward his prose surfaced in the presentation of the volume, which is remarkably halfhearted, hardly a hard sell. "I offer this book, as the title implies,"
Eliot wrote in the preface, "only as a miscellaneous collection, having no greater
unity than that of having been written by the same person."[23] Five months later,
Harcourt Brace published an American edition, with deletions only in the preface,[24] but the edition was to be another ingredient in the recipe for a major publishing error.

There were to be no more collections of Eliot's essays for fourteen years, but
on 6 April 1949 another young editor at Harcourt Brace, Robert Giroux, wrote
to Eliot about the state of his books in America. *Selected Essays* was still in print,
though the stock was nearing depletion. As Eliot's most recent volume of prose,
Essays Ancient and Modern, was now out of print, Giroux proposed to reprint it.
Eliot replied on 19 April that he was "perfectly agreeable" to the reprinting,

> unless you prefer to do an enlarged edition of *Selected Essays* with a selection
> from *Essays Ancient and Modern* and two or three more recent ones. But I had
> rather wanted to keep the more recent ones, notably *The Music of Poetry* and
> *Milton*, for a new volume of essays on poetry which would include my two lec-
> tures on *The Development of Shakespeare's Versification* and my two lectures on
> Johnson's *Lives of the Poets* when I was able to find the time to rewrite them.[25]
> (HBA)

Giroux replied on 27 April that they would prefer to publish the new volume
of essays on poetry when ready rather than add the new essays to an enlarged edition of *Selected Essays*. For the present, however, they preferred to publish an enlarged edition with a selection from *Essays Ancient and Modern* rather than reprint
the latter. Accordingly, on 1 July Eliot sent Giroux a copy of the American edition
of *Essays Ancient and Modern*, indicating his selections (with dates provided by John
Hayward) and their positions in *Selected Essays*: "Religion and Literature," "The
Pensées of Pascal," "Modern Education and the Classics," and "In Memoriam."
"When these four essays are included," he wrote, "there will only be left two out of
those in *Essays Ancient and Modern* which I want to scrap" (HBA).[26] He also expressed his wish to include his essay "Byron as a Scottish Poet," but because he had
no copy he would have to borrow the book in which it appeared before sending it
on. On 24 October he finally informed Giroux of his conclusion "that it is not
quite good enough to be worth including."[27]

To celebrate and take advantage of the fact that Eliot received the Nobel
Prize for Literature in December 1948, Harcourt Brace had planned to bring out
a Nobel Prize edition of *Selected Essays*. Eliot had even sent over a new contents
page with dates of publication, but the project was abandoned. That contents
page, which evidently contained the misdatings of "The Humanism of Irving
Babbitt" and "Second Thoughts about Humanism," was now brought forward to
date the essays in the new edition. Giroux may have had a copy of the second
English edition, for he informed another editor that the dates in the title of *Selected Essays 1917–1932* were to be dropped, because the dates were wrong and had
been dropped from the English edition. If he did have the second English edition

before him, he failed to compare the new proofs with the 1934 contents page, which would have revealed a glaring omission. Eliot received proofs only from the end of section 5 to section 7, which contained the corrected plates for the added essays. Even so, he was advised by Giroux on 21 April that they were "simply for reference purposes and, unless you want to, it is not necessary to read them for correction, since they are being most carefully proofread on this side"(HBA).

The second American, or "new edition," issued by Harcourt Brace on 5 October 1950 preceded the third English edition by eleven months. The preface for the American edition was simply redated for the English edition. Writing the preface in July 1950, Eliot was wholly unaware that two distinctly different editions were in preparation, and he was later baffled by how the discrepancies could have occurred.[28] Faber and Faber based theirs on the revised second English edition of 1934, which had been reprinted six times by 1949; Harcourt Brace took the plates of their 1932 edition, substituted Eliot's revised contents page with newly misdated essays, incorporated the four essays from their edition of *Essays Ancient and Modern,* and thus published an unrevised text lacking the essay on "John Marston." Hence, for over sixty years American scholars with *Selected Essays* in their hands unknowingly have been playing with corrupt cards and a short deck.

I confess that I was unaware of these matters until I was well into editing Eliot's *Varieties of Metaphysical Poetry* (1993). I had been conveniently keying page numbers to the American editions of Eliot's prose when Faber and Faber asked me to use English editions. When I could not locate a third English edition of *Selected Essays* in libraries of the southeastern United States, I asked the firm to send me a copy. Most American libraries simply purchase the Harcourt Brace editions and do not duplicate with English editions. A forty-page discrepancy in the pagination for the same quotations in the American and English editions led me to turn the pages one by one until, after "Philip Massinger," to my astonishment, I came not to "Dante," as in the American edition, but to "John Marston." When Marston came crashing in to reveal his sixty-year absence in my edition of *Selected Essays,* and when I looked at the cold facts of the second English edition of 1934, I realized that my prized, career-long copy was, as an edition, a bag of nails, a miscrossed hybrid of textual transmission that had affected the reading and scholarship of a major text. Of course, the only remedy to this unscholarly textual situation is a much-needed standard critical edition of *Selected Essays.*

IV

I turn now to Eliot's Charles Eliot Norton Lectures, which he delivered at Harvard University during the 1932–33 academic year and published as *The Use of Poetry and the Use of Criticism.* Editorial discussion of the textual characteristics of Eliot's lectures eventually leads to the topic of misquotation, which, we are beginning to discover, is endemic in modernist texts.[29] Eliot had a vast literary memory, and certain passages of poetry and prose, particularly those of Dante and Shakespeare, he had by heart, or almost by heart, and when he summoned them to illustrate his lectures he seldom bothered to check their accuracy later. In some instances the misquotations affect his commentary, and in every instance it is of interest to observe how he held and transformed and returned to certain key passages in his memory. The misquotations thus become an integral part of the text, and it is not surprising to find several of them in his Norton Lectures.

The terms of the Charles Eliot Norton Lectures specify: "Within six months after their delivery, the manuscript of these lectures shall be delivered to Harvard University, whose property this manuscript shall then become." Late in December 1932, when Eliot learned that Oxford University Press ordinarily received the English rights to the lectures, he petitioned Harold Murdock, director of Harvard University Press, to grant the English rights to him for publication by Faber and Faber. On 28 December Murdock made the request on Eliot's behalf to President A. Lawrence Lowell, and at a meeting of the president and fellows of Harvard College on 9 January 1933 the request was approved.[30]

Eliot concluded his Norton Lectures on 31 March 1933 and returned to England in June to begin revising for the September deadline. The English and American editions of *The Use of Poetry and the Use of Criticism* were published simultaneously on 2 November 1933. "Contents as in the first edition (English)," Gallup writes of the American edition, "except that the dedication is printed on page [v]" (*Gallup* 52), so the conscientious critic should feel free to use whichever edition is at hand. Would that it were so! Once again there are marked differences between the English and American texts, and the situation was to be compounded in the second edition of 1964. An English reader who knows his Byron and Shelley, for example, might notice the interesting misquotations from *Don Juan* and *Epipsychidion* in the first edition, but an American reader would notice only the latter in his.[31] Those same readers would find misquotations only from *Don Juan* in the second English edition, only from *Epipsychidion* in the second American. There are other significant variations to account for, but unfortunately, and inexplicably, there is a gap in the correspondence of the Harvard University Press archives from 1932 to 1937. Eliot's corrected page proofs, however, have survived to tell much of the story.[32]

Eliot appears to have given the proofs a once-over, making about twenty-five corrections and emendations in ink. Among other minor oversights, he failed to check the misquotations and overlooked the missing hyphen in *Ash-Wednesday*. After these proof corrections were sent to America, further unreported corrections were made for the English edition, including restoration of the title hyphen. More noticeably, Eliot dropped the second of three footnotes on page 131 and incorporated the note into the text.[33] Thus, the two texts had gone awry even before the proofs reached Randall Hall.

In July 1932, just before Eliot began his tenure as Norton Professor, the Harvard University Press moved from its old offices in Randall Hall to new quarters on Quincey Street. The proof room, however, remained in Randall Hall, which the Press historian Max Hall characterized as "not only a place for correcting typographical errors but the nearest thing to an editorial department that the Press had."[34] The proof room was headed by "an aggressive man" named Joseph Tuckerman Day, a Harvard graduate, journalist, and editor who had worked at the *New York Times*, the Associated Press, and Ginn and Company before joining the Harvard Press in 1929. As an editor, Day carried on the nineteenth-century tradition of correcting and improving the author's prose, and he enjoyed the authoritative presence of Professor George Lyman Kittredge, a syndic of the Press who gave freely of his boundless editorial energy. As Hall recounts, "Harvard's Press seems to have been slower than most in establishing an editorial department in the modern sense, possibly because its proof room was populous and versatile, possibly also because many of its books benefited from editing by the University departments or by Professor Kittredge." Theodore Spencer, a Harvard English instructor who assisted Eliot in his course on contemporary literature, and who is acknowledged for his assistance with the volume, may also have been called into Randall Hall to read the proofs. In any event, such was the editorial climate when Eliot's corrected proofs arrived in October 1933.

The editors in Randall Hall entered all Eliot's proof corrections (except for rejecting Eliot's inserted hyphen in "field-work," p. 148n), corrected some additional typos, and then proceeded to edit the text. Eliot did not intend to misquote Byron, reasoned Joseph Day or another editor, and Harvard University Press would be institutionally remiss not to make the correction. The Shelley misquotation, however, escaped all editorial eyes. The editor removed several paragraph indentations, took liberties with some of Eliot's phrasing ("Addison observes that:" changed to "Addison observes:"), and altered the punctuation in several instances. The editor was generally unrestrained, even changing titles and rearranging textual material: at the end of two lectures, Eliot appended a formal note directly below his text, separated from it only by a double space, in the first instance entitled, "Note to Chapter I / On the Development of Taste in Poetry" (p. 32). In the American edition, each note has been removed from the bottom of the text and set on a new page, with an independent title and an imposed emphasis of its own: "Note on the Development of 'Taste' in Poetry" (p. 24).[35] With the author unawares, the result, in short, was another hybrid American edition.[36]

The first American edition later had every opportunity to improve itself, but its character was too deeply set. In 1964 Faber brought out the second English edition of *The Use of Poetry*, for which Eliot wrote a new preface. "The eight lectures in this volume," he wrote after making his revisions, "seem to me still valid. At least, I am ashamed neither of the style nor of the matter. Not having looked at them for many years, I found them, after two readings, acceptable enough for me to hope that republication in the present form may justify itself" (p. 10). Eliot retained his original 1933 preface but silently dropped a note that had appeared in the first English edition (p. 137): "With the influence of the devil on contemporary literature I shall be concerned in more detail in another book." He corrected the Shelley misquote but overlooked the Byron once again. He italicized a word for emphasis ("whether the attempt to teach students to *appreciate* English literature should be made at all," p. 36) and made other minor changes of punctuation, but he did not incorporate any emendations from the first American edition. It is clear that Eliot never saw the revised proofs of the first American edition and that he never referred to it when revising the second English edition.

The second American edition of *The Use of Poetry*, published by Harvard University Press in 1964, is only technically a second edition; in effect, it is merely a second printing of the first American edition, compromised by the absence of the original preface and by the presence of the new preface to the revised text of the second English edition. Harvard incorporated the new preface "by arrangement with Faber and Faber Ltd.," but the Press did nothing more than dust off the plates of their first edition, making none of the deletions, emendations, and corrections that Eliot had made for the second English edition. By appending to the unrevised text Eliot's new preface, with his expressed concern for the publication of the volume in its "present form," the Harvard edition leads American readers to believe that the corrupt form before them is the one to which Eliot refers. But the second American edition is nothing more than the hybrid first in new, more deceptive clothing (handsomely reprinted in 1986). Of course, the only remedy to this unscholarly textual situation is a standard critical edition of *The Use of Poetry and the Use of Criticism*.

V

Though there are still several volumes of prose before us, with still more troubling differences between the English and American editions, the dramatic point has been made, and as space is limited their textual histories must be recounted elsewhere. Some of the serious problems with later volumes, such as *After Strange Gods* and *Notes towards the Definition of Culture*, are often as much contextual as textual, and we sorely need critical editions with historical and contextual introductions to these works. As the later volumes of prose appeared, the communication/distribution gap between the English and American editions remained wide open, leading to major scholarly oversights. The Faber and Harcourt editions of *Notes towards the Definition of Culture*, for example, appeared in 1948, but in 1962, with no response from America, Faber brought out a "new English edition" in its paper-covered series. Eliot not only wrote an important new preface; he made a significant alteration: "One footnote," he remarks, "on page 70, I have re-written: it may still be that I have tried to say too much too briefly, and that the notion needs further elaboration."[37] That rewritten footnote comes out of his conscious reflection on previous allegations of anti-Semitism in his work and is important to any study of those allegations. There were 15,800 copies of the edition printed in England, many times the number of earlier prose editions, but the only copy I have located in American research libraries is in the Widener Library at Harvard. The unavailability of this paper-covered edition in America consequently exacts its toll on American scholarship.

There was also an attempt by Eliot's friend John Hayward to introduce and popularize Eliot's critical writings in England during and after World War II, first in a Faber edition entitled *Points of View*, where with Eliot's approval he selected extracts from his prose and gave them separate titles. In 1953 he expanded this collection as *Selected Prose*, in an edition of forty thousand copies published by Penguin and expressly "Not for sale in the U.S.A." It contained substantial extracts from "Reflections on *vers libre*," "What Dante Means to Me," "Virgil and the Christian World," and "Yeats," and though the essays would all find their way into later collections, the material was not available on the American market for several years. Frank Kermode's *Selected Prose* (1975) is the contemporary counterpart of these earlier selections, and though it was designed, as the blurb says, "for use by students in Universities" both in England and America, it brought to the tip of the iceberg several additional extracts from the submerged mass of Eliot's uncollected prose.

As the trade editions of Eliot's selected prose moved forward in his lifetime, he cast off essays from earlier selections as he shaped and solidified his canon, and he seized the opportunity in new selections to retrieve earlier pieces that he had neglected. Hence, in *On Poetry and Poets* (1957) he rescued from *TLS* "Sir John Davies" (1926), whose poems had influenced *Four Quartets*, and in his last collection, *To Criticize the Critic* (1965), he honored many requests by reaching back to 1917 to recover both "Reflections on *vers libre*" and *Ezra Pound: His Metric and Poetry*. Eliot's prose provides a rich landscape for the study of canon formation, but there are pitfalls for the student of canons if he does not secure every fugitive edition of Eliot's prose, especially the 1956 American edition of *Elizabethan Essays*, published as *Essays on Elizabethan Drama* twenty-two years after the English edition. For this volume Eliot returned once again to section 3 of the third English edition of *Selected Essays* with some serious second thoughts and a sharp pair of scissors, cutting from the canon "Shakespeare and the Stoicism of Seneca," "Hamlet and His Problems," and "Four Elizabethan Dramatists." "All three of these essays," he wrote in the preface,

> on re-examination embarrassed me by their callowness, and by a facility of unqualified assertion which verges, here and there, on impudence. The *Hamlet*, of course, had been kept afloat all these years by the success of the phrase "objective correlative"—a phrase which, I am now told, is not even my own but was first used by Washington Alston. . . . Instead, I have included *Seneca in Elizabethan Translation*, which seems to me to deserve its place as the first "essay in Elizabethan drama." (p. 6)[38]

These were very serious firings and promotions indeed, but when a "new English edition" was published in 1963, two years before his death, he reaffirmed the shakeup.[39] Had we seen a fourth English edition of *Selected Essays*, these early foundation pieces of section 3 probably would have been excluded.

It may be true that the state of the editions of an author is in direct relation to the state of scholarship on that author. Eliot is among our greatest prose writers—he is a Prose General of our age—but as the century comes to a close his many essays are dispersed and in editorial disarray. And this unordered situation is reflected on the field of scholarship, where endless essays and monographs on Eliot fail to make an impact at the forward line, or sink to the bottom of the sea of print, because their links are cut to the archives and vast stores of research materials on which significant breakthroughs depend. Does it not seem that 90 percent of the essays on Eliot are written without an awareness of 90 percent of his work? There will be a major advance in Eliot studies when we create the textual conditions for first-rate scholarship, when we have all his work firmly and precisely in place. As Eliot wrote of Baudelaire:

> It is now becoming understood that Baudelaire is one of the few poets who wrote nothing, either prose or verse that is negligible. To understand Baudelaire you must read the whole of Baudelaire. And nothing that he wrote is without importance. He was a great poet; he was a great critic. And he was also a man with a profound attitude toward life, for the study of which we need every scrap of his writing.[40]

It could not be said better for Eliot himself. We need—and I do not even mention the needs of the poetry—collections of his unpublished prose, of the numerous presently restricted essays and lectures. We need volumes of his uncollected prose—of those six hundred–plus items in the Gallup bibliography and many others since discovered and unrecorded. We need editions of his introductions and prefaces to the works of other authors. We need an edition of his *Criterion* commentaries from 1922 to 1939. We need every scrap of his writing, and we need standard scholarly editions of his published works. Valerie Eliot and Faber and Faber are strongly aware of these needs, I believe, and the recent critical editions of Eliot's Clark Lectures and early poems are positive indications that we are at the threshold of a new textual age for organizing and presenting Eliot's texts, and that they will accompany those of Lawrence and Woolf and Yeats and other modernists into the next century with a new precision and in a greater human context. That in itself will open a rich new world of Eliot studies. And I say confidently to young scholars that we are now at the threshold of a new age for the study of all modernist literature, that there is no richer time to be a modernist teacher and scholar, and that many of the riches are yet to be found in the untapped archives and in the unexamined histories of modernist texts.

NOTES

Prelude. The Dark Angel

1. *The Poems of Matthew Arnold,* ed. Kenneth Allott; 2nd ed., ed. Miriam Allott (London: Longman, 1979), p. 163; hereafter abbreviated *PMA* in the text.

2. *The Complete Prose Works of Matthew Arnold,* vol. I, ed. R. H. Super (Ann Arbor: University of Michigan Press, 1960), p. 1; hereafter abbreviated *CPW1* in the text.

3. *Autobiographies* (London: Macmillan, 1955), p. 314; hereafter abbreviated *Aut* in the text.

4. Text as quoted in *Autobiographies,* p. 314. Yeats omits the second stanza:

> Because of thee, no thought, no thing,
>
> Abides for me undesecrate:
>
> Dark Angel, ever on the wing,
>
> Who never reachest me too late!

The succeeding nine stanzas appear as epigraphs to chapters in this book (except chapter 5); the text is as printed in *The Collected Poems of Lionel Johnson,* 2nd and rev. ed., ed. Ian Fletcher (New York: Garland, 1982) pp. 52–3. "The Dark Angel," written in 1893, first appeared in *The Second Book of the Rhymers' Club* (London: Elkin Mathews and John Lane, 1894).

5. *The Oxford Book of Modern Verse* 1895–1935, ed. W. B. Yeats (Oxford: Clarendon Press, 1936), pp. ix–x; hereafter abbreviated *OBMV* in the text.

6. *The Variorum Edition of the Poems of W. B. Yeats,* ed. Peter Allt and Russell K. Alspach (New York: Macmillan, 1966), pp. 135–6; hereafter abbreviated *VP* in the text.

7. *Memoirs: Autobiography—First Draft: Journal,* ed. Denis Donoghue (New York: Macmillan, 1973), pp. 91–2. Eliot was later to publish in the *Criterion,* (hereafter abbreviated *Cr* in the text), in "Some Letters of Lionel Johnson," Johnson's self-revealing account to Louise Imogen Guiney of Beardsley's conversion to Catholicism: "I can say, emphatically, that his conversion was a spiritual work, and not an half-insincere aesthetic act of change, not a sort of emotional experience or experiment: he became a Catholic with a true humility and exaltation of soul, prepared to sacrifice much. He withdrew himself from certain valued intimacies, which he felt incompatible with his faith: that implies much, in these days when artists so largely claim exemption, in the name of art, from laws and rules of life. His work, as [*sic*] himself declared, would have been very directly religious in scope and character: he would have dismissed from it all suggestion of anything dangerously morbid: he would have made it plain that he was sometimes a satirist of vices and follies and extravagancies, but not, so to say a sentimental student of them for their curiosity and fascination's sake. There was always in him a vein of mental or imaginative unhealthiness and nervousness, probably due to his extreme physical fragility: this he was setting himself to conquer, to transform into a spiritual and artistic source of energy. . . . I ascribe all in his work, which even great friends and admirers find unwelcome, partly to his febrile, consumptive, suffering state of body, with its consequent restlessness and excitability of mind; partly to sheer boyish insolence of genius, love of audaciousness, consciousness of power. He was often ridiculed, insulted, misconstrued: and he sometimes replied by extravagance. But despite all wantonness of youthful genius, and all the morbidity of disease, his truest self was on the spiritual side of things, and his conversion was true to that self. . . . This, I think, is the strict truth" (*Cr* 3: 361–3).

8. Quoted in R. F. Foster, *W. B. Yeats: A Life* (Oxford: Oxford University Press, 1997), p. 413.

9. "Friends of My Youth," lecture notes edited by Joseph Ronsley in *Yeats in the Theatre,* ed. Robert O'Driscoll and Lorna Reynolds (Niagara Falls, N.Y.: Maclean-Hunter Press, 1975), p. 73; hereafter abbreviated *YT* in the text.

10. "On Teaching the Appreciation of Poetry," *Critic* 18 (1960), 78.

11. "Tradition and the Practice of Poetry," a 1936 lecture published in *T. S. Eliot: Essays from the Southern Review,* ed. James Olney (Oxford: Clarendon Press, 1988), pp. 13–14; *IMH* 395.

12. *Saltire Review* 4 (Summer 1957), 57; quoted in *IMH* 397.

13. Slightly misquoted ("Sovegna vos a temps de ma dolor") from *Purgatorio* 26, lines 147–8, translated by Eliot in "Dante" (1929): " 'be mindful in due time of my pain.' / Then dived he back into that fire which refines them" (*SE* 256).

14. Wilde's portrayal of the Sphinx, "a songless tongueless ghost of sin" whose "poisonous melodies" wreck his persona's spiritual life, anticipates Johnson's "The Dark Angel." "Hideous animal, get hence" he cries to the Sphinx,

> You wake in me each bestial sense, you make
>   Me what I would not be.
>
> You make my creed a barren sham, you wake
>   foul dreams of sensual life,
> And Atys with his blood-stained knife were
>   Better than the thing I am.

The canceled passages of "Prufrock" also recall the relation of sensual abandonment and spiritual terror in Wilde's "The Harlot's House," where, despite the warning of a phantasmal *danse macabre,* the poet's love is enchanted into the illicit house, leaving him with a vision of his terrible loss: "Love passed into the house of lust." See my "Wilde's Dark Angel and the Spell of Decadent Catholicism," in *Rediscovering Oscar Wilde,* ed. George Sandulescu, (Savage, Md.: Barnes and Noble, 1994), pp. 371–96.

15. Sebastian, a third-century Roman centurion, was sentenced to death by Diocletian when he was discovered to be a Christian. Though Sebastian was shot with arrows, they did not kill him; he was eventually stoned to death. As Eliot's lecture notes for his 1909 Harvard course, "Florentine Painting" (Fine Arts 20b), reveal, he had begun his study of Sebastian with Antonio Pollaiuolo's fifteenth-century painting of the martyr.

16. Eliot would include the motto ("only the divine endures; the rest is smoke") from Mantegna's painting, which he saw in the Palazzo della Cà d'Oro in Venice in 1911, in the fragmented sequence of phrases that constitute the epigraph for "Burbank with a Baedeker: Bleistein with a Cigar" (1919). The painting is reproduced in Lyndall Gordon's *Eliot's Early Years* (New York: Oxford University Press, 1977), plate 9, facing p. 80.

17. *The Inferno of Dante Alighieri,* Temple Classics edition (London: J. M. Dent, 1909), pp. 168–9. Ricks notes that Eliot marked this line in his copy (Houghton) of this edition (*IMH* 220).

18. "Critical Note" to *The Collected Poems of Harold Monro,* ed. Alida Monro (London: Cobden-Sanderson, 1933), p. xv.

19. "Where in broad daylight the spectre grips the passer-by!" Eliot quoted the French line in his note to line 60 of *The Waste Land* (*CPP* 76).

20. In a letter to *TLS,* no. 1719 (10 January 1935), Eliot responded to a suggestion by the reviewer of Ernest Dowson's *Poems* that Eliot got the phrase "Falls the Shadow" in *The Hollow Men* from the opening lines of Dowson's best known poem, "Nom sum qualis eram bonae sub regno Cynarae":

I cried for madder music and for stronger wine

But when the feast is finished and the lamps expire,

Then falls thy shadow, Cynara!

"This derivation had not occurred to my mind," replied Eliot, "but I believe it to be correct, because the lines he quotes have always run in my head, and because I regard Dowson as a poet whose technical innovations have been underestimated" (p. 21).

21. "Poet and Saint . . ." *Dial* 82 (May 1927), 427. Eliot's review was of the American edition (New York: Albert and Charles Boni, 1926) of Symons's translation of Baudelaire's *Les fleurs du mal, Petits poèmes en prose, Les paradis artificiels* (London: Casanova Society, 1925). The review was reprinted, with deletions and revisions, as "Baudelaire in Our Time" (*FLA* 86–99, here 90).

22. Eliot evidently came across the passage (p. 44) when he was seeing through the press C.W. Everett's edition of *The Letters of Junius* (London: Faber and Gwyer, 1927). The epigraph appears in the draft reproduced in a program of readings, *Stage Sixty Theatre Club Presents Homage to T. S. Eliot: A Programme of Poetry, Drama and Music* (Globe Theatre, London, 13 June 1965).

23. The python had appeared in one of Eliot's earliest poems, "Circe's Palace" (25 November 1908): "Along the garden stairs / The sluggish python lies" (*CPP* 598).

24. Eliot had made such a relational observation in "The 'Pensées' of Pascal" (1930), where he observes that Pascal had "received his illumination from God in extremely poor health; but it is a commonplace that some forms of illness are extremely favourable, not only to religious illumination, but to artistic and literary composition. A piece of writing meditated, apparently without progress, for months or years, may suddenly take shape and

word." He concludes in personal terms, "I doubt whether these moments can be culti-vated by the writer; but he to whom this happens assuredly has the sensation of being a vehicle rather than a maker" (*SE* 405).

25. *The Collected Poems of Harold Monro,* p. xiii.

26. Ibid., pp. xv–xvi.

27. I am indebted to C. K. Stead's initial discussion of "Eliot's 'Dark Embryo'" in *The New Poetic* (London: Hutchinson University Library, 1964), pp. 125–47.

28. *The Collected Poems of Lionel Johnson,* p. 291.

29. *The Collected Poems of Harold Monro,* p. xiv. In an interview in the *Paris Review* 21 (Spring/Summer 1959), Eliot stated (p. 50) that when he got to London "There was really nothing except the people of the 90's who had all died of drink or suicide or one thing or another" (*IMH* 398).

30. Paul Elmer More, who was to become a close friend of Eliot, had compared Yeats unfavorably with Lionel Johnson in "Two Poets of the Irish Movement" (1903). Where he found in Johnson "something of the classic saint," he found in Yeats, in his re-cent works, not only a "sickliness" and "wasteful revery" but "a sense of failure and decay, rather than of mastery and growth." More further alleged that "the real kinship of Mr. Yeats's present style is with that of Arthur Symons, himself a disciple of the French deca-dents; only one must add in justice that no taint of moral degeneration has appeared in the Irish writer—and that is much to concede to a decadent." *Shelburne Essays. First Series* (1904; rpt. New York: Phaeton Press, 1967), pp. 177–92.

31. Eliot's recent dissociation of himself from a broad sweep of late Victorians is evi-dent in his letter (Yale) of 22 December 1924 to Ezra Pound: "Probably the fact that Swinburne and the poets of the nineties were entirely missed out of my personal history counts for a great deal. I never read any of these people until it was too late for me to get anything out of them, and until after I had assimilated other influences which must have made it impossible for me to accept the Swinburnians at all. The only exception to the above is Rossetti. I am as blind to the merits of these people as I am to Thomas Hardy" (*IMH* 394–5).

32. Eliot points specifically to George Bernard Shaw, H. G. Wells, and Lytton Strachey, not only as members of the generation that "skipped" the 1890s but as part of "the progeny of Huxley, and Tyndall, and George Eliot, and Gladstone. And with this gen-eration Baudelaire has nothing to do; but he had something to do with the 'nineties, and he has a great deal to do with us" (*FLA* 87).

33. Tom Paulin, "Undesirable," review of Anthony Julius, *T. S. Eliot, Anti-Semitism and Literary Form,* in *London Review of Books* (9 May 1996), p. 15. Though I am not in schol-arly agreement with the motives, methods, and conclusions of Julius's extensive brief on the alleged anti-Semitic basis of Eliot's art, I have not attempted to include a counter-ar-gument in this study. His is only the latest of several books dating back to Stanley Edgar Hyman's *The Armed Vision* (New York: Knopf, 1948), and including George Bornstein's *Transformations of Romanticism in Yeats, Eliot, and Stevens* (Chicago: University of Chicago Press, 1976), that bring the charge or attempt to make a case with familiar and limited ma-terials. When presently restricted materials become available for a full scholarly investiga-tion of the matter, a book-length study rather than a chapter will be required, and a larger context than Julius and previous critics have provided.

34. See Warwick Gould and Thomas F. Staley, eds., *Writing the Lives of Writers* (New York: St. Martin's Press, 1998), p. ix.

35. Ibid., pp. 24, 41, 111, 155.

36. *W. B. Yeats: A Life,* p. xxvii.

37. *Theory of Literature* (New York: Harcourt, Brace, 1948), p. 68.

Chapter 1. In the Lecture Halls

1. *Harvard College Class of 1910. Seventh Report* (June 1935), p. 219.

2. The courses offered were "Tendencies of Contemporary French Thought" (6), retitled "Modern French Literature" on the 1916 syllabus; "Contemporary French Poets and Novelists" (6); "Six Nineteenth-Century Thinkers: Chateaubriand, Michelet, Sainte-Beuve, Comte, Taine, Renan" (6 or 12); "The Novel in France" (6 or 12); "French Literary Criticism" (6 or 12); "Contemporary Literary Movements" (6). In each of its Extension centers the Oxford Delegacy had a Local Committee through which applications for courses offered were made by local organizations. The number of lectures given, six or twelve, depended in part upon the subsidiary funding of the course. Eliot's six courses remained on the Delegacy's list until 1919–20, but there were no further requests after 1916. As early as 1919, in a course of six lectures on "Georgian Poets" by L. U. Wilkinson of St. John's College, Cambridge, Eliot was himself the subject of an Extension lecture. Wilkinson discussed the "Necessity of taking into account the more revolutionary school of modern verse. The values and the significance of the Vers-librists, with special reference to the 'Imagists', Mr. Richard Aldington, 'H. D.', and Mr. T. S. Eliot."

3. A copy of Eliot's syllabus is in the Department of External Studies, Oxford University, together with Delegacy records containing his reports. Another copy of the syllabus is in the Houghton Library, the copy sent to his brother, Henry Ware Eliot, to whom he wrote on 6 September 1916: "I am working at my lectures. I will send you the syllabus when it is out" (*L1* 151).

4. Just as he began his course of lectures Eliot published a review of Victor Boudon's *Avec Charles Péguy, de la Lorraine a La Marne (août-septembre, 1914)* (1916), writing that "it was not until his death that the full significance of Péguy and his life was realised, that he was seen as a national, a symbolical figure, the incarnation of the rejuvenated French spirit. . . . His work hardly demands, perhaps would not bear, close analysis. There may be passages in his verse which are pure poetry; there are certainly passages in his prose which are of the best prose. . . . There is not a great deal, certainly, of the finest verse; and his prose is not marked, as a rule, by excess of subtlety. One would hardly call him a "thinker." His style even is questionable. It is not a style to think in; it is too emphatic, too insistent. His sentences a dozen pages long convey an emotion, but thought is submerged. But two things are certain: His style is not decadent. . . . Péguy represented something which was real and solid. He stood for a real re-creation, a return to the sources, the peasant soil, which was not obscurantist; a peasant genius educated but unspoilt. . . . He was not primarily a writer of this or that review, redactor of this or that journal. He was a man of the people—more than Hugo, of whom he wrote so well." *New Statesman* 8 (7 October 1916), 19–20.

5. Eliot later wrote, "In 1910, when I had my first introduction to literary Paris, Claudel was already a great poet in the eyes of a younger generation—my own generation. He had published *Connaissance de l'Est, Art Poétique,* and those plays which appeared in one volume under the general title of *L'Arbre*: and I am not sure that these three books do not constitute his strongest claim to immortality" (*IMH* 408).

6. Eliot, who spent the 1910–11 academic year in Paris, later wrote to Shiv K. Kumar: "I was certainly very much under his (Bergson's) influence during the year 1910–11, when I both attended his lectures and gave close study to the books he had then written" (*IMH* 412).

7. Eliot's list of books precedes the lecture outlines in the printed syllabus. Some initials have been expanded and some first names inserted. Eliot noted at the bottom of the list: "Inquiries are being made as to other translations than those given above."

8. Pound's "Approach to Paris" had appeared not as a book but as a series of seven articles in *New Age* from 4 September to 16 October 1913. The series included studies of Remy de Gourmont, Jules Romains, Charles Vildrac, Laurent Tailhade, Henri de Régnier, Tristan Corbière, Francis Jammes, Arthur Rimbaud, Paul Fort, André Spire, Henri-Martin Barzun, and others.

9. The syllabuses for Eliot's tutorial classes are now bound and lodged in the University of London Library, Senate House. Copies of the syllabuses for the first and third years are in the Houghton Library. His class reports are in the Department of Extra-Mural Studies, University of London.

10. In a 1919 lecture, "Modern Tendencies in Poetry" (*Shama'a* 1 [April 1920], 9–18; see note 32), Eliot placed Browning and Victorian poetry in contemporary perspective: "The history of poetry is by no means a series of triumphant discoveries; in England particularly, it has been largely a history of experiments that have failed, of successful experiments that have been overlooked, and of men trying to do something else than that for which they were fitted. The greater part of Victorian poetry was a *piétinement sur place*. The one Victorian poet whom our contemporary can study with much profit is Browning. Otherwise, almost all of the interesting developments in poetry are due to Frenchmen: Baudelaire, Gautier, Mallarmé, Laforgue, Corbière, Rimbaud" (pp. 12–13).

11. Midway through the course, Eliot wrote to his mother: "Lately I have been at a point in my lectures where the material was unfamiliar to me: I have had to get up the Brontës for one course and Stevenson for the other [see p. 42 below]. Of course I have developed a knack of acquiring superficial information at short notice, and they think me a prodigy of information. . . . But I am looking forward to lecturing on Dickens. I found *Jane Eyre* and *Wuthering Heights* amazingly good stuff, but I cannot endure George Eliot" (*L1* 219).

12. Eliot wrote to his mother on 11 April 1917 that his lectures "are now on Ruskin and involve some reading in political economy . . . I have been doing some writing—mostly in French, curiously enough it has taken me that way—and some poems in French will come out in the *Little Review*" (*L1* 175).

13. Eliot later wrote in the introduction to his Norton Lectures, "I can recall clearly enough the moment when, at the age of fourteen or so, I happened to pick up a copy of Fitzgerald's *Omar* which was lying about, and the almost overwhelming introduction to a new world of feeling which this poem was the occasion of giving me. It was like a sudden conversion; the world appeared anew, painted with bright, delicious and painful colours." In the fifth lecture, however, he declared that "I can still enjoy Fitzgerald's *Omar*, though I do not hold that rather smart and shallow view of life" (*UPUC* 33, 91).

14. As he approached the end of his first-year tutorial, Eliot wrote to his cousin Eleanor Hinckley on 1 April 1918 about the novels: "Meredith knew what he was doing, but unfortunately it wasn't worth doing, don't read him" (*L1* 228). Eliot had borrowed a line from Meredith's "Lucifer in Starlight" for "Cousin Nancy" (1915), "The army of unalterable law," and there is a striking resemblance between the scene in the hyacinth garden in *The Waste Land,* where Eliot's persona says: "I was neither / Living nor dead, and I knew nothing, / Looking into the heart of light, the silence" (lines 39–41), and stanza 8 of Meredith's "Hymn to Colour," where Love shows Meredith's persona Life and Death and describes Death to him as

> the heart of light, the wing of shades,
> The crown of beauty: never soul embraced
> Of him can harbour unfaith; soul of him
> Possessed walks never dim.

Eliot used the same phrase to describe a mystical moment in *Burnt Norton:* "The surface glittered out of heart of light" (*CPP* 172).

15. In this list some first names and the editors of volumes have been inserted; some initials and shortened titles have been expanded.

16. Statistical information on student attendance and success in Eliot's Southall classes is provided by W. E. Styler, "T. S. Eliot as an Adult Tutor," *Notes and Queries,* n.s. 19 (1972), 53–4.

17. Graham Wallas, professor of political science at the London School of Economics, had put Eliot in contact with Frederick Samuel Boas, formerly professor of English at Queen's University, Belfast, and now Divisional Inspector for Higher Education for the London County Council. "Mr. Boas has been very kind to me," Eliot had written to Wallas on 23 March 1917, "and hopes to get me some evening work next autumn. What I should like especially would be another tutorial class, but there seems faint hope of that" (*L1* 167).

18. A copy of the syllabus is in the Greater London Record Office, bound in *Evening Institute Handbills, 1917–18.* Styler states that Eliot taught two courses at Sydenham ("T. S. Eliot as Adult Tutor," p. 53), but there is no record of a second course in the Record Office. Eliot wrote that he was invited to offer a course of lectures on "The Development of English Poetry" in 1918–19, but because of the low fee and lack of expenses he decided it was not worth his while (*L1* 230). Unfortunately, Eliot's dossier has been destroyed.

19. Eliot was to comment on Meredith's philosophy in his review of J. H. E. Crees's *George Meredith: A Study in his Works and Personality* (1918): "Mr. Crees speaks of Meredith's 'profound philosophy.' Of course it is the first duty of a philosopher to be clear and logical and simple, and he can then afford to let the profundity take care of itself; but the fact is that most of Meredith's profundity is profound platitude. His blood and brain and spirit trinity may be a profound analysis; he has left the clarity and precision to Plato, who had already conceived a somewhat similar anatomy." "Studies in Contemporary Criticism," *Egoist* 5 (October 1918), 114.

20. Eliot wrote to his mother on 4 March 1918: "I have been cramming George Eliot for the last two weeks in preparation for a lecture on her on last Friday. I was surprised to enjoy her so much. Of course there is a great deal of endless prosing, and I think my memory of pleasure is based chiefly on one story—*Amos Barton*—which struck me as far and away ahead of the rest. I read the *Mill on the Floss, Scenes of Clerical Life, Adam Bede* and *Romola* in preparation for this one lecture. This week is Meredith, whom I have lectured on before" (*L1* 221).

21. "I am busy reading Emerson," Eliot wrote to his mother on 19 September 1917. "He strikes me as very wordy. He has something to say often, but he spreads it out and uses very general terms; it seems more oratory than literature. His biography is interesting and contains many familiar names" (*L1* 196).

22. On 24 October 1917 Eliot described to his mother a weekend trip with Vivien to a farm in the Surrey hills: "I took down books and prepared my lecture on William Morris. I no longer *write* them—I set down about three pages of notes. Vivien says I am getting better and better as a lecturer" (*L1* 203). In "Reflections on Contemporary Poetry," [3] published in the next issue of the *Egoist* (November 1917), Eliot remarked: "The style of William Morris is a 'style like speech,' only it is the speech of Morris, and therefore rather poor stuff. The 'Idylls of the King' sound often like Tennyson talking to Queen Victoria in heaven; and the 'Earthly Paradise' like an idealized Morris talking to an idealized Burne-Jones" (p. 151).

23. "*The Way of All Flesh,*" Eliot wrote to Eleanor Hinckley, "was written by a man

who was not an artist and had no sense of style; it is too long, and the beginning of the book and the adventures of Ernest are dull, but the character of Christina is amazing. Butler (read his *Notebooks*) just happened to know this phase of English life particularly well; Christina is one of the finest pieces of dissection of mental dishonesty that I know anywhere; Butler pursues her relentlessly to her death. It is a book you must read" (*L1* 228).

24. In this list short titles have been expanded.

25. Eliot had reviewed Duffin's book in the *Manchester Guardian* (23 June 1916), characterizing it as "in substance a good set of Extension lectures" and concluding that "Mr. Duffin's enthusiasm atones for many faults. Most of his praise of 'Jude' and 'The Mayor of Casterbridge' is just enough, but to rank Hardy with Fielding and Thackeray as the greatest masters of the English novel is the privilege of such enthusiasm" (p. 3).

26. Eliot described the problems of the class in his own report: "At the beginning of the Session the Class found that it had lost several of its best members through death, removal and more essential work. . . . The influenza epidemic during November, and the December elections were disturbing factors and reduced the attendance. I believe we shall have the attendance at 10 to 12 during the winter. The amount of reading done has been very satisfactory, and the *average* merit of papers (fewer than for this period last year) is, I think, higher than a year ago." At the end of the year, the support for a literature class at Southall was discontinued. In terms of the grants paid by the Board of Education (see Styler, " T. S. Eliot as an Adult Tutor," p. 54), Eliot was a costly tutor for the Extension Board. He was paid £60 for the first year, £70 for each of the two subsequent years, and claimed £3 traveling expenses each year.

27. The parenthetical numbers to the right of the first eleven subject titles represent what appear to be Eliot's holograph renumbering of the subjects as lectures on the Houghton Library copy.

28. As a Harvard senior Eliot was a student in George Pierce Baker's "English 14: The Drama in England from the Miracle Plays to the Closing of the Theatres," in which his *Development of Shakespeare as a Dramatist* (1907) was a standard text.

29. Eliot wrote to his mother on 26 January 1919: "I am lecturing on Elizabethan Lyric verse tomorrow—Shakespeare, Jonson, Campion, Barnfield etc. Then I go on to the Sonnet and afterwards to prose—Sidney, Raleigh, Bacon etc. I think I sent you the syllabus. I hope to get some of the material for a book on Elizabethan blank verse out of the course" (*L1* 270).

30. Eliot evidently drew upon the structure and substance of his lectures on Jonson for his review of Percy Simpson's edition of *Every Man in His Humour* (1919), in which Eliot expresses "some regret that 'Every Man in his Humour' should be the best known of Jonson's plays. There appears to be some accepted belief that you can get the essentials of Jonson from this play: all that you need, perhaps, for culture. 'Every Man in his Humour' is the first mature work of Jonson, and the student of Jonson must study it; but it is not the play in which Jonson found his genius: it is the last of his plays to read first. If one reads 'Volpone,' and after that re-reads the 'Jew of Malta'; then returns to Jonson and reads 'Bartholomew Fair,' 'The Alchemist,' 'Epicœne' and 'The Devil is an Ass,' and finally 'Catiline,' it is possible to arrive at a fair opinion of the poet and dramatist. . . . [Jonson's] type of personality found its relief in something falling under the category of burlesque or farce. . . . It is not, at all events, the farce of Molière: the latter is more analytic, more an intellectual re-distribution." "The Comedy of Humours," *Athenaeum,* no. 4672 (November 14, 1919), 1180–1.

31. "Professional, Or . . ." *Egoist* 5 (April 1918), 61.

32. *Shama'a* (Urur, Adjar, India) 1 (April 1920), 9. This, one of the most fugitive of

Eliot's uncollected essays, was delivered to the Arts League of Service in Westminster and reserved by its secretary for publication in the new review in India. Eliot wrote to his mother that he planned "to develop the various parts of it, divide it into separate essays or chapters, and make a small book of it" (*L1* 346). An important complement to "Tradition and the Individual Talent" (1919), the essay describes the importance of Laforgue, Corbière and Mallarmé to modern poetry. "Great success," wrote Vivien Eliot in her diary (Bodleian) after the lecture. An extract from the essay appears in *IMH,* 403–04.

33. For example, topic 16, "Bacon," in the Elizabethan literature syllabus, includes "Survey of prose from Bacon to Hobbes, Sir Thomas Browne," and in July 1923 Eliot published "Contemporary English Prose: A Discussion of the Development of English Prose from Hobbes and Sir Thomas Browne to Joyce and D. H. Lawrence" in *Vanity Fair.*

Chapter 2. Hulme of Original Sin

1. "T. S. Eliot and His Relation to T. E. Hulme," *University of Toronto Quarterly* 2 (April 1933), 380–96.

2. *The Critical Ideas of T. S. Eliot* (Tartu, Estonia: K. Mattiesen, 1932), p. 118.

3. *The Achievement of T. S. Eliot,* 3rd ed. (New York: Oxford University Press, 1958), p. 71.

4. See Michael Roberts, *T. E. Hulme* (London: Faber and Faber, 1938), p. 208; David Daiches, *Poetry and the Modern World* (Chicago: Chicago University Press, 1940), p. 91; Stanley Edgar Hyman, *The Armed Vision* (New York: Knopf, 1948), p. 98; Kristian Smidt, *Poetry and Belief in the Work of T. S. Eliot* (Oslo: Jacob Dybwad, 1949), p. 38; rev. ed. (London: Routledge and Kegan Paul, 1961), p. 23; W. K. Wimsatt, Jr., and Cleanth Brooks, *Literary Criticism: A Short History* (New York: Vintage, 1957), p. 660. Marion Montgomery, in *T. S. Eliot: An Essay on the American Magus* (Athens: University of Georgia Press, 1969), follows Matthiessen but argues (pp. 2–3) that the kinship between Eliot and Hulme has been exaggerated, especially in regard to their attitudes toward the relation of aesthetics and metaphysics in their conceptions of the image. John D. Margolis, in *T. S. Eliot's Intellectual Development* (Chicago: University of Chicago Press, 1972), asserts that though Eliot read Hulme's poetry before 1924 he was not familiar with Hulme's essays or critical theory until after the publication of *Speculations.*

5. "T. S. Eliot and the Romantic Heresy," *Yale French Studies* 13 (1954), 5.

6. *From Gautier to Eliot* (London: Hutchinson, 1960), pp. 163, 157.

7. Seán Lucy, *T. S. Eliot and the Idea of Tradition* (London: Cohen and West, 1960), p. 33.

8. *Poetry and the Modern World,* p. 91.

9. T. S. Eliot, *A Sermon* (Cambridge: Cambridge University Press, 1948), p. 5.

10. Unsigned review of *Group Theories of Religion and the Individual,* by Clement C. J. Webb, *New Statesman* 29 (July 1916), 405. Hulme abandoned Bergson in 1911 after a visit to Pierre Lasserre, who convinced him "that Bergsonism was nothing but the last disguise of romanticism" (*CWTEH* 165).

11. *New Age* 13 (8 May 1913), 38.

12. *Blasting and Bombardiering* (London: Eyre and Spottiswoode, 1937), p. 108.

13. "This Hulme Business," *Townsman* 2 (January 1939), 15. John Gould Fletcher sheds some light on Pound's later diminishment of Hulme's influence in *Life is My Song* (New York: Farrar and Rinehart, 1937): "I noted, however, that he [Hulme] avoided meeting Pound, for a reason which he did not state. To tell the truth, there was bad blood between them, a resentment similar to that which I myself had felt since Ezra had decided to write his series of notes on the French symbolists. Hulme felt that Ezra was simply ex-

ploiting ideas which he had originally given to him, and was claiming them for his own. Ezra felt that he was making sufficient acknowledgment of his own indebtedness to Hulme by printing the small handful of poems which Hulme had written, as an appendix to his own most recent book. Thus the queerly compounded alliance between the young English student and the American expatriate was already at an end, though neither spoke of the fact, and always remained outwardly polite to the other" (p.76). After Hugh Kenner published *The Poetry of Ezra Pound* (1951), James Laughlin wrote to him on 30 August 1951 that he "had an interesting talk with Herbert Read about it. He likes it, but feels that you didn't give enough credit to T. E. Hulme in the early part about Ezra's life in London. Read is of the opinion that Ezra got a lot of his best ideas out of Hulme, and then rather disowned him" (Texas).

14. Arnold Dolmetsch (1858–1940) developed principles and techniques for the recovery of early instrumental music in modern times. He achieved international reputation with his book *The Interpretation of the Music of the 17th and 18th Centuries* (London: Novello, 1915), which Pound counseled all "anti-versilibristi" to read. See Pound's "Vers Libre and Arnold Dolmetsch," *Egoist* 4 (July 1917), 90.

15. Roberts says the wound occurred "early in March" (*Hulme,* p. 32).

> And ole T. E. H. he went to it,
> With a lot of books from the library,
> London Library, and a shell buried 'em in a dug-out,
>   And a bullet hit him on the elbow
> . . . gone through the fellow in front of him,
> And he read Kant in the Hospital, in Wimbledon,
> in the original,
> And the hospital staff didn't like it.

> *The Cantos of Ezra Pound* (New York: New Directions, 1948), p. 71.

16. T. E. Hulme, *Speculations,* ed. Herbert Read (New York: Harcourt, 1924), p. x.

17. *The Scene Is Changed* (London: Macmillan, 1942), p. 41.

18. Letter to the editor, *TLS,* no. 2893 (9 August 1957), 483.

19. There has been some confusion over the authorship of the poem, which appears under the signature "T E. H." with the title "Poem: Abbreviated from the Conversation of Mr. T E. H." There is a copy of the poem, with the title "Trenches, St. Eloi," among Hulme's papers (University of Keele), and A. R. Jones (*Life and Opinions of T. E. Hulme* [London: Victor Gollancz, 1960], p. 151) says that the poem "was reprinted by Ezra Pound as his own poem and without the signature T. E. H. in . . . *Umbra* (1920). It is probable that Ezra Pound actually wrote the poem on the basis of one of Hulme's conversations during the period 1914–15 and credited Hulme with the authorship in his *Catholic Anthology*." A closer examination of *Umbra* (London: Mathews, 1920) clarifies the confusion. The title page contains a general description of the contents: "All that he now wishes to keep in circulation from 'Personae,' 'Exultations,' 'Ripostes,' etc. With translations from Guido Cavalcanti and the late T. E. Hulme." Included in the volume are the five poems that make up "The Complete Poetical Works of T. E. Hulme," together with "Poem / Abbreviated from the Conversation of Mr. T.E.H.," as printed in *Catholic Anthology* (London: Elkin Mathews, 1915). The presence of this poem is explained by Pound in a statement prefacing Hulme's poems: "Hulme's five poems were published as his *Complete Poetical Works* at the end of *Ripostes* in 1912; there is, and now can be, no further addition, unless my abbreviation of some of his talk made when he came home with his first wound in 1915 may be half counted among them" (p. 123). Though the poem is only "half"

Hulme's, he was in London and associating with Pound at the time of its publication, and, as Jones points out, Hulme's friends certainly credited him with the authorship.

20. Ezra Pound, "T. S. Eliot," in *We Moderns . . . 1920–1940* (New York: Gotham Book Mart, catalogue 42, 1939), p. 24.

21. Samuel Hynes, in his introduction to Hulme's *Further Speculations* (Minneapolis: University of Minnesota Press, 1955), confirms that after Hulme was released from the hospital he began "hanging around the Café Royal, talking to his friends" (p. xxvii). Hulme's friend Ramiro de Maetzu, who spent 1915 in London, says that Hulme could always be found at the Café Royal, where "me monstraba la inmensa transcendencia de la doctrina del pecado original." *Autobiographia* (Madrid: Editora Nacional, 1962), p. 149.

22. "Orage: Memories," *New English Weekly* 6 (15 November 1934), 100.

23. *The Autobiography of Bertrand Russell*, vol. 2 (London: Allen and Unwin, 1968), p. 19.

24. Quoted in Ray Monk, *Bertrand Russell: The Spirit of Solitude* (London: Jonathan Cape, 1996), p. 440.

25. Ibid., pp. 55–6.

26. Jones, *Life and Opinions*, p. 89.

27. Each of Hulme's "War Notes" in the *New Age* from 27 January to 2 March 1916 was reprinted, under a different title and with minor textual revisions, two days later in the *Cambridge Magazine*. Some of Russell's replies there were reprinted in the *New Age* and are included in appendix A of *Further Speculations*, pp. 209–13. When Russell first replied, Hulme wrote to C. K. Ogden: "I am glad that Russell has replied, particularly as it's a letter that quite gives him away" (*CWTEH* 474).

28. Eliot and Russell were conscious of their antithetical temperaments. From the moment Eliot encountered Russell in London in 1914 he stated openly that he was "not a pacifist," and in a statement indicative of his philosophical-spiritual position during this period, he later revealed his own critical attitude toward "A Free Man's Worship": "I am sure that for me the strongest outside influences were negative. Observation of the futility of non-Christian lives has its part; and also realization of the incredibility of every alternative to Christianity that offers itself. One may become a Christian partly by pursuing scepticism to the utmost limit. I owe . . . something, in this way, to Bertrand Russell's essay, *A Free Man's Worship*: the effect this essay had on me was certainly the reverse of anything the author intended" (*A Sermon*, p. 5). In a March 1918 review in the *Nation* of Russell's *Mysticism and Logic*, which contains "A Free Man's Worship," Eliot expressed long familiarity with Russell's *Philosophical Essays* (1903, 1910), in which the essay earlier appeared. Eliot's antagonism toward Russell's writings would only increase in the next decade: as he wrote to Richard Aldington on 24 February 1927 about the difficult and necessary emancipation of philosophy from science, "read any of the more recent philosophical works of Bertrand Russell, and see what a dark age of gross superstition we still live in" (Texas).

29. Hulme's preface was deleted in subsequent editions of Sorel's book. The earlier American edition (1914) did not contain the preface.

30. See Alan Cohn, "Some Early Reviews by T. S. Eliot (Addenda to Gallup)," *Papers of the Bibliographical Society of America* 30, (third quarter, 1976), 421. Eliot's reviews were signed in accordance with Jourdain's practice that the reviewer sign only with the Greek initial of his last name, in Eliot's case "η"(the Greek letter eta).

31. *Monist* 27 (1917), 478–9.

32. "On TSE," in *T. S. Eliot: The Man and His Work*, ed. Allen Tate (New York: Delta-Dell, 1967), p. 4. "The Embankment" (1909), as reprinted in Pound's *Riposes* (1912):

(The fantasia of a fallen gentleman on a cold, bitter night.)

Once, in finesse of fiddles found I ecstasy,

In the flash of gold heels on the hard pavement.

Now see I

That warmth's the very stuff of poesy.

Oh, God, make small

The old star-eaten blanket of the sky

That I may fold it round me and in comfort lie.

33. Grover Smith asserts that Eliot, after reading Hulme's poems in *Ripostes,* modeled his "The Death of Saint Narcissus" (1915) on Hulme's "Conversion," "which must have been fresh in Eliot's recollection." *T. S. Eliot's Poetry and Plays,* second edition (Chicago: University of Chicago Press, 1994), p. 34.

34. "The New Elizabethans and the Old," *Athenaeum,* no.4640 (4 April 1919), 134.

35. "A Brief Treatise on the Criticism of Poetry," *Chapbook* 2 (March 1920), 2.

36. *TLS,* no. 2893 (9 August 1957), 483. Eliot continues, denying that Hulme was thinking of him, Pound, Joyce, and Lewis when Hulme wrote in 1914 that "we are in for a classical revival": "If Hulme associated Joyce with anything in the nature of a 'classical revival,' it could only have been on the evidence provided by *Dubliners,* if that book was available to him. But Hulme had certainly never heard of myself; and as nothing of mine was published until the summer of 1915 (and then only in *Poetry Chicago*) there was no evidence whatever." Eliot had in fact met Pound and Lewis in the autumn of 1914 (see p. 55), but he did not meet Joyce until Lewis introduced them in Paris on 15 August 1920. "I had almost forgotten that episode," Eliot later wrote of the meeting, misremembering it for the summer of 1921, "until my memory was revived by Lewis's account [in *Blasting and Bombardiering*]. . . . My memory is a feeble one, whether for scenes or for conversations, and I envy Lewis's ability to conjure up pictures from the past." "Wyndham Lewis," *Hudson Review* 10 (Summer 1957), 168.

37. In his foreword to Father William Tiverton's *D. H. Lawrence and Human Existence* (London: Rockliff, 1951), Eliot wrote that Lawrence "was an impatient and impulsive man (or so I imagine him to have been; for, like the author of this book, I never knew him)" (p. x). However, Eliot had written to Sydney Schiff on 25 July 1919, "What little I have seen of [D. H.] Lawrence lately makes me think him thoroughly *dégringolé* [run down]" (*L1* 324).

38. Many years later, Read wrote in his memoir of Eliot, "I do not think that Hulme's *Speculations,* when they were published in 1924, made any difference to Eliot's political idealism or philosophical faith, but his convictions were immensely strengthened. As the man who had rescued Hulme from a probable oblivion I had earned Eliot's deep gratitude." *The Cult of Sincerity* (London: Faber and Faber, 1968), p. 104.

39. "Charleston, Hey! Hey!" *Nation and Athenaeum* 40 (29 January 1927), 595.

40. *TLS,* no. 1412 (21 Feb. 1929), 136.

41. Ashley Dukes, *The Scene Is Changed,* p. 41.

42. "Types of English Religious Verse" (1939; twenty-one page typescript), p. 20.

43. For a general description of the course, see Ronald Bush, " 'As If You Were Hearing It From Mr. Fletcher or Mr. Tourneur in 1633': T. S. Eliot's 1933 Harvard Lecture Notes for English 26 ('Introduction to Contemporary Literature')" *ANQ* 11 (Summer 1998), 11–20.

44. Eliot was to take a later critical perspective of Hulme's poems in the draft (King's) of an undelivered lecture, "The Last Twenty-Five Years of English Poetry" (1940), in which he says of his quotation of Hulme's "The Embankment": "This is not a perfect poem, and the last line ["That I may fold it round me and in comfort lie"] is definitely

weak in construction. But, in the world of 1910 or so, this and a dozen poems one might choose . . . were evidence of a radical change in the whole practice of verse" (*IMH* 389).

45. The early drift away from Bradley is implicit in numerous places, including Conrad Aiken's *Ushant* (Cleveland, Ohio: Meridian-World, 1962), pp. 214–16. Aiken, describing the growing distance between himself and Eliot during the war years, says that "from this [Eliot's] remarkable thesis [on Bradley], which had contributed much to the 'fixing' of D.'s [Aiken's] implicit intellectual or philosophic position, adding, as it did, the basic 'why' as to the values of knowledge, the Tsetse [Eliot] was gradually to retreat, as if that magnificent vision, into the apparent chaos which blazed and swarmed and roared beyond the neat walls of Eden, was one he found insupportable" (p. 215). In his review of Russell's *Mysticism and Logic* (see note 28) Eliot states: "As a philosopher Mr. Bradley attains a perfection which is so emphatically a perfection of destruction, the most valuable part of his work is so purely sceptical, that his greatness is due rather to a consummation of dialectical technique than to a single vision" (p. 770).

46. "A Prediction in Regard to Three English Authors," *Vanity Fair* 21 (February 1924), 29, 98. This is the revised English text of "Lettre d'Angleterre," *Nouvelle Revue Française* 21 (1 November 1923), 619–25.

47. In the third of a five-part series, "Notes on Bergson," (1911–12), Hulme develops his idea of doubt, belief, and the modern "saint," who "in every generation has to struggle with an obstacle which stands in the way of any idealist or religious interpretation of the universe" (*CWTEH* 143). It directly parallels Eliot's own conception, which he developed primarily in his essays on Baudelaire, particularly in "Baudelaire in Our Time" (*FLA* 86–99).

48. "Mr. P. E. More's Essays," p. 136.

49. See especially "An American Critic," *New Statesman* 7 (24 June 1916), 284; "Mr. Leacock Serious," *New Statesman* 7 (29 July 1916), 404–5; and the unsigned review of Webb, *Group Theories of Religion and the Religion of the Individual*.

Chapter 3. Laforgue and the Personal Voice

1. Eliot informed Edward J. H. Greene of the fact and effect of his first reading of Baudelaire in 1907 or 1908, as Greene recounted in *T. S. Eliot et la France* (Paris: Boivin, 1951), p. 18. Eliot explained in a letter of 12 April 1928 to René Taupin that when he discovered Laforgue in 1908 he was "already familiar with the work of Baudelaire," and in a subsequent letter of 17 January 1930 to Taupin he reaffirmed that his first poems "were almost pure Laforgue, with a little Baudelaire." Printed in R. A. Gekoski (bookseller), *Catalogue 23* (London, 1997), p. 6.

2. "Modern Tendencies in Poetry," *Shama'a* 1 (April 1920), 13.

3. The quatrain is preceded by three widely spaced lines from the opening of *Inferno* 3, the inscription of the gate of hell (misquoted from memory): "Justitia mosse il mio alto fattore / Mi fece la divina potestate / La somma sapienza e il primo amore" (see *IMH* 83, 281).

4. Warren Ramsey, *Jules Laforgue and the Ironic Inheritance* (New York: Oxford University Press, 1953), p. 199. In *The Pound Era* (Berkeley: University of California Press, 1971), Hugh Kenner says that Laforgue "was first of all a role for Eliot," and that "Laforgue was the first of a succession of poets whom Eliot does not so much imitate as face toward, by way of locating his own structures of words set free, liberated in magnificent but sober

nonsense, which however beat upon will not disclose 'meaning' " (pp. 134–5). Peter Dale shares Kenner's view in the introduction to his edition of *The Poems of Jules Laforgue* (London: Anvil Press Poetry, 1986): "Eliot took on the role of Laforgue as Laforgue took on the role of the clown" (p. 18).

5. Tom Paulin, "Undesirable," review of Anthony Julius, *T. S. Eliot, Anti-Semitism and Literary Form*, in *London Review of Books*, 9 May 1996 p. 15.

6. Leonard Unger, "A Tribute: T. S. Eliot: The Intimate Voice," *Southern Review* 1 (Summer 1965), 733.

7. "Eliot and the Tradition of the Anonymous," *College English* 28 (May 1967), 559.

8. "Modern Tendencies in Poetry," pp. 10–11.

9. Trans. Mark Wardle, intro. T. S. Eliot (London: R. Cobden-Sanderson, 1924), pp. 12, 14.

10. Introduction to G. Wilson Knight, *The Wheel of Fire* (London: Methuen, 1930; rev. and enl. ed. 1954), pp. xii–xix.

11. Eliot's interpretive theory and his general critical practice anticipate the theoretical formulations of Georges Poulet, Marcel Raymond, and Jean Rousset, who attempt to define the process of apprehending the inner experience below objective form. See Richard Macksey and Eugenio Donato, eds., *The Structuralist Controversy: The Languages of Criticism and the Sciences of Man*, (Baltimore: Johns Hopkins Press, 1972), pp. 56–72.

12. "Donne in Our Time," in *A Garland for John Donne*, ed. Theodore Spencer (Cambridge: Harvard University Press, 1931), pp. 15–16.

13. "Reflections on Contemporary Poetry [IV]," *Egoist* 6 (July 1919), 39.

14. This observation about the relative absence of a personal voice in Yeats's early poems led Eliot to address the apparent contradiction in his criticism: "I have, in early essays, extolled what I called impersonality in art, and it may seem that, in giving as a reason for the superiority of Yeats's later work the greater expression of personality in it, I am contradicting myself. . . . I am willing to leave the point unsettled—but I think now, at least, that . . . [t]here are two forms of impersonality: that which is natural to the mere skilful craftsman, and that which is more and more achieved by the maturing artist. . . . The second impersonality is that of the poet who, out of intense and personal experience, is able to express a general truth; retaining all the particularity of his experience, to make of it a general symbol. And the strange thing is that Yeats, having been a great craftsman in the first kind, became a great poet in the second." What Eliot says of Yeats's personal pattern in relation to his earlier and later work may stand as characteristic of his own: "It is not that he became a different man, for . . . one feels sure that the intense experience of youth had been lived through. . . . But he had to wait for a later maturity to find expression of early experience; and this makes him, I think, a unique and especially interesting poet" (*OPP* 255).

15. "Nocturne," "Humouresque (After J. Laforgue)," and "Spleen" were collected in *Poems Written in Early Youth* (New York: Farrar, Straus and Giroux, 1967); "Suite Clownesque" has only recently been published, as reconstructed by Ricks (*IMH* 32–38).

16. "Reflections on Contemporary Poetry [IV]," p. 39.

17. "Modern Tendencies in Poetry," p. 13.

18. In a letter to E. J. H. Greene, quoted in "Jules Laforgue et T.S. Eliot," *Revue de littérature comparée* (July–September 1948), 365.

19. "On a Recent Piece of Criticism," *Purpose* 10 (April–June 1938), 92.

20. After Laforgue went to Germany in 1881, he fell under the philosophical influence of Arthur Schopenhauer (1788–1860) and especially of his disciple, Eduard von Hartmann (1842–1906), whose *La Philosophie de l'inconscient* (1869) became Laforgue's temporary Bible and provided the language for his poetic personae, who in the face of

nothingness (*le néant*) in the external world continuously seek the Absolute (*l'absolu*) in the Unconscious (*l'inconscient*).

21. Quoted in *Selected Writings of Jules Laforgue* ed. and trans. William Jay Smith (New York: Grove Press, 1956), p. 38.

22. So clearly had Eliot associated the moon with the egoistic search for absolute truth within the self that in a review of James Huneker's *Egoists* in 1909 he characterized aspects of the romantic philosophical genius as "perverse and lunary." See *Harvard Advocate* 88(5 October 1909), 16.

23. The immensely popular song "By the Light of the Silvery Moon" was introduced in 1909 by the child singer Georgie Prince as part of Gus Edwards's vaudeville sketch *School Boys and Girls* (see *IMH* 171).

24. George Santayana, *Three Philosophical Poets* (Cambridge: Harvard University Press, 1910), p. 177. Eliot evidently drew upon Santayana's interpretation of Goethe's episode of Faust, Helen, and their offspring Euphorion in this book, which was comprised of lectures that Eliot had heard in Santayana's courses at Harvard (see *VMP* 48). "The product of this hybrid inspiration," writes Santayana, "will be a romantic soul in the garb of classicism, a lovely wild thing, fated to die young. . . . It is an evidence of Goethe's great wisdom that he felt that romantic classicism must be subordinated or abandoned" (p. 178).

25. Though space does not permit their inclusion and consideration here, *Inventions of the March Hare* contains additional Laforguean poems in which Eliot plays variously and ironically with marionettes, the moon, the Absolute, and the Unconscious. See especially "Convictions," "Goldfish," "First Debate between the Body and Soul," and "Afternoon," in the last of which a group of art-loving ladies gathered in the British Museum on a Sunday afternoon are seen to move "beyond the Roman statuary / Like amateur comedians across a lawn / Towards the unconscious, the ineffable, the absolute" (*IMH* 53; *L1* 89).

26. "Modern Tendencies in Poetry," p. 13.

27. When Bonamy Dobrée submitted an essay on Laforgue to the *Criterion* in 1924, Eliot wrote to Dobrée on 4 May of his desire to see a critical treatment of Laforgue's romantic mind: "It would be extremely interesting if you could go into the philosophical basis of Laforgue's thought, which so far as I know has never been properly done. Of course no discussion of Laforgue would be complete without an analysis of his technical innovations in verse" (Brotherton).

28. Laforgue had been in Berlin for four years as French Reader to the Empress Augusta when in 1886 he met and took English lessons from Leah Lee (1861–1888), an English girl who had served as governess to the Empress Augusta's children. They married in London on 31 December and moved to Paris, where Laforgue died of tuberculosis in August 1887; Leah died of the disease the following June.

Chapter 4. The Savage Comedian

1. Conrad Aiken, "King Bolo and Others," in *T. S. Eliot: A Symposium,* compiled by Tambimuttu and Richard March (Chicago: Regnery, 1949), p. 22.

2. *Pound/Lewis: The Letters of Ezra Pound and Wyndham Lewis,* ed. Timothy Materer (New York: New Directions, 1985), p. 8.

3. The bawdy poems excised from his early poetic notebook are included in appendix A of *IMH* (305–21); additional Bolo poems are in the Pound archive at the Beinecke Library, Yale University. Eliot continued to write about Bolo for years, circulating the poems among James Joyce, Bonamy Dobrée, Theodore Spencer, and other trusted friends.

In a letter to Dobrée of 6 August 1941 Eliot indicated that the Bolovian period had ended (Brotherton). However, in a 1959 interview, when asked by Donald Hall if he still wrote in the Bolo vein, Eliot replied: "Oh yes, one wants to keep one's hand in, you know, in every type of poem, serious and frivolous and proper and improper. One doesn't want to lose one's skill." *Paris Review* 21 (Spring/Summer 1959), 59.

4. Immanuel Bekker's edition, *Aristophanis Comoediae: cum scholiis et varietate lectionis,* 5 vols. (London: Whittaker, Treacher, and Arnot, 1829), was among the books in an inventory (1934) of Eliot's library that was slipped into a private album of Vivien Eliot (Bodleian).

5. Henri Bergson, *Laughter: An Essay on the Meaning of the Comic,* trans. Cloudesley Brereton and Fred Rothwell (New York: Macmillan, 1911), p. 51.

6. "On the Essence of Laughter, and Generally of the Comic," in *Baudelaire: Selected Writings on Art and Artists,* trans. P. E. Charvet (Harmondsworth: Penguin, 1972), pp. 141–42.

7. "London Letter," *Dial* 70 (June 1921), 688–9. Eliot quotes from Baudelaire's French: *"Pour trouver du comique féroce et très-féroce, il faut passer la Manche et visiter les royaumes brumeux du spleen . . . le signe distinctif de ce genre de comique était la violence."*

8. "The Romantic Englishman, the Comic Spirit, and the Future of Criticism," *Tyro* 1 ([Spring 1921]), p. [4].

9. Review of *Tarr,* by Wyndham Lewis, *Egoist* 5 (September 1918), 105. On 22 March 1921 Virginia Woolf recorded a conversation with Eliot after missing their train. " 'Missing trains is awful,' I said. 'Yes. But humiliation is the worst thing in life' he replied." *The Diary of Virginia Woolf,* vol. 2, ed. Anne Olivier Bell (New York: Harcourt Brace Jovanovich, 1978), p. 103.

10. "Contemporary English Prose," *Vanity Fair* (New York) 20 (July 1923), 51.

11. Lewis's self-portrait, "Mr. Wyndham Lewis as Tyro" (1920–21; Ferens Art Gallery, Hull, England), attempts to portray the grotesquely savage element of human consciousness.

12. Review of *Tarr,* p. 105.

13. Robert H. Bell first broke the news in "Bertrand Russell and the Eliots," *American Scholar* 52 (Summer 1983), 309–25. Though he was unable to quote from the letters, he drew upon and paraphrased Russell's extensive correspondence in the McMaster University archives to disclose the nature of the affair, citing one of Russell's specific admissions of sexual relations and showing that they were intermittently lovers from October 1917 until Vivien wrote to him on 18 January 1919 that she "disliked fading intimacies and wished to break completely." Though Bell's essay appeared just in time for inclusion in Peter Ackroyd's *T. S. Eliot: A Life* (1984), Ackroyd made surprisingly little of it, noting Russell's "claim" that he made love to Vivien and viewing the alleged seduction as a one-off incident that Eliot likely knew of but remained silent about: "It was the pointless and messy end of what had been an intense but 'platonic' relationship, and the intimacy between Vivien and Russell came to an end" (p. 84).

14. *Bertrand Russell: The Spirit of Solitude* (London: Jonathan Cape, 1996), p. 482.

15. Letter of 29 December 1916, quoted in ibid., p. 487.

16. Intentionally or accidentally, Eliot broke off the last phrase of Aspatia's exclamation, misquoting "Look, look, wenches!" misleadingly turning her melancholic hysteria to male sexual expectation.

17. "American Literature," a review of *A History of American Literature,* vol. 2, ed. William P. Trent et al., *Athenaeum,* no. 4643 (25 April 1919), 237.

18. Eliot was to write again of "The wrong'd Aspatia" in "Elegy," a canceled fragment of *The Waste Land* (*WLF* 117).

19. Eliot may have confided more about the poems to his brother, who wrote to his friend Henry B. Harvey on 16 September 1944 to encourage an article by his wife, the poet and critic Dorothy Dudley: "However, have a meaty tip for Dorothy: she might write an essay on the influence of surrealism on TS Eliot. It's there, sticking out like a barber pole, but no critic has touched it . . . TSE's short earlier poems are certainly partly inspired by Picasso (et al). I think he [Eliot] was one of the earliest surrealist poets. Critics have floundered around in interpreting his Sweeney, etc. poems without discovering the surrealism which is the key to their understanding. Tell D to give it a thought" (Chapel Hill: *MS* 12009).

20. The play appears in C. F. T. Brooke's edition of *The Shakespeare Apocrypha* (Oxford: Clarendon Press, 1908), which Eliot included on the reading list for his syllabus on Elizabethan literature.

21. The epigraph was not used when the poem first appeared in the *Little Review* 5 (September 1918), 10–11.

22. Stanzas 4–7 of "Sweeney Among the Nightingales" are remarkably similar in diction and imagery to Bertha's impression of Kreissler in Wyndham Lewis's *Tarr,* the single passage quoted by Eliot in his review of *Tarr,* in which he discussed its distinctive English humor; the review appeared in the same month in which "Sweeney Among the Nightingales" appeared in the *Little Review.* To Eliot, the scene is "as good as anything of the sort by Dostoyevsky": "She saw side by side, and unconnected, the silent figure drawing her and the other one full of blindness and violence. Then there were two other figures, one getting up from the chair, yawning, and the present lazy one at the window—four in all, that she could not bring together somehow, each in a complete compartment of time of its own." Review of *Tarr,* p. 105).

23. F .O. Matthiessen, *The Achievement of T. S. Eliot,* 3rd ed. (London: Oxford University Press, 1958), p. 129.

24. "The Silver Bough," letter in *Times* (London), 6 April 1958, p. 4.

25. "The Noh and the Image," review of *Noh, or Accomplishment, a Study of the Classical Stage of Japan,* by Ernest Fenollosa and Ezra Pound, *Egoist* 4 (August 1917), 103.

26. Saint Augustine, *Confessions* 3.1, quoted in *The Waste Land,* note to line 307 (*CPP* 79).

27. The manuscript record belies Eliot's tongue-in-cheek remark in an interview with Maura Laverty on 25 January 1936 for Irish Broadcasting that *Sweeney Agonistes* "was written in two nights. Working from ten o'clock at night until five the next morning I succeeded, with the aid of youthful enthusiasm and a bottle of gin in completing the work in what believe must have been record time. Unfortunately, as one grows older, gin and enthusiasm seem to lose some of their value as mental stimulants" (Houghton: AC9.El464.Zzx, Box 8, folder 15; partially quoted in A. Walton Litz, "Tradition and the Practice of Poetry," *Southern Review* 85 [Autumn 1985], p. 875).

28. Eliot's two-page holograph outline of the play was reproduced in *The Stage Sixty Theatre Club Presents Homage to T. S. Eliot: A Programme of Poetry, Drama and Music* (Globe Theatre, London, 13 June 1965), pp. 4–5. The manuscripts and typescripts related to *Sweeney Agonistes,* including the scenario of an early draft entitled *The Superior Landlord,* are in the Hayward Collection, King's College, Cambridge University.

29. Michael J. Sidnell, *Dances of Death: The Group Theatre of London in the Thirties* (London: Faber and Faber, 1984), p. 264.

30. Eliot icily drew on Brutus's speech to Lucilius in *Julius Caesar* (4.2.20–7) in writing "The Hollow Men," parts of which originate in "Doris's Dream Songs" (1924), probable fragments of *Sweeney Agonistes:*

When love begins to sicken and decay,

It useth an enforcèd ceremony.

There are no tricks in plain and simple faith;

But hollow men, like horses hot at hand,

Make gallant show and promise of their mettle;

But when they should endure the bloody spur

They fall their crests, and, like deceitful jades,

Sink in the trial.

31. The fact that Eliot was not directly involved in Vivien's committal to the nursing home after her mental health worsened is made clear in letters from Vivien's brother, Maurice Haigh-Wood, to Eliot on 14 July and 14 August 1938, made public by Valerie Eliot in an interview with Blake Morrison, "The Two Mrs Eliots," *Independent*, 24 April 1994, in *Sunday Review*, pp. 4–9. In the latter letter Maurice describes to Eliot, who was away in the country, how he had taken Vivien to see two different doctors, Dr. Hart and Dr. Mapother, and the subsequent committal: "Both doctors felt strongly that she should be put into a home. They handed me their certificates. I then had to go before a magistrate to obtain his order. I got hold of one in Hampstead. I then went to Northumberland House, saw the doctor there, & arranged for a car to go with 2 nurses to Compayne Gardens that evening. The car went at about 10 pm. Vivienne went very quietly with them after a good deal of discussion" (p. 5).

32. Quoted in Hermione Lee, *Virginia Woolf: A Biography* (London: Chatto and Windus, 1996), p. 451.

33. There is a copy of the publication, which was printed before 15 August 1939, in the Houghton Library. Eliot's anonymously printed poems include "How to Pick a Possum," "The O'Possum Strikes Back," "The Whale and the Elephant: A Fable," "Ode to a Roman Coot," "Three Sonnets," "Vers pour La Foulque: feuillet d'album" [in French], "Translation into English of 'Verses for the Coot,' Album Leaflet," and "Abschied zur Bina" [in German].

Chapter 5. In the Music Halls

1. Sickert's painting appeared in the first volume of the *Yellow Book* (April 1894), 85.

2. *Men and Memories,* vol. I (London: Faber and Faber, 1931), p. 237.

3. *Mainly on the Air* (New York: Knopf, 1947), p. 49. Beerbohm's famous obituary of Dan Leno (1904) and other essays on the music halls were collected in *Around Theatres* (1924; rpt. New York: Simon and Schuster, 1954).

4. Letter of 15 February 1932 to the music-hall historian J. B. Booth, printed in Booth's *The Days We Knew* (London: T. W. Laurie, 1943), p. 30.

5. *Men and Memories,* p. 275.

6. *Letters to the New Island,* new ed., ed. George Bornstein and Hugh Witemeyer (Basingstoke: Macmillan, 1989), p. 58. Yeats was himself averse to music-hall lyrics, as he revealed in a letter to his father of 14 March 1916: "I separate the rhythmical and the abstract. . . . In poetry they are not confused for we know that poetry is rhythm, but in music-hall verses we find an abstract cadence, which is vulgar because it is apart from imitation. This cadence is a mechanism, it never suggests a voice shaken with joy or sorrow as poetical rhythm does. It is but the noise of a machine and not the coming and going of the breath." *The Letters of W. B. Yeats,* ed. Allan Wade (New York: Macmillan, 1955), p. 609.

7. "Prologue: In the Stalls," lines 1–4, from *London Nights* (London: Leonard C. Smithers, 1895).

8. *Egoist* 4 (December 1917), 165. This letter, signed "Muriel A. Schwarz," is one of five composed by Eliot as a correspondence filler.

9. *Egoist* 5 (March 1918), 47.

10. Eliot wrote to Virginia Woolf on 2 June 1927: "I am free for tea on Wednesday or Thursday or for dinner on Wednesday. And if any of those times suited you I should be very glad to show you what little I know about the Grizzly Bear, or the Chicken Strut" (Berg). Quoted in Hermione Lee, *Virginia Woolf: A Biography* (London: Chatto and Windus, 1996), p. 453.

11. Eliot was a strong supporter of the Phoenix Society, founded in 1919 under the auspices of the Stage Society specifically for the production of Elizabethan and Restoration drama. Its performances became increasingly important to Eliot in working out his theory of poetic drama.

12. *Tyro* 1 ([Spring 1921]), p. [4].

13. *Dial* 70 (June 1921), 687.

14. Ibid., p. 688.

15. Ibid., pp. 687–8.

16. Lionel Trilling, observing Eliot's interest in "the public intention and the music-hall tradition of Kipling's verse," was the first to observe that "anyone who has heard a record of Mr Eliot reading *The Waste Land* will be struck by how much that poem is publicly intended, shaped less for the study than for the platform or the pulpit, by how much the full dialect rendition of the Cockney passages suggests that it was even shaped for the music hall, by how explicit the poet's use of his voice makes the music we are so likely to think of as internal and secretive." "Kipling" (1943), rpt. in *Kipling's Mind and Art,* ed. Andrew Rutherford (Edinburgh: Oliver and Boyd, 1964), p. 89. Trilling's observation was recently confirmed by actress Fiona Shaw's dramatic reading of the poem to packed audiences in Wilton's Music Hall, London, January 1998.

17. B. R. McElderry, Jr., first identified Eliot's lines as being adapted from the 1912 hit song "That Shakespearian Rag," in "Eliot's 'Shakespeherian Rag,'" *American Quarterly* 9 (Summer 1957), pp. 185–6. Originally published by Joseph W. Stern and Co. in 1912, the lyrics were written by Gene Buck and Herman Ruby, the music by Dave Stamper, for performance at the Ziegfeld Follies: "English Theatre and Music Hall rights strictly reserved." "The publishers of the song," writes McElderry, "listed it fourth among ten titles in a *Variety* advertisement for July 19, 1912 (p. 25) adding this comment: 'If you want a song that can be acted as well as sung send for this big surprise hit.'"

Valerie Eliot has identified adaptations of several other songs, all popularized in vaudeville and minstrel shows in the early 1900s, in the canceled opening lines of *The Waste Land,* including "Harrigan," from George M. Cohan's musical play, *Fifty Miles from Boston* (1907); "By the Watermelon Vine" (1904) by Thomas S. Allen; "My Evaline" (1901) by Mae Anwerda Sloane; "The Cubanola Glide" (1909) by Vincent Bryan; and "The Maid of the Mill" by Hamilton Aïdé (lyrics in his *Songs without Music,* 1889), music by Stephen Adams. Eliot had earlier adapted popular college songs, such as "The Maid of Phillipopolis" ("She was a beau-ti-ful Bul-ga-ri-an, / Oh! Such a light and fair-y air-y 'un"), for his Bolo poems: "King Bolo's big black basstard kween / That airy fairy hairy un" (*L1* 125). See Lockwood Honoré, comp., *Popular College Songs* (Cincinnati, Ohio: John Church, 1891), pp. 30–1.

18. See Jewel Spears Brooker's broad discussion of Eliot's principle of collaboration in "Common Ground and Collaboration in T. S. Eliot," *Centennial Review* 25 (Summer 1981), 225–38.

19. *The Diary of Virginia Woolf,* vol. 2, ed. Anne Olivier Bell (New York: Harcourt Brace Jovanovich, 1978), p. 68. In "Notes on the Blank Verse of Christopher Marlowe," published in the autumn of 1919, Eliot had tried to characterize "the direction in which Marlowe's verse might have moved . . . [as] toward this intense and serious and indubitably great poetry, which, like some great painting and sculpture, attains its effects by something not unlike caricature" (*SW* 80). The "personal upheaval" evidently followed the appearance of *Prufrock and Other Observations* (1917) and may have involved discovery of Vivien's relationship with Bertrand Russell.

20. On one of his early experimental title pages, which he identified in the margin as "My typing. Probably precedes the fragments themselves," Eliot typed "FRAGMENT OF A MELOCOMIC MINSTRELSY," with the single epigraph from Paul Mazon's French translation (Paris: Société D'Edition "Les Belles Lettres," 1920) of Aeschylus's *Les Choéphores,* evidently the copy borrowed from Pound:

Oreste:

> Vous ne les voyex pas, vous,
> Mais, moi, je les vois. Elles
> Me pourchassent, je ne puis
> Plus rester. (p. 121)

21. "Eliot's Friends," *Observer,* 18 June 1967, p. 19. In "The Poetic Drama" Eliot had written theoretically about the importance of 'framework' for poetic drama: "The ideal condition is that under which everything, except what only the individual genius can supply, is provided for the poet. A *framework* is provided. We do not mean plot. . . . But a dramatic poet needs to have some *kind* of dramatic form given to him as the condition of his time, a form which in itself is neither good nor bad but which permits an artist to fashion it into a work of art. And by a 'kind of dramatic form' one means almost the temper of the age (not the temper of a few intellectuals); a preparedness, a habit, on the part of the public, to respond in a predictable way, however crudely, to certain stimuli." *Athenaeum,* no. 4698 (14 May 1920), 635.

22. Quoted in Donald Gallup, *T. S. Eliot and Ezra Pound* (New Haven, 1970), p. 28.

23. Cyril W. Beaumont, *The Diaghilev Ballet in London: A Personal Record,* 3rd ed. (London: Adam and Charles Black, 1951), p. 144.

24. "Modern Tendencies in Poetry," *Shama'a* 1 (April 1920), 17.

25. " 'The Duchess of Malfi' at the Lyric: and Poetic Drama," *Art and Letters* 3 (Winter [1919], 1920), 39.

26. "The Poetic Drama," p. 635.

27. Beaumont, *The Diaghilev Ballet in London,* p. 138. Massine describes the dance: "We began with the traditional high kicks of the cancan to the first staccato passage of the music, followed by elevation steps. Then, kneeling on one knee, I imitated with rapid pulse movements the lifting of the girl's skirt, while Lopokova passed her leg over my head, one knee bent, the raised leg revolving in a froth of petticoats. As the music swelled to a crescendo we each went into a series of pirouettes with our arms extended at right angles, until Lopokova collapsed for the final pose in a *grand-écart* split, I myself matching it and watching with horror and admiration Lopokova's shocking behaviour. . . . Perhaps it was the contrast between the fluttering, pink-petticoated, mischievous Lopokova, taunting and being taunted, and her greasy and sinister-looking partner, which caused the cancan to be so well received" (*My Life in Ballet* [New York: St. Martin's Press, 1968], pp. 137–8).

28. Eliot may have actually seen *Parade* the previous spring at the Alhambra, where it

was in the program as part of the Diaghilev repertoire ("first performances in England") with *La Boutique Fantasque, Le Chapeau Tricorne,* and other productions that he saw then.

29. Beaumont, *The Diaghilev Ballet in London,* p. 149. *Parade* (1917) was Cocteau's clarion call for a new drama. His essay "The Collaboration of 'Parade' " was included in *Le Rappel à l'ordre* (Paris: Stock, 1926), translated by Rollo H. Myers as *A Call to Order* (London: Faber and Gwyer, 1926), one of the first books that Eliot saw through the press after joining the firm, writing to Bonamy Dobrée on 23 June 1926 that "the one side of Cocteau's work which so far has shown itself to be of incontestable value and interest is his theatrical side" (Brotherton). Cocteau wrote of the public reception of *Parade* in his preface: "What I turned to the circus and music-hall to seek was not, as is so often asserted, the charm of clowns and negroes, but a lesson in equilibrium. This school, which teaches hard work, strength and discretion, grace and utility—which is, in fact a *haute école*—lost me the sympathies of many inattentive people" (p. viii). As Cocteau describes the conjuror's performance, "The Chinaman pulls out an egg from his pigtail, eats and digests it, finds it again in the toe of his shoe, spits fire, burns himself, stamps to put out the sparks, etc." (p. 53).

30. As Cocteau described Bronislava Nijinska's *tour de force* performance in *Les Biches* (1924), "See how she maintains her balance on the brink of caricature without ever falling into it, just as the musician, in spite of his easy manner, never lapses into mere facility" (*A Call to Order,* p. 70), an echo of Eliot's description of Marlowe's style: "this style which secures its emphasis by always hesitating on the edge of caricature at the right moment" (*SE* 124).

31. " 'The Duchess of Malfi' at the Lyric: and Poetic Drama," p. 39.

32. *Dial* 71 (August 1921), 214.

33. *Dial* 71 (October 1921), 453. The *Times* reviewer, who wrote that "a great deal of the ballet was for us merely a tedious posturing in sight and sound," may have contributed to the production being pulled after the third performance on July 1: "At last [Sokalova] deigns to move in a high-leaping, ungainly dance which is at least a triumph of calisthenic skill. The others leave her to herself; her dance becomes more extravagant, til at last she falls on the stage exhausted. That is all that happens, and through it all Stravinsky's orchestra tears its way in ever-increasing harshness" (29 June 1921, p. 8). When, three years later, Eliot anticipated the return of the Diaghilev Ballet to London, he recounted his own annoyance at the audience during the performance: "Let us hope that Sir Oswald Stoll will be able to provide at the Coliseum, other turns of sufficient liveliness to induce our London audiences to sit through the performance of the greatest mimetic dancer in the world—Massine—to the music of one of the greatest musicians—Stravinski. The writer of these lines recalls his efforts, several years ago, to restrain (with the point of an umbrella) the mirth of his neighbours in a 'family house' which seemed united to deride Sokalova at her best in the *Sacre de Printemp.* [*sic*]. May we at least tolerate a part of what Paris has appreciated!" (*Cr* 3:5).

34. Diaghilev eventually returned to London with a new company (lacking Massine) for a two-month season from 24 November 1924, and though their struggle for success prompted Eliot to devote his "Commentary" in the *Criterion* (January 1925) to a call for public support, he lamented the dispersement of former dancers, including Massine, to revue and music halls: "It is deplorable that Mr. Diaghileff has no longer the support of several of those dancers who played such important parts in the successes of several years ago; it is deplorable that dancers of genius should withdraw to the ordinary music hall turn. A dozen little troupes of self-directed dancers may tour the halls; but their efforts are wasted. . . . If dancers disperse, they diminish the importance of their art. It is . . . a public obligation . . . to continue to support Mr. Diaghileff's ballet, and use our efforts

so that on his next visit to London he may have the facilities for producing the *Sacre* and the newer work of Stravinski" (*Cr* 3:161–2).

35. Eliot read the original publication, which was collected and translated as "Professional Secrets," in *A Call to Order.* "The circus, the music-hall, the cinema, and those other enterprises which, since the advent of Serge de Diaghilev, have provided our younger men with great opportunities, are so many faces conspiring together, in an unconscious alliance, against the present-day theatre, which is now nothing but an old photograph album" (pp. 174–5).

36. Oreste Rastelli, born in Bologna, Italy, in 1900, began his acrobatic career as a boy at the Casino de Paris in 1909. He then joined his father's act in circus and variety, subsequently forming his own act, "The Rastellis," with his wife, son and two other male acrobats. Eliot evidently saw them perform in Paris, for they first appeared in London at the Palladium from 25 February to 4 March 1929, on a bill led by Nellie Wallace "at her best and most characteristic" (*Stage,* 28 February 1929, p. 13).

37. "The most ramshackle Guitry farce," Eliot wrote in "The Possibility of a Poetic Drama," has some paltry idea or comment upon life put into the mouth of one of the characters at the end. . . . The consummation of the triumph of the actor over the play is perhaps the productions of the Guitry" (*SW* 56, 58). "In order to make an Elizabethan drama give a satisfactory effect as a work of art," he wrote in "Four Elizabethan Dramatists," "we should have to find a method of acting different from that of contemporary social drama, and at the same time to attempt to express all the emotions of actual life in the way in which they actually would be expressed: the result would be something like a performance of *Agamemnon* by the Guitrys" (*SE* 112–3).

38. *Sleeping Partners* played for 129 performances at St. Martin's Theatre from 31 December 1917 to 20 April 1918. James Harding describes the action, in which a young man [played by Seymour Hicks] pursues a married woman: "There follows some excellent business when, in desperation, he tries to telephone her, performs acrobatics as he lights his cigarette with a box of matches from the other side of the room, and finds himself making intimate declarations on a crossed line to a housewife ordering cherries from her grocer. While he fumes into the receiver, pleading for a word from the beautiful subscriber, she appears silently in the doorway at his back and tiptoes over to him with a smile." *Sacha Guitry* (London: Methuen, 1968), p. 81. Barbara Everett attributes Eliot's use of the telephone to Ring Lardner in "The New Style of *Sweeney Agonistes,*" *Yearbook of English Studies* 14 (1984), p. 256.

39. During a reading from his works at Columbia University in April 1958, Eliot decided to read "Fragment of an Agon" to illustrate the rapid dialogue: "Again, I'm doing something I don't usually do. You'll just have to imagine the different speakers. I can't stop to indicate who is saying what, but Mr. Sweeney is saying most of what's of any importance. This was a work I never finished because it has to be spoken too quickly to be possible on the stage, to convey the sort of rhythm that I intended. It was much too fast for dialogue, really." "T. S. Eliot Talks about His Poetry," *Columbia University Forum* 2 (Fall 1958), 14.

40. Letter of 18 March 1933 to Hallie Flanagan (King's). In April 1916 Ezra Pound took Eliot to a private performance of Yeats's *At the Hawk's Well,* with the Japanese actor Mischio Itow in the role of the hawk. The performance made a strong impression on Eliot's view of symbolic drama, and he soon wrote on the importance of Noh in his review, "The Noh and the Image" (*Egoist* 4 [August 1917], 102–3), of *Noh, or Accomplishment* (1916), by Pound and Ernest Fenollosa. In the letter just quoted, he directed Hallie Flanagan's attention to this book and to Yeats's preface and notes to *At the Hawk's Well* in preparing her production of *Sweeney Agonistes.*

41 "The Beating of a Drum," *Nation and Athenaeum* 34 (6 October 1933), 12.

42. Swinley, who went on to become a distinguished Shakespearean actor, had played Jaffier in the Phoenix Society production of Thomas Otway's *Venice Preserved* (1921) and Amintor in its production of Francis Beaumont's and John Fletcher's *The Maid's Tragedy* (1922).

43. In a postscript to a 1927 letter (undated [late June], Berg) to Virginia Woolf, Eliot wrote that he had "just been to see Ernie Lotinga in his new play at the Islington Empire. Magnificent. He is the greatest living British histrionic Artist, in the purest tradition of British Obscenity. How did I get in? As I heard a Lady say a few days ago at the Kings Arms at 11:25 A.M.: 'I just Ambled in Unconscious.'" When Mrs. Ethelbert enters the church "*with marketing bag, hilariously*" in *The Rock* (London: Faber and Faber, 1934), she replies to her husband, who asks " 'ow on earth did you 'appen along?'", "Oh, I just ambled in unconscious" (pp. 65–6). Jacob Isaacs, a fan of Ernie Lotinga, wrote about the comic purgation in *Sweeney Agonistes*: "Whether this purgation came directly from Ernie Lotinga, who is not only bawdy, but a direct descendant of the phallic comedy of Greece and Rome, I do not know. This I do know, that if I have done nothing else for literature, I did at least take Mr. Eliot to see Mr. Ernie Lotinga at the Islington Empire" (*An Assessment of Twentieth-Century Literature*, p. 147). Lotinga, on tour with a play entitled *Convicts*, opened for a week at the Islington Empire on 20 June 1927. The critic for the *Stage* (23 June 1927) described the play as "a fruitful source of mirth, thanks to the many opportunities provided for Ernie Lotinga to display that very pleasant brand of humour peculiar to himself" (p. 11).

44. *The Rock,* pp. 67–8. The observant critic for the *Times* stated that "Mr. Eliot's pageant play looked first to liturgy for its dramatic form, though wisely imitating also the ready and popular stage modes, such as music-hall, ballet and mime. . . . Mr. Eliot ranges widely in his methods, freely borrowing wherever he pleases—there is even a pantomime interlude—but under the discipline of a traditional morality. All the same, he has created a new thing in the theatre and made smoother the path towards a contemporary poetic drama" (29 May 1934, p. 12).

45. The anonymous lyrics are actually Eliot's rendition of a song made famous by the music-hall comedian Tom Costello (1863–1945), who is best remembered as the henpecked husband in "At Trinity Church I Met My Doom, or That's What She's Done for Me," words and melody by Fred Gilbert (London: Francis, Day and Hunter, 1894). Chorus:

> She told me her age was five-and-twenty,
> Cash in the bank of course she'd plenty,
> I like a lamb believed it all,
> I was an M.U.G.
> At Trinity church I met my doom,
> Now we live in a top back room,
> Up to my eyes in debt for 'renty,'
> That's what she's done for me.

46. *Listener* 16 (25 November 1936), 994.

47. The tune for two verses and the refrain of "One-Eyed Riley," scored by Mary Trevelyan from Eliot's dictation, is printed at the end of the play (*CPP* 441). There are, of course, other more bawdy and vulgar versions of the song, including an English variation, "O'Reilly's Daughter":

Sitting in O'Reilly's bar
drinking rum and coca cola,
Suddenly there came to mind,
I'd like to shag O'Reilly's daughter.

Chorus: Hi yi yi—Hi yi yi
    The one-eyed Reilly,
    Rub it up, stuff it up, bum and all,
    Play it on your old base drum.

48. *The Making of a Play: T. S. Eliot's* "The Cocktail Party" (Cambridge: Cambridge University Press, 1966), p. 26.

49. *Poetry and Drama* (London: Faber and Faber, 1951), pp. 32–3.

50. Eliot elucidates this quality in "The Development of Shakespeare's Verse" (part 2, p. 12), comprised of two lectures (King's) delivered at Edinburgh University in 1937 and at Bristol University in 1941; copies of the lectures, unpublished in English, are in the Houghton Library, Harvard University. See appendix, note 25.

51. These lines, identified by Eliot only as being from a "Popular Song," are as yet untraced.

52. "T. S. Eliot and I," *Observer Review,* 20 February 1972, p. 21.

53. "Our Mr. Eliot Grows Younger," *New York Times Magazine,* 21 September 1958, p. 72.

54 Other scholars have begun to explore Eliot's use of popular culture, notably David Chinitz in "T. S. Eliot and the Cultural Divide," *PMLA* 110 (March 1995), 236–47. Chinitz also explores Eliot's attraction to the music halls in developing his argument that Eliot "developed a quite progressive theoretical position on the relation between high culture and popular culture and attempted repeatedly to convert his theory into art" (p. 237). In *Gendering Bodies/Performing Art* (Ann Arbor: University of Michigan Press, 1995), Amy Koritz studies Eliot's writings on music hall and the Russian ballet as reflections of his contradictory ideological commitments: "For example, on the one hand, the subordination of the performer to the text, and the value given to male performers, marks Eliot's commitment to a text-based and male-centered aristocracy of high art. On the other hand, Eliot's praise of a female music hall performer signals his simultaneous need to appropriate the vitality of that performer for his own art, as well as a desire to block the absorption of her working-class audience into the middle class" (p. 138). Manju Jaidka's *T. S. Eliot's Use of Popular Sources* (Lewiston, N.Y.: Edwin Mellen Press, 1997) surveys Eliot's interest in nonsense poetry, detective fiction, and the music hall/vaudeville tradition. Recent studies of Eliot and the ballet include Nancy D. Hargrove, "T. S. Eliot and the Dance," *Journal of Modern Literature* 21 (Fall 1997), pp. 61–88, and Terri A. Mester, *Movement and Modernism* (Fayetteville: University of Arkansas Press, 1997).

Chapter 6. The Horrific Moment

1. "For T.S.E.," in *T. S. Eliot: The Man and His Work,* ed. Allen Tate (New York: Delta-Dell, 1967) p. 89; rpt. in *Selected Prose 1909–1965: Ezra Pound,* ed. William Cookson (London: Faber and Faber, 1973), p. 434.

2. See *Ezra Pound: The London Years,* Catalogue of an Exhibition at Sheffield University Library, 23 April–13 May 1976, introduction and notes by Philip Grover, and Ezra

Pound, *A Walking Tour in Southern France,* ed. Richard Sieburth (New York: New Directions, 1992), pp. 14, 24.

3. A photograph of the wave pattern at Excideuil is reproduced in Hugh Kenner, *The Pound Era* (Berkeley: University of California Press, 1971), p. 337.

4. "Literature and the Modern World," *American Prefaces* 1 (November 1935), 20.

5. Prufrock's allusion to Lazarus, invariably misidentified as John 11:1–44, is to Luke 16:19–30 (Revised Standard Version): "The poor man died and was carried by the angels to Abraham's bosom. The rich man also died and was buried; and in Hades, being in torment, he lifted up his eyes, and saw Abraham far off and Lazarus in his bosom. And he called out, 'Father Abraham, have mercy upon me, and send Lazarus to dip the end of his finger in water and cool my tongue; for I am in anguish in this flame.' But Abraham said, 'Son, remember that you in your lifetime received your good things, and Lazarus in like manner evil things; but now he is comforted here, and you are in anguish. And besides all this, between us and you a great chasm has been fixed, in order that those who would pass from here to you may not be able, and none may cross from there to us.' And he said, 'Then I beg you, Father, to send him to my father's house, for I have five brothers, so that he may warn them, lest they also come into this place of torment.' "

6. *Manchester Guardian* 803 (23 June 1916), 3.

7. "Beyle and Balzac," *Athenaeum,* no.4658 (30 May 1919), 392.

8. *Egoist* 5 (January 1918), 10. Eliot was to express a similar sentiment about the American view of "Sweeney Among the Nightingales" and "Burbank" two years later: "I suppose I shall be thought merely disgusting" (*L1* 363). See p. 94.

9. "Shakespeare and Montaigne," *TLS,* no.1249 (24 December 1925), 895.

10. Ray Monk, *Bertrand Russell: The Spirit of Solitude,* (London: Jonathan Cape, 1996), pp. 510–1. Russell went on to say that the night was *"utter hell"* and had an indescribable "quality of loathsomeness about it," but this is less a statement of affair-ending physical revulsion (due to Vivien's chronic menstrual problems), as Peter Ackroyd suggests, and more Russell's way of indicating his preference for Colette, to whom he now wished to return: "I want you to understand that the one & only thing that made the night loathsome was that it was not with you. There was nothing else to make me hate it" (p. 511). Monk detects in the letter an element of Russell's growing self-disgust and "discovery of the moral depths to which he is capable of sinking" (p. 512).

11. Monk quotes Colette's description of the meeting: "We had tea on the kitchen table. I found him reserved and rather shut up in himself—remote. Extraordinarily erudite, of course. His eyes were most remarkable. One felt they might spring out on one at any moment—like a cat. His manner was detached and there was a certain frigidity about him. But underneath that frigidity, one felt there lurked a curiously deep despair. He talked in slow, hesitating fashion. It was difficult to think of him as an American." *Bertrand Russell: The Spirit of Solitude,* p. 539.

12. "Bertrand Russell and the Eliots," *American Scholar* 52 (Summer 1983), 321.

13. "Beyle and Balzac," p. 393.

14. See "Whitman and Tennyson," *Nation and Athenaeum* 40 (18 December 1926), 426.

15. Brutus, reflecting on his sleepless nights since Cassius first set him against Caesar, says, "Between the acting of a dreadful thing / And the first motion, all the interim is / Like a phantasma or a hideous dream" (2.1. 63–5). Eliot used this passage, misquoting "miasma" for "phantasma," as the epigraph for an unpublished scenario, "The Superior Landlord," a five-page typescript (Kings's) related to *Sweeney Agonistes*. Brutus continues:

The Genius and the mortal instruments
Are then in council; and the state of man,
Like to a little kingdom, suffers then
The nature of an insurrection (66–69).

16. "The Duchess of Malfy," *Listener* 26 (18 December 1941), 8.

17. "Beyle and Balzac," p. 392.

18. "London Letter," *Dial* 3 (September 1922), 331.

19. "The Lesson of Baudelaire," *Tyro* 1 (Spring 1921), 4.

20. "A Prediction in Regard to Three English Authors," *Vanity Fair* 21 (February 1924), 98.

21. In Poe's "Ligeia," when the dying second bride, Lady Rowena, begins her "hideous drama of revivification," the narrator falls into an extremity of horror: "Through a species of unutterable horror and awe, for which the language of mortality has no sufficiently energetic expression, I felt my heart cease to beat, my limbs grow rigid where I sat."

22. "Kipling Redivivus," *Athenaeum*, no. 4645 (9 May 1919), 297.

23. Eliot quoted these lines from *Inferno* 33, line 46, in the note to line 412 of *The Waste Land:* "*Dayadhvam*: I have heard the key" (*CPP* 74, 80), quoted earlier in a "London Letter": "To one who, like the present writer, passes his days in this City of London (*quand'io sentii chiavar l'uscio de sotto*) the loss of these towers, to meet the eye down a grimy lane, and of these empty naves, to receive the solitary visitor at noon from the dust and tumult of Lombard Street, will be irreparable and unforgotten." *Dial* 70 (June 1921), 691.

24. "A Brief Introduction to the Method of Paul Valéry," in Paul Valéry, *Le Serpent*, trans. Mark Wardle (London: R. Cobden-Sanderson, 1924), p. 13.

25. "A Study of Marlowe," *TLS*, no.1309 (3 March 1927), 140; partially quoted in *SE* 133.

26. *Abinger Harvest* (London: Edward Arnold, 1936), p. 91.

27. Introduction to Charles Williams, *All Hallows' Eve* (New York: Pellegrini and Cudahy, 1948), p. xv.

28. In this Norton Lecture "Matthew Arnold," Eliot went on to say: "The vision of the horror and the glory was denied to Arnold, but he knew something of the boredom" (*UPUC* 106). Eliot later clarified his sense of "boredom": "There is a very profound kind of boredom which is an essential moment in the religious life, the boredom with all living in so far as it has no religious meaning. The capacity for this boredom is latent in everybody, and it can never really be appeased by mere amusement." *Religious Drama: Mediaeval and Modern* (New York: House of Books, 1954), p. [12].

29. In *A Companion to Shakespeare Studies,* ed. Harley Granville-Barker and G. B. Harrison (Cambridge: Cambridge University Press, 1934), p. 295.

30. *An Assessment of Twentieth-Century Literature* (London: Secker and Warburg, 1951), p. 147. Isaacs attended a performance in the Group Theatre Rooms in January 1935 (not January 1933, as he misremembers). The producer, Rupert Doone, had written in the program that he saw Sweeney as "a modern Orestes (the three-dimensional character in the play). The rest are conventionalized conventional characters—the Eumenides or Bogies of Sweeney's persecution." Group Theatre Scrapbook 1 (Berg); printed in Michael J. Sidnell, *Dances of Death: The Group Theatre of London in the Thirties* (London: Faber and Faber, 1984), p. 324. Desmond MacCarthy characterized the play and production in the *Listener* (9 January 1935) as "the fragment of a drama of retribution translated into the terms of squalid modern crime . . . though it is the *feeling* of a haunted conscience that is most

powerfully conveyed in this strange little piece. . . . If you want to suggest in terms of actuality retribution for some sordid crime, could it be done better than this? Sweeney is speaking. You must imagine a man under a lamp sitting at a table, dressed with the careful colourless conventionality of a young clerk, and speaking the lines I am about to repeat, with unemphatic horror, speaking out of himself, out of an inner terror. He is addressing the girl opposite him, but he is also addressing us: it is half a sinister soliloquy, half a confession—or perhaps it is a threat to her: 'I knew a man once did a girl in . . .' Well, it certainly had a grisly impressiveness lifted above the matter-of-fact" (pp. 80–1). Eliot's puzzlement at the performance was astutely observed by Isaacs: though Eliot wrote to Auden that he was surprised by "the general level of intelligence" shown in the production (Sidnell, *Dances of Death*, p. 103), he was concerned with the discrepancy between the meaning of the production and his intended meaning. When the Group Theatre revived the play as a curtain-raiser to Auden's *Dances of Death* on 1 October 1935, Eliot wrote next to the clipping of an unidentified review, "This production was *completely* the reverse of what I meant!" (Houghton: AC9. El464.Zzx, box 4, folder 8).

31. "The Duchess of Malfy," p. 826.

Chapter 7. First-Rate Blasphemy

1. Eliot told E. J. H. Greene that he could not recall whether it was in 1919 or in 1920 that he returned to a study of Baudelaire's *Les Fleurs du Mal,* but it appears that Eliot had been reading Baudelaire even earlier, well before he actually appears in Eliot's poetry and criticism. See *T. S. Eliot et la France* (Paris: Bovin, 1951), p. 108.

2. "We must assume," says Eliot, "if we are to talk about poetry at all, that there is some absolute poetic hierarchy; we keep at the back of our minds the reminder of some end of the world, some final Judgment Day, on which the poets will be assembled in their ranks and orders. In the long run, there is an ultimate greater and less. But at any particular time . . . good taste consists . . . in approximating to some analysis of the absolute and the relative in our own appreciation." "Donne in Our Time," in *A Garland for John Donne,* ed. Theodore Spencer (Cambridge: Harvard University Press, 1931), p. 5.

3. Hulme may have been familiar with G. K. Chesterton's *Heretics* (1905) and *Orthodoxy* (1908), each of which went through several editions. Though Chesterton's use of the terms is somewhat more doctrinal, it is in the same spirit as Hulme's in that he sees contemporary "heresies" as springing from a belief in the Inner Light, a disbelief in Original Sin, a denial of absolute values, the fancy of the Superman, and correspondingly a mistaken view of man and his place in the world. Eliot had examined both books by July 1927, when he wrote in the *Criterion:* "In essays such as *Orthodoxy, Heretics,* or *The Defendant,* [Chesterton's] style is admirable for his purpose; he often has unique perceptions; but his mind is not equipped for sustained argument" (*Cr* 4:71).

4. In an unprinted letter of 31 March 1930 to the editor of the *Bookman,* concerning his ongoing controversy with the humanists, Eliot confirmed his adoption of Hulme's definition of humanism and the religious attitude: "On one point however I must say that your critic is near the truth. I do certainly associate the contemporary use of the word 'humanism' with that of T. E. Hulme. Hulme's use of the term is traditional and just; and if our new humanists mean something entirely different then they should call it by some other name." Quoted in Roger Kojecký, *T. S. Eliot's Social Criticism* (London: Faber and Faber, 1971), p. 75.

5. *New Statesman* 7 (29 July 1916), 405–6. Describing the book's central argument as "a chapter in the history of classicism and romanticism," Eliot sees Webb, who "stands for

the humane tradition," in an important struggle against those who stand for "the novelties of science" and who support the humanitarian "tendency to underestimate the value of the individual (the mystical heresy), and a tendency to regard religion as essentially a feature of primitive science, destined to disappear in a world of positive science."

6. "The Naked Man," *Athenaeum*, no. 4685 (13 February 1920), 208–9; reprinted, with revisions, as "Blake" in *The Sacred Wood* (*SW* 128–34).

7. "A French Romantic," *TLS*, no. 980 (28 October 1920), 703.

8. *Athenaeum*, no. 4653 (4 July 1919), 552–3.

9. "Mr. P. E. More's Essays," *TLS*, no. 1412 (21 February 1929), 136.

10. Eliot's dialogic essay, written as a preface for an edition of Dryden, *Of Dramatic Poesie* (London: Frederick Etchells and Hugh Macdonald, 1928), may be supposed, Eliot writes in this preface, "to have taken place between half a dozen fairly intelligent men of our time. And as the topics discussed by Dryden's party were issues of his day, so are mine issues of our day. . . . My dialogue represents the scraps of many actual conversations at divers times and in divers circumstances. . . . I have distributed my own theories quite indiscriminately among the speakers" (pp. ix–x).

11. "The Lesson of Baudelaire," *Tyro* 1 (Spring 1921), 4.

12. See, for example, Eliot's review of J. M. Murry's *Son of Woman: The Story of D.H. Lawrence*, where, in discussing Lawrence's "ignorance" and need of moral discipline, he states that the function of "true education" is "to develop a wise and large capacity for orthodoxy, to preserve the individual from the centrifugal impulse of heresy, to make him capable of judging for himself and at the same time capable of judging and understanding the judgments of the experience of the race" (*Cr* 10:771).

13. "Note sur Mallarmé et Poe," *Nouvelle Revue Française* 14 (1 November 1926), [524].

14. Eliot qualified the list, "et je crois avec Poe" (p. 525), revealing a stage in his ongoing reassessment of Poe's sensibility in numerous reviews and essays between "The Lesson of Baudelaire" (1921) and "From Poe to Valéry" (New York: Harcourt Brace, 1948).

15. "The Devotional Poets of the Seventeenth Century: Donne, Herbert, Crashaw," *Listener* 3 (26 March 1930), 552.

16. *Nation and Athenaeum* 41 (17 September 1927), 779.

17. This undated letter (Texas) should be dated [March 1927] by internal reference to Pound's periodical *Exiles*, first issued in spring 1927, and by Aldington's reply of 20 March 1927 (MS VE) to a line in the letter. The letter was quoted and misdated 1919 in Ernest J. Lovell, Jr., "The Heretic in the Sacred Wood; or, The Naked Man, the Tired Man and the Romantic Aristocrat: William Blake, T. S. Eliot, and George Wyndham," in *Romantic and Victorian*, ed. W. Paul Elledge and Richard L. Hoffman (Rutherford, N.J.: Fairleigh Dickinson University Press, 1971), p. 76.

18. "Archbishop Bramhall," *Theology* 15 (July 1927), 12. This passage was deleted when the essay was reprinted as "John Bramhall" in *Selected Essays* (London: Faber and Farber, 1932). Eliot's remarks on Machiavelli's lack of balance were qualified in "Nicolo Machiavelli," published in *TLS* the previous month. Eliot portrays him as "a man who accepted in his own fashion the orthodox view of original sin" and who was "no fanatic; he merely told the truth about humanity. The world of human motives which he depicts is true—that is to say, it is humanity without the addition of superhuman Grace. It is therefore tolerable only to persons who have also a definite religious belief; to the effort of the last three centuries to supply religious belief by belief in Humanity the creed of Machiavelli is insupportable" (*FLA* 62–3).

19. Eliot also sees an ontological-psychological divide between the twelfth-century mysticism of Richard of St. Victor and the sixteenth-century mysticism of St. Theresa and

St. John of the Cross: "I wish to draw as sharply as possible the difference between this mysticism of Richard of St. Victor, which is the mysticism also of St. Thomas Aquinas and of Dante, and the mysticism of the Spaniards, which . . . is the mysticism of Crashaw and the Society of Jesus. The Aristotelian-Victorine-Dantesque mysticism is ontological; the Spanish mysticism is psychological. The first is what I call classical, the second romantic" (*VMP* 104).

20. "Three Reformers," *TLS,* no. 1397 (8 November 1928), 818.

21. The blurb on the dust jacket of *The Waste Land* (New York: Boni and Liveright, 1922) contained an astute observation by Burton Rascoe, literary critic of the *New York Tribune,* on the blasphemous element in Eliot's early poetry: "His method is highly elliptical, based on the curious formula of Tristan Corbière, wherein reverential and blasphemous ideas are juxtaposed in amazing antithesis."

22. Quoted in Kojecký, *T. S. Eliot's Social Criticism,* p. 74.

23. *TLS,* no.332 (11 August 1927), 542.

24. *Virginia Quarterly Review* 10 (January 1934), 94. This essay was reprinted, with revisions, as part 3 of *After Strange Gods* (*ASG* 51).

25. "Le roman anglais contemporain," *Nouvelle Revue Française* 28 (1 May 1927), 671.

26. "Note sur Mallarmé et Poe," p. 525.

27. In *Egoists* (New York: Scribners, 1909), which Eliot reviewed in the *Harvard Advocate,* James Huneker astutely observed: "In Baudelaire, Barbey D'Aurevilly, and Villiers de l'Isle Adam, the union of Roman Catholic mysticism and blasphemy has proved to many a stumbling-stone. These poets were believers, yet Manicheans; they worshipped at two shrines; evil was their greater good" (p. 215).

28. *Against Nature,* trans. Robert Baldick (London: Penguin, 1959), p. 162.

29. From Eliot's unpublished lecture on Henry James, given at Harvard in the spring of 1933 in a course on contemporary literature (Houghton: MSAm 1691. 14[36]); quoted in F. O. Matthiessen, *The Achievement of T.S. Eliot,* 3rd. ed. (New York: Oxford University Press, 1958), p. 9.

30. Ibid., p. 24.

31. Eliot had jotted in his Harvard lecture notes: "Blasphemy: Lawrence incapable of." At the same time, in his Norton Lecture "Shelley and Keats," he clarified his view of Lawrence as being among certain romantic poets he considers "great heretics": "I should consider it a false simplification to present any of these poets, or Lawrence . . . simply as a case of *individual error,* and leave it at that. It is not a wilful paradox to assert that the greatness of each of these writers is indissolubly attached to his practice of the error, or his own specific variation of the error. Their place in history, their importance for their own and subsequent generations, is involved in it; this is not a purely personal matter. They would not have been as great as they were but for the limitations which prevented them from being greater than they were. They belong with the numbers of the great heretics of all times" (*UPUC* 99–100).

32. Tennyson, whose counter-romanticism and spiritual journey Eliot compares to that of Baudelaire, also belongs with Eliot's questing blasphemers. Though on the surface Tennyson, like Baudelaire, is very much the voice of his time, underneath is an abyss of sorrow and suffering and an emotional intensity that has been suppressed into a morbid melancholia and an imperfect vision. To Eliot, Tennyson is "desperately anxious to hold the faith of the believer, without being very clear about what he wanted to believe" (*SE* 334), but what is important is that Tennyson was not wholly deceived by the errors of an age that confused immortality with human perfectibility. Like Baudelaire, he was paradoxically "the most instinctive rebel against the society in which he was the most perfect conformist" (*SE* 337), and it is his religious struggle that makes him a "religious" poet: "*In*

Memoriam can, I think, justly be called a religious poem, but for another reason than that which made it seem religious to his contemporaries. It is not religious because of the quality of its faith, but because of the quality of its doubt. Its faith is a poor thing, but its doubt is a very intense experience. *In Memoriam* is a poem of despair, but of despair of a religious kind. And to qualify its despair with the adjective 'religious' is to elevate it above most of its derivatives" (*SE* 336). However, Eliot dismisses Tennyson as a "religious" poet after *In Memoriam* because he seems to have abandoned his incomplete spiritual journey: "The genius, the technical power, persisted to the end, but the spirit had surrendered. A gloomier end than that of Baudelaire: Tennyson had no *singulier avertissement*. And having turned aside from the journey through the dark night, to become the surface flatterer of his own time, he has been rewarded with the despite of an age that succeeds his own in shallowness" (*SE* 338).

33. In his ongoing battle with the humanists, Eliot wrote in a letter to the editor of the *Forum* 81 (February 1929), that certain anti-romantic phenomena "are evidences of a transition, a revolt against the paganism of progress of the nineteenth century, toward a re-discovery of orthodox Christianity. Even 'Freudianism,' crude and half-baked as it is, is a blundering step toward the Catholic conception of the human soul. . . . Perhaps the most interesting example . . . is the spectacle of the grandson of Thomas Huxley discovering that human nature is fundamentally corrupt. This seems to me a very healthy sign. Mr. Huxley is on the way toward orthodoxy" (p. xlvii).

34. *Bookman* 70 (November 1929), 232. In discussing the premises of the "Humanists"—Irving Babbitt, his American followers, and Ramon Fernandez in France—Eliot states "that the possession of clear literary standards must imply the possession of clear moral standards" (p. 230).

35. S. I. Hayakawa, "Mr. Eliot's Auto Da Fe," *Sewanee Review* 42 (July–September 1934), 367.

36. The terms occasionally reappear, as in Eliot's letter to the editors of the *Partisan Review* 9 (March–April 1942), concerning a lecture by Van Wyck Brooks on "Primary Literature and Coterie Literature." Stating that "Literature has at some times and in some places been condemned for infraction of laws of religious orthodoxy,★" Eliot appends the asterisk to note below that "Mr. Brooks, by the way, confuses heterodoxy with blasphemy" (p. 116).

37. In his Turnbull Lectures (1933), Eliot asserted that the function of the artist, whether he is heterodox or orthodox while the rest of society is the other, is "to bring back humanity to the real. . . . Greatness is not a state that poets really seek; greatness is a matter . . . of chance, of what happens afterwards when we are dead; and that depends upon a great many things outside of ourselves. It has often been said that no man is a hero to his own valet; what is much more important is that no honest man can be a hero to himself; for he must be aware how many causes in world history, outside of abilities and genius, have been responsible for greatness" (*VMP* 289).

Chapter 8. The Journey of the Exile in *Ash-Wednesday*

1. The earliest draft at King's College is entitled "All Aboard for Natchez / Cairo and St. Louis", with "*Perch' io non spero*" as an epigraph. A subsequent typescript in the Houghton Library is entitled "PERCH' IO NON SPERO," with succeeding words (mis-quoted) from Cavalcanti's opening lines dropped down as an epigraph, "di tornar piu mai / ballatetta, in Toscana . . ." Eliot has written on this draft, "to be published by Mar-guerite de Bossiano in *Commerce*." A later typescript (Texas) was temporarily retitled "BALLATA: ALL ABOARD FOR NATCHEZ, CAIRO AND SAINT LOUIS." with "Perch' io

non spero." as the epigraph. Eliot subsequently crossed out the title and epigraph of this typescript and printed the new title "PERCH' IO NON SPERO . . ." This draft, which was sent to Jean de Menasce for translation into French, bears the blue-pencil holograph of the editor or printer, "Commerce 13 ital" and is the English text as printed opposite the French translation in *Commerce* 15 (Spring 1928), 6–11.

2. Susan Clement recently provided the production details of the ten-inch 78 rpm sound recording of "The Two Black Crows, Parts I and II," produced in New York on 23 May 1927 (Columbia 935-D). See her " 'All Aboard for Natchez, Cairo and St. Louis': The Source of a Draft Heading of T. S. Eliot's *Ash-Wednesday* I," *Notes and Queries* 241 (March 1996), 57–9.

3. Lloyd Lewis, "The Two Black Crows," *New Republic* 54(14 March 1928), 124.

4. "On TSE," in *T. S. Eliot: The Man and His Work,* ed. Allen Tate (New York: Delta-Dell, 1967), p. 6.

5. In *The Early Italian Poets,* trans. D. G. Rossetti (London: George Newnes Limited, 1904), p. 276.

6. In his preface to the lectures, Eliot qualifies his study of the metaphysical poetry of the seventeenth century by stating that "the whole of my case turns upon my interpretation of the *Vita Nuova,* which is only hinted at in Lecture III, and my interpretation of the childhood of Dante. This must be developed very fully" (*VMP* 41).

7. "Two Studies in Dante," *TLS,* no. 1393 (11 October 1928), 732.

8. Grover Smith concludes in his *T. S. Eliot's Poetry and Plays* that the poem "is not innocent of what looks like wilful mystification. Its structure appears haphazard even where it is not, and its sheer verbosity at times is irritating"; 2nd ed. (Chicago: University of Chicago Press, 1974), p. 158. A. D. Moody, in his *Thomas Stearns Eliot, Poet* (New York: Cambridge University Press, 1979), is less mystified in his assertion that "the deeper difficulty with *Ash-Wednesday* is that it denies life with purposeful energy and positive feeling. . . . Somehow it achieves what should be humanly impossible, the celebration of death as a form of life. For myself, I can't say that I like it for that; but that is what it is and does, whether we like it or not" (p. 154).

9. Early in October 1928 Eliot sent this draft to Leonard and Virginia Woolf, anxious to read it to them. When the Woolfs went to the Eliots on the 17th, they were joined by Mary Hutchinson and McKnight Kauffer, the illustrator of Eliot's Ariel poems. Leonard recorded in his autobiography that "Tom began the proceedings by reading the poem aloud in that curious monotonous sing-song in which all poets from Homer downwards have recited their poetry" (*Downhill All the Way* [London: Hogarth Press, 1967], p. 10). Though each guest in turn responded to the poem, Eliot resisted most of the criticism. Virginia subsequently wrote in her diary (27 October) of her relief in "forgetting Mary & Tom & how we went to be read aloud to" (*The Diary of Virginia Woolf,* vol 3, ed. Anne Olivier Bell [New York and London: Harcourt Brace Jovanovich, 1980], p. 201).

10. This letter is reproduced in Stephen Parks, "The Osborn Collection: A Biennial Progress Report," *Yale University Library Gazette* 44 (January 1970), 25.

11. The volume (private) was described and offered as item 6 in Glenn Horowitz (Bookseller), *Catalogue 22: T. S. Eliot* (New York, [1990]), p. 4.

12. In a private paper written in the 1960s, Eliot wrote, looking back on his early marital situation, "I was still, as I came to believe a year later, in love with Miss Hale. I cannot however even make that assertion with any confidence: it may have been merely my reaction against my misery with Vivienne and desire to revert to an earlier situation" (*L1* xvii).

13. Letter of 17 April 1936 (Brotherton), printed in Tate, *T. S. Eliot: The Man and His Work,* p. 81.

14. William Force Stead wrote on the untitled draft in the Beinecke Library, "Early version of poem sent me by T. S. Eliot." This was the slightly emended text, with both epigraphs intact, for the first printing of the poem in the *Saturday Review of Literature* 4 (10 December 1927), 429. Before Eliot sent the copy to Stead, however, he crossed out the first epigraph, "The hand of the LORD was upon me," in pencil. He retained only the second epigraph, "e vo significando", and made further textual emendations before reprinting the poem a month later in the *Criterion* 7 (January 1928), 31–2. The single epigraph was dropped and the text was further revised for subsequent printings.

15. The quotation and translation are from the Temple Classics edition that Eliot possessed and used, *The Purgatorio of Dante* (London: J. M. Dent, 1910), pp. 300–1.

16. In an unpublished lecture, "The Bible as Scripture and as Literature" (Houghton), read before the Women's Alliance in King's Chapel, Boston, Massachusetts, on 1 December 1932, Eliot quoted Ecclesiastes 12: 5–12, and observed that "this book of *Ecclesiastes* . . . and this particular passage in *Ecclesiastes,* come I suppose as near to pure literature or pure poetry as anything in the Bible."

17. The title given to the poem in the manuscript sent to the Woolfs in October 1928, "Som de l'escalina," remained in place when a version of the poem was published separately with Jean de Menasce's French translation in *Commerce* 21 (Fall 1929), 100–3.

18. In "Bertrand Russell and the Eliots," Robert H. Bell recounts that "Once Russell casually inquired of a correspondent whether he had read Eliot's poem 'Mr. Apollinax.' 'He seems to have noticed the madness,' Russell noted, which in context suggests sexual madness" (*American Scholar* 52 [Summer 1983], 318). After Eliot left Vivien in 1932 he and Russell had no further contact until they exchanged brief notes in the 1950s.

19. This letter (Princeton) is quoted in Kojecký, *T. S. Eliot's Social Criticism,* p. 74.

Chapter 9. The Ignatian Interlude

1. Quoted in H. J. C. Grierson, ed., *Metaphysical Lyrics and Poems of the Seventeenth Century* (Oxford: Clarendon Press, 1921), p. xvii. Eliot's famous review of the anthology, "The Metaphysical Poets," appeared in *TLS* on 20 October 1921, and he used the volume as his primary text in his Clark Lectures.

2. Eliot had a copy of Thompson's *Hound of Heaven* in his library, and in his course on Victorian Literature in 1917 he lectured on Thompson as a "poet of religious faith" (see p. 40).

3. "An Italian Critic on Donne and Crashaw," *TLS,* no. 1249 (24 December 1925), 895.

4. "Reflections on Contemporary Poetry," *Egoist* 4 (September 1917), 118.

5. (Boston: Milford House, rpt. 1971), pp. 5–6.

6. (London: Burns and Oates, 1881), p. 96.

7. Eliot would have read of Southwell in Grierson's introduction to *Metaphysical Lyrics and Poems,* where he states that "Catholic poets . . . like Robert Southwell, learned from the Italians to write on religious themes in the antithetic, 'conceited', 'passionating' style of the love poets of the day" (p. xxxix), but he did not include any of Southwell's poems in the anthology.

8. "The Author of 'The Burning Babe,'" *TLS,* no. 1278 (29 July 1926), 508.

9. *The Preces Privatae of Lancelot Andrewes,* ed. F. E. Brightman (London: Methuen, 1903), p. li.

10. *Adelphi* 3 (March 1926), 652.

11. *Adelphi* 3 (February 1926), 593–4.

12. *Complete Poetry and Selected Prose,* ed. John Hayward (London: Nonesuch Press, 1929). Hayward wrote a "brief tribute of thanks" (p. xvi) to Eliot for his assistance in preparing the edition, which contained the first modern version of *Ignatius His Conclave.*

13. In *Humanism and America,* ed. Norman Foerster (New York: Farrar and Rhinehart, 1930), p. 110.

14. In April 1928 Father Yealey was given the option of receiving an M. Litt. or resubmitting the dissertation in a year. He chose the latter option, revising the text in Boston. He subsequently published a history of his native town, *Sainte Genevieve: the Story of Missouri's Oldest Settlement* (1935).

15. *Listener* 2 (3 July 1929), 22.

16. Ibid. Donne's "Sermon 80" was among the sermons included in *Complete Poetry and Selected Prose,* pp. 671–82.

17. *Listener* 3 (12 March 1930), 441-3.

18. Ibid., p. 443. Eliot refers to the translation of Jörgen Peter Müller's popular and frequently reprinted handbook of physical exercises, *My System: Fifteen Minutes' Work a Day for Health's Sake,* trans. G. M. Fox-Davies (London: Anglo-Danish Publishing, 1905).

19. In *A Garland for John Donne,* ed. Theodore Spencer (Cambridge: Harvard University Press, 1931), p. 5.

20. Ibid., p. 8.

21. Not until 1947, in "John Donne in Meditation: The *Anniversaries*" (*ELH: A Journal of English Literary History* 14 [December 1947], 247–73), did Louis L. Martz point out the structural relationship of the *Spiritual Exercises* and the *Anniversaries,* an observation developed further in Martz's *Poetry of Meditation* (New Haven: Yale University Press, 1954). Helen Gardner independently demonstrated the structural relationship between the *Spiritual Exercises* and the *Holy Sonnets* in *John Donne: The Divine Poems* (Oxford: Clarendon Press, 1952).

22. Eliot quotes from the second impression of *Practical Criticism* (London: Routledge and Kegan Paul, 1930), p. 290. The last sentence was dropped in subsequent impressions, perhaps because of Eliot's criticism here, noted by Richards in subsequent impressions (p. 291).

23. The five points that make up Richards's "frame of feelings" for meditating on a poem appear at the end of chapter 6, "Doctrine in Poetry," in *Practical Criticism*: "i. Man's loneliness (the isolation of the human situation). ii. The facts of birth, and of death, in their inexplicable oddity. iii. The inconceivable immensity of the Universe. iv. Man's place in the perspective of time. v. The enormity of his ignorance." Richards then offers the following instruction: "Taking these not as targets for doctrine, but as the most incomprehensible and inexhaustible objects for meditation, while their reverberation lasts pass the poem through the mind, silently reciting it as slowly as it allows. Whether what it can stir in us is important or not to us will, perhaps, show itself then. Many religious exercises and some of the practices of divination and magic may be thought to be directed in part towards a similar quest for sanction, to be rituals designed to provide standards of sincerity" (pp. 291–2).

Eliot was ever critical of Russell's essay "A Free Man's Worship"; see chapter 2, note 28.

Chapter 10. The Way to *Little Gidding*

1. "An Italian Critic on Donne and Crashaw," *TLS,* no. 1249 (24 December 1925), 878.

2. *Listener* 3 (26 March 1930), 553.

3. "George Herbert," *Spectator* 148 (12 March 1932), 360. Eliot originally planned the essay for *TLS* and for inclusion in *Selected Essays* (1932), as shown in the appendix.

4. "George Herbert," p. 361.

5. Quoted in Izaak Walton, *The Complete Angler & The Lives of Donne, Wotton, Hooker, Herbert & Sanderson* (London: Macmillan, 1906), p. 417.

6. "Christianity and Communism," *Listener* 7 (16 March 1932), 383.

7. *Criterion* 12 (October 1932), 40.

8. However discreet Eliot may have been about Vivien with Ottoline at this time, she had of course known of the affair from the beginning. After the affair ended in 1919, Vivien wrote nervously to Ottoline, who had become her close friend, about having confided to her at Garsington: "You know how rather frightened one feels after having talked unreservedly about a person. About Bertie, you know he was *extraordinarily generous* to me, I mean in *giving* things. So much so that it will always make me feel very mean for talking against him. I know you understand perfectly. But I think he was more generous to me than he has ever been to anyone. He really made a sacrifice. I shall never forget that, it makes a lot of difference to *everything*. I have really suffered awfully in the complete collapse of our relationship, for I *was* fond of Bertie (I think I still am). But it is of course *hopeless,* I shall never try to see him again." This undated letter (Texas) appears to follow Vivien's letter to Ottoline of 4 June 1919, in which she describes the final visit of Russell, who appeared at 18 Crawford Mansions in the early hours of a Monday morning "to fetch away another installment of possessions I had fetched from Marlow. He seemed dreadfully out of temper. Unfortunately I was not dressed, so had to shout to him from the bathroom, as cheerfully as I could. But the response was painful. . . . I thought we might have talked a little and come to, at any rate, amicable relations. But it is no good. I will make no more attempts at all. But it is strange how one does miss him! Isn't it hard to put him quite out of one's mind?" Quoted in Ray Monk, *Bertrand Russell: The Spirit of Solitude* (London: Jonathan Cape, 1996), p. 551. Monk suggests that Russell's emotional repression and guilt over the affair and Vivien's fate eventuated in an autobiographical story, "Satan in the Suburbs"(1953), in which a Mrs. Ellerker betrays her husband in an affair with Mr. Quantox. Russell's treatment of Mrs. Ellerker, says Monk in drawing out the parallels, "contrasts strikingly with that of the other minor characters in the story. . . . [S]he is a real person with real feelings. The reason for this, I feel sure, is that, in his portrayal of Mrs Ellerker, Russell was drawing on real life . . . on his affair with T. S. Eliot's wife. . . . After he has got from her what he wants . . . Mr Quantox deserts Mrs Ellerker, leaving her embittered and tormented by her guilty secret. Finally, she tries to confess her misdeeds, but, because of the public esteem in which Mr Quantox is held, she is disbelieved and committed to an asylum" (p. 432).

9. Eliot's letters to Emily Hale, said to number approximately a thousand and to date from about 1930 to 1957, are sealed at Princeton until 12 October 2019.

10. See William Baker, "T. S. Eliot and Emily Hale: Some Fresh Evidence," *English Studies* 66 (October 1985), 433.

11. Quoted in *T. S. Eliot: The Man and His Work* ed. Allen Tate (New York: Delta-Dell, 1967), p. 107. Eliot's marked copy (MS VE) of *The Poems of George Herbert,* with an introduction by Arthur Waugh, was in the World's Classics series (London: Oxford University Press, 1907).

12. Essay on "Liberty," *Time and Tide* 16 (19 January 1935), 89–90; from *The Ascent of Mount Carmel* 2.7.4.

13. Essay on "Liberty," p. 90; from *The Ascent of Mount Carmel* 2.5.7.

14. See Barry Spurr, "The Genesis of 'Little Gidding,' " *Yeats-Eliot Review* 6 (1979), 30.

15. *TLS,* no. 1800 (1 August 1936), 628.

16. Cambridge: Cambridge University Press, 1938, p. [xi].

17. "A Lay Theologian," *New Statesman and Nation* 18 (9 December 1939), 866.

18. *American Review* 8 (November 1936), 7.

19. "Paul Elmer More," *Princeton Alumni Weekly* 37 (5 February 1937), 373.

20. *Salisbury and Winchester Journal*, 27 May 1938, p. 12.

21. *Theology* 44 (February 1942), 13.

22. London: Routledge and Kegan Paul, 1973, pp. 283–4.

23. New York: Harcourt Brace Jovanovich, 1976, p. 183.

24. New York: Oxford Univ. Press, 1984, p. 224.

25. William Turner Levy and Victor Scherle, *Affectionately, T.S. Eliot* (Philadelphia: Lippincott, 1968), pp. 14–15.

26. "The compensations for being a poet are grossly exaggerated," Eliot had written earlier, "and they dwindle as one becomes older, and the shadows lengthen, and the solitude becomes harder to endure." Introduction to *The Collected Poems of Harold Monro*, ed. Alida Monro (London: Cobden-Sanderson, 1933), p. xvi.

27. *On Poetry* (Concord, Mass.: Concord Academy, 1947), p. 9.

28. *The Ascent of Mount Carmel*, trans. David Lewis (London: Thomas Baker, 1906), p. 298.

29. Essay on "Liberty," pp. 88–9

30. Quoted in F. O. Matthiessen, *The Achievement of T.S. Eliot*, 3rd ed. (New York: Oxford University Press), p. 195n.

31. Julian of Norwich, *Revelations of Divine Love*, 13th ed. (London: Methuen, 1952), p. 85.

32. *The Cloud of Unknowing*, ed. Dom Justin McCann (London: Burnes, Oates and Washbourne, 1924), p. 9.

33. Frank Morley, "A Few Recollections of Eliot," in *T.S. Eliot: The Man and His Work*, ed. Allen Tate, p. 107.

34. Brian Appleyard, "Interview: A Poet's Wife and Letters," *Times* (London), 17 September 1988, p. 35. Robert Lowell wrote to Valerie Eliot on 12 April 1965: "I'm sure everyone tells you that you gave Tom his greatest happiness. We all think this. Somehow I think, the long spiritual pilgrimage, that gruelling, heroic and yet inwardly at peace exploration and purgation—all that shines through Ash Wednesday and the Quartets was inevitably going to end in the surprise reward of a joyfull marriage [*sic*]." Robert Lowell, "To Valerie Eliot, a Letter," *Southern Review* 21 (Autumn 1985), 999.

35. Igor Stravinsky, "Memories of T. S. Eliot," *Esquire* 64 (August 1965), 92.

Appendix. American Publishers and the Transmission of T. S. Eliot's Prose

1. Eliot later explained that "Ezra was then known only to a few and I was so completely unknown that it seemed more decent that the pamphlet should appear anonymously" (*Gallup* 24). Eliot explained his anonymity more facetiously to William Levy: "Because I was a very young man then, just starting my writing career, and it would have been presumptuous of me to offer my opinions except on their own merits." Conversation quoted in William T. Levy and Victor Scherle, *Affectionately, T. S. Eliot* (London: J. M. Dent, 1968), p. 127. Eliot had written to Glenn Hughes on 4 April 1929 (Texas) that he found no reason to conceal his authorship.

2. *Egoist* 6 (December 1919), 71. The volume, scheduled for publication in the spring of 1920, never appeared.

3. "Bruce Lyttleton Richmond," *TLS*, no. 3072 (13 January 1961), p. [17].

4. Ibid.

5. *Anna Karenina and Other Essays* (London: Chatto and Windus, 1967), pp. 177–8. The Sussex ledger shows that of the two thousand copies of *Homage to John Dryden* printed at the Hogarth Press on 30 October 1924, 923 copies had been sold by the end of 1926.

6. Earlier in the preface Eliot had remarked: "The reader may be puzzled to know why I selected these articles and in this order. I wished to indicate certain lines of development, and to disassociate myself from certain conclusions which have been drawn from my volume of essays, *The Sacred Wood*" (*FLA* ix).

7. Eliot's three-page preface to the Faber and Faber edition of *Dante* recounts the process of his own reading of Dante, points to some previous studies that have been useful to him, and states his purpose "to persuade the reader first of the importance of Dante as a master—I might say, *the* master—for a poet writing to-day in any language. I should not trust the opinion of any one who pretended to judge modern verse without knowing Homer, Dante, and Shakespeare" (p. 12). The dropped epigraph reads: "In quella parte del libro de la mia memoria dinanzi a la quale poco si potrebbe leggere si trova una rubrica la quale dice: INCIPIT VITA NOVA [*sic*]". The dropped dedicatory inscription comes from the concluding sentence of Maurras's second chapter, "Beatrice": "La sensibilité, sauvée d'elle-même et conduite dans l'ordre, est devenue un principe de perfection" (Paris: Nouvelle Librairie Nationale, 1920), p. 39. Eliot wrote to Pound on 9 December 1929 (Yale) that the essay "is merely a small *auto*biographical fragment, not a contribution to scholarship for my Ph.D."

8. Charles Raymond Everitt (1901–1947), a 1923 graduate of Yale, had joined Harcourt Brace in 1924 after a postgraduate year at Oxford and was now editor-in-chief. Charles Alvin Pearce (1906–1970), a 1927 graduate of Hobart College, had joined the firm as a new editor in 1929. Alfred Harcourt (1881–1954) and Donald Brace (1881–1955) had left the publishing firm of Henry Holt in June 1919 to found Harcourt Brace in New York. Brace assumed the role of establishing relations with British publishers, agents, and authors and brought the firm its first major success with the American edition (1920) of John Maynard Keynes's *Economic Consequences of the Peace* (1919). Keynes or Virginia Woolf, the American editions of whose novels were published by Harcourt Brace, would have put Brace initially in touch with Eliot, who later dedicated *Essays on Elizabethan Drama* (New York: Harcourt Brace, 1955) "to the friend and publisher who introduced *Selected Essays* to the American reader in 1932" (p. x). "No American publisher," Eliot wrote in his obituary of Brace, "was better known or better liked in the literary world of my generation" (*Times* [London], 27 September 1955, p. 11).

9. "George Herbert" appeared not in *TLS* in February but as number 8 in the "Studies in Sanctity" series in the *Spectator* 148 (12 March 1932), 360–1.

10. "John Ford" appeared anonymously in *TLS*, no. 1579 (5 May 1932), 317–18.

11. "What Time Is It?" was never published; Valerie Eliot informs me that there is no manuscript by that title in Eliot's files.

12. "A Note on John Marston" was not published, but it was evidently incorporated into "John Marston" two years later when Eliot anonymously reviewed two recent editions of Marston's plays in *TLS*, no. 1695 (26 July 1934), 517–8.

13. The essay first appeared in Eliot's "London Letter" for the *Dial* 6 (December 1922), [659]–63, and had been reprinted, with revisions, as "In Memoriam: Marie Lloyd" (*Cr* 1:192–5), the text used for *Selected Essays*.

14. This essay, which originally appeared in *A Garland For John Donne*, ed. Theodore Spencer (Cambridge: Harvard University Press), pp. 1–19, has never been collected or reprinted.

15. A copy was "Inscribed to / the Library of Eliot House. / T. S. Eliot" (undated).

Eliot House, a residence hall named after Charles W. Eliot (1834–1926), a former President of Harvard University, was opened at Harvard in 1931. Eliot regularly presented copies of his works to the Library during and after his tenure as Norton Professor in 1932–33.

16. Harcourt Brace acted on all requests to reprint essays from the book until 1950, when, in a misunderstanding with Methuen about permission-granting rights, Eliot confirmed on 21 February that "there is no doubt that Methuen do hold the American as well as the British rights in all *The Sacred Wood* material" (HBA), and he asked that the two firms come to a general understanding and work out a nonduplicatory procedure for granting subsidiary rights. Faber and Faber recently acquired the rights from Methuen, resetting and reissuing the volume in 1997.

17. On 29 July Brace explained to Morley that if Faber and Faber published on that date, or on any date within fourteen days after Harcourt Brace, simultaneous publication would be effected and the copyright would be safe in both countries. He had long been sensitive to the dangers of intervals between the publication of the English and American editions, as revealed in his letter of 25 November 1924 to Leonard Woolf regarding the American edition of Virginia Woolf's *Jacob's Room*: "I wish, in fact, that we might publish the novel simultaneously in the two countries. If there is a long interval, copies of the English edition come in here in considerable numbers and not only cut down our sales but take the edge off the market" (Berg).

18. Eliot later wrote that the dating of essays in the table of contents "is a practice I like to observe in printing any collection of essays; but it is peculiarly important where the critical judgments may depend on the conclusions of current scholarship." *Elizabethan Dramatists* (London: Faber and Faber, 1963), p. 7. "Tradition and the Individual Talent" (1919), misdated 1917 in the first edition of *Selected Essays,* is repeatedly misdated in contemporary scholarship by critics who work from the first edition. Eliot could not unstick 1917 from his own memory, giving the essay that date again as late as 1964, in the preface to the second English edition of *The Use of Poetry* (*UPUC* 9).

19. In March 1909 the United States tightend the Chace law to require that the setting, printing, and binding of a foreign work had to be done in America to obtain U.S. copyright, and within thirty to sixty days of publication in Britain.

20. Gallup states that the total printing of the first American edition consisted of 4,080 copies (*Gallup* 34). The English edition had been reset in 1932 for the Faber Library series, and the revised sheets now contained the Greek epigraph added to "Mr. Apollinax"; the first of two epigraphs for "The Hippopotamus," however, had been dropped, to be restored in subsequent editions.

21. The *Chicago Daily Tribune* of 2 December 1933 published a drawing of Eliot by Theresa Garrett Eliot, describing him as a poet who "is the idol of the younger literates of Europe and is considered by many the greatest living English poet." The drawing is reproduced in *VMP* 230.

22. Since "John Marston" was published anonymously in *TLS*, only those American readers who acquired copies of *Elizabethan Essays* would have known of the essay's existence prior to the appearance of the Gallup bibliography. Gallup's 1947 checklist described only the first English and the first American editions of *Selected Essays* and did not describe the second English edition (1934) or its reprintings. The 1952 bibliography does not describe the second edition either, mentioning it only in a note to the third English edition: "The second English edition (1934) reprinted the essay 'John Marston' from *Elizabethan Essays* (1934) but contained no new material" (p. 19). This note remained unchanged, and the edition undescribed, in the revised edition (1969) of the bibliography (p. 49). There are no copies of the second English edition in such major American research repositories as the Houghton Library and the Berg Collection.

23. London: Faber and Faber, 1936, p. 7. Eliot alludes sardonically to the description on the dust jacket of *For Lancelot Andrewes*, which describes the volume as consisting "of seven essays which are selected from Mr Eliot's work of the last two or three years, and which he believes show some consistency. The subjects cover a wide range of literature, theology and philosophy; but taken together they have a unity of their own."

24. In the preface to the English edition Eliot explained specifically that he was "omitting two papers with which I was dissatisfied, on Machiavelli and on Crashaw," and he went on to explain the exclusion of a third essay: "And as the essay on Thomas Middleton is now included in another collection called *Elizabethan Essays,* there was no point in including that either" (p. 5). In the American edition, however, the explanations have been deleted, so that the reader is informed only that Eliot is "omitting three essays, those on Middleton, Crashaw, and Machiavelli" (New York: Harcourt, Brace, 1936, p. v). Eliot had explained his dissatisfaction with the essay on Machiavelli to Bonamy Dobrée in a letter of 13 September 1930: "I doubt myself whether good philosophy any more than good criticism or any more than good poetry can be written without strong feeling . . . my essay on Machiavelli, for instance, is not good, not because I did not know enough (which I didn't) but because I had not soaked deep enough in Machiavelli to feel intensely— therefore, in so far as there is any good in it, that is because it is not about Machiavelli at all" (Brotherton).

25. The two lectures that comprise "The Development of Shakespeare's Verse" (King's) were delivered at Edinburgh University in 1937, at Bristol University in 1941, and on Eliot's German tour in 1949. Unpublished in English, they were translated into German for periodical publication in *Der Monat* 2 (May 1950) and subsequently in *Der Vers: Vier Essays* (Berlin: Suhrkamp, 1952). "The Music of Poetry," "Milton II," and "Johnson as Critic and Poet" were eventually collected in *On Poetry and Poets* (1957).

26. The scrapped essays were "Baudelaire in Our Time" (1927), which had been carried forward from *For Lancelot Andrewes,* and "Catholicism and International Order" (1933).

27. The essay, which originally appeared as "Byron (1788–1824)" in Bonamy Dobrée's *From Anne to Victoria* (1937), was included in *On Poetry and Poets* as "Byron."

28. When Eliot put together *Essays on Elizabethan Drama* for Harcourt Brace's Harvest Series in 1955, he went back to the first American edition of *Selected Essays,* presumably for the first time. Finding "John Marston" absent, he explained in the preface that he was including the essay because it "was written just too late for inclusion in *Elizabethan Essays*" (p. 10). But of course it was included in *Elizabethan Essays,* and when *Essays on Elizabethan Drama* was reprinted as *Elizabethan Dramatists* in 1963 for the Faber paper-covered editions, he specifically used the third English edition of *Selected Essays* and dropped the explanation from the preface, probably having discovered what had happened less than two years before his death.

29. See Christopher Ricks's "Walter Pater, Matthew Arnold and Misquotation" (1977), collected in his *Force of Poetry* (Oxford: Clarendon Press, 1984), pp. 392–416, where he places Eliot in the modern "genre of misquotation."

30. This correspondence is in the papers of A. L. Lowell, Harvard University Archives. There is no correspondence related to Eliot's Norton Lectures in the files of the Chairman of the Norton Professorship.

31. The misquotations from *Don Juan* on p. 31 are from canto 4, stanza v, which Eliot had memorized imperfectly as early as 16 November 1914, when he first misquoted the last line in a letter to Conrad Aiken (*L1* 69): "Except perhaps to be a moment merry . . ."; this was corrected to "Unless it were to be a moment merry. . . ." in the American edition, along with other minor errors (p. 21). In the lecture "Shelley and Keats," Eliot

states that he is "thoroughly gravelled" by several lines from *Epipsychidion,* misquoting the first (line 160) as "True love in this differs from dross or clay" (p. 92); this was corrected in the second English edition to "True love in this differs from gold and clay."

32. The Harvard University Press archives are in the Pusey Library, Harvard University. The page proofs, corrected in Eliot's hand, of the first English edition of *The Use of Poetry and the Use of Criticism* are now in the Houghton Library (★AC9 El464 933ua). The proofs are dated 23–30 September 1933 by the printer for Faber and Faber, Robert MacLehose and Company, Glasgow, and were received at the library in January 1981 following purchase from the London bookseller Bernard Quaritch, Ltd.

33. The texts of the proofs (p. 131) and the American edition (p. 123) read, "I am sure, from the differences of environment, of period, and of mental furniture, that salvation by poetry is not quite the same thing for Mr. Richards as it was for Arnold; but so far as I am concerned these are merely two variants of one theological error." The corresponding footnote reads, "And different shades of Blue." The altered text of the English edition reads, "but so far as I am concerned these are merely different shades of blue" (p. 131).

34. Max Hall, *Harvard University Press: A History* (Cambridge: Harvard University Press, 1986), p. 58.

35. Similarly, the "Note to Chapter IV / On Mr. Herbert Read's Appraisal of the Poetry of Wordsworth" (p. 81) was removed from the end of the text to a new page and retitled "Note on Mr. Herbert Read's Appraisal of the Poetry of Wordsworth" (p. 74).

36. Eliot presented an inscribed copy of the American edition "to the Eliot House Library / from the author," signed and dated November 1933, but there is no evidence that he ever examined or compared the text. He later presented an inscribed (undated) copy of the second impression (1934) of the English edition to the Eliot House Library.

37. (London: Faber and Faber, 1962). The note is to a statement in the text: "In certain historical conditions, a fierce exclusiveness may be a necessary condition for the preservation of a culture: the Old Testament bears witness to this." The note reads: "It seems to me highly desirable that there should be close culture-contact between devout and practising Christians and devout and practising Jews. Much culture-contact in the past has been within those neutral zones of culture in which religion can be ignored, and between Jews and Gentiles both more or less emancipated from their religious traditions. The effect may have been to strengthen the illusion that there can be culture without religion. In this context I recommend to my readers two books by Professor Will Herberg published in New York: *Judaism and Modern Man* (Farrar, Straus and Cudahy) and *Protestant-Catholic-Jew* (Doubleday)."

38. "Seneca in Elizabethan Translation," placed in section 2 of all editions of *Selected Essays,* had not been included in *Elizabethan Essays.*

39. Published as *Elizabethan Dramatists* in the paper-covered series (London: Faber and Faber, 1963), p. 5.

40. "Poet and Saint . . ." p. 424. The opening paragraph containing this statement was deleted when the essay was collected and reprinted as "Baudelaire in Our Time" in *For Lancelot Andrewes* and subsequently in *Essays Ancient and Modern.*

INDEX